W9-AER-123

The Genuine Article

New Americanists

A Series Edited by Donald E. Pease

Paul Gilmore

The Genuine Article

Race, Mass Culture,

and American Literary

Manhood

Duke University Press

Durham and London

2001

© 2001 Duke University Press

All rights reserved

Printed in the United States of America on acid-free paper ∞

Designed by C. H. Westmoreland

Typeset in Adobe Garamond by Keystone Typesetting, Inc.

Library of Congress Cataloging-in-Publication Data appear on

the last printed page of this book.

Contents

Illustrations

Acknowledgments

Slightly different versions of the first two chapters (" 'De Genewine Artekil' " and "The Indian in the Museum") have previously appeared in *American Literature* 69 (December 1997) and *Arizona Quarterly* 54 (summer 1998), respectively. This book began as a dissertation under the direction of Bill Brown, Laura Rigal, and Ken Warren at the University of Chicago. I developed many of its central ideas in dialogue with them in classes and conversations. Their intellectual guidance, mentorship, and encouragement helped to sustain this project in its first stages, and their continued interest has helped it to develop more fully. Once, during a workshop at Chicago, they successively made cases for the future of American literary studies as a kind of cultural history, as a category of social history, and as intellectual history. Influenced by their different approaches, this book attempts to bring all three categories to bear in constructing a history of a particular literary formation. From the outset of this project, my friends from Chicago have read and commented on various sections and have offered emotional support and friendship. My thanks go out to Charley Davis, Will Pritchard, Christy Coch, Alexis Dudden, Aeron Hunt, Margaret Keller, Alison Landsberg, Jamil Mustafa, and Paige Reynolds. I have had the good fortune to have a collegial and supportive environment at both Mississippi State and Bucknell University. I would like to thank John Rickard, Glyne Griffith, and Saundra Morris, in particular, for reading and commenting on parts of this book. My life in Lewisburg has flourished as Joshua Harmon, Sarah Goldstein, Will Pritchard, and Mo Healy have lent companionship during the final revisions of the manuscript. I am particularly grateful to scholars at other institutions who have generously read and commented on parts of this book: Joan Dayan, David Leverenz, Alan Trachtenberg, and Terence Whalen. Their insightful readings as the project neared completion helped me work through some of the more complex arguments surrounding antebellum American literary culture. At Duke University Press, Donald Pease was instrumental in supporting this project, and Reynolds Smith has patiently responded to my many queries. Lynn Walterick provided close and careful copyediting with a light and generous hand. My parents and my sister, Kristin, have encouraged and supported my intellectual endeavors my entire life. More recently, Jane and Bob Cottingham have welcomed me into their lives with a warmth and generosity I did not know existed. Finally, Reid Cottingham entered my life at the moment this project changed from a dissertation into a book. Her presence in my life has led to an even greater transformation, encouraging me to become a better person as she helped me gain perspective and restored my sense of myself. Without her love and support, I would have finished this book, but it would not have mattered. With love, I dedicate it to her.

Introduction

Let him write like a man,
for then he will be sure to write like an American.
—Herman Melville, "Hawthorne and His Mosses" (1850)[1]

"Dat's de genuine article ob a gemman."
—Zeke in Anna Cora Mowatt, *Fashion* (1845)[2]

With these two epigraphs, speaking to one another across the divide of high and mass culture, I hope to elicit the central questions of this book: What role do mass cultural representations of race play in antebellum literary texts? How are those representations connected to questions of gender? How does the conjunction of mass culture and literature reflect on class formation in nineteenth-century America? Melville's notion of writing like a man comes from one of the most famous statements of the canonical American Renaissance's ideal of resisting the reading public, a public he implicitly defines as feminine. While feminine readers view Hawthorne as "a pleasant writer, with a pleasant style" (242), Melville realizes and celebrates Hawthorne's "great power of blackness" (243), his "short, quick probings at the very axis of reality" (244). Melville conceives of a model of masculine literary production through its resistance to a popular market characterized as feminine and shallow. Coming from exactly the kind of popular, sentimental culture Melville had in mind, the caricatured, blackfaced Zeke's comment reflects on Melville's ideas by indicating the difficulty of telling the genuine from the fake, placing both definitions of genuine manhood and those of race into question. Mowatt's play is centrally concerned with upholding middle-class gender ideals supposedly imperiled by the growth of a commodity culture. But Zeke, performed by a white man in blackface and speaking of a cook who has been able to pass himself off as a French count, suggests the instability of racial and gender identities, hinting, with the term "article," that such identities might be products of commodity culture. While Melville describes masculine writing as transcending feminized market demands through its plumbing of metaphysical and moral blackness, Mowatt's Zeke intimates the prominence of commercial, mass cultural representations of racial blackness to middle-class concerns about gender. Placing these two disparate texts in dialogue helps us to connect mass cultural representations of blacks and Indians and masculinized models of literary production through their similar concerns about gender roles in a market economy.

This book attempts to trace a dynamic relationship between these spheres, arguing that writers of the antebellum era defined literary authorship as a masculine profession through their invocation and manipulation of images of racial otherness from a variety of mass cultural forms—Indian melodrama, blackface minstrelsy, popular museum exhibits, and daguerreotypy. Moving beyond cultural historians such as Eric Lott who have highlighted the importance of ambivalent mass cultural figurations of race to white working-class manhood, I argue that writers drew on equally ambivalent figures from respectable, middle-class mass culture to construct their profession as masculine. Unlike Lott, I stress that race became an essential element for negotiating ideas of manhood not just for the working classes but also for the new middle class. Reconstructing how authors such as Nathaniel Hawthorne, Henry David Thoreau, and Edgar Allan Poe drew on mass cultural figures of racial difference to work through their own professional status as men and as authors, I read their ambivalence about both race and the market economy as suggestive of a more general ambivalence within mainstream, middle-class ideals of manliness. Importantly, this ambivalence allowed not just canonical white authors but also African American and Native American writers like William Wells Brown and Okah Tubbee to use mass cultural representations of blacks and Indians to create or negotiate a masculine ideal of professional authorship imagined to transcend mere market considerations. By articulating the role mass culture and race played in descriptions of the literary profession as a masculine realm, this study emphasizes the centrality of race to broader notions of middle-class manhood in mid-nineteenth-century America.

The rest of this introduction elaborates the central terms of this book—the genuine article and literary manhood. With the term "the genuine article," I attempt to capture mass culture's simultaneous production of race as a mutable and transferable commodity and as an absolute truth giving access to the deeper and darker realities of human existence. By literary manhood, I mean a series of strategies and processes by which certain authors defined themselves and their works as masculine in rather everyday terms of autonomy, strength, intelligence, and rationality. I develop these terms by placing this book within a larger framework of recent literary, cultural, and social histories of the antebellum era. By doing so, I want to emphasize that this project works primarily as a literary history in its reconstruction of a particular kind of distinctly masculine literary authority. In excavating this construction of a male literary sphere, this book necessarily engages with both broader cultural histories of different forms and institutions, specifically mass cultural forms, and recent social histories of gender and race in the nineteenth century. I take it as axiomatic that our modern notions of literature developed from within (even when defined against) the social and economic context of an emerging capitalist industrial order.[3] Yet rather than reading the texts I examine as simply reflecting this economic and social transformation, I privilege the literary for its ability to refract, illuminate, and reimagine its own cultural and social grounds of production. In other words, I regard literature as a semiautonomous sphere in order to foreground its potential to "reveal while veiling" the inherent contradictions of capitalism.[4] In particular, I argue that in the antebellum period such contradictions were potently displaced onto and displayed in mass cultural constructions of racial and gender difference. Through the play of authenticity and performance, identification and differentiation, mass culture not only provided powerful images of racial and gender differences but rendered those differences mutable. Antebellum authors, I argue, frequently took up and reworked these images and the audience dynamics that produced them in order to mediate the increasingly professional nature of authorship and commodified nature of literature. Recovering these strategies, this book describes how writers defined themselves as serious authors through a dialectic with mass cultural forms.[5] The market revolution and its transformation of the categories of race and gender were then determinate but not ultimately determining of these strategies.[6] Thus, this synthesis of the mass cultural and the literary reveals the historical contingency of distinctions between high and low, male and female, white, black, and red.

This book contends that writers of the antebellum period imagined and, in turn, attempted to negotiate the contradictory demands of an emergent model of middle-class manhood through the invocation of racialized figures from mass culture. Mass culture, in this book, will refer to the antebellum explosion of commercial, urban-centered amusements that depended upon drawing large numbers of paying (or potentially paying) patrons into communal, public spaces for the mass viewing of their attractions.[7] Giving birth to many modern advertising techniques and shaping a modern consumption-oriented culture, performances and exhibitions staged in the theaters, minstrel halls, popular museums, and daguerreotypal galleries of the antebellum era provided the groundwork for later mass cultural forms such as film. I use the term "mass culture" in order to underline these amusements' modernity, the standardization and commodification of their products, their dialectical relationship with notions of high culture, and their attempt to create or appeal to a vast, undifferentiated mass audience.[8]

Following the work of Eric Lott and others, I will argue that within these forums white American men came to understand their own manhood through an oscillation between identifying with and differentiating themselves from the gendered and racialized bodily experiences these institutions commercialized.[9] By simultaneously giving vent to and excising "black" and "red" passions through the play of race and gender as performance and essence, mass cultural forms produced "authentic" manliness as a complex of natural passions that had to be properly constrained and rechanneled. While Lott and historians like David Roediger have argued that in the years preceding the Civil War the minstrel show was largely a white working-class male subculture, their focus on mass culture as exclusively (or nearly exclusively) working class obscures the fact that the minstrel show's dynamic of "love and theft" was a much more pervasive, indeed cross-class, cultural logic at play in a variety of forms and texts.[10] Even though much recent work has focused on the changing class composition of commercial entertainment audiences in the nineteenth century, most of that work, such as Lawrence Levine's and Peter Buckley's, has focused on the antebellum development of a distinction between highbrow and lowbrow amusements.[11] I am interested, however, in those entertainments that attempted to occupy the vast cultural middle and whose representations of racial difference helped the middle class to figure itself, its relationship to the market revolution, and its ideas of gender.

I take the market revolution to encompass the wide-sweeping changes between the end of the War of 1812 and the outbreak of the Civil War that transformed the United States from an almost exclusively agricultural nation only beginning to cross the Appalachians into a burgeoning commercial and industrial giant whose population spanned the continent.[12] Throughout this book, in using the notion of the market, the marketplace, and the market revolution, I will be referring not so much to actual physical markets (with some exceptions) as to what C. B. Macpherson calls market society. In a market society, "labour has become a market commodity"—a man's "energy and skill are his own, yet are regarded not as integral parts of his personality, but as possessions"— and thus "market relations . . . shape or permeate all social relations."[13] When the northern United States (the central focus of this book) or the United States as a whole truly became a market society is a point of immense debate. What is more certain is that by the late antebellum era, the 1840s and 1850s, the market revolution had already transformed the northern United States immensely.

In the last twenty years, social historians have begun to describe the birth of the middle class, largely defined by its strict gender ideologies, as one of the most prominent products of this transformation.[14] As Stuart Blumin has argued, this middle class does not fit traditional Marxist notions of a class. Rather than being centrally defined by its relation to the means of production and united through a consciousness of common political and economic interests, this middle class developed through "the 'structuration' of certain types of social and cultural experience, to which expressions of class consciousness or awareness are related as a matter of secondary importance."[15] Perhaps the most important defining structure for the middle class in mid-nineteenth-century America was the ideal of gendered separate spheres. As a number of feminist historians have argued, the rise of capitalism in America in the early and mid-1800s went hand-in-hand with the idealization of a domestic, woman's world as a moral repository outside the competitive, amoral public men's world.[16] The figure of the self-made man provided the complement to this womanly domestic virtue. As E. Anthony Rotundo has summarized this new formation, "a man [now] took his identity and his social status from his own achievements, not from the accident of his birth. Thus, a man's work role, not his place at the head of the household, formed the essence of his identity."[17] Through the ideal of the separate spheres, the middle class defined manhood in terms of professional achievement. But while professional achievement differentiated the new middle class from an older patrician elite and an emergent working class, it simultaneously linked the *middle* class to these competing class formations: professional achievement supposedly would grant the economic and social autonomy of the older elite, but actually entailed entering the labor marketplace like members of the working classes.

A developing mass cultural sphere responded to and helped to figure these economic and social changes. In the late 1830s and early 1840s, as the theater came to be seen as a disreputable den of immorality haunted by boisterous working-class men, predatory pseudoaristocrats, and fallen women, entrepreneurs such as P. T. Barnum specifically began to advertise their attractions as respectable, middle-class alternatives. By appealing to both the rowdy tradition of working-class theater and emerging ideas of middle-class decorum and respectability, they attempted to be "all things to all people," bringing high and low culture and their related class constituencies together and creating an audience "unmapped in the contours of class interest."[18] In their synthesis of middle-class respectability and Bowery-born sensational entertainments, such as minstrelsy, these more middle-class-oriented mass cultural arenas provided a model for combining older artisanal and genteel paradigms of gender ideals within a highly commercialized realm. These amusements then constituted a sphere for the display and visual consumption of racialized bodies different from the raucous minstrel halls of the working class and theaters of the older elite. Unlike these venues, the more middle-class sites were seen as pacifying both viewer and object, while still allowing access to the primitive energy of the exoticized other. These forums thus produced blacks and Indians simultaneously as primitive embodiments of unruly masculinized behavior and as safe, sentimentalized commodities for a feminized middle-class audience.

Mass cultural forms often mapped these contradictory, gendered effects by making key distinctions not simply between "black" and "white" or "red" and "white," but between blackness and Indianness as forms of primitive embodiment. In the 1820s and 1830s, Indian melodrama tended to display Indians as noble, stoic, and naturally independent, often celebrating their savage manliness, while narrating their tragic, but necessary, disappearance. Blackness, in blackface performances of the same time, most often was figured as dangerous, erotically charged, and potentially even rebellious, as resistant to, but part of, the modern urbanizing and industrializing world. By the 1840s, however, in more middle-class minstrel shows, as in pseudoscientific romantic racialism and political debates over slavery, blacks were most often portrayed as femininely outside the burgeoning economy, as naturally religious and emotional, in need of protection and incapable of functioning in a competitive labor economy. In this way, by the mid-1840s, while blacks and Indians both represented a kind of anti-market authenticity, they tended to be gendered as polar opposites—blacks as femininely submissive and emotional, in need of protection from (or as victims of) the market, Indians as masculinely stoic and resistant to the market.[19]

As we will see, however, this gendered binary refused to remain stable. Placed within the domestic setting of middle-class-oriented museums, "savage" Indians could be read in sentimental terms. Similarly, the rebellious face of the minstrel mask continued to haunt even the most sentimental Stephen Foster minstrel tunes and their feminized representations of blackness. Thus, where in the sentimental realm Harriet Beecher Stowe evokes minstrel stereotypes in figuring Tom's inherent spirituality and goodness, in the arena of literary manhood William Wells Brown uncovers a revolutionary potential still buried within sentimental minstrelsy to figure a model of black manhood. Furthermore, because of the immense commercial success of minstrelsy, the commodification of actual blacks in slavery, and the metaphorization of self-commodification in the labor economy as slavery, blackfaced figures came to represent the very dangers of the marketplace, even as blackness itself often connoted an antimarket effeminacy or hypermasculinity.

By focusing on the various, sometimes contradictory roles mass cultural institutions and their representations of blacks and Indians played in articulating middle-class ideas of manhood, this book suggests the centrality of race to the construction of white manhood across class lines. As my study indicates, race became central to notions of manhood not only for working-class Northerners who were compared to slaves and were in direct economic competition with free blacks, but for middle-class Northerners who seemingly had less contact with blacks and Indians.[20] Such an emphasis forces us to reformulate our understanding of middle-class ideologies of manhood. In describing antebellum manhood, historians have tended to focus on mid-century middle-class advice guides, such as William Alcott's *The Young Man's Guide* (1833), and their calls for self-restraint.[21] Such histories contend that middle-class manhood only began to celebrate a kind of primitive, bodily manhood (supposedly embodied by "primitive" peoples such as blacks and Indians) at the end of the century. By reexamining the respectable entertainments of the antebellum era and emphasizing antebellum authors' identification with representations of blacks and Indians from these forums, this book suggests a more complex picture of antebellum middle-class manhood. Rather than seeing the more restrained manhood of William Alcott and his followers and this more passionate manhood of minstrel shows and other entertainments as two distinct formulations, I argue that they were in tension with each other from the outset of the market economy.[22]

In other words, it was not only working-class men who ambivalently encountered and resisted new forms of bodily discipline and alienation. If, as Georg Lukács writes, "the problems of consciousness arising from wage-labour were repeated in the ruling class in a refined and spiritualised, but, for that very reason, more intensified form," then the alienation of labor commodification, the splitting of the self into an alienable commodified self and a supposedly more authentic inner self, not only structured the consciousness of working-class men, but entailed the restructuring of the lived bodily experience of men and women of all classes.[23] In catering to a diverse audience and changing and competing gender ideals, such attractions as minstrel shows and museum Indian displays provided audiences with types of racialized primitive authenticity constructed as lying outside new forces of bodily restraint—bourgeois rules of decorum, stricter working-place discipline, self-objectification through labor commodification—even while such amusements were a key part *of* the new cultural marketplace.[24]

The emergence of the profession of authorship paralleled this development of a more middle-brow mass culture and placed literature and mass culture in direct competition. Authorship developed as a profession within the broader rise of the middle class and a culture of professionalism during the market revolution. Following the lead of William Charvat's groundbreaking work, critics such as Michael Gilmore, Michael Newbury, and Terence Whalen have described antebellum authors' responses to and representations of the transformation "from authorship as a genteel and financially irrelevant hobby to authorship as a career organized by increasingly complicated market mediations."[25] Up until 1820 or so, publishing in America was an expensive, limited enterprise. Most writers were members of an economically independent elite who often financed and published their own works and thus retained more control over their products. Rather than viewing writing as a profession from which to earn a living—most derived little or no income from their work—they tended to see their writing either as entertainment for a small coterie of friends or as a kind of public service, a noblesse oblige attempt at providing moral and political guidance to the masses. By 1850, owing to changes in attitudes toward reading as entertainment and massive growth in the population and literacy, the United States had become the largest reading market in the world. This growing market and technological innovations in transportation as well as production made publishing a more lucrative business and, in turn, gave rise to a number of large publishing houses that actively competed with one another through advertising and other modern market methods. As the *North American Review* remonstrated in 1843, "Literature begins to assume the aspect and undergo the mutations of trade. The author's profession is becoming as mechanical as that of the printer and the bookseller, being created by the same causes and subject to the same laws."[26] No longer independent producers, authors were now laborers in a large, market-oriented industry.

Like the rise of professions more generally, the transformation of authorship into a profession granted writers the possibility of gaining great wealth and autonomy, but also troubled older definitions of manly work by compelling their dependence upon the market in the form of publishers, reviewers, and readers. As Amy Dru Stanley has argued, the "conversion of human labor into a commodity. . . . confused traditional understandings of sexual difference" by placing supposedly economically and politically independent, free men in a position of dependence and servility previously reserved for women, children, servants, and slaves.[27] Furthermore, as David Leverenz, Leland Person, and Scott Derrick have noted, the profession of authorship presented male writers with a particular problem because writing tended to be seen as a feminine activity.[28] Finally, not only were "women writers . . . actually more professionalized than their male counterparts," as Lawrence Buell has pointed out, but the nonmanual labor of the middle class was already often seen as effeminate in comparison with the rugged, independent manual labor of an artisan past.[29] In sum, while professionalization served to offset the potentially emasculating effect of selling one's labor and helped to define a male public sphere, professional writing threatened one's self-definition as a man.

The prominence of women in the literary profession (despite the actual numerical and structural superiority of men) helps to suggest that separate spheres ideology, rather than actually describing a social reality, worked to shore up contested, sometimes fluid distinctions between private and public, female and male. In the past decade, social and literary historians have demonstrated that the idea of gendered separate spheres reconstructed in the 1970s and 1980s does not accurately represent the actual experience of most nineteenth-century Americans, especially for all those who were not white and middle class.[30] The idea of gendered separate spheres coercively and powerfully defined many Americans' lives, but we should not simply read those ideals as reflective of a static historical reality. Instead, in this book, I will read gender as a process, attending to the ways gender ideologies were not simply repressive but productive, examining how gender is constructed through the reiteration (and thus transformation) of idealized behavior, and exploring how people negotiated a cultural and social landscape that defined manhood and womanhood in a multiplicity of often contradictory ways.[31]

In terms of literary manhood, then, we need to be attuned to the constant breaking down of gender ideologies in the course of their iteration, especially in such an androgynous field as the literary (feminine) profession (masculine). In other words, we need to explore the process through which being a man, or discursively passing for a man, became central to wielding a kind of literary authority, even as literary practice itself often dismantled any simple distinction between masculine and feminine. In "Hawthorne and His Mosses," Melville constructs literary writing dealing with the black truths of life and covertly resisting readers' (and the market's) expectations as a distinctly masculine practice. That he would come to such conclusions in a review of Hawthorne's work would not be surprising to many, given Hawthorne's infamous proclamation against "a d——d mob of scribbling women."[32] Yet Hawthorne's gendered literary distinctions begin to blur when he turns his critical eye to individual writers. In his attack on the scribbling women, Hawthorne describes works such as Maria Cummins's *The Lamplighter* (1854) as "trash," whose success would make him "ashamed of himself if" he also succeeded.[33] In a follow-up letter to his publisher, however, after noting his previous "vituperation on female authors," Hawthorne proceeds to state that he has been reading Fanny Fern's novel *Ruth Hall* and has "enjoyed it a great deal."

> The woman writes as if the devil was in her; and that is the only condition under which a woman ever writes anything worth reading. Generally, women write like emasculated men, and are only to be distinguished from male authors by greater feebleness and folly; but when they throw off the restraints of decency, and come before the public stark naked, as it were— then their books are sure to possess character and value.[34]

Hawthorne maintains gendered literary distinctions between what is admirable and worth reading and what is successful trash, but that distinction does not neatly apply to actual men and women. In Hawthorne's eyes, most male writers write as if they were emasculated, like the vast majority of women writers. On the other hand, some women writers write in an unwomanly fashion, as though the devil were in them, a description that emphasizes their dangerous and sexualized transgression of gender norms, but also associates them with Hawthorne's description of *The Scarlet Letter* as "a h-ll-fired story."[35] According to Hawthorne, most men do not, in fact, write like men, while some women can and do, thus making them at once admirable in terms of literary achievement but offensive in terms of gender decorum.

Two of the women writers Hawthorne found both attractive and repulsive because of their "manly" writing, Fanny Fern (Sara Parton) and Margaret Fuller, similarly maintained, while manipulating, these gendered literary distinctions. In the autobiographical *Ruth Hall*, Parton satirizes readers and critics who argued that "the *female* mind is incapable of producing anything which may be strictly termed *literature*."[36] Yet in this novel and elsewhere, she implicitly calls for a more "manly" kind of writing through her critical portraits of Hyacinth (her brother, the dandyish poet N. P. Willis) and her celebration of *Leaves of Grass* as what an "effeminate world," full of "forced, stiff, Parnassian exotics," needed.[37] In a similar vein, the feminist Fuller distinguishes "male and female," "masculine energy" and "Femality," the "electrical" (poetic) genius of women, as the "two sides of the great radical dualism," even as she argues that "There is no wholly masculine man, no purely feminine woman."[38] For Fuller, the male artist naturally must embrace his feminine side. Yet because the antebellum era viewed the masculine nature of women and the feminine nature of men as unnatural, the woman who expressed a "masculine mind" of intellect was seen as "a manly woman."[39] In these terms, Fuller felt that "womanhood," as it was then defined, was "too straitly-bounded" to give women the proper "scope" of action.[40] Dismissing the sentimental fiction associated with most women (and many male) writers as lacking in "reality" and "flimsy beyond any texture that was ever spun or dreamed of by the mind of man," Fuller expressed a desire to write in a more manly fashion: "I have always thought that . . . I would not write, like a woman, of love and hope and disappointment, but like a man, of the world of intellect and action."[41] For Fuller, being a fully developed woman writer meant, in the terms allowed her by antebellum America, being more manly, meant writing in a more masculine style defined in opposition to (feminine) sentimentalism.[42]

My point is that when Melville calls for Americans to write like men he was participating in a discourse that defined literary manhood as a position that, under certain circumstances and at certain costs, women could inhabit and that men by no means automatically inhabited.[43] All this is not to reimpose a distinction between the literary and the non-literary in gendered terms, but to trace out the gendered definitions of different kinds of writing and how those gendered lines broke down. As Melville's discussion illustrates, even as most male authors used sentimental techniques, an idea of American literary manhood was being defined, in part, through the demonization of feminine, sentimental, literary mass culture and its feminine consumers. Against the market for the sentimental, Melville bases a masculine claim to cultural authority and autonomy on an ability to capture and reveal "reality" in all its depths for a more limited, culturally elite audience. If the market revolution meant, as Marx put it, that "All that is solid melts into air," many male authors positioned themselves as cultural authorities by promising access to a more solid ground beyond the market's illusions.[44] In contrast to domestic sentimentalism, which similarly promised a realm (most often the home) beyond the market, literary manhood encouraged the reformulation of the literary as a separate autonomous sphere, defined by its masculine independence and its "short, quick probings" at the darker depths of reality.

Like the ideal of self-made manhood, this ideal drew from older models of genteel manhood and artisanal independence in formulating a notion of autonomous self-creation. But the terms of such autonomy were, in the main, reversed. Where the average man proved himself through economic success, by making himself into a financially successful, independent man, being a manly writer meant resisting commercial demands. Because their profession and the literary market were largely imagined in feminine terms and because many of the most successful authors were women, male authors often oscillated between a desire for commercial success and a need to define themselves as independent creators resistant to a feminizing marketplace. But where their resentment of commercial success and their critique of middle-class materialism have often been read as placing these writers outside of middle-class norms, I read their ambivalence about the marketplace and the gender ideals it gave rise to as constitutive of the middle class, as revealing the contradictions inherent in middle-class ideology. Thus, while several of the authors I study—Cooper, Poe, Thoreau—attempted to maintain the pose of the gentleman author, they, like the middle class more generally, had to face the reality that their labor as writers placed them more squarely with the masses of working men whom they often denigrated than with economically independent dilettantes. Writers' ambivalence about working for another reflects a larger cultural uncertainty about the relationship between manhood and commodified labor. As Stanley argues, separate spheres ideology provided the terms for negotiating this uncertainty. Literary manhood, in its particularization of and difference from the wider ideals of the separate spheres and self-made manhood, then reveals the fissures within middle-class gender ideologies. In this way, American literary manhood's impossible ideal of achieving market success, without being beholden to or limited by market demands, participates in the problematic of middle-class gender ideals while in the process calling into question core cultural truths about gender.

Race, Mass Culture, Literature

This book traces the different effects of invoking mass cultural images of Indians and blacks to figure artistic practice, with the prologue and first three chapters emphasizing the more positive, although always ambivalent, possibilities of such identification and the final chapter elaborating the threat represented by such identification. According to the developing ideal of American literary manhood, the serious author was supposed to stand outside of the market and outside of middle-class ideas of decorum and respectability, yet he needed the market to support himself and his family and needed to be respectably middle class in order to wield cultural authority. With the term "the genuine article" I hope to capture the ways racial figures from mass cultural forms helped to articulate and resolve the problematic of literary manhood.[45] These commodified images of Indians and blacks transcended the market, yet were extremely profitable; they often represented an uncivilized passionate manliness, yet became a key element of popular sentimentalized attractions. Such figures were real—they were genuine expressions of the "truth" of racial difference—yet they placed that truth into question by revealing racial difference as a matter of performance. They offered a truth outside the market's demands—both blacks and Indians were imagined to embody traits eradicated by the market revolution—even while they achieved great market success. In this way, representations of blacks and Indians within these mass cultural forums became the perfect figures for thinking through the contradictions of the market revolution and middle-class gender ideologies, particularly for authors intent on proving their cultural autonomy while achieving market success. Replicating, criticizing, and expanding upon the racial dynamics of these mass cultural models, antebellum writers constructed and worked through the paradoxical demands of what I have labeled literary manhood.

Two examples can quickly suggest the ambivalence of this identification to ideals of literary manhood. In her 1842 discussion of "Entertainments of the Past Winter," Margaret Fuller cites " 'Jump Jim Crow' " as evidence that "All symptoms of invention [in the U.S.] are confined to the African race." She explains that because, "like the German literati, [they] are relieved by their position from the cares of government" and because "the Caucasian race have yet their rail-roads to make," African Americans represent the true position of the artist, beyond the mere material or political concerns of most Americans.[46] Yet Fuller's construction depends upon her romantic racialist view of Africans as having a feminized, essential "talent for melody."[47] Jim Crow, in her hands, stands for the independence that literary manhood stood for, but simultaneously effeminizes the artist. In an 1845 article titled "Who Are Our National Poets?" James Kennard Jr. satirizes Fuller's idea of African invention by citing James Crow and Scipio Coon as America's most truly national poets. He mocks the ideal of the artist being removed from society by citing slaves as those most truly "secluded" from the cares of the material world. Less sarcastically, however, he goes on to equate the economic position of American writers with slaves: "Alas! that poets should be ranked with horses, and provided with owners accordingly! In this, however, our negro poets are not peculiarly unfortunate. Are not some of their white brethren owned and kept by certain publishing houses, newspapers, and magazines?" While he lampoons the idea of black slaves being the nation's poets, Kennard simultaneously emphasizes the power of minstrelsy (and by proxy, mass culture), the fact that "the whole civilized world resound[s] with their names," thus suggesting his envy of their position.[48] From different perspectives, Kennard and Fuller illustrate that racial mass culture served to figure both the possibility of a popular art unburdened by material concerns and the possibility of art being nothing more than a commodity. Identifying the position of the artist with mass cultural representations of racial others enabled writers to imagine themselves outside mainstream middle-class ideals, as opposing the materialism of American society, even as it suggested their own degraded positions as slaves to publishing houses and reconnected them to highly commercialized culture.

Thus, by rendering gender and race matters of performance and matters of authentic or essential nature, these mass cultural forms occasioned the possibility of sympathetic cross-racial identifications. By momentarily or vicariously becoming black or red, white men not only buttressed a white male identity, but, occasionally, identified with the racial victims of American capitalist expansion. Because primitive racial manliness circulated as the genuine article, as a commodity offering authenticity to any willing (or capable) of paying, it created strict essential distinctions while subverting them. Crucially, then, this dynamic did not simply produce a monolithic ideal of white manhood. Rather, in the slippage between the cultural and biological notions of race, a limited space was opened within which Native American and African American (and occasionally Euro-American) writers and speakers could enunciate resistance to Indian removal policies and slavery.[49] Because of this constant oscillation between staging race as a mask and as essential character, writers and performers like Brown and Tubbee could reconfigure, in small ways, definitions of authentic racial and gender identities. This book, then, explores the tension between these constructions' repressive nature and their potential for providing gendered racial identities that could be reformulated by Native Americans, African Americans —and Euro-Americans—in opposing further economic and political exploitation.

Finally, by focusing on authors' deployment of mass cultural forms in constructing literary manhood and literary texts' mirroring—both reversing and replicating—of the gender and racial logics and tropes of these forms, this project sheds light on the interdependence of the literary and the mass cultural and on the internal workings of both. Viewing the literary as part of a larger cultural network of entertainment commodities, I use literary manhood to open up the category of antebellum middle-class manhood. Literary manhood, I argue, was a particular strategy for dealing with new economic, social, and cultural formations. Because literature articulates and imaginatively suspends the conditions of its own production, it does not simply reflect those formations but helps to unveil them and their contradictions. Read in this light, American literary manhood belies both the notion of completely determining structures of capitalism, sexism, or racism and the ideal of an aesthetic transcending such structures. By examining the intersection of race and manhood through the literary invocation of mass cultural forms, we can exhume antebellum race and gender ideologies in all their complexities, recovering the ever-present possibilities of their transgression and reconfiguration while insisting on their overarching power.

Let us start fair with the young night and take our first walk in Broadway. . . . Here we are at the American Museum, crowned with its · Drummond Light, sending a livid, ghastly glare for a mile up the street, and pushing the shadows of the omnibuses well-nigh to Niblo's [theater]. . . . Let us go up stairs and listen to the negro and Yankee abominations on the little stage in the garret, see the big anaconda, and watch the innocent wonder of those who come here principally and chiefly to be amused. . . . Not only here, but at the ice-cream saloons and Christy's Minstrels, and the Art-Unions and picture-galleries.
—George Foster, *New York by Gas-Light* (1850)[50]

The chapters of this book basically follow George Foster's gaze up and down Broadway as he points his readers to some of the best-known entertainments of the era—from the theater to minstrel halls to Barnum's museum and its various attractions to a particular kind of picture-gallery, the daguerreotypal parlor. In my prologue, "Staging Manhood, Writing Manhood: Cultural Authority and the Indian Body," I focus on *The Last of the Mohicans* (1826) and the genre of Indian melodrama, as epitomized by Edwin Forrest's portrayal of Metamora (King Philip). Both Cooper's novel and Forrest's performances envisioned the Indian as exemplifying authentic masculine embodiment. By invoking a kind of spectatorship associated with Indian melodrama, Cooper attempts to prop up a more genteel, patrician model of male authorship even as his immense success undermined such a model. After examining Forrest's and Cooper's parallel figurations of the Indian body, I conclude by describing how this model of cultural authority was displaced by the 1840s as dominant literary and mass cultural forms became more centrally identified with the emerging middle class. The chapters that follow then articulate how, in the transformed cultural and economic landscape of the 1840s and 1850s, writers defined a modified version of literary manhood through a similar dynamic with racialized mass culture.

The first chapter, " 'De Genewine Artekil': William Wells Brown,

Blackface Minstrelsy, and Abolitionism," turns to blackface minstrelsy, a dominant mode of representing blackness that replaced Indian melodrama as the most popular American dramatic form. I focus on Brown's *Clotel* (1853), the first novel by an African American, arguing that in the novel Brown appropriates minstrel show tropes and characters for antislavery purposes. In its oscillation between sympathy and dismissal, the minstrel show mirrored both the possibilities and limitations of antislavery forms, specifically in terms of producing positive images of black manhood. Brown works through the problematic status of black manhood in antislavery rhetoric and abolitionist literature by exploiting the minstrel show's fundamental ambivalence. Through his invocation of minstrelsy and its contradictory depictions of black manhood, Brown emphasizes the instability of race and gender in both the minstrel show and abolitionism. Brown's novel acknowledges minstrelsy's and abolition's strict equations of gender and race even as it exploits their fundamental fluidity to articulate a "genuine" black (and literary) manhood.

The next chapter, "The Indian in the Museum: Henry David Thoreau, Okah Tubbee, and Authentic Manhood," builds on the prologue and the first chapter by exploring the intersection between gendered images of blackness and Indianness. Thoreau considered popular museums like P. T. Barnum's American Museum effeminate, commercialized institutions that housed "dead nature collected by dead men," yet he returned to such museums again and again to experience the wild, masculine primitivism he found in exhibits of live Indians and Indian artifacts. Okah Tubbee was born a slave in Mississippi but claimed to be the stolen child of an Indian chief. After escaping slavery, he began to perform as an Indian in northern museums, such as Barnum's, both to support his family and to call for the reform of U.S. Indian policy. Tubbee's account of negotiating a more masculine Indian identity by rejecting a feminized black one within the space of the museum and in his autobiography helps to highlight the ways in which Thoreau's ambivalence about the museum—because of its contradictory gender effects—was tied to his pro-Indian and antislavery sentiments. Thoreau's ambivalent reactions to the popular museum and Okah Tubbee's biographies and performances reveal the popular museum as simultaneously offering a reinvigorating dose of primitive, masculine wildness to the city and taming that wildness for consumption by a more respectable, more familial middle-class audience. Thoreau's identification with the Indian as staged in such museums then helps to flesh out a racialized dimension to his ambivalence about what he saw as a feminized literary marketplace.

If the popular museum mapped its contradictory appeals to a masculinized sensational tradition and a domestic, feminine sentimentalism onto Indian and black bodies, Indianness and blackness as separate categories all but disappeared into an amorphous nonwhiteness in museum exhibitions of human abnormalities. With the third chapter, "A '*Rara Avis in Terris*': Poe's 'Hop-Frog' and Race in the Antebellum Freak Show," I return to the popular museum, focusing on the display of human anomalies and their implicit (and often explicit) references to ideas of racial difference. I place Poe's story of a misshapen dwarf jester and his revenge on an unappreciative audience in the context of both Poe's struggles with the literary marketplace and contemporary displays of abnormal humans such as Harvey Leach. In the museum's commodification of the racially exotic, Poe found a model for constructing himself as a male author simultaneously gaining revenge against (and thus imaginatively transcending) the demands of a corrupted marketplace, while cashing in on its desire for sensational effects.

In the fourth and final chapter, "Inward Criminality and the Shadow of Race: *The House of the Seven Gables* and Daguerreotypy," I turn to Nathaniel Hawthorne's novel and daguerreotypal galleries in order to suggest that these logics of racialized gender were at play in texts and institutions that did not explicitly address questions of race. Building on my readings of minstrel figures in previous chapters, I argue that in *Seven Gables* Hawthorne symbolizes the dangers of the marketplace to the middle-class family and the autonomy of literary manhood through a representative commodity, a Jim Crow gingerbread man. In order to situate the middle-class family and a model of artistic production outside the realm of market exploitation, Hawthorne turns to the daguerreotypal gallery's production of respectability through the revelatory rendering of interior character via visible, exterior signs. Through this exteriorization of character, the daguerreotypal gallery produced a vision of the United States as a homogeneously white, virtuous republic. This imaging of virtuous respectability through readable bodily signs necessitated a subsequent materialization of animalistic passions in ethnographic photographs of blacks and Indians. In parallel fashion, the transformation of Holgrave into a proper middle-class husband, on which the narrative and Hawthorne's ideal of an uncorrupted art depend, turns on the excision of the possibility that he contains the implicitly racialized masculine passions that the Jim Crow figures and the daguerreotypes of Judge Pyncheon reveal.

While the other chapters in this book explore a model of literary manhood that identified authorship with figures of racial difference, this chapter examines Hawthorne's attempt to avoid such racial identification by imaginatively abandoning the literary market altogether. The chapter then suggests that the oppositional possibilities inherent to literary manhood, the kind of possibilities exploited by Brown and Tubbee, were powerfully foreclosed. With my epilogue, "Electric Chains," I return to these possibilities by exploring the use of daguerreotypy to imagine a kind of cross-racial identification and politics in Walt Whitman's poetry and James Ball's daguerrian gallery. Through the prologue, the four chapters, and the epilogue, I provide a series of case studies that narrate a history of antebellum American literary manhood. This history emphasizes that, through its invocation of mass cultural images of blacks and Indians, this model of literary manhood produced different and sometimes contradictory political and aesthetic effects. These chapters suggest that this negotiation of, resistance to, and evasion of the literary marketplace and its demands through mass cultural figurations of racial difference exemplifies a wider cultural strategy. Mass cultural forms and their representations of race became a vehicle through which a number of antebellum writers—from Melville's evocation of the minstrel show in "Benito Cereno" and *The Confidence-Man* to Margaret Fuller's references to Jim Crow and the Chinese Museum to Emerson's allusion to the pit in the playhouse in "Self-Reliance"—envisioned their position as writers. Appropriating these figures, writers attempted to develop a literary aesthetic that contended with the market revolution's challenge to and reassertion of notions of both manly independence and racial authenticity.

Staging Manhood, Writing Manhood:

Cultural Authority and the Indian Body

With the publication of *The Pioneers* (1823), James Fenimore Cooper achieved a popular success previously unknown for an American writer. In the preface to the next Leatherstocking Tale, *The Last of the Mohicans* (1826), he attempted to limit that popularity by dissuading certain readers from pursuing the text further: "The reader, who takes up these volumes, in expectation of finding an imaginary and romantic picture of things which never had an existence, will probably lay them aside, disappointed." In particular, Cooper warns female readers that his "narrative" concerns "matters which may not be universally understood, especially by the more imaginative sex" who, "under the impression that it is a fiction, may be induced to read the book."[1] After providing historical background on Indian names and colonial warfare, Cooper concludes by reiterating that his book should have only a limited, male readership:

> As, however, candour, if not justice, requires such a declaration at his hands, [the author] will advise all young ladies, whose ideas are usually limited by the four walls of a comfortable drawing room; all single gentlemen, of a certain age, who are under the influence of the winds; and all clergymen, if they have the volumes in hand, with intent to read them, to abandon the design. He gives this advice to such young ladies, because, after they have read the book, they will surely pronounce it shocking; to the bachelors, as it might disturb their sleep; and to the reverend clergy, because they might be better employed. (3–4)

Instead of being a novel that can be read by the habitués of "a comfortable drawing room" (i.e., women and immature and effeminized men), *Mohicans* proclaims itself to be a book only for men who have the time and ability to give themselves over to its shockingly realistic scenes without being haunted by nightmares.[2] In the book that follows, Cooper attempts to redefine literature as a masculine province by linking his writing to a kind of authenticity embodied by the Indian.[3] This identification with the Indian body, I will argue, allows Cooper to unite patrician and lower-class men together in opposition to the artificial and emasculating drawing-room life of commercial society, thus securing his cultural autonomy and buttressing his own claims to manliness. Cooper's construction of a deferential model of cultural authority through the Indian body parallels a model of spectatorship connected to the theater of the 1820s and its presentation of the Indian body. Yet Cooper's very success, commercially and culturally, would help to undermine the class dynamics supporting his authority and help to give birth to a new kind of professional author.

In remasculinizing writing in his preface, Cooper contests the abilities of two groups central to the production of literature in the early republic—women and the clergy. Despite his prefatory denomination of his book as manly, Cooper consistently equates women and literacy in the text of *Mohicans*, giving voice to an anxiety that reading and education are feminine or effeminizing through Hawk-Eye's repetitive attacks on "schooling and passing a boyhood in the settlements" (220). From the first American novels in the 1790s onward, novel-reading had been seen as a particularly feminine pursuit, with cultural and social critics decrying its subversive and immoral effects.[4] While a number of American women wrote novels, most male writers, with a few notable exceptions such as Charles Brockden Brown and Hugh Henry Brackenridge, avoided the culturally suspect form.[5] Cooper began his career by trying to better the domestic novels of writers such as Jane Austen. With his *Precaution* (1820), he attempted to cater to what he envisioned as a genteel female audience, even, with a few essays, taking on the guise of a woman author.[6] In this light, Hawk-Eye's diatribes against a young man "misspend[ing] his days among the women, in learning the names of black marks" (31), and falling "into the hands of some silly woman, when he should have been gathering his education under a blue sky, and among the beauties of the forest" (224) suggest an anxiety on Cooper's part that his chosen career would emasculate him.[7]

With his preface, then, Cooper attempts to stave off this threat by defining his masculine "narrative" in opposition to feminine or emasculating fictions. Describing himself as a writer dealing with manly subjects for manly readers, Cooper casts his book as a different kind of literature, authentically real in its portrayal of Indians and Indian warfare and thus shocking to the more imaginative sex. Equating Indianness with a masculine sublime authenticity in opposition to civilized life, Cooper parallels contemporary characterizations of American Indian life as an alternative to commercial society.[8] Most notably, in *The Sketchbook of Geoffrey Crayon* (1819–1820), Washington Irving contrasts his portraits of English society with descriptions of "uncivilized" Indians' "savage virtue" and "proud independence."[9] Because of their simple economy, the fact that their "wants were few, and the means of gratification [were] within their reach," Indians had a more unrestrained, more authentic life far different from the "artificial life" of European commercial society:

> In civilized life, where the happiness, and indeed almost the existence, of man depends so much upon the opinion of his fellow men, he is constantly acting a studied part.... The Indian, on the contrary, free from the restraints and refinements of polished life, and, in a great degree, a solitary and independent being, obeys the impulses of his inclination or the dictates of his judgment; and thus the attributes of his nature, being freely indulged, grow singly great and striking.[10]

As the expropriation of Indian lands on the western frontier helped to fuel the economic growth that created the new literary markets for Irving's and Cooper's books, the Indian began to serve as a nostalgic representative of all that was imagined as being lost by early industrialization and commodity culture. For these early professional writers, the Indian came to represent an authentic kind of unified self set in opposition to a divided self characterized as femininely performative. Through this characterization, these writers implicitly contrast the self-identical Indian and his masculine self-sufficiency and bodily integrity with the self-objectification and commodification of a burgeoning market capitalism.

Although Cooper aligned his writing with a kind of masculine authenticity standing outside market society, he covertly acknowledges his dependence upon the market by deploring those (female) readers "who find a strange gratification in spending more of their time in making books, than of their money in buying them" (1).[11] Cooper, in other words, did not object to the market per se, but rather to the market's ability to undermine his autonomy by making him dependent on a female audience and by putting him in direct competition with women writers. Envisioning himself as an aristocratic artist producing moral tales for a democratic audience, Cooper desired to reach a wide audience without having to depend "upon the opinion of his fellow men" and thus act "a studied part." In an 1822 review of Catharine Sedgwick's *A New-England Tale*, he comments that "We love the artist who enters into the concerns and sufferings of the humble, whose genius condescends to men of low estate," but then describes the author's function as giving such men "a share of literary and moral instruction, as shall define their duties."[12] What threatens Cooper is not so much the market itself, but the way the market empowers a humble (or, worse, female) audience to question his definition of their duties by not spending their money on his books. The market, by freeing labor power from traditional restraints and unleashing more commodities to choose from, jeopardized an older cultural authority based on paternalistic deference and patronage.

In the first three Leatherstocking Tales, Cooper attempts to bolster this older model of cultural authority by appealing across class lines, while maintaining social hierarchies. He does so by linking his marginalized, lower-class hero Natty Bumppo to a series of upper-class, romantic heroes who, by learning from him, achieve or confirm their social and cultural authority within civilization. What these heroes learn from Natty are the manly lessons of the Indians and the sublime wilderness, a process paralleling Cooper's own attempt at remasculinizing writing and thus confirming his own class- and gender-based cultural authority. In *Mohicans*, Cooper identifies himself and his reader with Duncan Heyward, "a young gentleman of vast riches" (38), by consistently describing scenes and actions through his eyes.[13] Unlike the psalmist David Gamut, whose "ungainly" body has "all the bones and joints of other men, without any of their proportions" (16), Heyward has a "handsome, open, and manly brow" (23) and a "manly figure" (27). Yet Heyward has not completely escaped the effeminizing effects of an education in the settlements. After he has begun to suspect his Indian guide Magua of treachery and meets Hawk-Eye and the Mohicans, Heyward attempts to capture his guide, "trusting the result to his own manhood" (43) rather than entrusting the task to the experienced foresters. His failure, Magua's escape, and the central role Magua plays in repeatedly endangering their lives prove that, at least at this point, Heyward, like Gamut, "possess[es] the stature without the knowledge of men" (36).

Yet if Heyward has not yet proven his manhood and specifically lacks "the knowledge of men," Cooper provides both him and his readers with the perfect guides for gaining that knowledge. In the "unlooked for and unusual trial[s]" that follow Heyward's introduction to Hawk-Eye, he must "trust to the experience of men who know the ways of the savages" (132) by "imitating" the "deliberate examples of the scout and Uncas" (70) again and again.[14] This imitation and Heyward's transformation are most visible in his change in the second half of the novel from "clothes . . . which rendered him particularly conspicuous" (74) to Indian garb, "vestments adapted both in quality and colour, to their present hazardous pursuit" (182). Heyward's re-education culminates in his being able to pass as Hawk-Eye—"one whose skin is neither red nor pale" (291)—in front of the assembled Delaware tribe. Heyward's impersonation works because Cooper has already linked him with Hawk-Eye in terms of manhood, through their united attempt at rescuing the Munro sisters, "flowers, which though so sweet, were never made for the wilderness" (46), and their common identification with the idealized masculine Indian, the "unblemished specimen of the noblest proportions of man" (53). Although Hawk-Eye in the end proves "who is the better man" (296), both his "deference" (294) to and his "open admiration"(230) for the young major illustrate how Heyward has confirmed his social authority through this process of imitation. By identifying with Hawk-Eye through the Mohicans' manliness and their embodiment of both a natural nobility and a republican self-reliance, independence, and equality, Heyward gains Hawk-Eye's admiration and ratifies his leadership of the not-yet-independent nation.[15] In this way, Heyward mirrors Cooper's own attempt at ratifying a class-based, cultural authority in the new republic. In defining a masculine democratic art that will uphold a hierarchical social and cultural order against the upheaval of the market revolution, Cooper identifies his writing with the noble, masculine Indian and his embodiment of an authentic, autonomous manliness.

As the *Last* in the title indicates, however, Cooper was promoting Indianness not as an alternative to, but as a corrective of, Euro-

American civilization and, in particular, the feminine gendering of literary pursuits. Thus, while Heyward's survival depends on imitating the manliness of the Mohicans, becoming too much like the Indians, like Hawk-Eye, would end in his exile from civilization and his loss of social status.[16] In order to masculinize writing without surrendering claims to political and cultural power within civilization, Cooper needed a model for simultaneously embracing and separating himself from the primitive manliness of Indians. I want to suggest that the theater of the 1820s provided the perfect model for such a project. Not only did noble Indians become the favorite subject matter of American drama in that decade, but unlike reading, theater-going was seen as a particularly masculine practice that united all classes under the leadership of a patrician elite.[17] A famous article from 1827 called for the creation of a truly American drama precisely because it would provide the best medium for identifying with those masculine passions embodied by the Indian, without letting them overwhelm the Euro-American body. According to this article, the development of the theater is so important because

> it is by this mode of giving play and excitement to the mind, by mimic representations, that the force of the operations of the passions in real life is unquestionably tempered and restrained. . . . In witnessing them, we are excited by the passions of others instead of our own . . . and that stimulus, which may be pronounced to be one of the actual wants of our nature, is thus afforded to us, without any of the evil consequences resulting from an indulgence of the passions in our own proper persons.[18]

"Dramatic exhibitions" allow people to experience dangerous passions vicariously (and thus safely), and, just as important, because they "address themselves both to the understanding and the senses," they encourage a "wholesome, manly and vigorous taste" among "the ordinary classes of people." "Through the medium of their eyes" "all classes of mankind" could at once gain the natural pleasure of "manly" passions —"the actual wants of our nature"—while avoiding the danger to the body that the indulgence of such passions entailed.

In *Mohicans*, Cooper describes a kind of spectatorship, similar to that elaborated in this article, as a way of allowing Heyward and his readers to identify safely with the Mohicans' manliness. At the beginning of the second half of the novel, Heyward becomes "a deeply interested and wondering observer" (195), a "spectator" both "within" and "without" the "scene" (198), as he watches Hawk-Eye and the Mohicans debate the best way to pursue Magua. What Heyward observes is that Indianness, like the passions represented on the stage, is simultaneously both authentic and performed. He sees Hawk-Eye at one moment "affect the cold and inartificial manner, which characterizes all classes of Anglo-Americans" and at the next "assume the manner of an Indian" (199). After Hawk-Eye wins the argument and retires, Cooper reiterates the performative nature of Indian manners: "Left now in a measure to themselves," Chingachgook and Uncas "cast off, at once, the grave and austere demeanour of an Indian chief" and in place of "ferocity" display "gentle and natural feelings" that are "even feminine in softness" (200). This scene reveals to Heyward that Indianness and manliness are masks—in fact the same mask—that can be taken off and on by the Mohicans as well as Hawk-Eye, thus allowing him to realize that he, too, can take on this type of manliness as need be. Heyward recognizes that he can re-create an already performed role, and thus he "imbib[es] renewed confidence from" their performances because he can "imitate their example" (200), as he subsequently does throughout the second half of the novel. Paradoxically, by imagining Indian manliness as a performance, Cooper could posit it as an inimitable alternative to the false life of market society. By invoking a kind of spectatorship tied to the masculine theater of the era, Cooper allows himself and his readers to identify with his Indian heroes' authentic manliness without becoming savage themselves.

The contemporary staging of Indian bodies as sublime spectacle illuminates this oscillation between identification and distanciation, authenticity and performance. During the 1820s, plays about Indians came to dominate American playwriting, culminating with the immense success of Edwin Forrest's performance in John Augustus Stone's *Metamora, or the Last of the Wampanoags* in 1829.[19] As the play's subtitle indicates, Stone and Forrest drew upon the success and cultural status of Cooper's novel. Yet the theatrical staging of the Indian body epitomized by Forrest's performance in *Metamora* as "the grandest model of a mighty man" preceded Cooper's most famous novel.[20] Forrest was first celebrated for his "perfect portraiture of the highest type of the native Indians," for being "the genuine Indian," or, at least, a "counterfeit . . . [that] might have deceived nature herself," following his appearance in the rather minor role of the noble Indian chief in an 1825 production of M. M. Noah's *She Would Be a Soldier, or the Plains of Chippewa* (1819).[21] Thus, when Forrest held an 1828 contest for a play to capitalize on his increasing star status, he called for an American play featuring an "aboriginal" hero.[22] My point, then, is not to propose Forrest's performances as an exact influence on Cooper's depiction of Indians in *Mohicans*, but to suggest that the theatrical staging of the Indian as sublime masculine spectacle for a nearly all-male, cross-class audience, which Forrest's stardom exemplifies, provides a useful parallel for understanding Cooper's attempt to reconfirm a masculine cultural authority based on class deference.[23]

Like the campfire scene in *Mohicans*, *Metamora* foregrounds the audience's identification with a performance of Indianness embodying authentic masculine passions that artificial Euro-American society supposedly denies. As the prologue to the play puts it, the audience members' "bosoms" will "answer with responsive swell. . . . when passion's self stalk[s] living o'er the stage" (205). The play itself is dominated by the passionate exploits of Forrest's Metamora. He kills a wolf with his bare hands, murders a traitorous companion, vents his destructive rage on the colonists, slays his wife rather than letting her become a slave, and then finally falls to the guns of the colonists, cursing the white race with his last breath, all to the backdrop of spectacular waterfalls and mountains and properly timed bursts of thunder and lightning (see Figure 1). As in *Mohicans*, the demise of Forrest's noble savage shares the stage with a romantic subplot. Unlike Cooper's Heyward, the play's romantic hero, Walter, is a product of "poverty and toil and consciousness of lowly destiny" (208). Yet at the end of the play, he discovers that his adopted father is actually his real father and that he is not, in fact, a poor orphan but a true aristocrat. Central to this revelation is the way the play links Walter with the noble Metamora from the outset. Walter, who identifies Metamora when he makes his first appearance onstage, displays his manliness both by trying to get an honorable peace for Metamora and by fighting his Indian warriors. Furthermore, Metamora not only spares Walter's and his beloved Oceana's lives during his bloody rampage, but also slays Walter's rival, the evil aristocrat Fitzarnold, thus allowing Walter to "come stainless to [Oceana's] arms" (216).

Cooper's aristocratic hero proves his manhood and reasserts his social standing by uniting himself with the lower-class Hawk-Eye and the Mohicans and by learning how to perform as one whose skin is

1. Frederick S. Agate, *Metamora—The Last of the Wampanoags* (1832), from *Token and Atlantic Souvenir* (1842). *Courtesy of Department of Special Collections, the University of Chicago Library.*

neither pale nor red. In this way, Cooper and Heyward affirm their masculine authority by linking themselves with the lower class and Indians. Likewise, the theater of the 1820s helped to ensure a patrician cultural authority by providing a cross-class, masculine realm where "Patrician and plebeian urbanites alike assumed that they would encounter prostitutes, drunkards, noisy spectators, and occasional riots, as well as risqué spectacles on stage."[24] While most theaters delineated class divisions through ticket prices and seating—the pit, the box, the gallery—they depended upon their ability to appeal to and gain the patronage of lower-class patrons as well as the elite, upon providing an arena where men of different classes could mingle and participate in rowdy behavior.[25] Stone's play attempted to appeal to both working-class and elite theater audiences by staging Forrest as a noble yet republican Indian who helps the orphaned white hero overcome an aristocratic villain so that his true aristocracy can then be revealed. In this way, the play links those used to "poverty and toil" with aristocratic cultural authority through the authentic Indian body. Just as Metamora's actions allow Walter to remain stainless, so playgoers, because the theater can give "play and excitement to the mind" without "the evil consequences resulting from an indulgence of the passions," can safely "answer with responsive swell" Forrest's Metamora and his savage passions. Walter's role in the play is then to mediate the audience members' identification with Forrest's genuine masculine Indianness, so that they, too, become sutured to a deferential, cultural authority embodied in the ideal masculine Indian.[26]

Cooper and Forrest achieved previously unheard-of commercial success, becoming two of the United States' earliest cultural celebrities, by identifying their work with a kind of Indian masculine authenticity seen as antithetical to the everyday life of the emerging capitalist order. Through the idealized, masculine Indian body, as staged in productions such as *Metamora* and as celebrated in texts like *Last of the Mohicans*, and through a model of theatrical spectatorship that gave vent to the primitive passions associated with that body, Cooper and Forrest linked the lower orders of artisans and working men with a social and cultural elite. At a time when the market revolution and the speeding up of the American industrial revolution meant the interpellation of increasing numbers of Americans into a new economy with new forms of labor alienation and discipline, Cooper and Forrest use the Indian body to represent a nostalgic vision of masculine wholeness and authenticity. Through this identification, Cooper and Forrest (and their audiences) could mourn the passing of the Indian, even as they supported Andrew Jackson and his policies designed to make sure the Indian did disappear from the United States.[27] In turning to the Indian body, Forrest and Cooper united audiences of working men and patricians in their resistance to new market arrangements, even as their commercial success helped to transform their own professions into market-oriented capitalist enterprises.[28]

The dispersal of this cultural order built on the joint participation of elite and working men in supposedly "universal spaces" became violently apparent with the New York Astor Place Riot in 1849.[29] While the riot itself was precipitated by the rivalry between Forrest and English actor William Macready, at the time appearing at the elite Astor Place, it staged above all the complete dissolution of the cultural hegemony of the 1820s.[30] As Peter Buckley puts it, following the 1820s, "New York's culture grew along two routes: one course followed Chatham Street and then up the Bowery—the home of melodrama, menageries and the B'hoys of Edwin Forrest . . . the other followed the uptown march of fashion along Broadway . . . to the Opera House, the home of Macready."[31] This disintegration of a more unitary theater culture was accompanied by a correspondent shift in attitudes toward the theater. As Rosemarie K. Bank has argued, William Dunlap's 1832 *History of the American Theatre* (a book dedicated to Cooper) announces this shift by criticizing the theater as it then existed not for the immoral material found in drama (as most American clerical critics had), but for the disruptive, now class-marked behavior of audience members.[32] Where the reviewer in 1827 could call for a true American drama that would appeal to all classes by giving vent to manly, natural passions, in the 1830s best-selling reformers such as William Alcott began to delineate a respectable middle class by designating play-going as immoral, largely because it promoted such passions: "among the causes of vicious excitement in our city [New York], none appear to be so powerful in their nature as theatrical amusements."[33] While a cross-class, deference-based model of cultural authority reigned in the theater of the 1820s, in the 1830s the theater became marked as distinctly unrespectable, an immoral den for ill-mannered lower-class men and prostitutes.

The fortunes of Forrest and Cooper reflect this transformation of the cultural field. While the Indian body as performed by Forrest in the raucous theaters of the 1820s could provide an outlet for a cross-class male audience, during the 1830s that raucous behavior and Forrest's Indian body began to be seen as disreputable in terms of class. As the respectable classes stayed away from the theater in the 1830s and the elite increasingly defined themselves through their attendance of European forms and stars, Forrest's violently rebellious republican heroes— not just Metamora, but Spartacus and Jack Cade—were increasingly identified with the unmannered behavior of the artisanal and laboring audiences of such forums as the Bowery.[34] A review article on American dramatic literature from September 1830 provides an early example connecting Forrest and his Indian performances to unruly theater activities. The author notes that Forrest's performance as Metamora "is nightly witnessed by crowded theatres, applauding with strange enthusiasm the reckless cruelties of a bloody barbarian, who . . . delights the white men of the present day, by burning the villages of their forefathers, and involving women and children in one indiscriminate massacre." The author's anxious remarks about this "strange enthusiasm" over the gory deeds of "most bloody and barbarous ferocity" conclude with the "hope, for the honour of humanity, that this applause is bestowed on Mr. Forrest, rather than the ferocious savage whom he personates." This fear that the audience has overidentified with the barbarous pleasures of the Indians against other whites (and specifically women and children) becomes a fear that in their "strange enthusiasm" the audience will become just as "reckless" as the Indian character whom they applaud. The playgoers' "strange enthusiasm" or "vicious excitement" (Alcott) undermines the boundary separating civilized whites from savage Indians, erecting in its place a racialized boundary between respectable and brutish classes defined by the amusements they attend.[35]

If Forrest's authentic portrayals of the noble Indian provided a safe outlet for his audience to express their primitive manly passions in the 1820s, by the 1840s Forrest's performances were seen as encouraging manly passions that endangered women and children and whose expression distinguished the lower orders from the respectable middle class. As the cultural ground upon which he built his career—first the cross-class audiences of the 1820s and then the working-class audiences of the 1830s and 1840s—was reevaluated in the dominant terms of respectability, Forrest no longer was seen as embodying "the grandest model" of American manhood. Rather than being an authentic embodiment of the noble American Indian and American manhood, Forrest—with the conclusion of Eastern Indian removal, the ignominy of the Astor Place Riot, and his scandalous divorce a few years later— became an inauthentic blowhard: "If, in 1831, it was felt Forrest's Metamora was 'a remarkably and highly finished picture of the American Indian,' in 1855, his 'feathers, beads, moccasins, and red-ocher' were seen as the only 'Indian characteristics' of the role."[36]

Similarly, although Cooper was still celebrated as one of the greatest

American authors, his fortune had also declined as the social grounds of cultural authority shifted. In place of "a pre-industrial, aristocratic concept of the artist," Cooper had helped to establish the American literary profession, bringing about "the transition from the gentleman-amateur-author phase of American letters to the professional and commercial phase."[37] In the 1820s, Cooper had basically functioned as his own publisher, using his own capital to hire the work of printers. By the 1840s, in large part because of his success, but also as a result of the expansion of the reading public and the decreasing costs of publication with the transportation revolution and new technologies like the steam press, publishing had become an industry much like others revolutionized by the economic changes of the Jacksonian era. No longer able to control publishing arrangements as he previously had, Cooper essentially became an employee of publishers, "a tired hack, forced to grind out two novels a year for much smaller returns than he had received in the twenties for one novel a year."[38] While Cooper continued to adhere to "the code of the gentleman," a code that "required that he be completely independent, that he be beholden to nobody," he had helped to create a democratic, commercial audience and a kind of American professional authorship that guaranteed that the kind of elite paternalistic cultural authority he hoped to wield was an impossibility.[39] This shift is reflected in Cooper's reimagining of the link between Indians and class. Through the mediation of the figure of the noble Indian, Cooper had united the lower-class Hawk-Eye with a series of aristocratic heroes in defending a model of independent, masculine cultural authority. With *The Redskins; or, Indian and Injin* (1846), however, Cooper attempts to uphold class distinctions by distinguishing between nearly extinct noble Indians and the anti-renters who masked themselves as Injins. The Indian no longer could provide a vehicle for a now-outdated form of cultural authority; instead the Injin was simply a lower-class Hawk-Eye in redface attempting to overturn the old social order.[40]

Thus, the second generation of professional authors in America, those associated with the American Renaissance and coming of literary age in the 1830s and 1840s, faced a far different publishing world than Cooper did in the 1820s. Yet, I will argue, those writers continued to draw upon racial images from mass culture in trying to imagine authorship as a masculine sphere independent of the mass democratic market.

The writers I examine found themselves in direct competition not only with extremely popular sensational and sentimental literature but also with new urban amusements that attempted to draw the amorphous middling classes by combining the sentimental and the sensational. While in the 1830s the theater had come to be defined in class terms as a masculine space unsafe for respectable women, the 1840s gave birth to a variety of commercial entertainment forms that explicitly "re-gendered" their audiences by advertising themselves as respectable.[41] Marking the shift "from the elite paternalism of the 1820s to business-class respectability in the 1860s," the purveyors of the new amusements of the 1840s, such as P. T. Barnum, defined their attractions as safe for women and children by claiming to police the behavior of their pa-trons.[42] Yet as they defined their attractions as feminine in order to assure respectability, these entrepreneurs incorporated the overly mas-culine, sensational entertainments of the Bowery in order to draw as wide an audience as possible.[43] By incorporating lower and more elite forms while distinguishing themselves from both more elite audiences (through a democratic rhetoric and low ticket prices) and the unman-nered behavior of lower-class environs, these commercial amusements, by the time of the Astor Place Riot, not only had achieved financial success, but had also been accepted by many of the middle-class re-formers who had spoken out against the theater in the 1830s.[44] Balanc-ing more feminine, sentimentalized attractions with a hint of the lurid, masculinized, sensational attractions of the more corrupt theater, these commercial amusements conquered the cultural middle ground be-tween the elite Astor Place and the lowly Bowery, so that, as Bruce McConachie puts it, "the culture of liberal capitalism, a nexus of be-liefs and behavior centered on male individualism, female domesticity, and social respectability, could emerge as fully hegemonic in the mid 1850s."[45]

The writers I focus on in the rest of this book needed middle-class respectability and patronage in order to be accepted within culturally dominant terms, yet aspired for the status of autonomous literary art-ists opposed to bourgeois materialism and the corrupt tastes of the literary marketplace. I argue that one of the ways such writers con-structed their identities as male writers working within, but against, market demands was by identifying with and distinguishing them-selves from the representations of racial others in respectable mass cultural forms such as the popular museum, daguerreotypal parlors, and sentimental minstrel shows. Because such amusements attempted to cash in on the sensationalistic effects and popularity of Bowery-identified, masculine amusements like Indian melodrama and minstrelsy by taming them for respectable audiences, they could provide these writers with a vehicle for establishing a kind of masculine, aesthetic independence. In their transgression of "feminine" bourgeois norms in terms of racial difference, such images provided writers a way of both acceding to the market's demands and establishing themselves beyond them. Attempting to establish themselves as independent masculine authors in an industry increasingly run like other capitalistic enterprises and still often characterized as a feminine province of successful women authors and domesticated readers, these writers invoked respectable amusements as an alternative model for gaining cultural authority over (and independence from) the increasingly dominant middle class. Cooper's novel and Forrest's performances from the beginning of the Jacksonian era help to suggest the ways in which these dynamics of authenticity and performance, race and gender, would continue to circulate throughout American mass cultural and literary forms of the pre–Civil War era, even as the kind of deferential cultural authority their identification with noble Indians guaranteed was replaced by a more middle-class, business-oriented hegemony.

"De Genewine Artekil"

William Wells Brown, Blackface Minstrelsy, and Abolitionism

In 1856, in addition to continuing to deliver lectures, former slave and "professional fugitive" William Wells Brown began to read dramatic pieces of his own composition at antislavery meetings.[1] His first play—the first play known to have been written by an African American—was titled either *The Dough Face* (a common epithet for "Yankees") or *Experience, or, How to Give a Northern Man a Backbone* and provided a satirical reply to Boston clergyman Nehemiah Adams's proslavery *A South-Side View of Slavery* (1854).[2] There is no extant text of this play, but two years later Brown published *The Escape; or, A Leap for Freedom,* another dramatic piece he often delivered to antislavery audiences. One of the central characters of this play is Cato, a slave characterized in the first two acts as a comic buffoon who toadies to his master and spies on his fellow slaves. In the second scene of the first act, Brown dramatizes Cato in an incident that he claimed was autobiographical and that he had already used in his novel *Clotel* (1853): When Cato attends to slaves in the place of his doctor-owner, in a bit of slapstick humor he accidentally pulls out the wrong tooth of a fellow slave. In the third act, however, Brown reveals a different side of Cato when he is left alone: "Now, ef I could only jess run away from ole massa, an' get to Canada wid Hannah, den I'd show 'em who I was." At this point in his dramatic readings, the light-skinned and eloquent Brown would, after a soliloquy full of malapropisms and dialect, break into an antislavery song set to the minstrel standard "Dandy Jim"—Cato's "moriginal hyme"—which Brown had already published as part of his *Anti-Slavery Harp* (1848):[3]

Come all ye bondmen far and near,
Let's put a song in massa's ear,

It is a song for our poor race,
Who're whipped and trampled with disgrace.

CHORUS
My old massa tells me, Oh,
This is a land of freedom, Oh;
Let's look about and see if it's so,
Just as massa tells me, Oh.[4]

As one contemporary reviewer put it, at such moments "you lose sight of the speaker" and in place of the educated Brown see the caricatured Cato.[5] This moment epitomizes Brown's performance of blackness—essentially a putting on of blackface—and is emblematic of how black abolitionists like Brown were necessarily engaged with blackface minstrelsy, the most popular entertainment form of the time.[6] Whether in narratives, lectures, or fiction, professional fugitives were called upon to prove their authenticity by providing, as Frederick Douglass recalled his white supporters putting it, "a *little* plantation manner of speech."[7] At the same time, however, black abolitionists were expected to mirror the ideal traits of middle-class, white manhood —intelligence, eloquence, self-restraint, and, above all, literacy—in order to exemplify black capacity for freedom. The professional fugitive was, in essence, required to embody the social meanings of blackness and whiteness simultaneously, to be both the illiterate plantation slave of the minstrel stage and an eloquent defender of his race.

In this chapter, I will use this episode from *The Escape* as a starting point for reading Brown's *Clotel*—the first novel by an African American—as a reworking of the ways both the minstrel show and the antislavery movement constructed strict racial definitions through the display of race as a matter of masquerade. As in Cato's scene from *The Escape*, Brown "blacks up" in *Clotel* by invoking minstrel show stereotypes when fictionalizing incidents from his own life through dark black male characters. Through multiple blackfaced characters, Brown links antislavery and minstrelsy, highlighting the antislavery possibilities in minstrelsy. Brown defended his appropriation of such theatrical effects on the grounds of gaining financial and popular support— "People will pay to hear the Drama that would not give a cent in an antislavery meeting."[8] He did not, however, turn to the minstrel show simply because of its popularity, but because in the early 1850s it provided perhaps the best forum through which to construct a viable representative black manhood. For Brown, the minstrel show offered particularly expansive representational possibilities because its commercialized images foregrounded the slippage between performative and essential notions of blackness and manliness.

In both abolitionism and the minstrel show, the production of race as a sort of mask depended upon the simultaneous construction of ideas about gender. The minstrel show was obsessed with the black male body, producing it as the embodiment of both a hypermasculine bestiality and a sentimental, effeminate childishness; antislavery rhetoric consistently circulated around either the proposition that slavery's chief crime was the destruction of true gender relations based in the domestic family unit or the idea that the effeminate, more spiritual African race should be saved from the masculine, aggressively materialistic Anglo-Saxon one. In the strictest terms, despite important political and iconic differences, the economies of race and gender at play in the minstrel show and the most prominent antislavery forms similarly equated manhood with whiteness. In this way, both forums attempted to use gender distinctions to anchor the slipperiness of race. Through Brown's redeployment of minstrel tropes, he reveals how the markers of manliness and whiteness were dependent on and constantly in play with those of blackness and femininity, so that gender and racial traits were at once strictly defined and, to a limited extent, transmutable.[9] In writing the first African American novel, Brown turns to fiction *not* to escape the problematic of stereotyped black representability, but to negotiate the objectification and commodification of the black image by revealing its instability. Combining the minstrel show with the sentimental novel, Brown highlights the dependence of middle-class manhood on images of blackness, thus opening the possibility of creating a blackfaced version of literary manhood.[10]

"The Public's Itching Ears"

The parallel courses of the minstrel show and abolitionism begin in the early 1830s. White actors had appeared in blackface on the American stage as early as a 1769 production of the play *The Padlock*, but the minstrel craze did not begin in earnest until T. D. Rice "jumped Jim Crow," first in the old northwest (perhaps Cincinnati, Pittsburgh, or

Louisville), sometime between 1829 and 1831, and then on the New York stage in 1832. At essentially the same time that Rice was first performing Jim Crow, the immediate emancipation movement emerged onto the political scene, inaugurated by William Lloyd Garrison's founding of *The Liberator* in 1831 and following on the heels of David Walker's *Appeal* (1829) and Nat Turner's revolt (1831). By the late 1830s, the demand for "black" male bodies had increased significantly—in the slave markets of the old southwest as laborers, in theaters and other entertainment sites as blackface performers, and in the abolitionist movement as antislavery lecturers. What these sites had in common was a focus on the black male body in slavery, on its status as a valuable economic article. Both the abolitionist platform and the minstrel stage attempted to evoke the reality of the Southern plantation by capturing and reproducing the truth of black life in the slave South. Neither minstrel shows nor abolitionism, however, exclusively focused on blacks in the South. Minstrel shows combined representations of the plantation slave Jim Crow with those of the Northern dandy Zip Coon; abolitionists demonstrated the connection between slavery in the South and racial prejudice in the North. Yet when defending their claims to authenticity by citing experience as the basis for their testimony or representations, both abolitionism and the minstrel show consistently set that experience either in the South or in some border region that granted access to the South.[11]

In attempting to reveal "American Slavery As It Is," both the minstrel show and the antislavery movement produced and exploited what one abolitionist called "the public['s] . . . itching ears to hear a colored man speak, and particularly a *slave*."[12] As antislavery groups began to employ black men to give authentic testimony about slavery in the late 1830s and early 1840s, minstrel performers began to claim that they gave a true picture of African American life through skits, songs, and dances.[13] In 1842 and 1843, western New York witnessed both the beginning of William Wells Brown's career as an antislavery agent and what Edwin Christy claimed was the first complete minstrel show. While Brown and other fugitive slaves tried to represent black manhood to white Northern audiences through their experiences in the slave South, ads and reviews proclaimed that white performers like Christy, Rice, and Dan Emmett were "the negro, par excellence," "the best representative of our American negro," "the perfect representative of the Southern Negro Character."[14] The minstrel show spectacularized black bodies for commercial purposes; antislavery groups put former slaves on display—"curiosit[ies] from the South," "specimen[s] of the fruits of the infernal system of slavery"—primarily for political ends.[15] Yet both forums staged black bodies precisely because they did draw. The minstrel show has most often been characterized as an extremely racist caricature of blacks and black lifeways that served to legitimate slavery and racial prejudice, but as scholars like Eric Lott and Robert Toll have argued, despite its racist content, the minstrel show was a complicated production in which various, at times contradictory, racial and political logics came into play. In fact, as Toll has pointed out, the minstrel show, at least prior to 1850 or so, "presented virtually every argument abolitionists used."[16] The emergence of these arguments in the minstrel show points toward a deeper connection between the minstrel show and abolitionism, specifically, the way in which in commodifying the black body both the minstrel show and antislavery rhetoric linked the construction of racial and gender distinctions to racial and gender confusion.

It was these representational limitations and possibilities that Brown faced in writing the first African American novel. Inspired by the phenomenal success of Harriet Beecher Stowe's *Uncle Tom's Cabin* (1852), Brown wrote *Clotel* in 1853 while living in England as an exile from the Fugitive Slave Law of 1850.[17] Rather than being a coherent narrative consistently centered on Clotel, the president's daughter (as the title implies), Brown's novel is a fragmented, episodic overview of slavery from Virginia to New Orleans to Mississippi.[18] Part of its patchwork quality derives from Brown's incorporation of stories from his *Original Panoramic Views* of slavery (1850) and his travel book, *Three Years in Europe* (1852), incidents from his slave narrative (1847), and whole sections lifted verbatim from Lydia Maria Child's "The Quadroons" (1842). The book begins with an introductory, third-person "Narrative of the Life and Escape of William Wells Brown." Written by Brown, and often quoting Brown's previously published first-person slave narrative and travel narrative, this introduction has regularly been read as marking the transition from autobiography to fiction in early African American literature. By taking the place of the authenticating letters of white abolitionists usually found preceding slave narratives, Brown's introduction, as a number of critics have shown, authorizes Brown as a writer of fiction.[19]

Most important for my argument, this narrative places Brown in a position of literary authority—of literary manhood—by focusing on his acquisition of the traits of middle-class manhood—specifically, literacy and economic success—through his ability to put on multiple masks. Brown stresses the importance of economic independence by arguing that, unlike other fugitive slaves who have come to England on "begging missions," he has "maintained himself and family by his own exertions—by his literary labours, and the honourable profession of a public lecturer."[20] It is through his literary endeavors that he has proven himself in the middle-class male role of family provider. In describing his first literary endeavor, his learning how to write, Brown narrates how he *acted* as though he could write in order to get young boys to teach him (37–38). By performing literacy, he, in fact, became literate. The next episode he relates emphasizes the market value of creating one's self as an authority, further linking his story of acquiring literacy to economic success and the construction of a male identity. Soon after escaping from slavery, Brown becomes a barber in Michigan, falsely advertising himself as a "Fashionable Hair-dresser from New York, Emperor of the West" (39). By taking on a popular and fashionable role, Brown is able to establish himself financially.

Building upon this success, Brown then sets up a wildcat bank, issuing printed bank notes, "Shinplasters," on the basis of the capital he already earned. After taking great care in printing the notes—"studying how I should keep the public from counterfeiting them" (41)—and worrying about having enough hard money to back his notes, Brown realizes that he need not bother with having hard money at all, because he "can keep cashing [his] own Shinplasters." Rather than actually needing to be solvent, Brown learns that he must act as if he is. By "putting in circulation the notes which [he] had just redeemed" (42), by keeping his shinplasters, his "printed" goods, in circulation, he becomes solvent. When he comments in the next paragraph about his concern "for the redemption of his race from personal slavery" (42), Brown links the redemption of his race to the redemption of "worthless paper" (40). Through his introduction, Brown suggests that it is through acting as though one fit middle-class images of manhood and by invoking popular images and keeping them in circulation that he, as a former slave, can both maintain his own family and redeem his race from slavery, that he can pursue his goals as a producer of printed goods.[21]

Brown's descriptions of his acquisition of literacy and his successes as a barber and a banker establish his central strategy for dealing with images of blackness and slavery in his novel. As a banker, he is at first concerned about backing up his notes with hard money, with the real thing, but then realizes that the way to stay afloat is simply to continue redeeming printed images with more images. In the novel itself, he keeps in circulation two of the era's most prominent images of blackness—the tragic mulatta of sentimental fiction and the male plantation slave of the minstrel stage—producing multiple examples of the same character types.[22] While Brown ostensibly focuses on the histories of Currer, her daughters by Thomas Jefferson, Clotel and Althesa, and her granddaughters—all beautiful mulattas who, with one exception, come to tragic ends—he does so through a series of often disconnected (or only slightly connected) scenes reminiscent of the segmented program of a minstrel show. In these episodes, Brown not only recalls the minstrel show's formal aspects, but also introduces a number of minstrel-like male characters who form a second thematic line parallel to the tragic mulatta stories. While the impact of slavery on the "fairer" sex—and, in this novel, they always are fairer—provides Brown's starting point, he doubles the racial confusion caused by his apparently white but really black heroines through a number of black male characters who, by invoking and reworking the minstrel show, similarly reveal the markers of their blackness as constructed.[23] Brown combines the standard sentimental abolitionist account of tragic mulattas, a form often directed specifically at white women, with the more masculine form of the minstrel show. Doing so, he foregrounds the performative nature of race and gender in both abolitionism and minstrelsy, thus creating a space from which to articulate a black male literary voice.[24]

Following his introduction, Brown opens the novel itself by setting up these two narrative lines, distinguishing between the "fearful increase of half whites"—like his heroines and himself—and "the real Negro," who "does not amount to more than one in every four of the slave population" (59). This distinction first arises in the diegesis following the sale of Currer and her daughters in an auction block scene set in Virginia. When taken south via the Mississippi River, Currer meets Pompey, the personal slave of the slave-trader Walker. Pompey's duties include "getting the Negroes ready for market" (70) as they are transported down the river. In his introductory narrative, Brown recounts how he was hired out to a slave-trader—also named Walker—who would buy gangs of slaves in Missouri and then transport them down the river to New Orleans. One of Brown's jobs under the "soul-driver" was "to prepare the old slaves for market." In doing so, he had to shave old men and "pluck out the grey hairs where they were not too numerous; where they were, he coloured them with a preparation of blacking. . . . After having gone through the blacking process, they looked ten or fifteen years younger" (21). Pompey, who "clearly showed that he knew what he was about," has similar duties and instructs the slaves that they "must grease dat face an make it look shiney" (71) when they go into the market. Neither Brown's "blacking process" nor Pompey's "greas[ing]" up is exactly equivalent to the corking of the minstrel show, but in his narrative Brown recalls having to set slaves in the New Orleans market "to dancing, some to jumping, some to singing, and some to playing cards. . . . to make them appear cheerful and happy" (*N* 194). What Pompey's "greas[ing]" up and Brown's "blacking process" indicate is the constructedness of the black body as a commodity. Just as Brown produces himself and his shinplasters as the real things in order to survive in the capitalist North, so blacks are artificially turned into merchandise in the slave South. Slaves are not simply what they appear to be on the auction block; rather they must be coerced into performing their roles as valued (because of their youth, demeanor, strength) objects.[25]

Yet this implicit recognition of the performative nature of those traits most valued in the marketplace does not reveal race as an illusion. Instead, it seems to lead to strict racial distinctions.[26] Brown notes that Pompey is, like all other male slave characters in *Clotel* (with one exception), "of real Negro blood." He "was of low stature, round face, and, like most of his race, had a set of teeth, which for whiteness and beauty could not be surpassed; his eyes large, lips thick, and hair short and woolly." Pompey "would often say, when alluding to himself, 'Dis nigger is no counterfit; he is de genewine artekil'" (70–71). Yet Pompey, like Brown, is a master of counterfeiting, especially the counterfeiting of such valuable articles as slaves. This episode demonstrates that *appearing* as the "genewine artekil," like Pompey, involves masquerade, in essence, putting on blackface; it reveals race as an illusion, as a mask that one puts on, while acknowledging the ways in which that mask makes race very real. What then does it mean for the light-skinned Brown to fictionalize himself in basically the same way, blacking himself up as a character (Pompey) described as a minstrel caricature? In narrating his own complicity with a slave-driver in the form of a caricatured black figure, Brown could be, and often has been, accused of being "colorist"—of espousing the idea that the worst slaves were the "real Negro[es]" and that the ones most deserving and capable of freedom and its responsibilities were light-skinned, like his mulatta heroines and himself.[27] Yet, while Pompey's actions show no resistance to slavery, the blackfaced characters who follow in the novel complicate the idea of his complicity by forming a composite representative black male character who resists slavery through acts of subterfuge and masquerade. By describing the submission and resistance of his male slaves as different masks—as different ways of blacking up—Brown demonstrates both how masquerade creates them as "genewine artekil[s]" through strict racial definitions and how the performative nature of that masquerade allows them to redefine what it means to be a "genewine" black man.

Through these multiple black men, Brown reveals a different face on the standard caricature of the happy black slave. Jean Fagan Yellin places Brown's characterization of these figures within the trickster tradition in African American culture.[28] I am more interested, however, in the ways in which Brown was invoking and critiquing the minstrel show. This is not to say that Brown was not drawing upon African American traditions of the trickster figure; instead, it is to insist on the ways in which representations of such "folk" figures were already mediated by mass cultural representations.[29] Because of this mediation, the slave, per se, could not be represented. Brown frequently described this problem in his lectures: "I may try to represent to you Slavery as it is . . . yet we shall all fail to represent the real condition of the Slave. . . . Slavery has never been represented; Slavery never can be represented. . . . The Slave cannot speak for himself." At the same time, however, Brown realized that, on the abolitionist stage, he "represent[ed]" the "system of Slavery."[30] Or, as he put it in another lecture, "I stand here as the representative of the slave to speak for those who cannot speak for themselves."[31] In attempting to "speak for" the slaves still in bondage, the former slave entered into public debates over race and slavery. But to do so, he had to cast off the markers of both his past enslavement and his racial difference and take up the language and figures articulated by the dominant culture.[32]

I will argue that Brown turns to the minstrel show in order to reclaim the blackness that he had to abandon in order to enter into the public sphere.[33] In this way, he was able to produce a model of literate black manhood that could be read as representative of slaves in general, even while undermining any simple notion of "the Slave." In *Clotel*, Brown recognizes and demonstrates the possible uses and limitations of appropriating minstrel figures for explicitly antislavery purposes, but his appropriation does not amount to the complete transformation of a monolithically negative form. Instead, Brown is able to use minstrelsy for his antislavery purposes because of the ambivalence within the form itself, because the minstrel show, in both negative and positive ways, mirrored the representational logic and problematic of the abolitionist platform. Brown does not undermine the minstrel show in order to reveal a true representation of black manhood; rather he undermines the idea of one authentic representation of black manhood by insisting on the instability of both white and black manhood and by pointing to the ways in which race and gender were always being performed and being performed together.[34]

"African Nature . . . Full of Poetry and Song"

In the last decade, increasing critical attention has focused on the minstrel show in antebellum American culture. While the various studies differ in a number of important ways, a revisionist picture of the minstrel show has emerged. Led by Eric Lott's work in *Love and Theft*, cultural historians have argued that despite its racist content, blackface, at least in its earlier Jacksonian incarnations of the 1830s and 1840s, was much more than simply a defense of slavery or a racist projection used to consolidate a white identity.[35] Instead, it at times provided a forum where white and black working-class cultures intermingled and where the possibility of interracial solidarity was imagined. According to these studies, early blackface engendered the formation of a subversive, Northern white working-class male subculture by giving voice to some distinctly working-class concerns through imagining cross-racial union. While respectable audiences and critics dismissed the blackface craze of the 1830s, by the end of the 1840s minstrel shows had begun "to attract the patronage of the most respectable citizens," as indicated by their incorporation into the more middle-class attractions—like Barnum's American Museum—of Broadway.[36] According to historians like Lott, W. T. Lhamon Jr., and Dale Cockrell, as it became increasingly acceptable to these middle-class audiences, blackface was drained of its subversive content: the focus shifted from possibly antislavery materials and dangerous images of Northern black dandies like Zip Coon and potentially rebellious slaves like Jim Crow to sentimentalized visions of slaves happily singing on the old plantation. As blackface performances became more strictly organized—into minstrel shows and concerts—and were taken up by more middle-class venues, the radical nature of the form was dissipated.[37]

By 1850 the minstrel show and its basic conventions—its racial masquerade, its caricatures of slaves, and its burlesque of high culture pretensions—had come to structure the ways in which a broad cross-section of white Northern Americans confronted and constructed ideas of black character and came to understand and live their own raced and gendered identities. In its earlier incarnation, in the 1830s and early 1840s, the minstrel show was nearly an all-male affair (men would continue to play almost all roles throughout the century), which foremost staged the interplay between black and white manhood. As Lott has demonstrated, the "main achievement" of the minstrel show's white male audiences and performers was the "simultaneous production and subjection of black maleness."[38] While recent historians have tended to read the acceptance of minstrelsy by more middle-class, mixed-gendered audiences in the 1840s as yet another (or the first) example of the cooptation of a truly oppositional, working-class popular culture into a commodified, bland, simplistic, and hegemonic mass culture, I am interested in how Brown was able to mine the more respectable minstrel show of the 1850s for antislavery ends. In other words, becoming a mass cultural form neither completely drained minstrelsy of all of its antislavery content nor totally eradicated its evocation of possibly subversive cross-racial identification. Rather, because of the ways in which minstrelsy continued to stage blackness in conjunction with characteristics of dominant (white middle-class) ideas of manhood, Brown could draw on its commodified interplay between whiteness and blackness to suggest the black capacity of taking on the traits of white, middle-class manhood that, according to a certain antislavery logic, blacks had to demonstrate in order to prove their humanity.[39]

Specifically, whereas in the 1830s elite and middle-class critics disparaged blackface and its audiences, in the 1840s and early 1850s they began to celebrate the minstrel show as an antidote to or an escape from the increasingly complex and disciplined world arising with industrial, market capitalism and urbanization.[40] Most famously, perhaps, Margaret Fuller read "the African race" and their "African melodies" such as "Jim Crow" as a cultural corrective for "the Caucasian race [who] have yet their rail-roads to make."[41] Similarly, as Y. S. Nathanson put it in 1855, the popularity of "Jim Crow" extended to "Merchants and staid professional men," prompting them "to unbend their dignity."[42] By providing white audiences with models of "African nature . . . full of poetry and song," minstrel shows could revitalize an overly refined and business-oriented white existence. Because "[African] joy and grief are not pent up in the heart, but find instant expression in their eyes and voice," "these simple children of Africa," though "inferior to the white race in reason and intellect," offer a valuable "lesson" in "lighten[ing] the anxiety and care which brood on every face and weigh on every heart."[43] In the figure of the simple plantation slave, middle-class audience members could appreciate the joys of a bodily existence undisciplined by the market and developing ideals of decorum, while at the same time maintaining some distance from that bodily enjoyment as mandated by the emerging discourse of middle-class manhood.[44]

In order to maintain the proper bodily (dis)engagement to appreciate the pleasures associated with these images of natural freedom in slavery without succumbing to them, the minstrel show oscillated between acknowledging its performative nature and claiming unmediated authenticity. Although critics admitted that "We at the North hear these songs only as burlesqued by our Negro Minstrels," commentary on the minstrel show often obscured the distinction between "Negro Minstrels" and actual African Americans.[45] Numerous stories circulated about naive viewers who believed that the performers were actually black, a confusion that could easily spring from the ubiquitous references to white performers as "Negro songsters" or "Negro dancers."[46] But at the same time, performers and audiences emphasized the artifice of performances, the fact that underneath the burnt cork were white men: lyrics, skits, and sheet music illustrations frequently alluded to the white identity of performers.[47] Accordingly, minstrel performers simultaneously displayed characteristics that marked them as black and as white. And by extension, in attending minstrel shows and learning the "lesson[s]" of black bodily and emotional freedom from such "Negro" entertainers, white audience members were imagined to replicate this logic by internalizing the characteristics of blackness while remaining white themselves: audience members "lighten[ed]" their "brood[ing]" "face[s]" by vicariously "blacking up." In this way, minstrelsy was driven by an oscillation between the celebration and denigration of black men, a dance of identification and differentiation that simultaneously foregrounded and disavowed the dependence of middle-class white manhood on notions of black manhood.

"A Million of Counterfeit Jim Crows"

Accounts of the most famous black minstrel entertainer of the period, William Henry Lane, demonstrate that this oscillation between authenticity and artifice produced strict racial distinctions and at the same time rendered those distinctions nonsensical. The story of Lane, who, like Brown, lived in England from 1848 to 1852, exemplifies the dual movement of the minstrel show that allowed Brown to articulate his antislavery argument.[48] In the early 1840s, because his more respectable audiences would "have resented . . . the insult of being asked to look at the dancing of a real negro," P. T. Barnum "greased" and "rubbed" Lane's face "with a new blacking of burnt cork" before letting him appear on his stage. According to contemporary accounts, although "a genuine negro"—"the genuine article"—Lane needed to become a "seeming counterfeit" in order to gain a place on the minstrel stage.[49] This description highlights the way in which the minstrel show produced authenticity through counterfeits.[50] Lane could only be accepted as black on the minstrel stage if he appeared to be a white man in blackface. Just as Pompey had to "grease" the face of slaves and use a little "blacking" to make his owner's slaves "de genewine artekil[s]" for the slave market, Lane had to become a "counterfeit" in order to reveal himself as "the genuine article." In order to appear real—and gain commercial success—Lane had to perform the blackness that he supposedly embodied naturally.

As Lane's fame grew, his actual race became well-known, and, apparently, he began to appear on stage without blacking up. But even without blackface, the type of imitation and repetition staged by the minstrel show rendered Lane's race simultaneously a mask and his essential identity. According to flyers from the period, at the climax of his performances, Lane would perform an "Imitation Dance . . . in which he will give correct Imitation Dances of all the principal Ethiopian Dancers in the United States. After which he will give an imitation of himself—and then you will see the vast difference between those that have heretofore attempted dancing and this WONDERFUL YOUNG MAN."[51] In this series of imitations, as he imitates white men in blackface who claim they are imitating black men, Lane ends up imitating himself, conflating the authentic and the counterfeit and making any idea of the authentic appear bankrupt. This multiplication of Jim Crow–like images to the point of unreality is at the center of the most famous description of Lane's dancing, that of Charles Dickens. In his *American Notes* (1842), Dickens describes seeing Lane during a trip into the underworld of the Five Points district of New York: "the greatest dancer known. He never leaves off making queer faces. . . . dancing with two left legs, two right legs, two wooden legs, two wire legs, two spring legs—all sorts of legs and no legs. . . . he finishes . . . with the chuckle of a million of counterfeit Jim Crows, in one inimitable sound!"[52]

Lane's performances verge on the unreal, as he becomes a counterfeit of a counterfeit and his body both multiplies and disappears. This is not to say, however, that the unreality created through this multiplication of images undermines the idea of authenticity. Instead, while it does deconstruct the possibility of finding a stable center of authenticity, it also enables the authentic to be reinvoked. Reviews used Lane's imitations of imitations not to reveal how the blackness he represented was also an imitation, but to argue for the purity of previous dancers: "the Nigger Dance is a reality. . . . [Otherwise] how could Juba enter into their wonderful complications so naturally?" Lane was able to copy other dancers "so naturally" because they had reproduced "real" black dancing practices in their "Nigger Dance[s]" so well. Lane's performances were "far above the common performances of the mountebanks who give imitations of American and Negro character," because he embodied "an ideality . . . that makes his efforts at once grotesque and poetical, without losing sight of the reality of representation."[53] Through his performances, Lane both places the idea of authentic black identity into question by appearing as a "counterfeit Jim Crow" and provides a possible site for its reinterpretation. His example emphasizes how the minstrel show produced race and gender as authentic, as real, by repeatedly staging their defining traits as matters of masquerade.[54]

As Lane's story also demonstrates, the minstrel show simultaneously produced black men as white and white men as black, thus making the differential markers of white and black manhood interchangeable while creating notions of essential racial difference and authentic racial identity. Because minstrel performers embodied characteristics of both black and white manhood, the minstrel show, at times, staged black men who displayed characteristics of white manliness that blacks supposedly lacked. In particular, this slippage produced minstrel representations of the possibility of slave resistance even as the minstrel show of the 1850s actively discounted such possibilities. Early versions of "Jim Crow," for example, raised the possibility of emancipation and slave revolt in reference to the Nullification crisis:

Should dey get to fighting,
Perhaps de blacks will rise,
For deir wish for freedom,
Is shining in deir eyes.

. . . .

I'm for freedom,
An for Union altogether,
Aldough I'm a black man,
De white is call'd my broder.[55]

This desire for freedom, by whatever means necessary, including violence, often appeared in the lyrics of early minstrel songs like "The Raccoon Hunt": "My ole massa dead and gone, / A dose of poison help him on / De debil say he funeral song."[56] Such moments depended upon racial slippage. In singing of slave resistance, the performer of "Jim Crow" is at once black—"I'm a black man"—and white, or at least the white man's equal, his "broder."[57]

First performed in New York less than a year after Nat Turner's failed revolt, "Jim Crow" evokes the image of "the Spartacus of the Southampton revolt."[58] Such explicit antislavery statements and allusions to slave revolt began to disappear from blackface performance as it was incorporated into a more middle-class entertainment industry in the 1840s. Yet as Lhamon has stated, "the multiple aspects of the minstrel mask preserved contradictory meanings" even as "the industrial economy of the Atlantic world and the microeconomy of minstrel theatre producers reversed the original Jim Crow engagement" and "P. T. Barnum, Sam Sanford, E. P. Christy, Charles White, and other ever more middle-class entrepreneurs gradually realigned the disturbances of this identification."[59] Even as the noise of working-class blackface was turned into music for middle-class audiences, the possibility of manly black rebellion and cross-racial resistance to slavery and capital remained as an undercurrent.[60] For example, "Uncle Gabriel, the Darkey General," a song performed by the respectable Christy's Minstrels, celebrated Turner's revolt while conflating it with the Gabriel Prosser–led conspiracy of 1800—"He was the chief of the Insurgents, / Way down in Southampton. / Hard times in old Virginny."[61] By simply invoking the memory of two of the best known American slave revolts, such songs gave evidence against the image of the happy plantation slave that was central to Southern propaganda and many minstrel skits. Yet by referring to the slave leader as an "Uncle" and by focusing on his punishment—"And there they hung him and they swung him"— the song simultaneously attempts to contain the specter of slave revolt by reinscribing black manhood as either submissive or disempowered.[62] In staging race and manliness as fluid and performed, the minstrel show, at least temporarily, enabled the union of blackness and manhood, pointing to a way of constructing black manhood through the instability of race and gender.

"And So Did I Pretend"

In the slippage created by this constant repetition and performance of difference, the constant oscillation between whiteness and blackness, Brown was able to produce a representative black manhood through his own "million of counterfeit Jim Crows." In *Clotel*, Brown foregrounds this possibility of using the minstrel show to enunciate slave resistance in his characterization of Sam, the novel's second black male character. Pompey "*appeared* perfectly indifferent to the heartrending scenes" (70, emphasis added) of slavery and seemed simply to submit to its structures while displaying the stereotyped characteristics of the minstrel slave; yet Brown's description of him points toward the elements of masquerade in his appearance. With Sam, Brown turns that masquerade into an explicit critique of slavery.[63] A slave with Currer on Reverend Peck's plantation in Mississippi, Sam is essentially an earlier incarnation of *The Escape*'s Cato. In the chapter "A Night in the Parson's Kitchen," Sam seems to be nothing more than comic relief in the form of a minstrel burlesque: he wishes he were lighter ("He was one of the blackest of his race"[131]), fawns over his master and mistress, treats his position in the household with an overabundance of pride and dignity, and is overly concerned with his dress ("he was seldom seen except in a ruffled shirt"[131]). Despite his ability to read, Sam still believes in fortune-tellers, and Brown explicitly links his prejudice against blacks (he claims his mother was a mulatta) to "ignorance" (133). Finally, "A Night in the Parson's Kitchen" ends with Sam telling of his experience as a doctor's assistant, including the story of pulling the wrong tooth that Brown later used in *The Escape*: "We once saw Sam taking out a tooth for one of his patients, and nothing appeared more amusing" (134). With the accompanying illustration of minstrelized blacks (see Figure 2) and Brown's use of the inclusive "we"— indicating a communal viewing—the novel stages a scene that could have come directly from a minstrel show, a skit that represents blacks as inherently comic and incapable of performing the more intellectual tasks involved in professions such as medicine.[64]

At this point, Brown has shown his black male characters as buffoons and toadies who buy into the master's ideology. Yet as he develops Sam more fully, "we" realize that we have only seen the stereotyped laughing black face, not the critical, freedom-yearning face that coexists alongside it. We next encounter Sam after Reverend Peck's death. As Peck's abolitionist daughter Georgiana and her friend Carlton walk over the plantation grounds, trying to decide what to do with the slaves, they hear "how prettily the Negroes sing." After Georgiana informs Carlton that the slaves will stop singing if they realize they have an audience, the pair decide to remain secluded and "stop, and . . . hear this one." Leading the singing is Sam, and at first it seems that he is still the simple minstrel caricature who is "always on hand when there's any singing or dancing" (154). The setting of this song recalls numerous sentimental minstrel songs of the early 1850s, perhaps most recogniz-

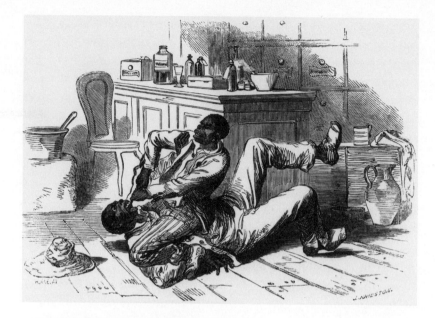

2. "Negro Dentistry," from William Wells Brown, *Clotel* (1853). *Courtesy of The Newberry Library, Chicago, Illinois.*

ably Stephen Foster's "Massa's in De Cold Ground" (1852): "Down in the corn-field / Hear that mournful sound; / All de darkies am a weeping—/ Massa's in de cold, cold ground."[65] But instead of expressing their sorrow and love for their master, as Foster's song seems to do and as both the two lovers and "we" the readers would expect, Sam and the other slaves celebrate their master's death, singing of his many cruelties and their own pretended sadness:

> He will no more trample on the neck of the slave;
>> For he's gone where the slaveholders go.
>
> . . . .
>
> Mr. Carlton cried, and so did I pretend;
>> Young mistress very nearly went mad;
> And the old parson's groans did the heavens fairly rend;
>> But I tell you I felt mighty glad.
>
> . . . .
>
> He no more will hang our children on the tree,
>> To be ate by the carrion crow;
> He no more will send our wives to Tennessee;
>> For he's gone where the slaveholders go. (154–55)

Here, Brown redeploys the standard conceits of the minstrel show—slaves singing and dancing on the plantation—in order to uncover its antislavery possibilities. Brown's rewriting of Foster's "Massa's in De Cold Ground" makes its possibly subversive meaning explicit. In Foster's song, "all de darkies am a weeping," yet the natural world, and specifically the mockingbird, with which blacks were often aligned in minstrel songs, is joyous—"mockingbird am singing, / Happy as de day am long." And though the "days were cold/ . . . [and] hard" while master was still alive, now, "summer days am coming." Finally, Foster's song raises the possibility that the slaves are faking their sorrow in order to gain respite from work: "I cannot work before to-morrow, / Cayse de tear drops flow." Foster's sentimental songs explicitly encouraged one type of antislavery argument, as made clear by Harriet Beecher Stowe's invocation of "Mas'r's in the cold, cold ground" in *Dred* (1856), through their depiction of blacks as more emotional and spiritual, in fact, more feminine.[66] Yet, like earlier blackface songs such as "Jim Crow," the more sentimental, middle-class "Massa's in De Cold Ground" also depends on the slippage between characterizing its singers as childishly sentimental—as "black"—and cunningly subversive—as intelligent and courageous (or at least treacherous) *men*. In his novel, Brown emphasizes such songs' implicit reference to the possibility of manly black resistance. By making this immanent critique from within minstrelsy of the 1850s explicit, Brown shows another side to both the minstrelized Sam and the minstrel show in general. In particular, this scene demonstrates that the slave's submission cannot be taken at face value and that representations of the male slave depend on occasionally revealing his unexpected resistance to oppression. But what Brown also makes clear is that, "from these unguarded expressions of the feelings of the Negroes," his two white abolitionist characters can "learn a lesson" (156). Specifically, what Carlton, Georgiana, and other abolitionists can learn is a different way of approaching one of the central problems of antislavery rhetoric, the problem of representing black manhood.

"A White Man . . . Within"

Antislavery rhetoric consistently spoke of the debilitating effects of slavery in gendered terms. During the antebellum period, rising middle-class ideologies of the family foregrounded gender—as defined by strictly distinguished traits—as an essential quality of being human.

Hence, as Kristin Hoganson has argued, despite its radical sexual politics, Garrisonian abolitionism attempted to show both how slavery deformed true gender relations and how blacks demonstrated their humanity by still maintaining these gender roles.[67] These contradictory impulses come together in the most famous antislavery topos—the ubiquitous "am I not a man and a brother"—which Brown reproduced with both his *Panoramic Views* pamphlet and his *Anti-Slavery Harp* (see Figure 3).[68] The emblem emphasizes that the slave is a man—is human—while placing its declaration in the form of a question and focusing on the disempowered, enchained, and imploring figure of the un-manned male slave.[69] While the accompanying text implies the slave's common manhood, the illustration strips the black man of the markers of manhood; with his body exposed both to the gaze of all onlookers and to the whips at his feet, his hands chained, his head turned up in supplication with his question, the figure represents the black male as dependent on the sympathy and good will of others, an object to be pitied and acted on, rather than a subject who acts. Such emblems seemed to indicate that under slavery a man could not truly be a man and a woman could not truly be a woman. Yet abolitionists needed to show that blacks were capable of such gendered identities. As Richard Yarborough has argued, "the crucial test of black fitness" for freedom came "to be whether or not black men were, in fact, what was conventionally considered 'manly.' "[70]

Abolitionists faced two primary problems in representing black manhood: first, slavery was constructed as antithetical to the ideal attributes of manhood, and second, because the construction of blackness was so intrinsically tied to ideas of enslavement, blackness came to be seen as essentially unmanly. The position of former-slave orators highlights this first problem.[71] Professional fugitives like Brown displayed the markers of genteel middle-class manhood—intelligence, eloquence, and especially literacy—but in becoming educated they were seen as less and less representative of the majority of the slave population. As Frederick Douglass recounts in his 1855 autobiography, "People doubted if I had ever been a slave. They said I did not talk like a slave, look like a slave, nor act like a slave. . . . 'he is educated, and is, in this, a contradiction of all the facts we have concerning the ignorance of the slaves.' Thus, I was in a pretty fair way to be denounced as an impostor."[72] As Henry Louis Gates Jr. and others have pointed out and as Douglass's and Brown's descriptions of acquiring literacy emphasize,

A DESCRIPTION

OF

WILLIAM WELLS BROWN'S

ORIGINAL

PANORAMIC VIEWS

OF THE

SCENES IN THE LIFE OF AN AMERICAN SLAVE,

FROM HIS BIRTH IN SLAVERY TO HIS DEATH OR HIS
ESCAPE TO HIS FIRST
HOME OF FREEDOM ON BRITISH SOIL.

FICTION.

"We hold these truths to be self-evident: that all men are created equal ;
that they are endowed by their Creator with certain inalienable rights, and
that among these are LIFE, LIBERTY, and the PURSUIT OF HAPPINESS."—
Declaration of American Independence.

FACT.

"They touch our country, and their shackles fall."—COWPER.

LONDON:

PUBLISHED BY CHARLES GILPIN,

5, BISHOPSGATE STREET WITHOUT;

AND TO BE HAD OF ALL BOOKSELLERS.

3. Title page of William Wells Brown, *A Description of William Wells Brown's
Original Panoramic Views* (1850). *Courtesy of the Boston Athenaeum.*

literacy came to represent the chief trait a black man needed in order to gain freedom and thus prove his manhood. Yet in achieving such literacy and freedom, he came to be seen as an exception to black ignorance and submission.[73]

It was not just that the former slave did not mirror accepted images of the slave; former slaves themselves often interpreted their acquisition of freedom as a complete transformation of their old selves. Douglass's paradigmatic narrative underlines the gendered nature of this transformation. There, he describes how his resistance to Edward Covey not only "rekindled the few expiring embers of freedom," but also "revived within [him] a sense of [his] own manhood." For Douglass, regaining manhood meant that "however long I might remain a slave in form, the day had passed forever when I could be a slave in fact" and "that the white man who expected to succeed in whipping, must also succeed in killing me."[74] Through active, physical resistance to slavery, Douglass becomes a man by ceasing to be a slave in fact. Brown narrates similar feelings in his introduction to *Clotel*: "I was no more a chattel, but a MAN. . . . The fact that I was a freeman—could walk, talk, eat, and sleep as a man, and no one to stand over me with the blood-clotted cowhide —all this made me feel that I was not myself" (34). But Brown also critiques Douglass's construction of a black voice and black manhood through physical resistance. In the second chapter of his 1847 narrative, Brown remembers a slave named Randall, who, like Douglass, "declared, that no white man should ever whip him—that he would die first" (*N* 181). Randall stakes his claim to manhood on physical resistance, and thus is a slave only "in form." Yet rather than eventually escaping to freedom, Randall is finally "subdued" (*N* 182) by the cruel overseer. In Brown's narrative, active resistance to the mechanisms of slavery does not make one a man, as Douglass insisted; instead it leads to one's being completely unmanned.[75]

Brown's critique of Douglass's model of black manhood also points to the problem of representability. Douglass proves his own manhood through his resistance and eventual escape, but his narrative also emphasizes his exceptionalism. And this exceptionalism characterizes the majority of slaves as "brute[s]" who demonstrate their "want of manhood" in not making "at least one noble effort to be free."[76] As Douglass phrased it in his 1855 autobiography, "I was *nothing* before; I WAS A MAN NOW. . . . A man, without force, is without the essential dignity of humanity." Importantly, in this version of Douglass's autobiography, his reclamation of manhood and freedom erases racial distinctions—"I now forgot my *roots*, and remembered my pledge to *stand up in my own defense*. . . . The very color of the man was forgotten."[77] At the moment of becoming a man, race disappears because achieving middle-class standards of manliness—autonomy, freedom, self-control, and, most important, literacy—was seen as antithetical to the servitude with which blackness had become so forcefully bound. It is only by denouncing his slave past that Douglass can fully become a man. In achieving freedom and the literacy and eloquence required to gain access to the public stage, the former slave was able to prove his manliness, but by doing so he could no longer be representative of black manhood; he might be black, but he was not "really" black, not like most blacks. As Frantz Fanon phrased it a century later, white acceptance was premised on the idea that "At bottom you are a white man," "You have nothing in common with real Negroes."[78]

In trying to prove black humanity by demonstrating black manhood, antislavery rhetoric did not simply face the problem that slavery seemed antithetical to manly attributes of physical self-possession, family protection, and powerful activity. Instead the supposed absence of these traits among slave men was consistently seen—often even by antislavery advocates—as essential to black character. The focus in antislavery fiction and forums on light-skinned characters and speakers highlights this problem. Certainly one of the reasons that Brown and Douglass became so influential was because white abolitionists viewed their light complexions as potentially more acceptable to the unconverted and as proof of the sexual degradations of slavery.[79] But as often happened in Brown's case, the light black spokesman's manly attributes —especially his eloquence and intelligence—were seen as evidence of his white blood: "He is far removed from the black race, being just the 'color of mahogany,' and his distinct enunciation evidently showed that a white man 'spoke' within, although the words were uttered by the lips of a redeemed slave"; "eloquent, humorous and interesting, showing clearly the white blood of his father."[80] As Douglass put it, "an intelligent black man is always supposed to have derived his intelligence from his connection with the white race. To be intelligent is to have one's negro blood ignored."[81] In being recognized as intelligent and eloquent, the professional fugitive was accepted as manly, but that manhood made him "white."

This logic of mulatto exceptionalism—the idea that blacks displayed admirable traits because of their "Anglo-Saxon blood"—appears in gendered terms in abolitionist fiction. Attempts to reveal slaves as either true women or real men—attempts to engender the black body—often ended up turning that body white. As Karen Sánchez-Eppler has put it more generally, "The problem of antislavery fiction is that the very effort to depict goodness in black involves the obliteration of blackness."[82] The central role of tragic mulatta figures in antislavery fiction in general and in *Clotel* in particular illustrates this problem. Such characters embodied the ideals of middle-class true womanhood and illustrated the dangers of slavery to the virtue and modesty deemed essential to this idealized femininity. Yet in rendering female slaves true women, such stories erased all but the most minute trace of their blackness.[83] A similar problem obtained in depicting male slaves in antislavery fiction. As Nancy Bentley has shown, black heroes of antislavery fiction who displayed the masculine traits of self-reliance and physical resistance to the degradations of slavery were almost invariably nearly white, like George Harris in Harriet Beecher Stowe's *Uncle Tom's Cabin*.[84] The contrast between such mulatto characters and black slaves distinguished fully gendered white slaves from more androgynous black characters. Specifically, mulatto heroes underlined a gendered racial distinction between the more active, masculine white race and the more passive, feminine black race.[85]

Even when writers characterized black men as heroes, they were burdened by this equation of race and gender. In "The Heroic Slave" (1853), a fictionalized account of the 1841 slave revolt on board the *Creole*, Frederick Douglass attempts to depict Madison Washington as a traditional hero who retains a black identity. Douglass's story suggests, however, that the display of manliness racially transformed even an explicitly *black* man. Douglass first introduces Madison Washington by his voice, a move that denies his black body. When Washington appears, Douglass's first narrator describes him as " 'black, but comely' " with a "sable" "manly form."[86] While these descriptions stress the blackness of Washington's skin, the first begins to feminize his "manly form" with its use of an adjective usually reserved for women and its allusion to the bride of Solomon.[87] More telling, in the second narrator's depiction of the revolt's climax aboard the *Creole*, Washington's heroism all but transmogrifies him into a white man: "I forgot his blackness. . . . It seemed as if the souls of both the great dead (whose names he bore) had entered him" (161). While this second white narrator's point has been to correct the "ignorance of the real character of *darkies* in general" (157) by showing their true nobility and courage, at the moment of these traits' clearest manifestation he erases not only Washington's black body, but also his black soul. Douglass could be emphasizing the racism of his second narrator, but this moment clearly echoes Douglass's 1855 account of achieving manhood by fighting Covey: "the very color of the man was forgotten." As the commentator on Brown's oratory might put it, both Douglass's and Washington's manliness reveals a white man acting from within.

"As Good As White Folks"

In the early 1850s, to depict a black man as a man required either painting him white—as with mulatto heroes—or stripping off his blackness to reveal a white interior—as with Madison Washington.[88] But both solutions replicated the racial distinctions they attempted to question—whiteness made one a man, blackness, by itself, left one less than a man. In *Clotel,* Brown uses his mulatto hero, George Green, to point toward a way out of this conundrum, thus enabling him to define himself as both a writer and a black man. Specifically, George's story helps Brown expand and elaborate his understanding of race and gender as masquerade by revealing the performative nature of white manhood. Yet as with his black male slaves and mulatta heroines, Brown uses his mulatto hero not only to render racial lines fluid but also to demonstrate that the performance of race and gender makes them very real. By demonstrating the fictive nature of race and gender, Brown is able to construct a literate black manhood as a reality. Brown introduces George Green near the end of the novel as both a participant in Nat Turner's rebellion and the betrothed of Clotel's daughter Mary. Like Stowe's rebellious George Harris, George Green "was as white as most white persons" (224). Whereas Stowe saw slave rebellion arising from an "infusion of Anglo Saxon blood," Brown offers a more environmentalist understanding of his mulatto hero's rebelliousness.[89] Green's mixed-blood does, in part, enable him to become an insurgent. But it does so because his complexion makes "his condition still more intolerable" (224)—both blacks and whites treat him harshly—and because it grants him greater opportunities for realizing what freedom means: "George's opportunities were far greater than most slaves. Being in his master's house, and waiting on educated white people, he had . . . heard his master and visitors speak of the down-trodden and oppressed Poles. . . . fired with love of freedom, and zeal for the cause of his enslaved countrymen, [he] joined the insurgents" (224).

Brown further undermines the idea that black rebelliousness arises from an "infusion of Anglo Saxon blood" by making it clear that Nat Turner—"respected by the whites, and loved and venerated by the Negroes"—was "a full-blooded Negro" (213). And the only other slave rebel Brown mentions is the Maroon Picquilo, "a large, tall, full-blooded Negro, with a stern and savage countenance" (213). But Picquilo points up yet another problem of representing black male resistance. George—whether because of his greater educational opportunities or because of his "Anglo Saxon blood"—can denounce the slave system and cite European wars of liberation as examples for his own activities. Picquilo, on the other hand, stands mute, "a bold, turbulent spirit" whose "revenge imbrued his hands in the blood of all the whites he could meet" (214). George rebels because of his "love of freedom"; Picquilo fights for "revenge" because of his "barbarous. . . . character" (213–14). Middle-class manhood was based upon the ideal of control over one's own body, and fighting for one's freedom—as Frederick Douglass did—could demonstrate this power. But unless it could be defended in rational terms, physical conflict came too close to undisciplined bodily expression, an attractive but threatening prospect.[90] Thus, while white men became men by waging war for their freedom, black men who did the same were irrational, primitive brutes.[91] Picquilo becomes an animalistic spirit rising out of the Virginia swamps, the black, atavistic Nat who formed the mirror image to the submissive Sambo in Southern ideology.[92] Because Picquilo cannot speak or write for himself, because he must always be represented, he cannot account for his actions. Readers might temporarily identify with Picquilo's embodiment of primitive manliness, his "savage" rebellion—as minstrel show audiences might have identified with the singer of "Uncle Gabriel"—but emerging discourses of manhood encouraged them to disavow such embodiment. While minstrel show representations of black resistance might similarly be interpreted as displaying blackness as atavistic, the minstrel show undermined any easy reading of this form of embodiment as essentially black, as anything more than yet another mask. Through its constant interplay of blackness and whiteness, the minstrel show made it unclear whose atavism was whose, whose body was out of control through rebellion and whose was the tool of rational and righteous revolt.

Brown uses George to suggest this kind of racial (and gender) confusion as an alternative to equating manhood with resistance—an equation that eventually turned the black male into a white man or a primitive brute. After George is sentenced to death for his part in the rebellion, Mary visits him in prison and suggests that they exchange clothes so that he can leave the prison unnoticed as a woman. When eventually discovered, Mary will be punished, but not executed, and George will have escaped. George finally accepts Mary's plan and succeeds in escaping (Mary is sold south for her part in the plan), but he tellingly must remain "in the dress of a woman" (229) until well into the free states.[93] Eventually, George emigrates to England where he becomes a successful clerk, while passing for white. Then, through improbable twists, George meets Mary in France, soon after she has become a widow, and the two are finally married. Brown's denouement underlines masquerade—both of a gendered and racial nature—as a route to achieving a freedom that regrounds the basis of manhood. It is by putting on a feminine face of obsequiousness and acceptance that the black man can eventually gain the markers of (white) manhood: economic and political freedom and a family truly his own. Brown shows that George's "white" manhood—his ability to resist slavery—depends on being a "black" woman, his ability to act as a "slave woman" (229). Through George's escape, Brown underscores the idea that race and gender—specifically white manhood—are matters of masquerade, while using that masquerade to create a representative black manhood.

Though antislavery rhetoric and conventions, like the minstrel show, relied on destabilizing racial and gender distinctions, their logic of revealing black men as truly "white" (whether spiritually or physically) tended to maintain a basic racial equation of gender. Douglass's Madison Washington troubles any distinctions between blackness and whiteness by containing both, but his whiteness still marks his manhood and resistance to slavery, his blackness his emasculating inability to escape. Brown, through his multiple minstrel "heroes" and through George Green's story of masquerade, not only destabilizes notions of blackness while conjuring up "authentic" representations of it, as Lane's performance as Juba did; he also reveals the instability of whiteness and the dependence of white manhood on blackness. Brown suggests this interdependence not just through George Green's escape, but also in his characterization of Sam. Sam acts as a matchmaker between Georgiana and Carlton, enabling a marriage that he knows must take place for their plan of emancipation to come to fruition. Carlton is by far the most learned and intellectual character in the novel (see, for example, 94), but Brown traces how he must come to realize the limitations of his learning. By standing in for the desire that Carlton's "high spirit" (161) will not allow him to speak of, Sam enables Carlton to escape pauperism and take possession of the markers of middle-class manhood: economic independence and a beautiful, religious wife. By granting him access to the body—the desires of which he cannot speak and which his overly mental training have deprived him—as the minstrel show was imagined to do, Sam's agency allows Carlton to become a man. But Sam's actions also grant him access to manhood. By steering the couple together, Sam reveals his "general intelligence" (165) and is rewarded for his work by gaining a position of power in the new economic dispensation—he becomes the foreman over the incredibly productive, soon-to-be-freed slaves. Sam's intelligence and work earn him economic success and freedom, thus mirroring the dream of self-made manhood on which middle-class manhood was founded. By figuratively putting on blackface, Sam not only enables the flowering of white manhood, but also demonstrates the possibilities of black manhood.

Finally, with his last dark black slave, William, Brown reiterates this logic and returns us to its manipulation of minstrel conventions. William, "a tall, full-bodied Negro, whose countenance beamed with intelligence" (171), escapes from slavery with Clotel through a scheme Brown borrowed from the real life story of Ellen and William Craft.[94] In order to escape, Clotel poses as an invalid white man and William poses as her faithful servant. With this plot device, Brown not only emphasizes the instability of white manhood—a "black" woman can become a white man—but underscores the performative nature of the faithful slave—William begins to speak in dialect and "play[s] his part well" (172). When they reach the North, Clotel decides to return to Virginia in order to save her daughter Mary (Clotel is captured and commits suicide). Meanwhile, William confronts the prejudice of the North when he is told he must ride in a train's "Jim Crow" car (176). Because "Slavery is a school in which its victims learn much shrewdness, and William had been an apt scholar" (176), he accepts his identification as Jim Crow, as simply an object only fit for riding with the luggage, but reconfigures that identification to his economic advantage by only paying for his weight as an article of freight. In this way, he achieves the freedom associated with manhood, demonstrating that he is "as good as white folks" (177) by reconfiguring his status as a "Jim Crow"–like slave.

I have argued that by similarly embracing his status as a Jim Crow, as a mass-circulated, commodified stereotype, Brown is able to draw on the ambivalence of that stereotype and the form to which it gave birth to create himself as a black male author. Brown's multiple black male characters in *Clotel* reveal how the performative nature of both race and gender allowed the negotiation of a type of black manhood dependent on covert resistance and isolated moments of subversion rather than on heroic, but fatal, attempts to prove manhood through physical rebellion. The masquerades of George, Sam, and the other black male characters do not enable Brown's novel to escape the need to oscillate between blackness and whiteness in order to create black manhood— Sam, for example, sings his subversive song without a touch of dialect. Rather, *Clotel* emphasizes, through its invocation of the minstrel show, that white manhood was similarly indebted to an analogous oscillation between whiteness and blackness, thus demonstrating the instability of both race and manliness as markers of identity. Like Lane's performances as Juba, Brown produces a plethora of "counterfeit Jim Crows" ✷ —Pompey, Sam, William, Jack, Cato—all of whom seem to be unreal reflections of each other even as each is simultaneously "de genewine artekil." Implicitly drawing on his experience as a wildcat banker, Brown does not redeem his race by substituting a singular "real" picture of slavery for the minstrel show's depiction; instead he constantly keeps minstrel images in circulation, multiplying them ad infinitum and thus rendering blackness unreal even as he redefines it. Through "real Negro" men—who are "real Negro" men through masquerade— Brown reveals to his white audience the numerous minute ways in which black men in slavery grasped power, if only temporarily, and hence reveals the ways in which black men conformed to middle-class ideas of manliness—and thus proved their humanity—even while remaining slaves. In this way he mirrors both the constant interplay of artifice and authenticity within the minstrel show *and* the minstrel show's own critique of slavery. By turning to the minstrel stage, Brown demonstrates the inherent instability of representations of race and gender and points toward the possibility of a representative black manhood that, while depending on the instability of blackness and manhood, denies neither. Putting on the blackface of the minstrel show, Brown creates himself as a self-sufficient manipulator of the literary marketplace and its dependence on mass cultural images of blackness, thus authorizing himself as a black model of literary manhood.

The Indian in the Museum

Henry David Thoreau, Okah Tubbee,

and Authentic Manhood

In the 27 February 1843 edition of the *New York Herald*, P. T. Barnum advertised his American Museum as providing a "COMBINATION OF UN-EQUALLED AND UNPRECEDENTED ATTRACTIONS." An "Ethiopian Extravaganza" and "THE INDIAN CHIEFS, WARRIORS, AND SQUAWS" headline the list of attractions Barnum provides to back up his claim. These Indians, the ad assures, are "no miserable, degraded half breeds, but the Wild Warriors of the Far West," and thus, "however high curiosity may be raised, the anticipation cannot come up to the reality."[1] Such a combination of attractions was, despite Barnum's boast, far from unique. In the 1840s and 1850s, popular museums often featured representations of Native Americans and African Americans together. Promotions such as the following were, in fact, fairly common: "the greatest wonder of the age, CHOC-CHU-TUB BEE, an Indian Chief of the Choctaw tribe. . . . in conjunction with those Sable Sons of Apollo, the original ETHIOPIAN AND VIRGINIA SERENADERS."[2] From the opening of Peale's Museum in Philadelphia in 1786, popular museums in the United States had featured both displays of materials "from . . . the Indian, African, or other savage people" and exhibits of living persons identified as either black or Indian.[3] Whether it was through white men in black (or less often red) face, actual African Americans or Native Americans, or various collected artifacts and objects on display, early American museums constructed both blacks and Indians as primitive others, located somewhere in the natural order between the rest of "brute creation" on display and white audience members.[4]

Although museums represented Indians and blacks in complex, multivalent ways, they tended to make a core distinction between the two races, producing racial distinctions not simply between undifferentiated blacks or Indians and white audience members, but also between Indians and blacks. As noted in the previous chapter and as evidenced in the ads referred to above, in the 1840s, popular museums began incorporating minstrel shows into their variegated programs. These minstrel shows, in keeping with Barnum's and other museum operators' attempts at respectability, primarily depicted blacks as sentimentally or humorously childlike and emotional, but not particularly dangerous.[5] On the other hand, museum displays revealed Indians—represented neither by "degraded half breeds" nor by whites in face-paint, but by "wild" Indians uncorrupted by white culture—as stoically vanishing in the advance of a white civilization to which they would not submit.

The antebellum museum, in this way, mapped race along a gender axis—blacks represented effeminate submission and feminine sentiment, Indians manly resistance and self-reliance. At the same time, such museums became important sites for the inculcation of gender ideals among a new white constituency. In particular, these museums attempted to define themselves as respectable forms of moral and educational entertainment against the more disreputable, lower-class, male-dominated entertainments of areas such as the Bowery. Throughout the antebellum period middle-class reformers disparaged theaters and minstrel halls as institutions of iniquity that gave too free a rein to the passions. In response, popular museums portrayed themselves as places of rational amusement where women and children of the rising middle class could be safely entertained and educated.[6] Yet in attempting to draw as broad an audience as possible, the popular museum continued to stage the sensational, salacious attractions of the Bowery in a space marked as particularly domestic. This tension highlights the instability of mid-century middle-class gender ideas. While antebellum middle-class manhood has been characterized in terms of an ideal self-restrained familial provider, this ideal was constantly in tension with anxieties that American men needed to recover a more physical, "authentic" manhood supposedly exemplified by the lives of "primitive" peoples.[7] The antebellum popular museum staged these tensions through its more "feminine" sentimentalism and more "masculine" sensationalism, finally resolving them, however tenuously, through black and Indian bodies. By constructing blacks as effeminate and

Indians as hypermasculine, the museum could, in racialized terms, provide its patrons—both men and women—with the kind of polarized gender distinctions that the cross-gendered nature of its audience possibly disturbed. The antebellum popular museum thus foregrounded interconnections between race and gender in a commercial but domestic setting, becoming a particularly important forum in which the categories of gender and race were constantly being constructed and deconstructed.

In this chapter I focus on the performances and writings of Okah Tubbee (advertised above as Choc-Chu-Tub Bee) and the writings of Henry David Thoreau as a way of describing how antebellum popular museums provided men with a model for constructing an authentic, yet literary, masculine self. Where William Wells Brown needed to demonstrate his literacy and professional achievement in order to assert his status as a man, the professionalization of literature threatened Thoreau's manhood by potentially enslaving him to the demands of the marketplace. By simultaneously identifying themselves with the figure of the primitive Indian and distancing themselves from the figure of the enslaved black man as staged in the museum setting, both Thoreau and Tubbee negotiated a male identity in the market economy. Thoreau is well-known for both his celebration of the Indian and his antislavery sentiments and throughout his writings makes numerous references to visiting museums, often disparaging them as dead institutions. Tubbee was born a slave in Mississippi, but claimed to have been the stolen child of a Choctaw chief. After escaping slavery, he supported himself and his family by playing a variety of instruments and speaking on behalf of Indian causes at museums in the late 1840s. Thoreau's ambivalence about the museum derived from the ways in which it erected and disturbed racial and gender distinctions through its commodification of an idealized masculine Indian; Tubbee exploited these paradoxical effects to secure his own Indian identity. In their different uses of and reactions to the Indian in the museum, Thoreau and Tubbee underline the ways in which the museum did not simply detach Native Americans and their objects from some original cultural context—thus fragmenting and embalming such cultures—but *constructed* such cultures as authentic, so that both whites *and* Native Americans could reappropriate Indianness for different political and aesthetic ends.[8] By similarly describing a type of essential Indianness—

Indian in the Museum   69

as staged in the commercial museum but framed as antithetical to the capitalist economy—as a model of authentic manhood, Thoreau and Tubbee point to the ways in which the museum became a site where both spectator and performer, respectable author and marginalized musician, could imagine a kind of antimarket manhood within the cultural marketplace.[9]

"The Happy Family"

In the 1840s and 1850s, the most famous—and infamous—museum in the United States was P. T. Barnum's American Museum in New York City. Despite its proprietor's reputation for such humbuggery as the Feejee Mermaid, Barnum's museum was recognized by scientists such as Louis Agassiz for its contributions to the propagation of natural history.[10] While other more exclusive and more scientific institutions such as Philadelphia's Academy of Natural Science and the new Smithsonian Institution did exist, most museums in the United States, like Barnum's, depended on drawing paying audiences by combining amusement with education.[11] As such, antebellum museums exhibited much more than natural history cases full of stuffed animals and various artifacts: "educated dogs, industrious fleas, automatons . . . tableaux, gipsies, Albinoes, fat boys, giants, dwarfs . . . pantomime, instrumental music, singing and dancing in great variety, dioramas, panoramas, models of Niagara, Dublin, Paris, and Jerusalem . . . mechanical figures, fancy glass-blowing, knitting machines and other triumphs of the mechanical arts; dissolving views, American Indians, who enacted their warlike and religious ceremonies on the stage."[12] Gathering a wide variety of materials and attractions together, such popular museums strove to become acceptable forms of entertainment for an equally wide variety of patrons.

In particular, museum proprietors focused on rendering their attractions acceptable to the new urban middle class. One way they attempted to do so was by taming the chaotic effects of their variegated collections through written, often dramatic, guidebooks. By presenting the museum's attractions in more digestible, less threatening form, and by broadly defining museum audiences as respectable in terms of both dress and behavior, guidebooks helped museums to overcome continuing prejudices against public entertainment. Such guides specifically emphasize the ways in which the museum mirrors the traditionally feminine sphere of the home. Both an 1848 guide to Moses Kimball's Boston Museum and an 1849 guide to Barnum's museum feature an older male relative (an uncle in one, a grandfather in the other) leading a group of youngsters through the halls full of natural phenomena and manmade marvels. In the course of their tours, the elder relatives reveal exhibits as object lessons in temperance, Christianity, and patriotism as well as science. These guidebooks describe the museum as an urban analogue to, if not an outright substitute for, Christian institutions—"a kind of Noah's ark . . . bigger than the biggest church you ever saw." There, things which would make you "jump out of your skin" in fright—including "the scalping knives, and medicine bags, and wampum belts, and tomahawks, and pipes of our Indians"—are made safe for children and grandfathers to play with.[13] At the end of the fictional tour of Barnum's museum in *Sights and Wonders in New York* (1849), the anonymous author reiterates the museum's safe, familial qualities by noting that "such regulations are established and enforced, as render it perfectly safe and pleasant for LADIES and CHILDREN to visit the Museum though unaccompanied by gentlemen."[14]

The later *Illustrated Catalogue and Guide Book to Barnum's American Museum* (1864) is even more explicit, if less dramatic, about the domesticating effects of the museum. Barnum's museum is "unquestionably, from its position, character and popularity, as well as from its attractions of the most amusing, instructive and moral character, the special place of FAMILY AMUSEMENT IN THE UNITED STATES." By promising "to keep the Museum always free from every objectionable feature . . . to use the same precaution to protect any visitors while in the Museum that I would my own family," Barnum guarantees "that any lady or child shall be as safe here as in their own house."[15] Exhibits like the "Happy Family"—"[a] miscellaneous collection of beasts and birds (upwards of sixty in number), living together harmoniously in one large cage, each of them being the mortal enemy of every other, but contentedly playing and frolicking together, without injury or discord" (102)—epitomize the museum as a whole. Through "healthy amusement blended with valuable instruction" (back cover), the museum's exhibits present "an amusing picture of the harmony which care and kindness may produce in brute creation" (4), a harmony then replicated in the families in attendance (see Figure 4).

All three of these illustrated guides (figures 5 and 6) suggest that a

No. 884.—CASE—THE HAPPY FAMILY. A miscellaneous collection of beasts and birds (upwards of sixty in number), living together harmoniously in one large cage, each of them being the mortal enemy of every other, but contentedly playing and frolicking together, without injury or discord. At the time of the issue of this book, the family comprises 8 doves, 4 owls, 10 rats, 2 cats, 2 dogs, 1 hawk, 3 rabbits, 1 rooster, 8 Guinea Pigs, 1 Raccoon, 2 Cavas, 1 Cuba Rat, 3 Ant Eaters, 7 Monkeys, 2 Woodchucks, 1 Opossum, 1 Armadilla, &c., &c.

The Happy Family.

4. The Happy Family, from *Sights and Wonders in New York . . .* (1864). *Courtesy of the University of Minnesota Libraries, Minneapolis, Minnesota.*

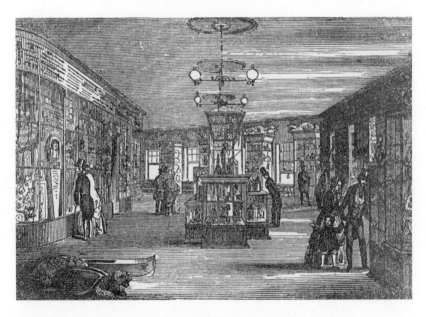

5. Sixth Saloon, from *Sights and Wonders in New York . . .* (1864). *Courtesy of the University of Minnesota Libraries, Minneapolis, Minnesota.*

6. Grand Entrance to the Boston Museum, from *Tom Pop's First Visit . . .* (1848). *Courtesy of the Boston Athenaeum.*

family could walk as safely through the graceful halls as through their own homes, and that in doing so, they would become another "Happy Family" on display, an example of the highest achievement of God's ordered creation. As an article from 1854 put it, the museum "has now become a kind of compromise between the theatre and the Church, it is a neutral ground upon which all parties and conditions may, and do meet."[16] Yet even as it mingled high and low, rational and salacious amusements for a cross-class, cross-gendered audience, the museum, as the family in figure 4 indicates, continued to differentiate and hierarchize, particularly along gendered lines—the two men stand together on one side, while the woman and child stand on the other. In other words, museum proprietors used a sentimental and educational literary format to tame their possibly disruptive collections, in particular those forms they had imported from such regions as the Bowery, yet they attempted to maintain the gender distinctions such comingling of attractions seemed to undermine. Through written promotions such as guidebooks and advertisements, museums created a family-oriented mode of amusement and education that simultaneously collapsed and resurrected strict gender distinctions.[17]

"Dead Nature Collected by Dead Men"

Thoreau focused his contempt for the museum on precisely what these guidebooks foreground—its role in domesticating the wild for mass, urban consumption. Seven months after the February 1843 *New York Herald* advertisement, Barnum was still featuring a troupe of "Ethiopian Serenaders" alongside his "Moving Dioramas" and ethnographic and natural history attractions.[18] His main attraction, however, was once again a group of Indians. Barnum boasted of their popularity to Kimball: "they will draw," "they could fill your room *that* night to overflowing, as it *fills* the people with enthusiasm to see the Indians beat their opponents as they will at the Boat Race."[19] On 1 October 1843, while living on Staten Island, Thoreau wrote his mother about this boat race: "A canoe race 'came off' on the Hudson the other day, between Chippeways and New Yorkers." As he continues, he compares the race to Barnum's other most recent scheme, the Great Buffalo Hunt of August 31—"it must have been as moving a sight as the buffalo hunt which I witnessed." After praising, perhaps sarcastically, the moving effect of wild Indians and buffaloes on the cityscape, Thoreau, as with most of his letters from New York, turns to a condemnation of the masses: "But canoes and buffaloes are all lost, as is everything here, in the mob." The effect of constantly "seeing so many people," "mere herds of men," is a lessened appreciation for the body—"one comes to have less respect for flesh and bones, and thinks they [the masses] must be more loosely jointed, of less firm fibre, than the few he had known."[20] The kinds of attractions Barnum exhibited and promoted were not simply humbuggery; rather, they became worthless because of the urban context within which they were shown, a context within which the material body came to have less true substance, less power to evoke nature and its mysteries.[21]

A week earlier, Thoreau had recorded his feelings about museums in his journal:

> I hate museums. . . . They are dead nature collected by dead men. I know not whether I muse most at the bodies stuffed with cotton and sawdust or those stuffed with bowels and fleshy fibre outside the cases. Where is the proper herbarium, the true cabinet of shells, and museum of skeletons, but in the meadow where the flower bloomed, by the seaside where the tide cast up the fish, and on the hills and in the valleys where the beast laid down its life and the skeleton of the traveller reposes on the grass?[22]

Although Thoreau does not specifically mention visiting Barnum's museum while living on Staten Island, his familiarity with Barnum's attractions and his later visits—he mentions going to Barnum's museum on three other occasions in his journal—make it likely that Barnum's American Museum was a referent for his remarks.[23] Thoreau's commentary here encapsulates the attitudes he consistently exhibits toward museums. He begins with disdain for the whole museal project—it is simply another institution of a dead culture that deadens everything it touches—and places the museum in direct opposition to the wild life of nature. Yet by the end of the passage, Thoreau is speaking of a "true" museum, thus embracing the idea of the museum by converting all of nature into a "proper" one. While the improper museum separates both observer and object from the reality of nature, thus rendering them both similarly moribund, the true museum would grant access to the truths and reality of nature lying behind and uniting and revivifying both live and dead bodies.[24] The true museum would help unveil the life in objects, both living and dead, rather than turning living things into dead objects.

Thoreau elaborates this distinction between the museum and nature further in a passage from the "Ktaadn" section of *The Maine Woods*. Upon ascending the mountain, Thoreau expresses his sense of awe at the sublimity of the scene:

> I most fully realized that this was primeval, untamed, and forever untamable *Nature*. . . . It is difficult to conceive of a region uninhabited by man. . . . And yet we have not seen pure Nature, unless we have seen her

thus vast and drear and inhuman, though in the midst of cities. Nature was here something savage and awful, though beautiful. . . . It was a place for heathenism and superstitious rites,—to be inhabited by men nearer of kin to the rocks and wild animals than we. . . . *What is it to be admitted to a museum, to see a myriad of particular things, compared with being shown some star's surface, some hard matter in its home!* [emphasis mine] I stand in awe of my body, this matter to which I am bound has become so strange to me. I fear not spirits, ghosts, of which I am one,—*that* my body might,—but I fear bodies, I tremble to meet them. What is this Titan that has possession of me? Talk of mysteries! Think of our life in nature,—daily to be shown matter, to come in contact with it,—rocks, trees, wind on our cheeks! the *solid* earth! the *actual* world! the *common sense! Contact! Contact! Who* are we? *where* are we?[25]

Thoreau seeks for "Matter, vast terrific,—not his Mother Earth" (*MW* 70). In its contrast to that wild matter, the museum stands as a weak, unreal substitute for contact with a more masculine "pure Nature"—"the *actual* world"—and one's body. Even in sublime nature, however, that contact is ever present, yet ever just beyond one's reach. This split between the untamed "hard matter" of nature (and the body) and the "ghosts" of subjectivity actually creates both sublime wonder and the desire for "the *solid* earth." In *Walden*, Thoreau more explicitly states that it is through this desire for the unreachable that the "tonic of wildness . . . refresh[es]" and renews us: "At the same time that we are earnest to explore and learn all things, we require that all things be mysterious and unexplorable."[26] We can never fully come in contact with nature or our own bodies, but in striving to do so, we can become more deeply aware of the divided, limited status of "our life in nature." In experiencing "untamable *Nature*," we become more aware of both our boundedness to and our separation from nature and our own bodies.

The museum, like other forms of commercialized amusements such as the theater (with which it was intimately connected), can only pretend to recreate such moments of insight.[27] Such "artificial amusements" as "theatres and operas" only "intoxicate for a season" and are "nothing compared to [our] pursuits" in nature (*J* 10:145). Thoreau acknowledges the possibility of gaining life-affirming contact with nature even "in the midst of cities," yet he denounces the village and its attractions for "only producing numbing and insensibility to pain"

(*Walden* 167).[28] Thoreau singles out commercialized entertainment because its visual and aural attractions, by being commodities, become inauthentic—"The too exquisitely cultured I avoid as I do the theatre. Their life lacks reality. . . . They are surrounded by things that can be bought" (*J* 4:154). While the sublime splendor of nature awes and invigorates us with its "mysteries," commodified entertainments lack life and reality. Wild nature, like Walden, remains "too pure to a have a market value" (*Walden* 199) and grants us (limited) access to and connection with transcendent mysteries; the museum's "myriad of particular things," by becoming visual commodities, become unreal, become detached, in their particularity, from nature as a whole.

Thoreau's objections to the museum are thus tied to its commercial nature, its place within the burgeoning market economy, and, in this way, are part of his critique of market relations in general.[29] For Thoreau, the museum, like the marketplace, did not simply deaden and derealize; it also emasculated. As the museum increasingly became a commercialized space designed for respectable women and families, it became, like other civilized institutions, a part of the urban landscape that makes "our lives . . . domestic in more senses than we think" (*Walden* 28). In fact, if a man "resigned himself to [the] tender mercies [of civilized institutions] he would soon be completely emasculated" (*Walden* 37). As Thoreau makes clear in his 1837 Harvard commencement address, it is the commercial spirit of the age that leads men to a "blind and unmanly love of wealth" and that keeps them from leading "manly and independent lives."[30] In sum, "In civilization . . . man degenerates at length," but "to make a man. . . . Give me a wildness whose glance no civilization can endure."[31] Thus, while the institutions of commercialized civilization emasculate man, closer contact with wild nature—whether at Walden, in the Maine woods, in the far west, or possibly even "in the midst of cities"—could help reinvigorate manhood by offsetting the deadening effects of the market and other "domestic" institutions.

"Independent Men . . . Not Tamed and Broken by Society"

According to Thoreau, there are other men, "nearer of kin to rocks and to wild animals than we," who have already achieved greater intimacy with nature and its truths: "how much more conversant was the Indian with any wild animal or plant than we are. . . . The Indian stood nearer to wild nature than we" (*J* 10:294).[32] The Indian's life in nature is the antithesis of the museum. In *Walden*'s "Economy," Thoreau warns his reader that in constructing a dwelling he must be careful, "lest after all he find himself in a workhouse, a labyrinth without a clue, a museum, an almshouse, a prison, or a splendid mausoleum" (28). Thoreau contrasts this museumlike dwelling with the "Penobscot Indians . . . living in tents" (28–29) and the simple wigwams of other Indians not yet "degraded by contact with the civilized man" (35). For Thoreau, it is this intimacy with nature that makes the Indian so fascinating and such a perfect model for renewing manhood: "The charm of the Indian to me is that he stands free and unconstrained in Nature, is her inhabitant and not her guest, and wears her easily and gracefully" (*J*1:253). While the emerging capitalist economy and commodity culture alienated a man from the products of his bodily labor and distorted his physical needs, thus separating him from an authentic self and nature, Thoreau found in the Indian the transcendent union of body and soul, nature and spirit, that he felt his culture had lost.[33]

Thoreau's deep investment in the study of Native American cultures and in the figure of the noble Indian is well documented. Besides the numerous references to Indians in his journals and published prose, he spent the last twelve to fourteen years of his life compiling his Indian notebooks, 2,800 pages of quotations from a wide variety of sources on Indians and Indian lifestyles.[34] The notebooks have led scholars to posit that Thoreau was planning to publish a lengthy treatise on North American Indians that would have, as Richard Fleck puts it, "correct[ed] the myopic view of nineteenth-century Euro-American historians."[35] Some less celebratory critics have noted the clearly "savagist" thinking that dominates Thoreau's earlier work, but they have tended to claim that his experience with Joe Polis near the end of his life helped him to move beyond a simply romantic or primitivist understanding of Indians.[36] Yet the majority of Thoreau's writings on Indians, and certainly at least some of the sections of *The Maine Woods* on Polis, reflect the very kind of romantic "savagism" we most often identify with writers such as James Fenimore Cooper. For Thoreau, race becomes "reality":

> Who can doubt this essential and innate difference between man and man, when he considers a whole race, like the Indian, inevitably and resignedly passing away in spite of our efforts to Christianize and educate

them? . . . Everybody notices that the Indian retains his habits wonderfully,—is still the same man that the discoverers found. The fact is, the history of the white man is a history of improvement, that of the red man a history of fixed habits of stagnation. (*J* 10:251–52)[37]

The Indian is essentially different from the white man; he is wild, primitive, untamable, "Another species of mortal man, but little less wild to me than the musquash [he] hunted" (*J* 1:337). For Thoreau, the Indian did not simply provide an example of a more authentic, natural existence in which body and soul were more integrated; instead, as in the museum, the Indian also could provide proof of the essential, scientific truth of racial difference.[38]

The Indian, like nature itself, can only be approached, not fully embraced because of "that strange remoteness [apparently biological as well as cultural] in which [he] ever dwells to the white man" (*MW* 158). Yet throughout his life and his writings, Thoreau attempted to breach this remoteness by identifying with Indians, if not outright imagining himself as one.[39] Whether the explicit example of the Indian he follows at points in both *A Week on the Concord and Merrimack Rivers* (1849) and *Walden* or the Indian guides Joe Aitteon and Joe Polis of *The Maine Woods*, Thoreau tries to emulate Indians because they are those "original and independent men . . . wild,—not tamed and broken by society" (*J* 2:448). Thoreau's identification with and celebration of the Indian marks not simply a desire for a simpler, more natural existence, but a desire for a more masculine self. As he puts it in *Walden*, "If, then, we would indeed restore manhood," we should do so by "truly Indian . . . or natural means"—"let us first be as simple and well as Nature ourselves . . . and take up a little life into our pores" (78). Indians' "wildness" makes them more truly men by making them untamable by commercialized culture.

Thus, in confronting the commercial failure of *A Week*, his first book, Thoreau identifies himself with the seemingly misdirected Indian who has woven a "basket of a delicate texture," but who has not yet realized "that it was necessary for him to make it worth the other's while to buy them." Like primitive Indians, rather than "studying how to make it worth men's while to buy [our] baskets," we should study "how to avoid the necessity of selling them" at all (*Walden* 19). While the basket-selling Indian has attempted to enter into the marketplace, what he really needs to do is return to his primitive, savage past and avoid the market altogether.⁴⁰ In this passage, Thoreau suggests the Indian not simply as a model of antimarket manhood, but as a model for anti-market, masculine literary production. Earlier, in *A Week*, he had similarly equated writing with Indian skills: "The talent of composition is very dangerous,—the striking out the heart of life at a blow, as the Indian takes off a scalp" (329). Writing, at its best, approximates the manly work of primitive Indians in its dangerous approach to the heart of nature and its avoidance of the marketplace. In following the Indian's model of manhood, Thoreau attempts to return to nature and thus avoid the entrapments of a feminized, commercial culture epitomized by the museum. By writing as the Indian takes off a scalp, Thoreau hopes to avoid the necessity of selling his baskets at all, or at least of selling himself in the process.

"Manly in the Extreme"

While Thoreau opposed the commercialized museum with the wild masculine alterity of the Indian, Okah Tubbee was able to escape from what he saw as an effeminized African American identity by playing such an Indian on the stage of the museum. By casting himself as closer to nature, more impassioned, and primitive in the very space Thoreau denigrated, Tubbee links these "essential" Indian traits *with* the museum. In doing so, he points both to the ways in which the museum produced primitiveness and to the ways in which the construction of the Indian as a model of primitive manliness depended upon a definition of blackness as effeminacy. Whereas William Wells Brown was able to draw on the suggestion of slave resistance and black manliness still implicit in more middle-class minstrel shows, Tubbee defines his masculine Indian identity against the images of effeminized blacks more common to such forums. Tubbee's self-production in the museum as a commodity embodying Indian manliness reverses, while replicating, Thoreau's construction of Indianness as a type of primitive manliness lying outside both the market economy and the museum. In this way, Tubbee's ability to construct himself as an Indian not only shows how the museum and its market logic enabled the articulation of a masculine Indian identity through the feminization of blackness, but also helps to reveal how Thoreau's celebration of the Indian as a model of antimarket literary manhood depended on the market economy and the museum.

Tubbee was only one of numerous Indians whom Barnum featured in his chain of museums along the eastern seaboard.[41] Dressed in Indian garb, Tubbee and his wife and child captivated large audiences wherever they went. During his performances, Tubbee would play various instruments of his own invention, call for the reform of U.S. Indian policy, and recite his own extraordinary story. Although illiterate, Tubbee produced a number of promotional biographies with the help of his full-blooded Mohican wife, Laah Ceil Manatoi Elaah (see Figure 7). These accounts grant us insight into his stage performances, as most sections read as transcriptions of set pieces which could be spoken or acted out.[42] According to his biographies, Tubbee was born in Mississippi in 1810 or 1811, and as a child was called William (or Warner) McCary. Raised in slavery by a black woman reputed to be his mother, Tubbee claimed to have discovered as a teenager that he was actually the stolen child of a well-known Choctaw chief—Mosholeh Tubbee—and not the mulatto child of his owner. Tubbee recounts how he used his musical skills to gain favor with a number of prominent citizens in the Natchez area and how, exploiting this favor, he convinced them of his Indian ancestry and then used this Indian identity to escape from slavery. After living in New Orleans, performing aboard Mississippi River steamboats, and finally settling in Missouri, Tubbee began appearing at northeastern entertainment venues such as Barnum's museums in order to promote Indian causes and to support his family.

Tubbee may very well have been a charlatan—a figure like Melville's mutable confidence man of 1857, able to play the role of Black Guinea at one turn, plead for the asylum of Seminole widows and orphans the next, and discourse on the metaphysics of Indian-hating elsewhere.[43] His indeterminate "actual" race, however, is not particularly important. Instead, what is important is the way in which his biographies and performances reveal how his self-commodification in the museum depends both on the instability of notions of racial difference *and* on the maintenance of strict racial lines. All of the various versions of Okah Tubbee's biography begin with a section titled either "An Essay Upon the Indian Character" or simply "Indian Character." This section, probably written by Lewis Leonidas Allen, the editor of the first edition of Tubbee's story and a minor travel writer, follows the basic lines of characterization set down by a plethora of writers of the period: The Indian is of "A noble race, with high and exalted notions of honor, he scorns anything which is low and mean."[44] But like other savagist texts, this celebration of the Indian's nobility is offset by the idea that "the Indian race is fading away, their palmy days being gone."[45] In the first half of the narrative itself, Tubbee relies on the essential traits of Indian character—as put forward in this introduction and by writers such as Thoreau—in order to prove his own Indianness. In the second half, however, he attempts to show that the Indian is not necessarily "fading away," but instead can become a productive member of advanced civilization. In this way, Tubbee attempts to escape the narrative of the vanishing American by implying that Indian character is not a matter of racial essence, but rather a matter of stage of civilization.[46]

Tubbee uses anecdotes from his childhood in order to prove that he is an Indian. In particular, he relies upon the idea—so prominent in Thoreau's writing—that Indians are closer to nature, and thus have some innate intimacy with wild creatures. Early in his narrative he recalls that while traveling through the wilds of Mississippi as a young child, he became separated from his companion and stumbled upon a bear family: "I expected they would kill me, but after examining me they turned and walked away" (19). Tubbee ascribes his salvation to "Providence" (20), but coming right after his description of his "proud heart" as "so characteristic of the red man" (18), the implication is clear—the bears, if not everyone else, realize, upon "examining" him, that he too is one of the "simple children of the woods" (58), truly "the son of the broad forest Chief" (43). Tubbee must be an Indian because it is the Indian who, in Thoreau's words, is "more conversant . . . with any wild animal." This recognition of his lineage does not end with the wild beasts of the forest, but extends to other "children of the woods," other Indians, and his reactions to them. Tubbee remembers that the first time he ever saw Indians he could not control himself. He felt "nailed to the spot" (30), and as they approached him, he became "wild with delight," finally "address[ing] them in a language . . . unknown [to him] before" (31). As he grew older and traveled throughout the South, he realized that he "had always loved the red people" (82), and it became clear to him that he felt this love because he was one of them. In his travels, all Indians, eventually, if not immediately, confirmed his conviction about his heritage. They "seemed to regard me as a companion; they did not even ask for or look for other blood in me" (32). Tubbee argues that his acceptance by other Indians was one of the

A SKETCH OF THE LIFE

OF

OKAH TUBBEE,

(CALLED)

WILLIAM CHUBBEE,

SON OF THE HEAD CHIEF, MOSHOLEH TUBBEE, OF THE
CHOCTAW NATION OF INDIANS.

BY LAAH CEIL MANATOI ELAAH TUBBEE, HIS WIFE.

TORONTO:
PRINTED FOR OKAH TUBBEE,
BY HENRY STEPHENS.

1852.

7. Title page of *A Sketch of the Life of Okah Tubbee* (1852). *Courtesy of Yale Collection of Western Americana, Beinecke Rare Book and Manuscript Library.*

strongest proofs of his origins and had "great bearing in the minds of many, knowing that one Indian can tell another" (40).

In convincing his readers—and museum audiences—of "the redness of [his] skin" (39), Tubbee embraces an understanding of race as biologically determinant. Despite being raised by a black woman in slavery, his racial lineage—the fact that his biological parents were Indians—determines his character and makes him act as an Indian. Hence, as Tubbee argues, his "exalted and noble ideas" and "manners . . . manly in the extreme" (29) had to "have been original," had to have come from nature because he "had received no education, either moral, mental, or physical" (30). For Tubbee, being an Indian means more than acting in certain ways; specifically it means not being black.[47] As a young boy, Tubbee climbed "a bluff, which no other boy dared to." When his false black mother punished him, she told him "that this was the way Indians and all wild savages lived, and could not be tamed; that the white people could not make as much service of them, as they could of the blacks, for they would not work for them, but spent their lives in wandering about in the woods, both day and night, living with the wild beasts." According to this story, Tubbee's black mother began his lessons in the fundamentals of racial difference—the blacks can be enslaved, the Indians cannot—ending her description with "what is bred in the bone will be in the marrow" (23). In proving himself a manly, noble Indian, Tubbee must demonstrate that, unlike blacks, he is untamable.

Throughout the rest of his stories of his childhood in Natchez, Tubbee attempts to make it clear that he must be of Indian rather than black blood because of his unwillingness to submit to authority and to take abuse. From the beginning of his enslavement, he had "to be whipped into obedience" and, because of his "proud heart," he refused to be abused by other black and white boys with "ill name[s]": "I could not and would not submit to such gross insults without defending myself, which is so characteristic of the red man" (18). The racial nature of this passionate refusal to be abused becomes most evident in an incident he recounts early in his narrative—when called a "nigger, all [his] Indian nature was aroused."[48] This "violent and unconquerable temper" indicates his Indian "spirit" that will not be "tamed" (27). All these examples point to Tubbee's ability to become red by differentiating himself from blacks. In attempting to reclaim the "freedom in which [he] was born" (45), he must argue that "the white man's blood possesses no more freedom than [his], [although] they have made no distinction between [him] and the negro slave" (43). By reinstating that distinction Tubbee can achieve freedom. By acting a certain way—both in his everyday life in the South and on the museum stage in the North—he gives proof of the biological truth of his race.

"Dancing at his Labor" vs. "The War Dance"

Tubbee was able to construct an Indian identity in his biographies and performances because racial distinctions between Indians and blacks already circulated in the museum and in the writings of Thoreau and others. By playing on the distinction already made between "Ethiopian Serenaders" and "Wild Warriors," Tubbee could escape being a slave (a commodified body) and gain the relative freedom of being an Indian in the museum (a self-commodified visual, aural, and literary product). Barnum's descriptions of his attractions highlight this racial distinction. His museum primarily represented African Americans and their culture through performances by white men in blackface. When Barnum did display actual black persons, his focus tended to be not so much on them as representative of black character as on the uncertainty of their humanity or of their blackness. Barnum began his career in entertainment in the 1830s by purchasing Joice Heth, a black woman who, he claimed, was 161 years old and had been owned by George Washington's father. While Barnum originally promoted Heth's mammylike relationship with George Washington, he spurred further interest in her by planting stories claiming that she was inauthentic—that, in fact, "she was made of india rubber, whalebone, and hidden springs."[49] Later attractions featuring actual African Americans similarly did not display them as representatively black. The only blacks mentioned in his 1864 museum guidebook are "What is It?" and a family in which "each alternate child . . . has been white and black; the white children's features being so decidedly Ethiopian as to preclude the possibility of doubt as to their being purely African."[50] The family of albino children followed in a long line of "white negroes" exhibited in American museums and often used to suggest the instability of racial distinctions.[51] "What is It?," on the other hand, featured William Henry Johnson, a short black man with strange facial features, as a subhuman link between men and apes, an exhibition that intimated the nearly subhuman status of Africans, without commenting directly on African American character.[52] In Barnum's museum, actual African Americans were curiously not representative of real black people; rather genuine blacks and representations of authentic black character could be seen in his minstrel shows. As Barnum's need to blacken black minstrel performer William Henry Lane's face seems to indicate (see chapter 1), his audiences expected representations of black character to be counterfeit.

Yet whether "the connecting link between humanity and brute creation" or minstrel caricatures, blacks in Barnum's museum were represented as inferior and childlike, though not particularly wild or threatening.[53] Barnum expressed his own feelings and summed up the exhibitionary logic of antebellum popular museums in regard to African Americans in *Struggles and Triumphs*: "The black man possesses a confiding disposition, thoroughly tinctured with religious enthusiasm, and not characterized by a spirit of revenge."[54] On the other hand, Barnum promoted his Indians, even when actually whites in facepaint, both as authentic and as "sufficiently blood-curdling to satisfy the most exacting reader of a penny-dreadful."[55] Whether white men in masquerade or actual blacks and Indians, the essential racial distinctions made were the same. Blackness was a childlike mask consisting of burnt cork and India rubber; Indianness was savagely real, even when performed by whites.[56]

In presenting himself as an Indian and claiming "manners . . . manly in the extreme" (29), Tubbee exploited the museum's tendency to reinforce the kind of racial distinctions that he made between Indians and blacks. To be taken as both authentic and masculine in the museum, he had to be Indian rather than black. A similar distinction operates within Thoreau's writing. Despite his antislavery stance, Thoreau's identification with the Indian as a masculine model depended on his characterization of blacks as effeminate. Thoreau's antislavery views are as well-known as his celebrations of Indian lifeways. From his refusal to pay the taxes of a government that supported slavery to his various eulogies for John Brown, Thoreau repeatedly condemns slavery in his writings. Few critics, however, have attempted to elaborate the connections between Thoreau's antislavery and pro-Indian sentiments in any depth.[57] Thoreau's most explicit statement linking blacks and Indians occurs in an early journal entry: "The African will survive, for he is docile, and is patiently learning his trade and dancing at his labor; but the Indian does not often dance, unless it be the war dance" (*J* 1:446). Although such moments of explicit racializing are infrequent, throughout Thoreau's work an implicit distinction between "docile" blacks and "war"like Indians lies behind his construction of the Indian as a model of antimarket literary manhood. Tubbee's biographies and performances reveal the antebellum museum's deployment of this bifurcating racial logic. In light of Tubbee's story, Thoreau's ambivalence about the museum emerges as a reaction to how the museum's production of race and gender as visual commodities simultaneously erected and challenged gender and racial distinctions. The museum's commodity logic at once hyperbolized racial and gender difference—providing Thoreau with the clear model of primitive Indian manhood he yearned for— and at the same time rendered such distinctions seemingly unreal, simply a matter of facepaint and India rubber.

For all his antislavery sentiment, Thoreau's writings contain few explicit statements about African Americans.[58] Thoreau mentions helping fugitive slaves, both in his journal and in *Walden*, but on the whole, his antislavery commentary focuses either on the impact of the institution upon Massachusetts or, later, on John Brown. Thoreau's explicit statements about, and against, slavery indicate that, despite his sympathy for enslaved African Americans, he conceived of them as less manly than himself. The main thrust of "Slavery in Massachusetts," for example, is an indictment of the "million slaves in Massachusetts" who will enforce the Fugitive Slave Law and thus attempt to "put a restraint upon [my] manhood."[59] His comments in this essay echo his earlier condemnation of Massachusetts and the majority of its citizens in "Resistance to Civil Government": "we should be men first, and subjects afterward."[60] By being "the *slave's* government" (67), Massachusetts is a "slut" (68), with "hardly one" (70) man within her borders. While the state and its adherents are "timid as a lone woman" (80), "the true place for a just man is . . . a prison" (76). Otherwise, through a wounded conscience, "a man's real manhood and immortality flow out, and he bleeds to an everlasting death" (77). Thoreau clinches his point by arguing that "I do not hear of *men* being *forced* to live this way or that by masses of men" (81, his emphasis). As he puts it in one of his lectures on John Brown, it is not even slavery that is the chief "foe," but rather "the want of vitality in man."[61] It is by opposing slavery that we can reinvigorate manhood, for slavery is not simply the absence of freedom, but of manhood as well. Helping to support slavery, conversely, is the same as being a slave, and hence being a slave is a matter of giving in to the effeminate government's or degraded masses' ignoble demands, something a true man would never allow himself to do.[62]

By couching his protest against the institution of slavery in terms of its threat to manhood and by equating slavery with emasculation, Thoreau's rhetoric collapses the distinction between the metaphoric slave in Massachusetts and the actual slave in Mississippi. In either case, any man who allows himself to be a slave is less of a man.[63] Thoreau specifically makes this point in a passage from *Walden* on the Egyptian pyramids: "As for the Pyramids, there is nothing to wonder at in them so much as the fact that so many men could be found degraded enough to spend their lives constructing a tomb for some ambitious booby, whom it would have been wiser and *manlier* to have drowned in the Nile" (58, emphasis added). Only a degraded, less manly man would allow himself to be a slave, whether in Thoreau's Massachusetts, ancient Egypt, or antebellum Mississippi. At the end of "Resistance to Civil Government" Thoreau suggests a racial component to this condemnation of men who allow themselves to be enslaved—morally, physically, or otherwise—when he remarks that his neighbors who help support the "*slave's* government" (67) are "a distinct race" (83) from himself. While blacks will survive, even in slavery, because they are "docile," real men like John Brown and Indians, "in teaching us how to die, have at the same time taught us how to live."[64]

Thoreau's reference to docile Africans "dancing at [their] labor" recalls central tropes of the minstrel show; reconstructing Thoreau's feelings about minstrel shows suggests another element to his distinction between Indians and blacks. For Thoreau, both the museum and slavery connoted emasculation, and thus the minstrel in the museum would have been a figure of particular contempt for him. In *A Week*, a few pages after equating writing with the Indian's taking a scalp, Thoreau celebrates the young men "Running hither and thither with appetite for the coarse pastimes of the day, now with boisterous speed at the heels of the inspired Negro from whose larynx the melodies of all Congo and Guinea Coast have broke loose into our streets." But this celebration of rural "love for Nature" cannot stand the touch of commerce inherent in the museum (337). The "natural" music from birds or the Congo and Guinea Coast remains authentic and "inspired" among boys and in the woods, but when performed in the space of the museum, whether by Jenny Lind or the Ethiopian Serenaders, such music becomes degraded: "The chickadees sing as if at home. They are not travelling singers *hired* by any Barnum. Theirs is an honest, homely, heartfelt melody. Shall not the voice of man express as much content as the note of a bird?" (*J* 12:386, emphasis added).[65] It is not simply the space of the museum that degrades such music; it is the fact that it is bought and sold. "The cities import [wildness] at any price" ("Walking" 224), but, because "trade curses everything it handles" (*Walden* 70), such wildness is thus rendered both impotent and unreal. Just as the wild cranberries are "*jammed*, to satisfy the tastes of lovers of Nature" (*Walden* 238) in Boston and New York, so primitive music is produced in the museum to satisfy a similar taste. But as "the ambrosial and essential part of the fruit is lost with the bloom which is rubbed off in the market cart" (*Walden* 173), so wildness in the museum is domesticated, losing its immortal essence. The slave stands in contrast to the Indian not simply because he follows the orders of other men, but because he is a commodity and has had the "essential part" of his manhood "rubbed off in the market." The black man and the songs of the Guinea Coast become inauthentic in the museum, a caricature in blackface or a mound of India rubber and springs. The Indian, on the other hand, by standing outside the market, maintains his primitive essence.

The Indian who is inscribed within the market economy, however, loses this essence and is transformed in terms of both race and gender. Thoreau catalogues such effects in *The Maine Woods*, the book in which he most fully confronts living Native Americans. Thoreau describes the first male Indian he sees as "a short, shabby, washerwoman-looking Indian— . . . [with] the woebegone look of the girl that cried for spilt milk" (6). The degraded Indian does not simply become a laboring woman; he appears as if in blackface. On his next trip, Thoreau's moment of greatest disappointment with his Indian guide, Joe Aitteon ("apparently of unmixed blood" [90]), comes when he hears him "whistling 'O Susanna,' and several other such airs" (107). "O Susanna" is, of course, one of the most lasting of several sentimental tunes by Stephen Foster originally performed by middle-class, more respectable blackface minstrel groups like Christy's Minstrels. Thoreau has set up this moment by scorning the idea of blackface at the beginning of "Chesuncook." There, he attacks the practice of shoe-shining on boats, ending with the retort of "They might with the same propriety insist on blacking your face" (84). Blacking one's face then epitomizes the absurdity of overcivilized Euro-American culture, and Thoreau's Indian guide turning into a blackface performer illustrates the great extent to which he has fallen away from truly masculine Indian ways, the fact that unlike his ancestors he cannot subsist "wholly on what the woods yielded" (107). Singing or whistling "O Susanna" is like being a "shabby washerwoman"; it links one to the degraded and effeminate unskilled labor of servants and slaves. And labor of this sort precludes one from being a man: "the laboring man has not leisure for a true integrity day by day; he cannot afford to sustain the manliest relations to men" (*Walden* 6).[66] Thus, the freedom of the primitive Indian's integrated life with nature stands in opposition to laboring for another, to the alienation of labor in the capitalist economy. While the Indian's free life in nature "was as far off from us as the heaven is" (*J* 10:294–95), the "negro" realizes that "slaves" will even "be obliged to work in heaven" (*J* 9:215).[67] The primitive Indian stands outside the market—neither consumer nor laborer—authentically masculine in his wildness, thus providing a model of antimarket literary manhood; but the "civilized" Indian becomes an effeminate, blackfaced slave to the market.

"The *Real* Thing"

We might expect Thoreau to view the Indian in the museum as similarly corrupted. Yet, despite his attacks on museums for being dead, effeminate institutions, Thoreau celebrated the contact with the Indian's primitive wildness that museums provided. This paradox derives not from some idiosyncrasy or inconsistency in Thoreau's thinking, but rather from the often conflicting racial and gender effects produced by the commodifying logic of the museum. While the museum came to play a key role in the feminization of urban culture, it also continued to produce displays that attempted to conjure up the kind of primitive sublimity that Thoreau and others often identified with both the Indian and manliness. In refashioning his identity, Okah Tubbee exploited this tendency of the museum to construct the Indian as commodified, wild spectacle. Barnum specifically focuses on this production of a sense of wildness in his accounts of his Indian performers. In *Struggles and Triumphs*, he describes the performance of the Indians in the following way:

> They gave their dance on the stage in the Lecture Room with great vigor and enthusiasm, much to the satisfaction of the audiences. But these wild Indians seemed to consider their dances as realities. Hence when they gave a real War Dance, it was dangerous for any parties, except their manager and interpreter, to be on the stage, for the moment they had finished their war dance, they began to leap and peer about behind the scenes in search of victims for their tomahawks and scalping knives! Indeed, lest in these frenzied moments they might make a dash at the orchestra or audience, we had a high rope barrier placed between them and the savages on the front of the stage.[68]

Lydia Maria Child described the same exhibition similarly: "I was never before so much struck with the animalism of Indian character, as I was in the frightful war-dance of these chiefs. . . . altogether they looked and acted more like demons from the pit, than anything I ever imagined. . . . [Their voices] clove the brain like a tomahawk."[69] As Barnum explained in reference to another group of Indians he exhibited in 1864, "My patrons were of course pleased to see these old chiefs, as they knew they were the '*real* thing'" because they were "blood-thirsty . . . treacherous."[70] Barnum needed his Indians to be wild enough to meet up with and exceed all the "curiosity" and "anticipation" that his eastern urban audience had formed about Indians. By terrifying their audiences, Barnum's Indians could prove themselves masculinely "real."

The conjunction of Ethiopian Serenaders with Wild Warriors of the Far West served to underline a gendered distinction between blacks and Indians. Yet at the same time, this union could have the opposite effect, putting a check on both the sense of reality and the savage wildness conjured up by Indian performances. The setting of the museum, and specifically the lecture room, imparted both a domestic air and an aura of performance, of unreality. The lecture room was not only used for lectures, ethnographic displays, and minstrel shows, but, beginning in the late 1840s, moral dramas—theatrical performances with sentimental themes, such as the blockbuster *The Drunkard*. In part, the difference of the Indians from these other types of performances—the sheer difference, for example, between weeping families or smiling and dancing blackface performers and tomahawk-wielding, screaming Indians—helped to underline their primitive wildness. Yet at the same time, the location of these displays raised questions of the theatrical, such as the distinction between the authentic and the performed.[71] The separating rope barrier then foregrounded the performative—theatrical—nature of the Indians' war dance and at the same time was essential to the dance's illusion of authenticity and reality.[72]

Child's oscillation between sympathy and fear highlights these paradoxical effects and complicates Barnum's description of the terror produced by his Indian exhibitions. Her first reaction is one of horror: "In truth, that war-dance was terrific both to eye and ear. I looked at the door, to see if escape were easy, in case they really worked themselves up to the scalping point." Yet Child goes on to say that "instantly I felt that I was wronging them in my thought. Through paint and feathers, I saw gleams of right honest and friendly expression and I said, we are children of the same Father, seeking the same home" (189–90). Child's overall feelings, however, are ones of sadness. She recognizes the Indian "as noble a specimen of manhood as I ever looked upon" (184) and thus remarks that "it always fills me with sadness to see Indians surrounded by the false environment of civilized life; but I never felt so deep a sadness, as I did in looking upon these western warriors; for they were evidently the noblest of their dwindling race, unused to restraint, accustomed to sleep beneath the stars" (187).

Child's sadness resonates with Thoreau's attacks on the fatal effect of the museum. She at first feels fear, but by stripping the Indians of cultural markers ("paint and feathers"), she realizes that they are merely in search of the same heavenly "home." Yet domesticating Indians—making them part of the museum's "Happy Family," by placing them in the same "home" with other "fellow children"—brings "sadness" because "the *false* environment of civilized life" restrains the "western warriors'" nobility, freedom, and manhood, their "authentic" Indianness. Child's reading of the museum's effect on Indians mirrors her own rendering in *Hobomok* (1824) of her title character as a noble masculine Indian sadly fading into the wilderness in the face of advancing civilization. The roping off of the Indian dancers at Barnum's museum is then similar to the effects of the sentimental novel; it domesticates wild

Indians and encourages readers' sympathy by making them part of the same happy family, but in doing so it renders them members of a dead (or "dwindling") race.[73] As Child is moved to sadness rather than fear by "Indians surrounded by the false environment of civilized life," so does Thoreau come to despise the Indian degraded by civilization. But, because of the paradoxical effects that Child recounts, because the museum does not merely make Indians "children of the same Father" but reveals them at "the scalping point," Thoreau could draw upon the museum and its practices as a model for accessing wildness, as a model for his own literary scalping.

"A Wild and Refreshing Sound"

The museum, in fact, played an integral part in Thoreau's attempts to recapture an Indian primitiveness. One of the chief ways Thoreau expressed his interest in Indians was through the collecting of arrowheads and other relics—"As much as sportsmen go in pursuit of ducks, and gunners of musquash, and scholars of rare books, and travellers of adventures, and poets of ideas, and all men of money, I go in search of arrowheads when the proper season comes round again." Here, Thoreau suggests his arrowhead hunting as parallel to or an alternative to both literary and economic pursuits. He argues that "I come nearer to the maker of [each arrowhead] than if I found his bones" and that from "these signs [these "fossil thoughts"] I know that the subtle spirits that made them are not far off" (*J* 12:88–91).[74] Through arrowheads, Thoreau comes in contact with an Indian spirit, thus moving closer to the Indian and the natural life beyond the reach of the market that the Indian exemplified. Thoreau not only collected arrowheads on his own, a collection that would at his death go to the Boston Society of Natural History's museum, but often went to museums to see such artifacts. Thoreau's journal is full of references to visits to various museums throughout the northeast, including a visit to the Academy of Natural Sciences in Philadelphia, where he saw Samuel Morton's collection of Native American crania.[75] As he put it on a day he visited Davis's museum in Concord, "I love to see anything that implies a simpler mode of life and greater nearness to the earth" (*J* 14:87–88). Arrowheads and other artifacts, as objects in the commercial museum, grant Thoreau contact with a masculine primitive wholeness he associates with Indians and opposes to the marketplace, allowing him to imagine linking poets' pursuit of ideas and all men's pursuit of money.[76] Despite and, paradoxically, because of their domesticating and commodifying effects, museums granted Thoreau access to Indian primitiveness through the artifacts they displayed and a possible model for pursuing literary goals in the economic realm.

Thoreau found a reservoir of primitiveness not only in arrowheads or the "Wild Warriors of the Far West" featured in popular museums, but also in the educated (or "civilized") Native Americans like Okah Tubbee and George Copway who often lectured in museum settings.[77] Thoreau's reaction to a lecture given by a Chippewa speaker in 1858 reveals a sense of "contact" with primitive wildness similar to that which he records in "Ktaadn." From Thoreau's description, the lecture on Indian folkways and traditions was similar to the type of lecture and performance both Tubbee and Copway gave to large museum audiences in the late 1840s and early 1850s. The lecture had such an impact on Thoreau that, in addition to his lengthy journal entry about it (*J* 10:291–95), he included his reactions to it in *The Maine Woods*. In his journal, Thoreau records that he "Went to hear a Chippeway Indian, a Doctor Mung-somebody," and that he felt that "There was so much of unsubdued Indian accent resounding through his speech, so much of the 'bow-arrow tang!'" (*J* 10:291). While Thoreau is at once commenting on the speaker's troubles with the English language, he is also celebrating the access to wildness that the "natural" language of the "unsubdued" Indian provides for him. This encounter led Thoreau to marvel at "how much more conversant was the Indian with any wild animal or plant than we are" (*J* 10:294–95). The version in *The Maine Woods* makes this sense of the wild even more explicit: "I have once heard a Chippewa lecture. . . . It was a wild and refreshing sound, like that of the wind among the pines, or the booming of the surf on the shore" (169).[78]

The lecturing—or performing—Indian in the museum can bring a reinvigorating dose of wildness to the city. And since "Life consists with wildness. . . . Not yet subdued to man, its presence refreshes him" and "in Wildness is the preservation of the World" ("Walking" 226, 224), the museum and its commodified attractions, rather than being death-wielding tools of effeminate civilization, become the remasculinizing saviors of that very civilization. The Indian, standing in for that wildness that is "too pure to have a market value" (*Walden* 199), remains outside the effeminizing sphere of the museum and its capitalistic logic, even when in the midst of the museum. The museum, paradoxically, in its commodification and exhibition of the Indian, in the rupture it creates between the masculine Indian body and the observer, between commodified racial other and paying museum patrons, with both physical (rope) and economic barriers, replicates the sublime sense of distance and contact that Thoreau locates between himself and nature (and his own body) at Ktaadn.[79] Thoreau collapses the distinction between an effeminizing civilization and a masculine nature by finding that nature "in the midst of cities." Just as "there is all of civilized life in the woods" (*J* 1:252), so Thoreau can find that wildness which "cities import . . . at any price" ("Walking" 224), but which is "too pure to have a market value," in the commercialized entertainments of civilization. Through the museum and its articulation of racial difference, Thoreau can mine the wildness of nature, the Indian, and his own body—a wildness always at one remove—in imagining a kind of masculine literary production resistant to the market yet dependent upon the market itself.

"The Savage Heart"

Okah Tubbee used the museum's tendency to objectify the Indian as innately wild in order to reproduce himself anew; yet, at the same time, he made a case for the possibility that Indians could become civilized. Okah Tubbee's problem in both his performances and his biographies was to claim an Indian heritage by playing up the wildness that the museum produced, but then to claim that this wildness was, in fact, not essential, that Indians, such as himself, could overcome their primitive roots and eventually become assimilated into Euro-American culture. Hence, Tubbee had to use the idea of race as essential in order to claim to be an Indian, yet denied such an essentializing logic in order to argue that the Indians were not necessarily doomed to extinction.

Tubbee's chief strategy in arguing that Indians need not "suffer themselves to be exterminated" (57), that the "entire extinction of the race" (78) could be avoided, was by advocating, in redface performances alongside blackface minstrelsy, that Indians "assume the habits of the pale face" (77). As with William Wells Brown, Tubbee's ability to manipulate literary and mass cultural conventions was essential to his negotiation of such masks in creating a masculine identity. In particular, Tubbee's ability to use both music and written texts allowed him to succeed in linking red and white faces and distinguishing himself from black ones. In addressing both Indians—in the hope of convincing them that some form of reservation system was their only alternative to extinction—and whites—in the hope of gaining support for the reformation of U.S. Indian policy—Tubbee created new instruments, including one out of a tomahawk: "I thought if the tomahawk, the Indian's most deadly weapon, could be made into an instrument of music, it would be coming nearer to the Indian's heart"; "the harmony might melt the savage heart" (86). Tubbee "softened down ["their hearts"] with melody" (92), so "that they might be refreshed and saved" (87). While the voice of the Indian in the museum was "refreshing" to Thoreau because, as Child put it, it "clove the brain like a tomahawk," Tubbee hoped that turning the tomahawk into a musical instrument would "refresh" his Indian brethren by making them less wild. The refreshing sound of music then parallels the museum's dual movement toward wildness and civilization, sensation and sentiment. Through music, Tubbee tried to domesticate, tame, and preserve the Indian outside the museum by making him at the same time pale and red.

Tubbee's musical talents certainly could have been a threat to his Indian identity, possibly serving to reidentify him with the ("primitive") singing and dancing slaves of plantation fiction and the minstrel stage. In order to articulate a position in favor of assimilation over extermination, while maintaining his allegiance to essential Indian characteristics—so as not to become black—Tubbee combined his museum performances and his music with a written form. Just as museum proprietors turned to written guidebooks to domesticate both audiences and attractions, to make "tomahawks" less threatening, so did Okah Tubbee use his written biographies to render himself and his tomahawk-flute more civilized at the same time as marking himself as *not* effeminately black, but rather masculinely wild. The collaborative nature of his biography makes this negotiation of identity possible. Producing a written biography not only helped Tubbee promote himself as an orator, performer, and doctor; it also helped him prove his point about the capacity of Indian peoples to become "civilized." But by having his wife actually write the text, Tubbee could maintain a pose of being outside civilization. By being both a musical performer and the subject of a biography written by another Indian, Tubbee could take advantage of both the conception of Indians as innately primitive and the idea that Indians' primitiveness was simply one stage on a path to their eventual civilization. By articulating his story both in the museum and on paper, Tubbee could begin to consolidate his identity as both Indian chief and American man, both as innately primitively wild savage and as civilized breadwinner for his family. Through the museum and his biography, he was at once domesticated and naturalized, to paraphrase Susan Stewart, becoming an object of sympathy and fear, thus allowing him to negotiate his manhood through an essential, wild "Indianness."

By turning himself into a popular entertainment commodity, Tubbee could claim to be wild, the very thing Thoreau claimed was unmarketable. Correspondingly, Thoreau could use the commercialized museum as a way to gain access to that unmarketable wildness. Thoreau identifies with the Indian in the museum, like Okah Tubbee, but unlike the basket-weaving Indian in *Walden*, this Indian is very aware that it is "necessary for him to make it worth the other's while to buy" his "basket of a delicate texture," his wild "authenticity." By both "importing" the wildness of the Indian into a domestic setting and sustaining an aura of primitive authenticity, the museum reveals that Thoreau was correct, that "true" wildness—in the form of racial difference—remains "too pure to have a market value," not despite, but because "the cities import it at any price."

A "*Rara Avis in Terris*"

Poe's "Hop-Frog" and Race

in the Antebellum Freak Show

In a letter to his close friend Frederick Thomas, dated 14 February 1849, less than eight months before his own death, Edgar Allan Poe wrote, "Literature is the most noble of professions. In fact, it is about the only one fit for a man." After being "quite out of the literary world for the last three years," Poe felt quite "savage." Having "*some* old scores to settle," he was ready to return to the critical battles that had made him infamous. As his just-completed review of James Russell Lowell's *A Fable for Critics* indicates, the target of his critical savagery, as it had been for much of his career, would be the Boston literary establishment.[1] A week before he wrote to Thomas, Poe completed "Hop-Frog," one of his last short stories, whose eponymous hero's parting shot—"This is my last jest"—has often been read as his own final jab at his critics and the literary marketplace. Publishing "Hop-Frog" in *Flag of Our Union*, a Boston weekly newspaper he described as "not a *very* respectable journal, perhaps, in a literary point of view, but one that pays as high prices as most of the magazines," Poe hoped the story would help him financially so he could start his own literary magazine, the *Stylus*. "Hop-Frog" was Poe's attempt to cash in on the public's demand for sensational tales in order that he might escape that very public. The target of Poe's critical savagery in his letter to Thomas, however, points to his story's being not simply an allegory of revenge against the literary marketplace, but also an attempt to establish a kind of savage literary manhood defined against both the literary mass market and the Boston literary elite.

In this chapter I argue that Poe attempts to negotiate the literary marketplace by drawing on one of the most popular commercial entertainment forms of the period, the presentation of human oddities for mass audiences. While "Hop-Frog," with its dwarf-jester, his midget friend, a king, and his ministers, may seem far removed from the United States of the 1840s, such characters would have been familiar to the audiences of popular museum attractions such as Tom Thumb (Charles Stratton). Most famously with Stratton, but more tellingly, I will argue, with attractions such as "What is It?," P. T. Barnum and other proprietors brought a variety of human anomalies to the centerstage. Drawing on such contemporary figures in constructing his fantastical revenge, Poe places himself squarely amidst scientific debates over human types, over human bodies and their meaning, and specifically over race. Poe uses the freak show to construct his allegorical revenge because of its commercial success, a success dependent on its ability both to exemplify and to stand outside the laws of science and, in particular, scientific descriptions of race. While not every "freak" displayed in antebellum popular museums was coded in racial terms, commentary and advertisements readily drew on notions of race to figure bodily difference. Because the racially exotic body in the museum was valuable in various, at times contradictory, ways, it occasionally transgressed racial lines and overturned the racial hierarchy of white mass market audience members and displayed racial other. Poe attempts to use this subversive element within the antebellum freak show to place himself outside the realm of mere commerce in a more purely aesthetic sphere, in the process appropriating racial difference to figure his artistic practice. By reading Poe's story through the popular museum and the popular museum through Poe's story, I explore both how Poe unwraps the commercial racial logic of the freak show, its commodification of the exotic, the different, and the abnormal, *and* how that logic offers us a different understanding of Poe's racial politics and aesthetics.

Unlike Thoreau, then, who draws on the museum's separation of gendered, racialized traits into categories of blackness and Indianness, Poe invokes the museum's use of race as a free-floating, imprecise category of difference from the normative white male body. Both Thoreau and Poe, however, take up the racialized body in the museum as a figure for thinking through and negotiating their position in the market economy as men and as producers of aesthetic commodities. With "Hop-Frog," Poe identifies the male artist with a commercialized, racial other in articulating a particularly masculinized model of aesthetic production.[2]

This model, however, is not simply defined as racially different and masculine. Rather, like Thoreau, Poe paradoxically invokes a commercialized racial figure in order to imagine an antimarket literary manhood, a type of masculine literary production imagined to elude the demands of the marketplace. Because the racialized, freakish body became valuable not only by substantiating an audience's claim to (white) normality, but by upsetting racialized notions of what the body signified and, thus, turning the tables on its audience, Poe could use it to fantasize his revenge against those who would simply render him a commodity. In attempting to create a space for a literary production more independent of the market, Poe embraces his commodified status through the freak show, realizing he has "no other capital to begin with than whatever reputation I may have acquired as a literary man."[3] In this way, Poe imagines Hop-Frog's escape as a model for escaping the mass market's demands and establishing himself as an aesthetic arbiter beyond both the market's fluctuations and an effete antislavery elite's power. In reacting to both the mass literary market and a white Northern antislavery literati, Poe, a self-identified Southerner, appropriates mass cultural racial difference in constructing a vision of literary manhood.

"My Last Jest"

"Hop-Frog: or, The Eight Chained Ourang-Outangs" is the story of "a dwarf and a cripple" captured "from some barbarous region" and enslaved by a king who makes him serve as his jester.[4] Upon the occasion of the story, the king is having a masquerade ball and calls upon Hop-Frog to contrive costumes for him and his ministers. One of the king's favorite "jokes" (the king is a great joker) is to require Hop-Frog to drink alcohol because of its potent effect upon him. The king forces Hop-Frog to drink a draught of wine and commands Hop-Frog to come up with "characters" for him and his ministers to assume. Shaken by the wine, Hop-Frog fails to respond. When the king tells him to drink more wine, Trippetta, a beautiful female dwarf who is the king's pet and Hop-Frog's sole friend (and fellow captive from the "barbarous region"), attempts to intercede on his behalf. The king tosses the wine in her face and pushes her to the ground. Following an inexplicable grating noise, Hop-Frog drinks more wine and elaborates his idea for the king and his courtiers to be costumed as "the Eight Chained

Ourang-Outangs" (*PT* 904). Hop-Frog helps them prepare for the masquerade, making their costumes out of tar and flax and chaining them together as apes caught in the jungle. At the height of the ball, the costumed "Ourang-Outangs" enter with great commotion, frightening most of the guests. Hop-Frog corrals the faux orangutans in the center of the ballroom and attaches them by their chain to a chain extending from a skylight. With a whistle, he leaps above the courtiers and, hanging onto the chain, is raised up by an unseen accomplice. Hop-Frog, now seething in anger, breaks the silence by emitting a low grating noise and then pretends to scrutinize the identity of the orang-utans by bringing his flambeau closer. Because their costumes consist of tar and flax, the courtiers erupt in flames and are quickly reduced to a charred mass. Hop-Frog describes the king's offenses to Trippetta, tells his stunned audience that "*this is my last jest,*" and then climbs out the skylight, presumably to join Trippetta in an "escape to their own country" (*PT* 908).

For years, critics have read Poe's story of revenge as an allegory either of a transhistorical battle of the imagination with reality or, more specifically, of Poe's own battles with the publishing industry and his American audience.[5] Throughout his literary career, Poe was teetering on the edge of financial ruin, and by the time he was writing "Hop-Frog" in January and February of 1849, his financial condition was especially precarious. As he told one friend, his primary reason for publishing the story was to "get out of [his] pecuniary difficulties."[6] At the same time, in addition to struggling to stay on his financial feet, Poe was also attempting to accumulate enough capital to start his own journal, the *Stylus*, a dream he had pursued since the early 1840s. As he described the journal in a letter to a potential subscriber in April 1849, only a month after the publication of "Hop-Frog," the *Stylus* would give the public "what they cannot elsewhere procure"; it would "aim high—address the intellect—the higher classes," thus allowing its editor to "exercise a literary and other influence never yet exercised in America."[7] In particular, Poe argued that such a magazine would fill a niche created by "the universal *disgust* excited by what is quaintly termed the *cheap* literature of the day," those magazines that consisted of "the ludicrous heightened into the grotesque; the fearful coloured into the horrible: the witty exaggerated into the burlesque: the singular wrought out into the strange and mystical."[8] Thus, at the time Poe was writing and publishing "Hop-Frog," his hopes had become almost singularly pinned upon the idea of raising enough subscribers to start his independent, elite journal.

In this way, "Hop-Frog" amounts to more than an attempt at escaping "pecuniary difficulties"; it was specifically part of an attempt to elude the very market that called for "terrible" tales such as "Hop-Frog" and that made "not . . . *very* respectable journal[s]" like *Flag of Our Union* so successful.[9] Read in this light, the story becomes an allegory of Poe's attempt to escape his own dependence on an unappreciative and exploitative mass audience. Just as Poe hoped that by producing a tale of the horrible, grotesque, and burlesque, such as the literary market called for, he could escape its power, so "Hop-Frog" tells the story of its "professional jester" (*PT* 899) giving his audience exactly what they want in order to escape their power.[10] Like Poe's mass audience, the king and his ministers have no time for the "refinements . . . of wit" (*PT* 899). "Over-niceties wearied them," as they can only appreciate "*breadth*," "*length*," and the "practical" (*PT* 899). Their attention is focused on the "*effect* produced"—especially "fright" (*PT* 904)—and they specifically call for literary/creative novelties rather than art: "We want characters . . . something novel. . . . We are wearied with this everlasting sameness" (*PT* 901). Poe not only characterizes this audience as incapable of seeing beyond "fright" and "effect" but also suggests their blindness derives from their focus on commercial matters. Throughout the story, the king's ministers respond in affirmation as a chorus with the refrain "Capital!," while the prime minister's lone enunciation consists of "And now to *business*" (*PT* 902, my emphasis) as he demands characters of Hop-Frog. Finally, Poe emphasizes this audience's limited capacity to appreciate Hop-Frog's creations by describing it as one undistinguishable, massive body. From the outset, Poe lavishes great attention upon the size of the king and his courtiers, their "large, corpulent" bodies, sarcastically distinguished by their "heavy wisdom" (*PT* 899). At the end, with his declaration that he knows "who these people *are*, now!" (*PT* 907, Poe's emphasis), Hop-Frog reveals them as "a fetid, blackened, hideous, and indistinguishable *mass*" (*PT* 908, my emphasis). In this way, Poe's king and his court—who respond with "Capital!" to the idea of "fright" (*PT* 904)—parallel the mass market that Poe, at times, felt himself financially required to appease. Writing "Hop-Frog" in the same month in which he wrote to

Thomas that literature was the only profession "fit for a man," Poe projects his anxieties of economic emasculation onto the body of Hop-Frog, then imagining himself, through Hop-Frog, gaining revenge against those who abuse beauty and truth. With "Hop-Frog," then, Poe attempts to create a space for a kind of intellectual aristocrat, a model of literary manhood defined by its defense of beauty—embodied, perhaps, in Trippetta's feminine form—against an unappreciative mass audience only interested in capital and fright.[11]

"Maltreatment Received at the Hands of the Populace"

Such an allegory—of the male artist (Hop-Frog) gaining revenge against an abusive audience (the king and his ministers)—nicely echoes the story of Poe as a writer who had to play to the sensational demands of the market in order to survive, but whose truly artistic tales transcend the market's power. Where apologists from Baudelaire to David Reynolds have read Poe in this way, critics such as Terence Whalen have more recently begun to argue that Poe's oeuvre, including his aesthetic critique of the marketplace, was, in fact, made possible by the commercialized nature of mass culture.[12] While Poe frequently denounced a purely economic basis for judging literature and lamented the way market considerations deformed literary works, he just as often accepted the economically driven nature of the antebellum publishing industry and often boasted of the growth in circulation that publications such as *Graham's Magazine* achieved under his editorship. In the early 1840s, he complained that "It seems that the horrid laws of political economy cannot be evaded even by the inspired" (*ER* 211) and argued that "if the popularity of a book be in fact the measure of its worth, we should . . . admit the inferiority of 'Newton's Principia' to 'Hoyle's Games'" (*ER* 225–26). Yet only a few years earlier he seemed to embrace those "horrid laws" when he argued that the "effect" of a tale "will be estimated better by the circulation of the Magazine than by any comments upon its contents" and that "truth and honor form *no* exceptions to the rule of economy, that value depends upon demand and supply."[13]

The tension between these seemingly paradoxical views comes to a head in Poe's dream of establishing himself as editor of an independent journal. When Poe commented on the fact that "The history of all

Magazines shows plainly that those which have attained celebrity were indebted for it to articles" of potentially "bad taste" consisting of "the ludicrous heightened into the grotesque; the fearful coloured into the horrible: the witty exaggerated into the burlesque: the singular wrought out into the strange and mystical," he was in fact defending his own tales, specifically "Berenice," in terms of their potential for helping a magazine's financial success.[14] Yet with the *Stylus* Poe apparently hoped that by gaining "a proprietary right" to his own magazine through the support of subscribers from "our vast Southern & Western Countries" he would escape his dependence upon the literate masses and a Northern literary elite, if not the literary marketplace.[15] Drawing on the commercial magazine form that had helped to place even "the inspired" at the mercy of "the horrid laws of political economy," Poe wanted to reinvent the form by appealing to an elite, regional audience and making it a vehicle for addressing ideas of truth and beauty. While critics have often read the *Stylus* as indicative of Poe's desire to inhabit an otherworldly aesthetic sphere outside the reach of the market, Whalen's work suggests that rather than trying to escape the market, Poe was simply trying to find the right market niche where the value of truth and beauty would fetch the best price.[16]

Thus, where David Leverenz has argued that "Hop-Frog" "satirizes emerging mass-market culture. . . . [and] capitalist constructions of manliness [and] individuality," we need to see this satire as being both critical of emerging mass culture and concomitant notions of manhood *and* deeply embedded within them.[17] "Hop-Frog" displays this dependence on mass market forms not simply in its sensationalism and its publication in a cheap weekly newspaper, but through its invocation of popular museum culture. Despite its seemingly fairy tale cast of a king, his ministers, and a jester, Poe's story of the display of half-man, half-beast orangutans, a deformed acrobatic dwarf, and a beautiful, talented midget to a mass audience would have resonated with American audiences familiar with the display and promotion of abnormal humans by popular museum proprietors like P. T. Barnum.[18] Dwarves and midgets not only had served as jesters in European royal courts throughout the sixteenth, seventeenth, and eighteenth centuries (and even, in a few cases, into the nineteenth century), but had appeared in popular, commercial forums such as Bartholomew Fair since the early seventeenth century.[19] Early American museums, such as Charles Willson

Peale's museum in Philadelphia, while taking a more scientific, democratizing approach, continued to display scientific abnormalities, and with Barnum's American Museum in the 1840s the American freak show, "the formally organized exhibition of people with alleged and real physical, mental, or behavioral anomalies for amusement and profit," came into its own.[20]

The antebellum freak show attracted patrons both by objectifying the bizarre and by making the bizarre seem normal. The most successful of Barnum's attractions, the young Tom Thumb, exemplifies this play between the familiar and the different. Throughout his career, Thumb performed as the American Yankee in miniature, "a perfect MINIATURE MAN, only TWENTY-EIGHT INCHES HIGH, perfect and elegant in his proportions, and weighing only FIFTEEN POUNDS!"[21] As Neil Harris argues, Thumb's popularity depended on the fact that, unlike most human oddities, "Crowds identified with him, rather than against him."[22] But Thumb's success was not simply dependent on his audience identifying with him; rather, it was his rendering of the familiar in *miniature*, with a difference, the fact that he seemed so familiar, yet so strange, that made him such a popular draw.[23] Audiences were delighted by Thumb's performances and recognized in him the middle-class traits they wanted to have themselves—intelligence, elegance, kindness, morality.[24] Yet they were reassured of their own normality not simply by his mirroring those traits, but also by his small size, by laughing not simply with him, but at his attempts at personating "large" world historical figures like Napoleon, Samson, and Hercules. In other words, as much as he was a petted favorite, like Trippetta, Thumb was still an object on display, to be laughed at and identified against, as with Hop-Frog.[25]

If Thumb's audiences tended to identify with him, even as his size marked him as abnormal and, consequently, them as normal, Barnum encouraged his audiences to view other strange humans he exhibited as different in terms of race. While in Europe developing the fame and reputation of his biggest star in the mid-1840s, Barnum also remained busy with other projects. In August 1846 he announced the London exhibition of what he called the "wild man of the prairies," or "What is It?" Claiming the creature had been captured in California or the mountains of Mexico, Barnum prompted his audience's reactions to the dark-skinned, hairy man with a series of questions: "Is it an animal?

Is it human? Is it an Extraordinary Freak of Nature? Or is it a legitimate member of Nature's Works? Or is it the long sought for link between man and the Ourang-Outang?"[26] It was quickly revealed, however, that this nondescript was actually the well-known American actor Harvey Leach, dressed in a hair costume with his skin stained underneath.

Leach stood only three feet, five inches tall, and, when he walked, he "waddled along, his hands touch[ing] the ground, in the manner of the higher primates," because one of his legs was six inches longer than the other.[27] Despite his deformity, Leach's "extraordinary muscular powers, especially in his arms" allowed him to "achieve some very remarkable feats of strength and agility."[28] Using his acrobatic skills, he had gained minor fame as Signor Hervio Nano on the New York and London stages in the early 1840s in roles such as Jocko, the Brazilian ape; Bibbo, the Patagonian ape; and "the Frog."[29] His best-known performance was as the Gnome Fly, wherein "he successively embodied a gnome, a baboon, and a fly," a performance that ended with his making "a wonderful flight, in magnificent costume . . . from the ceiling, back of the gallery, to the back of the stage."[30] Leach died only six months after his involvement in Barnum's "What is It?" hoax was revealed, and commentators of the day attributed his death to his embarrassment at his complicity in such a disreputable performance: "It killed Harvey Leach, for he took it to heart and died."[31] As one historian of the American stage put it in 1866, he died "from maltreatment received at the hands of the populace."[32]

The resemblance between Leach and Hop-Frog is striking. Like Leach, because of "the distortion of his legs," Hop-Frog "could only get along by a sort of interjectional gait—something between a leap and a wriggle." Similarly, despite his troubles walking, Hop-Frog is also a spectacular acrobat: "the prodigious muscular power which nature seemed to have bestowed upon his arms . . . enabled him to perform feats of wonderful dexterity, where trees or ropes were in question." And like Leach, who regularly performed as an ape, Hop-Frog, it seems, "resembled . . . a small monkey" (*PT* 900). Hop-Frog's narrative even seems to evoke Leach's most famous role, the "The Gnome Fly," in which he transformed himself from a gnome into a baboon and then into a fly; at the end of his story, Hop-Frog transforms his audience, rather than himself, into orangutans, but like Leach he escapes by making a "wonderful flight" far above an astonished crowd. Finally,

8. Le nain Americain, advertisement for Harvey
Leach (c. 1845). *Courtesy of Billy Rose Theatre Collection, The New York Public Library for the Performing Arts, Astor, Lenox and Tilden Foundations.*

Hop-Frog's story reverses the popular narrative of Leach's demise.
While Leach dressed up as an orangutan-type creature and was destroyed by his mass audience, Hop-Frog bedecks his audience as orangutans in order to destroy them. Even Leach's role as *génie du feu* (see
Figure 8), the fire genie, seems to recall Hop-Frog's final revenge.

I do not want to press these similarities too far and nominate Leach
as the precise model for Hop-Frog. Rather, I want to place these two
narratives together in order to indicate how "Hop-Frog" reverses a

standard antebellum tale of the abused, commercialized other by upsetting central distinctions between subject and object, normal and abnormal, civilized and brute, man and monster, master and slave. "Hop-Frog," in this regard, prefigures Tod Browning's film *Freaks* (1932) and its fantasy of the freakish object of attraction transforming the apparently normal into the monstrous. While the king proclaims he shall "make a man" (*PT* 904) of Hop-Frog, implying he is not yet one, the story reveals the king as a "monster" (*PT* 902) himself. Most important for this chapter, Poe's evocation of the popular museum and its commodification of the bizarre recalls his concern throughout his career with commercial culture and, especially, his concern with the commercial nature of literature and the commercial success of the literary grotesque. Poe's narrative reversal of the story of Harvey Leach suggests his investment in reversing the terms of popular museum culture and its commodification of its attractions, his desire to overthrow the categories of monster and man in establishing himself in a position of literary manhood. Such a reversal, I will argue, was already implicit in the antebellum freak show and had everything to do with its commercial nature. With the freak show, Poe was able to invoke the popular and sensational as a way of attempting to escape the popular market in sensational literature. Furthermore, as I will argue, by identifying himself with racial otherness, he could successfully and savagely satirize his literary foes.

"The Connecting Link Between Humanity and Brute Creation"

Drawing on popular museum culture to reconceive the literary marketplace, Poe turns to a figure of racial difference for constructing a fantasy of literary manhood. As Leach's exhibit exemplifies, the antebellum freak show was much more than a commercial attraction; it was a central site for the popularization of scientific ideas, especially scientific ideas about race. While cultural critics often complained of the tawdry, sensationalistic, and commercial nature of "museums" such as Barnum's, scientists like Louis Agassiz lent credibility to these institutions by celebrating their promulgation of natural science.[33] In fact, when Barnum's museum burned down in 1865, Agassiz and other scientists wrote a public letter lamenting the loss to the scientific community.[34] In particular, Barnum's display of amazing humans, including "wild" Indians from the western frontier, promoted the popular discussion and dissemination of scientific ideas concerning humankind.[35] As I have discussed in chapter 2, the popular museum brought together a cross-class, mixed gender, white urban audience, in the process normalizing ideas of the white middle-class family and decorous behavior. Recently, critics such as Rosemarie Garland Thomson and Leonard Cassuto have discussed how the antebellum freak show helped to police white normativity by defining the limits of the normal, white, rigidly gendered body in terms of race. By being both like and clearly unlike the almost exclusively white audience, such attractions shored up normative white identity at a time of immense social change.[36] Even Thumb, whose "perfect" white elegance and normality in miniature were central to his success, was often marked in terms of racial or gender difference in his performances—singing minstrel songs and wearing dresses—to emphasize his lack of a normal, white male body.[37]

Exhibits such as Barnum's "What is It?" more clearly reinforced the ideas of racial hierarchy put forth by texts such as J. C. Nott and George Gliddon's *Types of Mankind* (1854). With Leach, Barnum—as in his later and more famous "What is It?" exhibit featuring African American William Henry Johnson—refused to define precisely what his nondescript was: "The thing is not to be called *anything* by the exhibitor. We know not & therefore do not assert whether it is human or animal. We leave that all to the sagacious public to decide."[38] Yet as the exhibit of Johnson more explicitly foregrounds and as Leach's stained skin implies, such missing link figures clearly evoked a rather imprecisely defined racial order that ranked white audience members above darker-skinned, nearly subhuman others in some hierarchy of both humankind and creation itself. Confirming the racial science of the era, Leach's "What is It?" with his racially indeterminate exotic pedigree indicated to his audience that their normative white bodies were not just the standard for mankind, but were the superior models.[39]

Poe mirrors the racial coding of exhibits such as "What is It?" in describing Hop-Frog. Like Barnum, Poe is "not able to say, with precision, from what country Hop-Frog originally came." It was, he assures, "some barbarous region, however, that no person ever heard of—a vast distance from the court of our king" (*PT* 900). The racially other character of Hop-Frog is further suggested by his resemblance to black and Indian characters from elsewhere in Poe's work, almost all of whom are not simply of a different race, but horribly misshapen. For example, in *The Narrative of Arthur Gordon Pym* (1838), Dirk Peters, "the son of an Indian squaw" and "a fur-trader," is

> one of the most purely ferocious-looking men. . . . He was short in stature—not more than four feet eight inches high—but his limbs were of the most Herculean mould. His hands, especially, were so enormously thick and broad as hardly to retain a human shape. His arms, as well as legs, were *bowed* in the most singular manner, and appeared to possess no flexibility whatever. His head was equally deformed, being of immense size, with an indentation on the crown (like that on the head of most negroes), and entirely bald. (*PT* 1043)

Poe describes black characters similarly in *The Journal of Julius Rodman* (1840) and "How to Write a Blackwood Article" (1838). In *Rodman*, Toby is "as ugly an old gentleman as ever spoke—having all the peculiar features of his race; the swollen lips, large white protruding eyes, flat nose, long ears, double head, pot-belly, and bow legs" (*PT* 1242), while Pompey, in "Blackwood," is "three feet in height. . . . [and] had bow-legs and was corpulent. His mouth should not be called small, nor his ears short. . . . Nature had endowed him with no neck, and had placed his ankles (as usual with that race) in the middle of the upper portion of the feet" (*PT* 289). Rather than simply drawing upon grotesque stereotypes of blacks and Indians, Poe emphasizes their supposed biological difference through bowed legs, deformed hands, and short stature. Describing the dwarf Hop-Frog in terms of his exotic pedigree, distorted legs, "prodigious muscular power" (*PT* 900), and "large eyes" (*PT* 902), Poe all but defines him as yet another one of his deformed black or Indian characters.[40]

Poe's use of orangutans in "Hop-Frog" and elsewhere is particularly telling in this regard. Barnum advertised his own orangutan in 1846 as "the Grand Connecting Link between the two great families, the Human and brute creation," using almost the exact language he used to describe both Leach and Johnson as "What is It?": "the connecting link between humanity and brute creation."[41] Barnum displayed the costumed Leach and Johnson as links between human and orangutan because the orangutan already stood as a link itself between humans and other brutes. This liminal status of the orangutan is a recurring trope in Poe's oeuvre. Most famously, in "The Murders in the Rue Morgue" (1841) the murderer is thought to be an inarticulate madman or perhaps "an Asian" or "an African" (*PT* 416) before Dupin posits that it is an orangutan.[42] The orangutan was not simply seen as linking humans and other animals, but as being more closely related to irrational, inarticulate, primitive humans, specifically supposedly intellectually inferior Africans. Barnum drew upon this supposed relationship when he stated that the later "What is It?" was "found in the interior of Africa in a perfectly natural state, roving about like a monkey or Orang Outang," and was of "mixed ancestry" as indicated by the fact that "while his face, hands and arms are distinctly human, his head, feet and legs are more like the Orang Outang."[43] In both "Hop-Frog" and the "What is It?" exhibits, orangutans help to place the abnormal body in a racialized hierarchy, somewhere between fully human white audience members and lower animals. As Hop-Frog's revelation of his orangutans as a "blackened mass" iterates, the half-man, half-beast orangutan was, in the end, implicitly black or, at least, not-white.[44]

"Hop-Frog," however, reverses this racial coding. Instead of simply emphasizing the abnormality of its "dwarf" and "cripple" by demonstrating his close proximity to orangutans and blacks, the story reveals its ostensibly normal, fully human king and his ministers as monsters by displaying them first as orangutans and then as a blackened mass. "Hop-Frog," in other words, does not abandon the metonymic link between race and monstrosity, but rather reveals the supposed men as monsters while demonstrating the more powerful manhood of the exotic, abnormal other through his subtle plan of revenge. As Joan Dayan puts it, the story ends with "The epidermic curse—the fatality of being black, or blackened—[being] visited on the master race."[45] Yet what is most striking about this narrative is Poe's identification with, rather than against, the exotified other. Poe's racial attitudes have been debated much of late, with most of the focus centering on *Pym* and its description of the black Tsalalians and a review of two proslavery volumes that appeared in the *Southern Literary Messenger* under Poe's editorship in 1836 and that may or may not have been written by him.[46] What is clear by nearly all accounts is that whether Poe wrote the review, which states that "Domestic Slavery" is "the basis of all our institutions," or not, he embraced, at times, many of the "standard proslavery arguments of his day."[47] Most infamously, Poe's Pym describes the completely black Tsalalians as "among the most barbarous, subtle, and bloodthirsty wretches that ever contaminated the face of the globe" (*PT* 1150). Poe's exotic, deformed Hop-Frog, with his initial meekness and ready servitude that turn into sly revenge, closely resembles the subtle barbarians of *Pym* who initially appear meek and malleable, but then slaughter the crew of the *Jane*. Because of his customary slipperiness, Poe's precise attitude toward Pym and, by extension, the Tsalalians is as debatable as his racial attitudes, and his depiction of Hop-Frog has similarly evoked contradictory reactions. But what is more certain is that unlike the Tsalalians or Pompey, Toby, or even Dirk Peters (who only becomes "white" [*PT* 1156] in the context of the completely black Tsalalians), Poe describes Hop-Frog as a fully individuated and complex subject. In constructing a model of savage literary manhood in his fantasy of revenge against the literary marketplace, Poe identifies his aesthetic self with a character defined as racially other.

"A Triplicate Treasure"

How do we make sense of this identification? Dayan reads "Hop-Frog" as Poe's "envisioned revenge for the national sin of slavery," understanding the reversal of master and slave as deriving from Poe's "increasingly subversive concerns" with "the perils of mastery" and "the reversibility of supremacy."[48] While Poe may well have been obsessed with "the perils of mastery," his more explicit critical concerns during the period had to do with getting "the means of taking the first step" toward establishing the *Stylus* and settling "some old scores," specifically with the Bostonian literary elite.[49] More fully fleshing out Barnum's engagement with contemporary racial science grants one way of understanding how the figure of the freakish other offered Poe a vehicle both for commercial success and for allegorical revenge against the Bostonians. Specifically, the reversal at the end of the story, when the objectified Hop-Frog makes his mass audience the spectacle themselves and calls into question their own humanity, reveals and draws on a subversive element embedded within contemporary displays of the body in the museum and central to those displays' commercial success. In other words, Poe draws on the popular museum and its reversal of racial hierarchies because its exotification and disruption of racial differences had proven commercially successful and could be used to satirize what Poe saw as the hubris and hypocrisy of a Northern, anti-slavery, literary elite. The commercialization and subversion of racial difference and hierarchy in the popular museum becomes a mode through which Poe can create a popular story in attempting to escape the power of both the literary masses and a Boston literary elite.

Poe suggests the literary market value of race in a letter on the marketing of the *Stylus*, three months after the publication of "Hop-Frog." There, he explains his "awaiting the *best opportunity* for [the *Stylus's*] issue," by quoting Monk Lewis. Lewis, according to Poe, "once was asked how he came, in one of his acted plays, to introduce *black* banditti, when, in the country where the scene was laid, black people were quite unknown." He writes that Lewis's "answer was:—'I introduced them because I truly anticipated that blacks would have more *effect* on my audience than whites—and if I had taken it into my head that, by making them sky-blue, the *effect* would have been greater, why sky-blue they should have been.' "[50] Poe's point, it seems, is that the success of the *Stylus* depends on timing, on it producing the proper *effect*, an effect directly analogous to the sensation that racial others might cause in an audience of whites. Race sells because it produces a certain effect, namely fright, that is analogous to the effect produced by the right timing and right promotion in producing an elite literary journal. But it is not simply race that sells; it is the exotic, abnormal nature of the racial other that sells, the fact that he or she too is human, but does not appear to be.[51] Linking his elite literary journal to the appeal of racial difference, Poe identifies his aesthetic program with the market in the sensational and the sensational's transgression of the normal.

Poe fleshes out the commercial value of fright and exotified racial difference in describing Hop-Frog's value to his audience. Taking great care to describe that value precisely, Poe expands the literary market value of race that his citation of Monk Lewis suggests and complicates notions of the role of race in popular museums. As a "professional jester," Hop-Frog, Poe states, was a "triplicate treasure in one person" (*PT* 900). First, Hop-Frog gives the king "a jester to laugh *with*, and a dwarf to laugh *at*" (*PT* 899); Hop-Frog's objectified body allows the king both to identify with him in his jokes and to reconfirm his superiority through a bodily-marked hierarchy. Like Tom Thumb, Hop-Frog entertains his audience members, mirroring their own sense of themselves, and at the same time reinforces, through his deformed body, their sense of superiority. Yet Hop-Frog's body also marks him as different in another way. His diminutive size sets Hop-Frog apart because in "ninety-nine cases out of a hundred" jesters "are fat, round and unwieldy" (like the "mass[ive]" king and his ministers). Thus, "a lean joker [like Hop-Frog] is a *rara avis in terris*" (*PT* 899). According to Poe, then, Hop-Frog is a triplicate treasure (1) because his audience can identify with him and be entertained by him, (2) because his body seems to confirm their superiority by affirming the body as a stable marker of identity and cultural/racial hierarchies (they are civilized, he is barbarous), and (3) paradoxically, because his body does *not* confirm, but rather troubles such notions of stable bodily meaning, because he disrupts the linkage between jesters and rotundity. Unlike ninety-nine jesters out of a hundred, he is not fat.

While Hop-Frog's being a lean joker does not seem particularly subversive of antebellum ideas about the body, Poe's delineation of Hop-Frog's value, his status as a rara avis, suggests that part of the freak show's commercial success arose from its disruption of audience expectations about bodies and their meanings. We can use Hop-Frog's triplicate value then to understand the market value of Leach in "What is It?" better. One aspect of the cultural work of antebellum freakery was, as we have seen, its shoring up of the white bourgeois family as a normative standard for judging the world and other peoples, its confirmation of hierarchical, racialized divisions through its display of bodily difference. But as "Hop-Frog" indicates, this does not tell the whole story. In its invocation of what Neil Harris has called "the operational aesthetic," Barnum's exhibit leaves it "to the sagacious public to decide" precisely what "It" is and what "It" means.[52] Barnum first suggests that "It" upholds a natural order of things that consists of a great chain of being leading from God to civilized whites to displayed racial others to orangutans and then brute creation; that is, that as a link in the chain of being, It is "a legitimate member of Nature's works." Yet Barnum goes on to hint that It may not conform to the laws of nature at all, that it may be "an Extraordinary Freak of Nature." "Hop-Frog" emphasizes that one part of the freak's triplicate value was its subversion of such an order. Just as Hop-Frog's value is trebled because his body does not conform to the general law that jesters are "fat, round and unwieldy," so "What is It?" gains its commercial value, its power to attract paying customers, not simply by confirming their sense of superiority, but by challenging the order of nature that supposedly guarantees their superiority.

Because of the ways in which Barnum both courted scientific acceptance by providing specimens that confirmed scientific laws and needed sensational attractions that defied the laws of science, his exhibition of humans did not simply replicate given scientific theorems about race, but questioned the empirical grounds of those theorems. In particular, Barnum's exhibits displayed blackness both as nearly nonhuman and as potentially white, through both blackface minstrel shows, where whites became black, and the exhibition of albino African Americans or African Americans whose skins were turning white.[53] Barnum more directly addressed racial science in promotional biographies of Tom Thumb where he hinted that the American science of craniometry had little or no basis. Craniometry, as promoted by Samuel George Morton, was based on the idea that the interior volume of one's skull corresponded to one's intelligence. Morton used the measurement of skulls from ancient and contemporary skeletons to "prove" the continuation of racial stocks and the superiority of Caucasians. In this way, he became one of the chief theorists for the emerging American school of ethnology, the chief proponents of polygenism and strict, biologically understood racial distinctions in the antebellum period.[54] Barnum reasoned that while it may be "natural to suppose that the smallness of [Thumb's] brain should limit the development of his intellectual facilities," Thumb's intelligence implied that there was no correlation between brain size and intellect, thus disrupting the pseudoscientific assumptions underlying the racial hierarchy of the types of mankind.[55] While exhibits of people like Harvey Leach and Tom Thumb primarily served to substantiate their audience's claims to superiority and normativity, one part of their attraction was their calling into question the assumptions behind such norms, a questioning that simultaneously refocused attention on the "normal" bodies of the audience and empowered that audience, rather than a scientific elite, to be the arbiters of scientific truth.

"Hop-Frog" more fully plays out this reversal, but locates aesthetic and scientific power in the creative but disempowered individual rather than with the masses or the elite. Because Hop-Frog's body confounds the normative identity of jesters as fat, the focus shifts, as the story proceeds, from his body to the massive bodies of the king and his courtiers. The nature of this shift is possibly suggested by the fact that Hop-Frog's mental acuity, like Tom Thumb's, calls into question the assumptions of craniometry, assumptions implied by the story's description of the doltish king's "constitutional swelling of the head" (*PT* 900). Whether referring to craniometric standards or simply metaphorically referring to the king's ego, Poe's story emphasizes that the supposedly normative body does *not* correspond to intellectual superiority. Reversing the order of things in its conclusion, "Hop-Frog" inverts the chain of being that Hop-Frog's body supposedly substantiates —the chain from the skylight leads to Hop-Frog who hovers above the spectacularized and objectified blackened orangutan-courtiers below.

Poe's racist statements and his apparent belief in phrenology, a pseudoscience that provided the underpinnings for craniometry, would seem to trouble such a reading of "Hop-Frog."[56] Poe argued in an 1836 review that phrenology "ranks among the most important [sciences] which can engage the attention of thinking beings" (*ER* 329), and later in the same review, he quotes approvingly a passage that seems to contain the seeds of craniometry: "Idiocy is invariably the consequence of the brain being too small, while in such heads the animal propensities are generally very full" (*ER* 332). Yet as Dana Nelson has recently shown in a striking reading of Poe's "Some Words with a Mummy" (1845), Poe also satirizes racial science (and especially craniometry): Poe uses the mummy's account of the ancient Egyptians' scientific and technological superiority to undermine the scientific coterie's thesis that "we are to attribute the marked inferiority of the old Egyptians in all particulars of science, when compared with the moderns, and more especially with the Yankees, altogether to the superior solidity of the Egyptian skull" (*PT* 817).[57] Dismissing craniometry in order to poke fun at Yankee scientists and their ideas of progress, Poe suggests that he did not blindly accept racial science but rather saw it as evidence of hubris.

Elsewhere, in "The Literary Life of Thingum Bob, Esq." (1844), he uses the false sense of superiority granted by craniometry to satirize the literary market, and he further links craniometric and phrenological questions with aesthetic judgments in his criticism of Longfellow.[58] In one of his reviews of Longfellow, he specifically comments that "Not the least important service which, hereafter, mankind will owe to *Phrenology*, may perhaps, be recognised in an analysis of the real principles, and a digest of the resulting laws of taste" (*ER* 679). In another review of Longfellow, however, he qualifies his acceptance of phrenology by stating that while "Common observation . . . would suffice to teach all mankind that very many of the salient points of phrenological science are undisputable truths," he has little "faith in the marvels[,] inconsistencies. . . . [and] principles kindly furnished to the science by hot-headed and asinine votaries" (*ER* 760). From this passage, it might seem that Poe's dispute with racial science was part of a wider dismissal of science, fully exemplified in "Sonnet—To Science" (1829).[59] Yet Poe, most spectacularly in *Eureka*, but elsewhere as well, readily embraced certain scientific ideas and approaches. We might better understand Poe's skepticism by remembering that craniometry marked, as William Stanton has put it, a shift in early anthropology as "calipers replaced aesthetics."[60] As Poe argued in *Eureka*, rather than relying on so-called evidence, we should combine aesthetics and science, Poetry and Truth, as a "*perfect consistency*" (*PT* 1349), by foregrounding the importance of the imaginative or intuitive in scientific investigations. From this perspective, Poe criticizes phrenology and craniometry not for their racist insights and scientific hypotheses, but for their too precise reliance upon empirical measurement in shifting away from aesthetics.

In this way, "Hop-Frog" and its confutation of the relationship between bodies and their scientific meanings raises questions about the proper investigative techniques and attitudes that scientists should take in investigating man, about the relationship between science and aesthetics, and about the authority of scientific and other "votaries." Hop-Frog's success, like that of Tom Thumb, serves to undermine the idea of using purely mathematical, empirical devices for measuring human beings: the king and his courtiers' emphasis on "*breadth*" and "*length*" (*PT* 899) reveals that they, like racial scientists, incorrectly depend simply on measurements to decide what "make[s] a man" (*PT* 904). Just as Barnum's presentation of Leach in "What is It?" called on the imagination of the "sagacious public" rather than the measurements of a scientific elite to decide what "It" truly is, Poe's Hop-Frog uses his imagination to overturn the empirically minded king and his ministers and to show who is a man and who is not.

But "Hop-Frog" does not leave it up to the sagacious public to decide. Instead, it is not simply Hop-Frog's valuable exotic nature that makes him a *rara avis*, but his creative aesthetic imagination that sets him apart from an elite (the king and his ministers) and the masses (the guests at the masquerade who are duped by the orangutans). The term *rara avis* hints at this aesthetic nature, for Poe used the term in a version of his "Philosophy of Furniture" (1840) to describe those few with refined enough tastes to appreciate true art; and the phrase in both its sound, *rara avis*, and meaning, "strange bird," recalls Poe's most famous poem and nickname, "The Raven."[61] Hop-Frog's revenge, then, does not so much dismantle scientific racism as imply the importance of aesthetics rather than empirical data for judging what makes a (literary) man. In doing so, it links aesthetics with racial otherness against both the unthinking masses and an imitative and self-congratulating tyrant. As suggested by his satires of Yankee scientists and writers who use craniometry and phrenology to claim superiority, that tyrant, for Poe, was the Boston literati with whom he had so often waged war and who, he felt, used questions concerning race to substantiate their own aesthetic claims and authority.

"Our Literary Mohawk, POE!"

In closing, I will attempt to explore how identifying his own artistic and critical practice with racial otherness allowed Poe to imagine a revenge specifically against the Bostonians. Poe's identification with a racially indeterminate native of a barbarous region in "Hop-Frog" was not unprecedented. In fact, throughout his career, he embraced a characterization of himself as being a "savage Indian" in his critical practice. As early as 1836, the *Cincinnati Mirror* commented on Poe's "savage skill" in "us[ing] his tomahawk and scalping knife" as critic and editor for *Southern Literary Messenger*, a comment Poe subsequently reprinted in that magazine to puff its sales.[62] Later, in 1846, the image recurred when Poe was called "the tomahawk man" and "the Comanche of literature."[63] Then in January 1849, at the same time Poe was writing "Hop-Frog," A. J. H. Duganne lampooned Poe in "A Mirror for Authors" with the lines, "With tomahawk upraised for deadly blow, / Behold our literary Mohawk, POE!" (see Figure 9).[64] As noted earlier, in his letter to Thomas written soon after he finished "Hop-Frog" in early February, Poe invokes this characterization of his criticism. Being "quite out of the literary world for the last three years," during which time he has "*said* little or nothing," has made Poe "savage—wolfish"

With tomahawk upraised for deadly blow,
Behold our literary Mohawk, POE!

9. Edgar Allan Poe as "our literary Mohawk," from Motley Manners, esq. [A. J. H. Duganne], "A Mirror for Authors," *Holden's Dollar Magazine* (January 1849): 22. *Courtesy of Cornell University Library.*

and ready to settle "*some* old scores."[65] Calling himself savage, Poe proclaims himself ready to rejoin the "the race of critics," whom he elsewhere defines as exclusively "masculine—men" (*ER* 116). Identifying himself with a character figured as racially other in "Hop-Frog," Poe hoped to establish himself outside the reach of the literary mass market, just as identifying himself with another racial figure, the savage Indian, he hoped to settle some old scores, in particular those with antislavery Boston. With both, he hoped to clear a space for the *Stylus* and the authority it would wield, thus guaranteeing himself a place in the only profession "fit for a man."

About the same time Poe finished "Hop-Frog" in early February 1849, he completed a review of James Russell Lowell's *A Fable for Critics*, a satire of American letters that had appeared the previous October. In *A Fable*, Lowell had gently upbraided Poe for his criticism of Longfellow, but in Poe's letter to Thomas, where he states that he feels "savage," Poe points to the broader basis of his critique of Lowell: "Lowell is a ranting abolitionist and *deserves* a good using up."[66] It is not just Lowell who deserves a good using up; it is his entire Boston clique, "the Frogpondians":

> I wish you would come down on the Frogpondians. They are getting worse and worse, and pretend not to be aware that there *are* any literary people out of Boston. The worst and most disgusting part of the matter is, that the Bostonians are really, as a race, far inferior in point of *anything*

beyond mere talent, to any other *set* upon the continent of N. A. . . . I always get into a passion when I think about [it]. It would be the easiest thing in the world to use them up *en masse.* One really well-written satire would accomplish the business:—but it must not be such a dish of skimmed milk-and-water as Lowell's.[67]

Sharpening his critical tomahawk, Poe fixed his aim on his favorite target, those "servile imitators of the English," the Bostonians.[68] But as this letter suggests and as his review of Lowell's *Fable* and criticism of Longfellow reiterate, Poe's attacks were as grounded in sectional and political controversies over slavery and in his dismissal of their work as weak and effeminate ("skimmed milk-and-water") as in his sense that his foes' writings were imitative. In reviewing Lowell's *Fable* for *Southern Literary Messenger*'s Southern audience, Poe notes that "the grounds of the author's laudations" can only be understood by realizing that "Mr. Lowell is one of the most rabid of the Abolitionist fanatics," warning that "no Southerner who does not wish to be insulted, and at the same time revolted by a bigotry the most obstinately blind and deaf, should ever touch a volume by this author." Poe goes on to complain that Lowell's "prejudices on the topic of slavery break out every where in this present book" as he refuses to "speak well . . . of any man who is not a ranting abolitionist" (*ER* 819). According to Poe, Lowell's prejudice against Southerners is shared by most Bostonians: "It is a fashion about Mr. Lowell's set to affect a belief that there is *no such thing* as Southern Literature" (*ER* 819), and accordingly, "All whom he praises are Bostonians. Other writers are barbarians and satirized accordingly—if mentioned at all" (*ER* 820). Poe criticizes Lowell not just for his weak and imitative writing, but for what he sees as a regional bias revealed in his fanatical abolitionism.

Throughout his critical battles with the Bostonians, Poe used their abolitionist leanings as part of a broader attack on their aesthetics, a critique he enunciated in terms of region and gender. Earlier, during the "Longfellow War," Poe had defended his accusations against Longfellow of plagiarism by attacking Longfellow's defenders and their abolitionism: "In no literary circle out of Boston—or, indeed, out of the small coterie of abolitionists, transcendentalists and fanatics in general, which is the Longfellow junto—have we heard a seriously dissenting voice on this point" (*ER* 760). In reviewing Longfellow's *Poems on Slavery,* Poe more explicitly characterizes that group in effeminate terms, arguing that Longfellow's poems are "intended for the especial use of those negrophilic old ladies of the north, who form so large a part of Mr. Longfellow's friends." In the next sentence, Poe seems to allude to one of these "ladies" when he states "The first of this collection is addressed to William Ellery Channing" (*ER* 761–62). A few years earlier, in another review that attacked "Boston critics" (*ER* 461), Poe had argued that Channing was "like an honest woman" (*ER* 459). Poe attempted to clear a space for himself as literary arbiter for the nation and to suggest an alternative form of literary manhood by characterizing the Bostonians as a clique of womanish, imitative abolitionists who refused to see beyond their narrow bounds, who viewed all others, especially Southerners, as barbarians.

As I have argued, in "Hop-Frog" Poe identifies himself with a character from a "barbarous region" partly in order to gain the financial means to establish the *Stylus*, a journal he envisioned as breaking the stranglehold of the Boston literary clique. He specifically planned to raise subscribers in the South and the West, and repeatedly alluded to the *Stylus* and the Frogpondians in the same breath.[69] Even in his earliest plan for an independent literary journal in 1840, he stressed its independent nature by promising not to yield "to the arrogance of those organized *cliques* which, hanging like nightmares upon American literature, manufacture, at the nod of our principal booksellers, a pseudo-public-opinion by wholesale" (*ER* 1025). In attempting to establish the *Stylus*, Poe was not simply interested in controlling an independent journal that would place him beyond the mass market's demands and allow him to become arbiter of American literary taste; he was specifically attempting to gain independence from and revenge against the Boston clique of "abolitionists, transcendentalists and fanatics." As he put it, in reviewing his own work, he envisioned "the whole literary South and West . . . doing anxious battle in his person against the old time-honored tyrant of the North" (*ER* 1100).[70]

The title of "Hop-Frog" clearly resonates with Poe's epithet for his birthplace, Frogpondium, and Poe's central critical concerns with the Bostonian literary establishment, and his recent break with Providence poet Sarah Helen Whitman, which he blamed on her transcendentalist friends, suggests reading Hop-Frog's vengeful fury as directed at Boston and its literary establishment.[71] Consciously or unconsciously, the story draws some of its energy from Poe's distaste for the Boston literary clique. Identifying himself with a barbarian, as he had been recently described as "the literary Mohawk" and as he argued the Bostonians saw all others, Poe figuratively gains revenge over those he saw oppressing him, a group of tyrants whose aping ability recalls his characterization of Longfellow as "the GREAT MOGUL of the Imitators" (*ER* 761). Just as Poe had suggested that Longfellow deserved to be hanged (*ER* 717) for committing the "most barbarous class of literary robbery" (*ER* 678), that Channing should be "hung *in terrorem*" (*ER* 459), and that the entire Boston clique "hang[s] like nightmares upon American literature" (*ER* 1025), he has Hop-Frog hang the king and his ministers for their crimes against beauty and their abuse of his creative talents. Read in this light, "Hop-Frog" becomes the very satire Poe called for in his letter to Thomas.[72] With the horrified but delighted guests now standing in as a mass audience obsessed with the sensational, and the king and his ministers representing the tyrannical Boston literati, Poe's fantasy of revenge allows him to vent his rage against two groups he felt his art and his financial stability imperiled by: the literary masses and the elite Bostonian taste-makers.

In envisioning this revenge by making his Bostonian adversaries the victims of an imagined slave revolt, Poe also satirizes their racial politics and suggests their hypocrisy about racial matters. "Hop-Frog" echoes Poe's repetition of the standard Southern accusation against abolitionists of fomenting slave revolt. In response to Longfellow's poem "The Warning," Poe writes that it "contains at least one stanza of absolute truth" in its depiction of slave revolt: "One thing is certain:—if this prophecy be *not* fulfilled, it will be through no lack of incendiary doggrel on the part of Professor Longfellow and his friends" (*ER* 764). Poe reiterates this idea of abolitionist "incendiary doggrel" in his celebration of Robert M. Bird's proslavery novel *Sheppard Lee* (1836) for its "excellent chapters upon abolition and the exciting effects of incendiary pamphlets and pictures among our slaves in the South," an episode that ends "with a spirited picture of a negro insurrection, and with the hanging of Nigger Tom" (*ER* 399). The repetition of the word "incendiary" recalls the literally incendiary nature of Hop-Frog's final revenge, his destruction of the king and his ministers by hanging them by a chain and then burning them up, thus suggesting the link between the violence in "Hop-Frog" and abolitionist rhetoric.

This reversal of things—the identification of Yankee abolitionists with slaveholders as the victims of a slave revolt—underlines Poe's view of the Frogpondians as hypocrites. Throughout his criticism, Poe implies that Longfellow and other Bostonian abolitionist authors are as tyrannical in literary and other matters as the worst slaveholders and, perhaps, are as dependent upon the commercial value of race, in the literary market, as Southern slaveholders are in the slave market. In his review of Lowell's *Fable*, for example, Poe argues, "His fanaticism about slavery is a mere local outbreak of the same innate wrong-headedness which, if he owned slaves, would manifest itself in atrocious ill-treatment of them, with murder of any abolitionist who should endeavor to set them free" (*ER* 819). Similarly, in criticizing Longfellow's "The Quadroon Story," the story of "a slaveholder selling his own child," Poe comments that "a thing which may be as common in the South as in the East, is the infinitely worse crime of making matrimonial merchandise—or even less legitimate merchandise—of one's daughter" (*ER* 763). Longfellow, of course, is not literally making merchandise of his daughter; rather he is making literary merchandise out of the story of a daughter in slavery.[73] While Southerners hold slaves in bondage as a kind of property, Longfellow and his junto, according to Poe, abuse the slaves by turning them into a kind of inferior literary property. Poe emphasizes that the question is one of property rights, of economics, by commenting that "No doubt, it is a very commendable and very comfortable thing . . . [to] write verses instructing southerners how to give up their all with a good grace . . . but we have a singular curiosity to know how much of his own, under a change of circumstances, the Professor himself would be willing to surrender" (*ER* 762–63). The Boston abolitionists are willing to convert slave stories into merchandise, cashing in on the value of race in the literary marketplace, but would actually feel no sympathy for their own slaves and would be unwilling to give up their own (literary) property.[74] Just as the Yankee scientists in "Some Words with a Mummy" use craniometry to substantiate their own racialized superiority, and phrenological defenses of both Thingum Bob and Longfellow draw on scientific ideas of racial hierarchy to grant them literary authority, so Longfellow and his fellow Bostonians draw on their own innate sense of superiority in hypocritically turning the stories of slaves into literary capital, which in turn grants them authority. While the Boston clique covertly rely on race to substantiate their own economic position of literary authority in the marketplace, Poe turns to the commercial value of race, as displayed in freak show exhibitions, to satirize that dependence and cash in on the value of race himself.

Finally, in making an argument against an effeminized model of white middle-class manhood that he identifies with Boston's "negrophilic old ladies" like Longfellow, Lowell, and Channing, Poe turns to an antibourgeois figure, the non-normative, racialized body, in attempting to create an alternative model of literary manhood. To figure himself as a rara avis in the terris of antebellum literary culture, a culture he saw dominated by the mass market and by imitative and womanish Bostonians, Poe took on a savage persona that at once drew on and criticized the commercial success of sensationalized racial difference. Because such exhibits as "What is It?" depended not simply on substantiating racialized difference, but on titillating audiences with the possibility that such differences might be humbuggery, they could, at times, reverse the subject/object dichotomy, making audience members the object of scrutiny. It is because of this possible reversal that Poe turns to such figures for reimagining his struggle with the marketplace, in this way linking the artist with both racial otherness and slavery. "Hop-Frog" suggests that in the topsy-turvy world of the antebellum commercial museum, performances of racialized bodily difference did not simply stabilize hard notions of racial difference and racial hierarchy. Instead, because of their commodification of difference, because such attractions became triplicate treasures, they simultaneously underwrote and undermined both the bodily based racial hierarchies of contemporary science and the subject/object distinction they depended on. Because of the ways in which the exotified body in the museum transcended scientific laws—particularly those of race—in order to draw more attention and, thus, more money, the exotic, museal body becomes a perfect figure for Poe's attempt at transcending and exploiting the market and fantasizing an alternative model of white literary manhood. Identifying himself with a figure of racial otherness from one of the most popular and commercially successful attractions of the era in a sensational tale of slave revolt, Poe satirizes both the racial politics of the antislavery Bostonian literary circles and the mass market in sensational literature in an attempt to establish himself in a position of literary authority. Becoming the barbarian they imagine him to be, Poe appropriates racial otherness as a mode for reclaiming his position in the only profession "fit for a man."

Inward Criminality and the Shadow of Race

The House of the Seven Gables

and Daguerreotypy

Previous chapters in this book have explored how writers in the antebellum period conceived of literary manhood by invoking, while disavowing, the antimarket characteristics of Indians and blacks as presented in mass cultural forms. As commodities, such mass cultural figurations of race at once represented the dangers of being a commodity oneself, of becoming a virtual slave to anyone with money, and at the same time seemed to promise an unrefined masculine and aesthetic self outside the discipline of the market economy. In this chapter I argue that Nathaniel Hawthorne's *The House of the Seven Gables* (1851) similarly draws on mass cultural forms, specifically minstrelsy and daguerreotypy, in attempting to construct a model white middle-class family and a version of literary manhood. Unlike antebellum texts such as *The Last of the Mohicans, Uncle Tom's Cabin*, or even *The Maine Woods*, which foreground questions of race, *The House of the Seven Gables* seems, at first, to have little or nothing to do with race. Instead, at the center of Hawthorne's narrative is the historic conflict between two families, the aristocratic Pyncheons and the plebeian Maules, a conflict that resolves in the impending union of Phoebe Pyncheon and Holgrave, the last surviving Maule. But for that resolution to take place, Holgrave must prove his virtue by demonstrating that, unlike Jaffrey, the modern Pyncheon who reincarnates the economic and sexual desires of his Puritan ancestor, he does not mask an unconstrained, overly masculine self under his ever-shifting exterior. I argue here that Hawthorne draws on minstrelsy to figure the primitive traits that Jaffrey attempts to mask and then turns to daguerreotypy as a model for identifying and excising those racialized traits.

Jaffrey's overly masculine traits, which endanger the middle-class family and haunt Hawthorne's artistic practice, are intimately connected to the market economy. Although a number of critics have attended to the role of the market in this novel, few have noted the central role that a Jim Crow gingerbread man plays in Hepzibah Pyncheon's entrance into the marketplace. As a commodified representation of racial difference and slavery, the Jim Crow becomes a site where Hawthorne attempts to defuse his anxieties about the market with humor. But the racialized specter of exploitation, objectification, and commodification that the gingerbread man embodies returns throughout the novel to threaten Pyncheon women. The Jim Crow, in this way, prefigures the threat most fully represented in Jaffrey, a threat whose racial nature returns in Hawthorne's description of his novel's villain. For Hawthorne, race becomes the mode through which he can imagine moral judgments of manhood; it becomes the default category for materializing those manly, at times immoral, passions that endanger the bourgeois family that his narrative constitutes through the marriage of Phoebe and Holgrave. Because of the mass commercialization of blackness in the form of minstrelsy and the commerce in actual black bodies in slavery, blackness comes to represent the market revolution's potential disruption of gender and class identities and its commodification of everything, including literature. Racial difference and racial mixture, in this way, symptomatize the market's destabilization of a unified self and its destruction of an autonomous artistic practice. Unlike the other authors whom I have examined, then, Hawthorne invokes mass cultural images of racial difference not to imagine an alternative aesthetic, masculine realm outside the market, but to represent the very dangers of market society.

It is in this context that I attempt to understand Hawthorne's use of daguerreotypy. Much criticism of late has focused on the role of daguerreotypy in the novel, but, as with discussions of the market in *Seven Gables*, little of that work has explored the racial unconscious of daguerreotypal practices and daguerreotypal galleries.[1] These galleries displayed portraits of great men (and less frequently women) that were supposed to foster middle-class respectability by serving as models of emulation for urban audiences. Hawthorne's novel draws on the idea that daguerreotypy could reveal interior character, an idea that underwrote such exhibitions, to unmask Jaffrey's "black and damnable" traits underneath his benevolent smile.[2] Keeping the Jim Crow's role in prefiguring those traits in mind, I argue that Hawthorne characterizes Jaffrey's inherited, overly masculine nature in terms of not just moral blackness, but racial blackness. In this way, he echoes daguerreotypal practices that constructed white respectability both by displaying emulatory portraits and by producing the boundaries of respectability with very different photographs, specifically those of slaves in the South and Indians on the western frontier. Portraits in daguerreotypal galleries produced a unified vision of a progressive white nation, while ethnographic daguerreotypes recorded the racial and class differences that demarcated the respectable and civilized from the savage and uncivilized.

After invoking minstrelsy, a mass cultural form that in its earlier incarnation foregrounded the play of primitive manly passions embodied in racial others, Hawthorne turns to a more middle-class institution, the daguerreotypal parlor, and its strategies for interpellating a more refined, white middle-class manhood in an attempt to excise those potentially dangerous passions from the middle-class family. In the process, Hawthorne links the Jim Crow and Jaffrey with Holgrave's hypnotic story-telling power. Having Holgrave abandon his literary manuscript because of its potential to enslave Phoebe, and using the daguerreotype instead to unite Holgrave and Phoebe at the end, Hawthorne points to daguerreotypy as a less exploitative—and less market-driven and racially suspect—model for aesthetic production. Yet the specter of race and the visual commodification of identity (the fact that in the daguerreotypal parlor white manhood became a possession to be traded on) continues to haunt daguerreotypy. Finally, despite abandoning daguerreotypy, if not art itself, in its infamously unsatisfactory conclusion, Hawthorne's novel returns to those differences he tries to obfuscate, thus reiterating the centrality of commercial images of racialized difference to definitions of the white middle-class family and literary manhood.[3]

"The Sordid Stain"

When Hawthorne finally, "faint-heartedly," begins his story after "loitering . . . on [its] threshold" for several pages (34), he does so as a "disembodied" (30) viewer of Hepzibah's reopening of the cent-shop in the house of seven gables. Importantly, Hepzibah's old-fashioned cent-shop, located under one of the gables of the house, positions her in a liminal position, in terms of space and time, in relation to the burgeoning market economy of the 1850s. While Hepzibah, in her liminality, proves unable to compete in the modern marketplace, her reopening of the cent-shop suggests how a domestic, interior sphere was being invaded by the growing capitalistic market. In doing so, it maps Hawthorne's ambivalence about the market, sketching out the market's ability both to objectify humans (especially women) by treating them as little more than commodities and to revivify people by promoting "the invigorating breath of a fresh outward atmosphere" (51). As several recent critics have noted, then, this scene, with its playful, mocking tone, positions the marketplace at the center of the novel.[4] Few critics, however, have spent much time with the exact "commodities of low price" (35) that Hepzibah offers for sale and that Hawthorne so carefully catalogues. In particular, Hawthorne lingers over a "Jim Crow . . . executing his world-renowned dance, in gingerbread" (36), mentioning it by name twelve times over the next four chapters.[5] Through these multiple references, the Jim Crow (the first thing Hepzibah sells) comes to stand in for Hepzibah's commodities more generally, thus symbolizing her entrance into the marketplace. It is of no small matter that it is a *Jim Crow* gingerbread man that figures so prominently in the opening chapters of the novel. Rather, the Jim Crow, as a representation of black slavery and of mass cultural commodification, becomes so powerful for Hawthorne because of the way it incorporates the dangers of the marketplace to Hepzibah, women, and a domestic (interiorized) self more generally.[6] The gingerbread man represents both the threat that one will become a purchasable article that is nothing more than a slave to the will of another and, relatedly, the possibility that the market produces false selves, false faces, as the genuine article. Hawthorne's Jim Crow comes to embody the racialized, bodily passions that proper men were supposed to deny, the possibility such passions would enslave and degrade, by objectifying, women, and the danger that the market allowed respectable men, like Jaffrey Pyncheon, to hide such racialized and morally black passions under a false face.

Despite the fact that minstrelsy was the most popular entertainment form of the era, the Jim Crow's relative prominence in Hawthorne's novel is rather surprising. Politically, Hawthorne is best known for his refusal to address slavery or even the presence of racial others in the

United States.[7] Most notably, in his campaign biography of Franklin Pierce, Hawthorne championed his friend and classmate at Bowdoin for recognizing "slavery as one of those evils which divine Providence does not leave to be remedied by human contrivances, but which, in its own good time, by some means impossible to be anticipated, but of the simplest and easiest operation, when all its uses shall have been fulfilled, it causes to vanish like a dream."[8] As his hesitating, convoluted syntax might suggest, Hawthorne did not simply look to Providence to remedy slavery by making it "vanish like a dream." Instead, like many Northerners of the period, he hoped that the former slaves would also "vanish" from the United States—either by colonization, secession, war, or biological extinction.[9] This commitment to a racially homogeneous United States becomes evident in an 1862 letter from Hawthorne to Horatio Bridge. Hawthorne thanks Bridge "for a shaded map of Negrodom" (a map indicating racial proportions in the South) and then comments, "What a terrible amount of trouble and expense, in washing that sheet white!—and, after all, I am afraid we shall only variegate it with blood and dirt." In order to keep that sheet white, Hawthorne even maintains that he "should not much regret an ultimate separation" from "Negrodom," "if we can only put the boundary far enough south."[10] For Hawthorne, the Civil War (at its best) offers an opportunity to wash the United States white—both morally and racially—by either eliminating or expelling the sin of slavery and African Americans themselves. Hawthorne's nonfictional writings on slavery and race seem to indicate his inability to imagine an equitable multiracial society in the United States or, perhaps more exactly, his willful desire to fantasize the race "problem"—not simply slavery but the presence of African Americans in the United States—out of existence.[11]

In *Seven Gables* Hawthorne projects the threat of an unrestrained, market-driven manhood onto racial blackness, fantasizing the moral cleansing of middle-class and literary manhood through the disappearance of racial difference. This characterization of the dangers of the marketplace in terms of racial blackness becomes clear in the opening chapters with Hepzibah and the Jim Crow. Selling the Jim Crow gingerbread man does more than mark Hepzibah's entrance into the market; it destroys her fantasies of being a "lady." "Aided by the impish figure of the negro dancer," her little customer Ned Higgins demolishes "the structure of ancient aristocracy" (51), thus transforming Hepzibah from "the patrician lady . . . into the plebeian woman" (38). This transaction and Hepzibah's concomitant decline in class status endanger her moral self. As she reflects, "the shop [might] prove her ruin, in a moral and religious point of view" (55). While she dreams of appearing "unseen, like a disembodied divinity, or enchantress, holding forth her bargains to the reverential and awe-stricken purchaser, in an invisible hand," she realizes that "she must ultimately come forward, and stand revealed" to "every passer-by, whose eyes might be attracted by the commodities at the window" (40). In reopening the cent-shop, Hepzibah not only must put commodities on view, but must also put herself on view for any customer, thus rendering herself yet one more "piece" (54) of merchandise. In order to protect herself against the market's devouring appetite and prying eyes, she must present a false self; as Uncle Venner suggests, "Put on a bright face for your customers. . . . A stale article, if you dip it in a good, warm, sunny smile, will go off better than a fresh one that you've scowled upon" (66). In the market economy, it is not the article itself, but rather a false coating, that gives both goods and people themselves value.[12] Opening up the domestic sphere of the old house and putting herself on display through the sale of the Jim Crow, Hepzibah enters into the market, a realm that may prove her moral ruin by encouraging her to objectify herself for her customers or to present herself and her commodities falsely to them.

The Jim Crow materializes the anxiety that the marketplace's ability to put a price on everything and everybody will make everything unreal and false. Hawthorne elaborates this terror most fully in Hepzibah's nightmare vision of the modern stores with which she competes: "a kind of panorama, representing the great thoroughfare of a city, all astir with customers. . . . Groceries, toy-shops, dry-goods stores, with their immense panes of plate-glass, their gorgeous fixtures, their vast and complete assortments of merchandize, in which fortunes had been invested; and those noble mirrors at the farther end of each establishment, doubling all this wealth by a brightly burnished vista of unrealities" (48). Linking Hepzibah's vision to another contemporary commercial entertainment, the panorama, Hawthorne emphasizes the terrifying reproductive power of commodities and the marketplace. First duplicated by mirrors, then represented in panoramic form, the merchandise becomes a sea of "unrealities." Standing in for Hepzibah's merchandise more generally, the Jim Crow cookie reiterates this nightmare reproductivity. As in her vision of a panorama of mirrors of commodities, her gingerbread cookie is not simply a representation, but a representation of a representation—it is, after all, not a cookie of "a negro dancer," as Hawthorne puts it, but a cookie representing a white man's representation of an African American dancer. As in Dickens's reaction to William Henry Lane, it seems as though the very replicability of commodities, foremost figured by the Jim Crow cookie in these opening chapters, undermines the possibility of a true face, the possibility that anyone or anything is exactly what he, she, or it seems.

The Jim Crow is not just any mass cultural commodity; it is a representation and rematerialization of a particular kind of commercial racial exploitation and cross-racial identification. With the Jim Crow gingerbread man, Hawthorne links Hepzibah's cent-shop to the mass cultural marketplace, its performances of racial difference and suspension of clearly defined racial identity, *and* the slave market. In this way, he represents the moral danger of the marketplace in terms of both enslavement and racial transformation. Entering the marketplace means that Hepzibah loses a racially based, white aristocratic privilege and, in doing so, becomes a slave to her customers. As Hawthorne puts it, where the Pyncheons' claim to the Indian lands to the east had previously "caused the poorest member of the race to feel as if he inherited a kind of nobility" (19), Ned's purchase of the Jim Crow makes Hepzibah realize she no longer had anything "to do with [her] ancestry," that she might as well "take the map of her eastern-territory to kindle the kitchen-fire" (51). As we have seen in previous chapters, this fantasy of a "white" antimarket nobility becomes identified with a kind of Indian primitiveness. The whiteness of this lost racial "nobility" is revealed in Hepzibah's resentment toward a woman who resembles her old vision of herself, "a lady" whose "floating veil" and "swaying gown" made her seem disembodied, "an ethereal lightness": "Must the whole world toil, that the palms of her hands may be kept white and delicate?" (55). The Jim Crow cookie suggests a racial element to Hepzibah's descent into the "plebeian" class as "the sordid stain of that copper-coin" to her formerly "white" palm (51) transforms her into an "enslaved spirit" (42), like the Jim Crow itself, to whoever enters her shop.[13] In this way, Hawthorne draws on black slavery to figure Hepzibah's loss of her "white," aristocratic privilege of remaining "invisible" and "disembodied."

In spreading the contagion of market society, as figured in terms of slavery and blackness, the Jim Crow cookie enslaves and stains both Hepzibah and Ned Higgins. Ned's copper cent gives him power over Hepzibah—he is able to "stare at Hepzibah, a moment, as an elder customer than himself would have" (49–50), because he *is* a customer —yet he is simultaneously "irresistibly attracted" (58) by those commodities, like the Jim Crow, that Hepzibah sets in her window "to tempt little boys" (37). Their market transaction, in other words, simultaneously enslaves and empowers Ned (and her other customers) in a kind of visual economy as it does Hepzibah herself.[14] And, as with Hepzibah, the transaction transforms him in terms suggestive of racial difference. Ned is no longer the "same sturdy little urchin" who originally entered the shop; instead through his consumption of the Jim Crow, his "cannibal-feast," he becomes a "little cannibal," as the "discoloration . . . exceedingly visible" to his face demonstrates (50). This discoloration, like Hepzibah's enslavement, does not exactly turn Ned black, but smears or stains his cherubic whiteness. In other words, this little "urchin" not only is "aided by the impish figure of the negro dancer" (51) in destroying Hepzibah's claims to aristocracy, but, because of "his all-devouring appetite" (115), becomes the imp, "an evil spirit" (49), himself, as his consumption turns him into a "colored" cannibal. As Hawthorne articulated this master/slave dialectic in a sketch for a story in *The American Notebooks*, "the person who appears to be the master, must inevitably be at least as much a slave, if not more, than the other. All slavery is reciprocal."[15] If the cent-shop turns Hepzibah into an enslaved spirit, an enslavement hinted at in terms of race, it simultaneously enthralls Ned to his appetites, an enslavement similarly hinted at in terms of race. Hawthorne suggests that the market, especially the mass cultural market, does not simply objectify and commodify and, therefore, enslave women, but irresistibly turns the male viewers and purchasers who objectify women into slaves themselves, both to the commodities women display and to their own "all-devouring appetite[s]."[16]

By the 1850s the minstrel show had been tamed for a more promiscuous, middle-class audience. Yet it retained, as I have argued, a hint of its lurid past, of primitive unchained masculine passions, even as its commercial success rendered it a ready symbol of the market's power to commodify any and everything. Invoking a realm marked by a raucous, seemingly primitive male audience visually devouring a racialized other, a place where white men (audiences and performers alike) could act "black," yet remain white, the Jim Crow gingerbread man stands in for both the threat that market society unlooses primitive masculine passions to run wild and that it renders everyone a slave to market demands.[17] In this way, Hawthorne presents the dangers of the marketplace in terms of moral and racial blackness, in terms of the Jim Crow cookie rendering both Ned and Hepzibah, in their economic relationship with one another, slaves to their blacker selves. Doing so, he describes a moment of class transformation and possible class conflict in terms of race and gender. Through the Jim Crow gingerbread man, Hawthorne presents the danger that we might all be nothing more than commodities, unrealities, and that underneath our false fronts we might all be cannibals at heart.[18]

"To Look Black"

With Jaffrey, Hawthorne most fully imagines this danger, elaborating the distinctly masculine nature of the grasping economic self that Ned represents in childish form. While Ned has an "all-devouring appetite for men and things" (115), an "omnivorous appetite" that leads him to devour all of "natural history, in gingerbread" (67), the Judge's "ogrelike appetite" (275) allows him to "possess vast ability in grasping, and arranging, and appropriating to [himself], the big, heavy, solid unrealities" (229). For Ned, these "unrealities" come in the shape of gingerbread; for the Judge in the form of "such [things] as gold, landed estate, offices of trust and emolument, and public honors" (229). Ned purchases and devours a representation of slavery in gingerbread form, thus discoloring his own whiteness. Hawthorne suggests that Jaffrey, through his political connections to Daniel Webster (273) and his opposition to the Free-Soil party (275), identifies his own interests with those of slaveholders, and, as I will argue, similarly marks Jaffrey's economic and political grasping in terms of racial blackness.[19] Because he is a boy, the sexual dynamics of Ned's objectification of Hepzibah with his "stare" like that of "an elder customer than himself" (49) remain submerged. On the other hand, Jaffrey's grasping self is clearly defined in terms of being too masculine and too sexual. When he first meets his cousin Phoebe in the "gray medium" created by the "commodities at the window" of the cent-shop (117), he attempts to kiss her, terrifying her with his "dark, full-fed physiognomy" in which "the man, the sex, somehow or other, was entirely too prominent" (118). Emphasizing its overly masculine and sexual nature within the gray medium of the market—a place where white and black mix and mingle —Hawthorne represents the racialized economic danger of Ned and the Jim Crow in much more threatening fashion with Jaffrey.

Gobbling up everything in sight, Jaffrey repeats Ned's cannibalization of the Jim Crow, transforming himself, as Ned does, in terms of race. Just prior to commenting on Jaffrey's too-prominent manhood, the narrator describes Jaffrey's masquerade, his ability to hide his "dark, square countenance" and its "massive accumulation of animal sub-stance" under a look of "exceeding good-humor and benevolence" (116), as a kind of racial performance, a kind of reverse minstrelsy. Jaffrey's smile, the narrator tells us, "was a good deal akin to the shine on his boots . . . each must have cost him and his boot-black, respectively, a good deal of hard labor to bring out and preserve them" (117). The Judge's "mobility" of "countenance" is then like "the conscientious polish of his boots" (116), a type of blacking up, like the blacking up evoked by the Jim Crow figure that little Ned Higgins devours.[20] By polishing his face into a benign smile, the Judge can pass as "white," as "a man of eminent respectability" (228), hiding his "black and damnable" (312) interior under a layer of white respectability.[21] Hawthorne further suggests understanding this masquerade in terms of race by referring to the daguerreotypal removal of Jaffrey's mask as a "harlequin-trick" (64). As the harlequin's mask figured racial difference, was a type of blackface, so the Judge's mask is, in the end, figured as hiding an interior character coded as racially other because of its unrestrained passions and overly masculine desires.[22] Hiding his more primitive, masculine self, those "grosser attributes of [the] body" that "progress" is in the habit of "refining away" (121), the Judge essentially reverses the masking of white performers as minstrels and harlequins, painting a "white" face of re-spectability and restraint over his "black purpose[s]" (228).

Hawthorne plays up Jaffrey's atavistic nature, the primitive, racial characteristics of his dark self, by defining them in terms of biological inheritance. While Hawthorne's ostensible moral suggests a Gothic explanation—"the folly of tumbling down an avalanche of ill-gotten gold, or real estate, on the heads of an unfortunate posterity, thereby to maim and crush them" (2)—he explains the transmission of these masculine "bad passions" (119) from the Puritan Colonel to the antebellum Judge in the pseudoscientific terms of blood and race. Throughout the novel, Hawthorne denominates both the Maules (10, 25, 26) and the Pyncheons (17, 19, 22, 24 [twice], 69, 120) as "race[s]." "Race" in mid-nineteenth-century America had several meanings, one of which was simply "the lineage of a family."[23] Hawthorne suggests the more modern, restricted biological meaning, however, by stating that "the weaknesses and defects, the bad passions, the mean tendencies, and the moral diseases which lead to crime, are handed down from one generation to another, by a far surer process of transmission than human law has been able to establish, in respect to the riches and honors which it seeks to entail upon posterity" (119). Racial scientists of the era argued that men "are governed by certain psychological influences which differ among the species [races] of mankind as instincts vary among the species of lower animals" and that "these psychological characteristics . . . drive individuals and nations beyond the confines of human reason."[24] By emphasizing the irrational, criminal bad traits of the Pyncheon "race" and by comparing the Pyncheons with the "degenerated" but "noble race" (89) of Chanticleer and the chickens (see also 151–53), Hawthorne suggests emerging notions of innate racial character in describing the inherited nature of Jaffrey's black purposes.

The particular characteristics that make up Jaffrey's racial inheritance reiterate this connection. Although Jaffrey appears "a man of eminent respectability" (228) in public, "the woman's, the private and domestic view" whispers that like his ancestor he is "greedy of wealth" and has "fallen into certain transgressions" due to his "animal developement" (122). Like the Puritan who wore "out three wives, and, merely by the remorseless weight and hardness of his character in the conjugal relation," the Judge similarly delivered his wife's "death-blow in the honeymoon" (123), a blow revealing the "large sensual endowment" that makes him "a great beast" (275). As Holgrave's explanation of the curse at the end suggests, that inheritance is simply reducible to "blood" and "race": "Old Maule's prophecy was probably founded on a knowledge of this physical predisposition in the Pyncheon race" (304). According to racial scientists, what distinguished the Caucasian races from other "unhistoric" races was that "the fixedness of the unhistoric types of man" meant that they "cannot be forced to change their habits," that they cannot evolve beyond their ancestors' predispositions.[25] If, as Alan

Trachtenberg has argued, *Seven Gables* turns on whether Holgrave can break free from typological notions of character, Jaffrey's inability to do so, in the terms of racial science, marks him as distinctly non-Caucasian.[26] It is not that one's bad deeds magically curse one's offspring; rather a "race's" faults—its "moral diseases"—are transmitted biologically, through blood, as some pseudoscientific notion of racially inherited traits replaces the Gothic notions of a haunted house and a curse. Hawthorne then tracks the reembodiment of aristocratic family traits in a market-oriented, ambitious modern man by suggesting his moral failure in terms of a biological inheritance that draws on the dual notions of "race" at mid-century as family and as biological destiny. He marks, in this way, the transitional space between what Colette Guillaumin has called auto-referential and altero-referential systems of racism, the transition from class-stratified aristocracy to racially demarcated democracy.[27]

Hawthorne again suggests understanding these domineering and grasping masculine traits as racially black through Holgrave's temptation to replicate the behavior of his ancestors, as revealed in the imbedded story about Matthew Maule and Alice Pyncheon. Through his story-telling gesticulations Holgrave puts Phoebe in a state in which she could "live only in his thoughts and emotions" (211), and he realizes that with "but one wave of his hand and a corresponding effort of his will, he could complete his mastery over Phoebe's yet free and virgin spirit" (212). Holgrave can render Phoebe "no better than [a] bond-servant" to his will as generations of other "plebeian Maules" have done to Pyncheons in "the topsyturvy commonwealth of sleep"(26) and as Matthew does to Alice in the story itself. In this way, Holgrave's story raises the possibility that, like Jaffrey, he hides a darker self under the "mask" he wore over "whatever lay near his heart" (301).[28] Most important, just as the Jim Crow materializes Ned and Hepzibah's market relationship and prefigures Jaffrey's criminal, racial inheritance and masquerade, Hawthorne mediates this possibility of masculine dominance through another figure combining blackness and slavery.

Holgrave's story begins with the Pyncheons' black slave Scipio summoning Matthew Maule, a summons that leads to Matthew taking Alice's "delicate soul into his rude gripe" (210) and making her a "slave, in a bondage more humiliating, a thousand-fold, than that which binds its chains around the body" (208). As Ned's "childish gripe," aided by

the Jim Crow, "demolished" Hepzibah's "structure of ancient aristocracy" (51), the working-class Matthew crushes an aristocratic Pyncheon
woman in his masculine "gripe," making her, like Hepzibah, as much a
slave as Jim Crow or the "shining, sable . . . slave[s]" (191) Alice's father
owns. Like the Judge's masquerade, Matthew's enslavement of Alice
depends on his ability to hide his own "black" designs (188) under a
"dark smile" (195), a blackness that Holgrave connects to racial blackness
when Matthew asks Scipio if he "think[s] nobody is to look black but"
himself (188). Further, through this story, Hawthorne suggests that the
economic roots of the Pyncheons' power lie not only in the Colonel's
appropriation of the original Matthew Maule's land, but in his grand-
son's exploitation of slave labor and treatment of the younger Matthew
Maule as essentially a slave. Finally, Matthew makes Alice wait upon his
bride on his wedding night, and as she returns home in the snow and
rain, she catches her death cold. Just as the Judge delivered his wife her
"death-blow" on their wedding night, Matthew delivers a fatal blow to
Alice on his wedding night (210). With the embedded story of Alice and
Matthew, Hawthorne, for a third time, characterizes a sexual and class-
based male/female master/slave relationship in racial terms. Just as
Ned's consumption of the Jim Crow hints at his becoming a colored
cannibal himself and Jaffrey's "too prominent" sexuality and economic
grasping suggest an atavistically black character, so the immorality of
Matthew's enslavement of Alice is registered by equating his moral
blackness with Scipio's racial blackness. Through these repeated invoca-
tions of black figures, Hawthorne aligns brutish manliness, its enslavement of women, and its moral blackness with racial blackness and black
slavery, suggesting that if Holgrave replicates the sins of the past, if he
simply reembodies the bad traits of his ancestors, he will indeed turn
himself and Phoebe into "slaves . . . to by-gone times" (183), thus
revealing his character as essentially "black."

Finally, Holgrave's story, as numerous critics have noted and as indicated by the large-circulation magazines—*Godey's* and *Graham's* (186,
212)—for which he intends it, reveals Hawthorne's concern about his
own literary practice as potentially exploitative, as potentially enslaving
both him and his readers in a purely economic relationship. With this
embedded story, then, Hawthorne reinvokes racial categories to figure
the threat that Jaffrey (and perhaps Holgrave) hides under a mask of
respectability, linking it to literary production in the marketplace. In

other words, Hawthorne suggests that, at least in a market-driven economy, even a writer is likely to enslave others' bodies, especially those of women readers, with his commodities. Like Hepzibah, who must "dip" her articles "in a good, warm, sunny smile" (66) to make them sell, thus endangering her "in a moral and religious point of view" (55), so Holgrave's story intended for popular circulation endangers his moral state by placing him in a position to enslave (or at least control) Phoebe's and other readers' bodies, either by mesmerizing them or by provoking their "tears as an onion" (186) would. If, in "Who Are Our National Poets?" James Kennard Jr. equates American writers with Scipio Coon in terms of their enslavement to others, Hawthorne links Holgrave, through Matthew Maule, to Scipio and slavery, but then reverses the master/slave dialectic to place Holgrave in a potential position of mastery.[29] Literary manhood then potentially enslaves both writer and intended feminized audience in an economic transaction, like that between Hepzibah and Ned.[30] In the opening chapters of the novel, Hawthorne sets up a central theme of the marketplace and its dangers—its ability to enslave men and women, to foster a trade in false faces rather than true products, and to endanger the home in doing so—through the minstrel show and its commodification and performance of identity. Using the Jim Crow to figure the dangers of the marketplace, Hawthorne suggests that the market, and the literary market in particular, threatens to destabilize white identity and white privilege by rendering all involved morally black, a blackness figured in terms of both slavery and racial masquerade.

"Secret Character"

In the opening chapters of *The House of the Seven Gables*, Hawthorne defines the contemporary dangers of the marketplace in racial terms. Rematerializing the cannibal-like economic transactions embodied in the Jim Crow in Jaffrey, Hawthorne characterizes his villain through both mass cultural representations of racial blackness, slavery, and false identity *and* scientific racialism's definition of inherited character. With Holgrave's story, he hints that Holgrave too might contain the same villainous tendencies, suggesting that literary production itself might reproduce this racialized master/slave dynamic. In the end, however, after abandoning his manuscript to the flames, Holgrave refuses to mesmerize Phoebe, thus demonstrating that "amid all these personal vicissitudes, he had never lost his identity. . . . he had never violated the innermost man [nor anyone else's innermost self], but had carried his conscience along with him" (177). While Matthew Maule, Ned Higgins, and Jaffrey Pyncheon lose their identities because taking Pyncheon women into their masculine grasps transforms them in suggestively racialized terms, Holgrave, by resisting the "temptation" of "acquiring empire over" Phoebe's spirit, demonstrates his "reverence for another's individuality," thus assuring us of his character and revealing his true (white) identity (212).

It is in this context that Holgrave's profession as a daguerreotypist becomes important, for daguerreotypy was understood as counteracting those threats that Hawthorne materializes in the Jim Crow and that Jaffrey hides under his mask of "the sunniest . . . benevolence" (57). Figuratively abandoning a written narrative, which seems simply to replicate the sins of the past, Hawthorne instead uses daguerreotypy to establish a new, bourgeois Edenic family, uniting the previously class-separated Maules and Pyncheons in one respectable, domestic unit. He presents the economic and sexual threat of a too-masculine, "black" self through a figure from the most popular mass cultural form, minstrelsy, and then attempts to erase that threat by turning to a competing mass cultural form, daguerreotypy and daguerreotypal parlors. Minstrelsy often wore its commercial nature on its face, drew largely male audiences, and foregrounded cross-racial identification and the expression of "primitive" bodily masculine passions; Hawthorne turns to the daguerreotypal parlor because it figured itself as a more feminine, middle-class, noncommercial, aesthetic sphere for inculcating and policing a virtuous white republic. In *Seven Gables*, daguerreotypy functions to register and combat the commercial and sexual dangers of the marketplace and false identity, those threats represented by the Jim Crow and Jaffrey, by visualizing those characteristics in racial terms. In this way, Hawthorne suggests using daguerreotypy as a model for refiguring the potentially exploitative commerce of literary production.[31] Turning to daguerreotypy, Hawthorne hopes to escape the racialized dangers of commercial artistic production and the market destabilization of identity as represented in both the Jim Crow and Holgrave's mesmerizing story.

Hawthorne invokes the "new scope of mass identification opened up" by daguerreotypal galleries through Holgrave's display of "a daguerreotype of [Uncle Venner's] face . . . at the entrance of [his] studio" (157) and through his intention to have Jaffrey's portrait "engraved" (92).[32] As an itinerant daguerreotypist, Holgrave would not have had as glamorous a gallery as many in New York and Boston, but Holgrave's advertisement of his skill through displays of his work suggests his participation in more prominent daguerreotypal practices. In particular, as critics such as Alan Trachtenberg and Susan Williams have noted, Hawthorne draws on the emerging discourse about the pedagogical uses of daguerreotypy.[33] Holgrave famously restates the epistemology of character underlying these discourses when he argues that "There is a wonderful insight in heaven's broad and simple sunshine. While we give it credit only for depicting the merest surface, it actually brings out the secret character with a truth that no painter would ever venture upon, even could he detect it" (91). Daguerreotypy, according to antebellum theorists, not only displayed one's outward appearance, but disclosed, for better or worse, one's interior character.

In the late 1840s and early 1850s, this revelation of character was of a distinctly public nature. As Allan Sekula has put it, "The *private* moment of sentimental individuation, the look at the frozen gaze-of-the-loved-one, was shadowed by two other more *public* looks: a look up, at one's 'betters,' and a look down, at one's 'inferiors.' "[34] The first of these public looks emerged as a means of advertising, used by daguerreotypists simultaneously to attract patrons and to veil the commercial nature of their enterprise in a shroud of morality and aesthetics. Soon after the invention of daguerreotypy in 1839, the first portrait studios opened in the United States. By the mid-1840s, competition had become quite intense, and various daguerreotypists, especially in larger cities, began to display their most accomplished portraits, usually of famous men and women, as a way of attracting new patrons. By displaying portraits of famous people in luxuriously furnished, domestic parlor settings (see Figure 10), galleries (most famously, Mathew Brady's) soon became "primary objects of interest to visitors" to and inhabitants of cities like New York.[35] Such galleries did not actually charge admission; rather they were used to entice viewers to sit for their own portraits or to buy copies of those on the walls, a commercial intercourse often hidden away in back rooms. Although part of a large developing industry, daguerreotypal parlors promoted themselves as artistic, domestic realms

10. Ball's Great Daguerrian Gallery of the West, from *Gleason's Pictorial Drawing-Room Companion* (April 1, 1854): 208. *Courtesy of Department of Special Collections, the University of Chicago Library.*

outside the market economy, as defenders of middle-class decorum and privacy against the market's grasping and duplicitous nature.[36]

In particular, these portraits were supposed to act as a moral check in the rapidly changing world of mid-century urban America. As Marcus Root, one of the most prominent early theorists of photography, argued in 1864, "the great and the good, the heroes, saints, and sages of all lands and all eras are, by these life-like 'presentments,' brought within the constant purview of the young, the middle-aged, and the old. The pure, the high, the noble traits beaming from these faces and forms,—who shall measure the greatness of their effect on the impressionable minds of those who catch sight of them at every turn?"[37] Producing "lifelike 'presentments'" of "the great and the good" for the "impressionable" to emulate, the daguerreotypal parlor was understood as promoting the "pure" traits of the home in the new public spaces of urban America. But the daguerreotype's ability to index "human character" forwarded a "moral revolution" not only by providing models of moral conduct but also by unmasking those who refused such models, thus making the false

performance of virtue an impossibility.[38] At the same time that daguerreotypists were displaying portraits of moral exemplars in their
parlors, daguerreotypy was also being used for ethnographic purposes to
record, codify, and demonstrate the physiognomic features of criminals
and racial others. This second aspect of the daguerreotype's revelatory
power offered, as Root put it, "a valuable security for social order" by
"insuring, as it does, that men shall ultimately be known for what they
really are. . . . inward unworthiness, despite all effort, *will* glare through
the fleshly mask."[39] By identifying with the examples of respectability
on the walls of the gallery, the growing urban populace—and specifically
the large numbers of unattached, often transient young men new to the
city—were imagined to internalize lessons of middle-class restraint; if
they refused such models, other daguerreotypes would unmask their
"inward unworthiness."[40]

In *Seven Gables*, Jaffrey's daguerreotype should be of the type that
would hang in a gallery and serve as a model of all those "praiseworthy
qualities" that young men like Holgrave should strive for; instead it
reveals "the man, sly, subtle, hard, imperious, and, withal, cold as ice"
(92). The Judge's daguerreotype exposes his failure to fit ideals of
middle-class refinement and decorum, coding that failure, as we have
seen, in particularly masculinized and racial terms. The revelation of
the Judge's true physiognomy in his daguerreotype reemphasizes and
fully discloses the primitive (and racial) self he is attempting to hide.
While alive, the Judge has "spiritualized" (to a limited extent) his
ancestor's more "animal force" (121). The daguerreotype, however, removes Jaffrey's mask of respectability to reveal "his swarthily white
visage" (295). Just as the Colonel's "ruddy English hue" and "duskiness"
(121) reveal his animal force, so Jaffrey's swarthy visage becomes the
material sign of his "physical nature." "Swarthy" and "dusky" were
synonyms often used in describing racial complexion, and the Judge's
"swarthily white visage" mixes his brutish nature and mask of respectability in a figure of amalgamation, as implied by the narrator's "venture to marry these ill-agreeing words" (295).[41] Underneath his smiling
benevolence, as revealed by the daguerreotype, lurk the Judge's dark
"bad passions"—his ancestor's "duskiness"—which link him both to
the Colonel and to the ravenous Ned and the "blackness" of the Jim
Crow he devours. In displaying Jaffrey's heritage, his bad traits, to the
entire world, the daguerreotype suggests his questionable moral character, his departure from "white" respectability, in racial terms.

The daguerreotypal practices Hawthorne drew on imaged a type of middle-class respectability by distinguishing between exemplary portraits of great men and ethnographic studies of criminals and racial others, between, as Sekula puts it, "fully-human subject and less-than-fully-human object along vectors of race, sex, and class."[42] As galleries became important public sites for inculcating virtue, they constructed a vision of respectability through the exclusion of racial others and the primitive passions they supposedly embodied. As noted, scientific notions of racially inherited character were becoming commonplace during this period, and it is more than just a startling coincidence that Samuel George Morton's *Crania Americana*, which, by expanding physiognomy, established the science of craniometry and the American school of ethnography, was published the same year that the daguerreotype was invented. At root in both cases was the attempt to fix and characterize the world, including humankind, through scientific (and aesthetic) criteria.[43] In its reliance upon the legibility of exterior human features to reveal "wild" and "dark" interior character, daguerreotypy's moral project participated in a racialized understanding of character linked to the anthropometric sciences of phrenology and physiognomy.

While there is some new evidence to suggest more varied exhibitionary practices, the best-known daguerreotypal parlors rarely exhibited portraits of blacks and Indians.[44] At the same time, however, ethnological studies drew on the same logic of exterior features revealing interior character to capture and display the essential difference from white Americans that the "skins" of blacks and Indians supposedly signified.[45] The most striking group of daguerreotypes of this ethnological sort was explicitly conceived of as substantiating the precepts of scientific racism. In 1850, Louis Agassiz—perhaps the best-known scientist in the United States at the time—traveled from his Massachusetts home to South Carolina, where he delivered a paper in support of the American school of ethnography's ideas on the separate creation and eternal differences of the human races.[46] While there, he commissioned J. T. Zealy, a well-known daguerreotypist, to take a series of daguerreotypes (fifteen of which have survived) of nude or only partially clothed slaves, most of whom were born in Africa and illegally imported into the United States.[47] Agassiz hoped that by concentrating on native-born Africans and their children he could illustrate the eternal characteristics of the African race and demonstrate the continuance of these traits among African Americans in the United States. As the daguerreo-

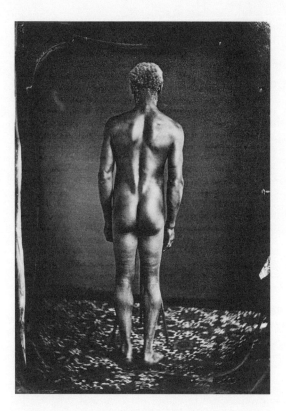

11. Daguerreotype of the slave Jem by J. T. Zealy (1850), original in Peabody Museum, Harvard University. *Courtesy of Peabody Museum, Harvard University.*

types themselves reveal, producing racial difference entailed the literal stripping of black bodies, so that nothing but the "primitive" body itself remained. In contrast to portraits of eminent white men that supposedly revealed their "pure" and "noble" traits through their faces and their dress, the daguerreotype of Jem (see Figure 11), by turning his face from the camera and focusing on his naked body, presented evidence of a racialized, primitive character different from that of respectable white viewers. By either omitting daguerreotypes of non-whites altogether or displaying only daguerreotypes that emphasized the primitively wild or uncivilized character of blacks and Indians, specifically through their bare or costumed bodies, dominant daguerreotypal practices worked hand-in-hand with racial science to define civilization and respectability in terms of whiteness.[48]

In *Seven Gables* the daguerreotype of Jaffrey does not exactly reveal a black body; rather his "swarthily white visage" hints at a racialized, black interior character underneath the outwardly white body. This daguerreotypal reading of interior character in terms of racial difference reappears in Dion Boucicault's successful tragic mulatta play *The Octoroon* (1859). Rather than revealing the race of Zoe, the eponymous heroine of the play, as audiences might expect from the title, the daguerreotype that appears in the final act reestablishes moral and racial order by revealing the crimes of the villainous Jacob M'Closky. The daguerreotype shows M'Closky murdering the slave boy Paul, a murder that has allowed M'Closky to buy Zoe at auction for his own lascivious pleasures. While attempting to escape from Paul's vengeful Indian friend Wahnotee, M'Closky stumbles across Scudder, the Yankee overseer, and asks him, as "a white man," to protect "one of [his] own blood" from "the red-skin." Scudder's reply indicates that the daguerreotype has revealed more than just M'Closky's murderous act; it has revealed that he can no longer make a claim based on his "blood," on his being a "white man": "Nature has said that where the white man sets his foot, the red man and the black man shall up sticks and stand around. But what do we pay for that possession. . . . in protection, forbearance, gentleness, in all them goods that show the critters the difference between the Christian and the savage. Now, what have you done to show them the distinction?"[49] M'Closky's murder of Paul, as captured by the daguerreotype, voids the implicit racial contract and demonstrates that he has become a "savage" himself.[50]

What Boucicault's play underlines is how the daguerreotype's ability to capture one's character was understood in implicitly racial terms even when used to differentiate the character of different "white" men; daguerreotypy delineated character through a racialized distinction between men who treated their "inferiors" with "protection, forbearance, gentleness" and those who did not. In this way, the play turns on the instability of "race" as a category in the 1850s—the fact that race did not only apply to the supposed differences between blacks, whites, and Indians—by racially distinguishing the low Irish character M'Closky from the Yankee Scudder and Anglo George Peyton.[51] In doing so, as in *House of the Seven Gables*, it exploits the ways in which daguerreotypy was understood as revealing a kind of criminal behavior demarcated in racialized terms. Playing on racialized notions of character, daguerreotypy delineated the boundaries of white middle-class respectability. Drawing on daguerreotypy's policing of middle-class norms through racialized character, Hawthorne removes the reverse minstrel mask of Jaffrey, thus expelling the masculine, economic, and sexual threat that both he and the Jim Crow represent.[52]

"An Instinctive Sense of Kindred"

In the closing chapters of *Seven Gables*, Holgrave's daguerreotype of the dead Judge clears Clifford's name by demonstrating that Jaffrey was culpable in the death of their uncle, thus revealing Jaffrey's "inward criminality" as "indeed black and damnable" (312). With this daguerreotypal evidence, Holgrave realizes that the old Maule curse "was probably founded on a knowledge of this physical predisposition in the Pyncheon race" (304), literally their tendency to choke on their own blood, but symbolically their evil, dark character that leads them to "trampl[e] on the weak" (123). Holgrave's daguerreotypy, in other words, helps to reveal, categorize, and remove the racialized, masculine grasping passions of Jaffrey. In the end, the daguerreotype of Jaffrey also allows Phoebe and Holgrave's love to mature. Yet for this love to flower, Holgrave must first abjure his own "black" passions, the possibility, as represented in his mesmerizing story, that he can enslave Phoebe to his will. Figuring those traits in terms of racial inheritance, the daguerreotype redefines the class conflict between the Pyncheons and Maules, allowing Holgrave to embrace the home and marriage as a shelter where he can reveal and renounce his own hidden ancestry, casting off the various "exterior[s]" he has worn in the market economy, and thus removing the "mask" he "habitually" wore over "whatever lay near his heart" (301). This final daguerreotype literally acts to bring Holgrave and Phoebe together in the chapter "The Flower of Eden," when it "separated Phoebe and [Holgrave] from the world, and bound them to each other," thus "hasten[ing] the development of emotions" that "it had been Holgrave's purpose to let . . . die" (305). The daguerreotype "draw[s] them together" (305) and allows their love to flower in an ahistoric Eden by separating them from the past—the racialized overly masculine traits of the Pyncheons as reembodied in Jaffrey—and the present of the outside world. Race, rather than class, or, perhaps more properly, race understood in terms of middle-class morality, now defines respectability, so that the historical class differences separating

Phoebe and Holgrave no longer matter, thus leading Holgrave to simply abandon his critique of bourgeois institutions and become a "conservative" (315, see 84 and 179–85 for his radicalism).[53]

Marking Holgrave's refusal to replicate the conflict between the Pyncheons and the Maules by having him commit his manuscript to the flames and using daguerreotypy to unify Holgrave and Phoebe, Hawthorne seems to indicate that narrative itself must be abandoned because like minstrelsy and the unrestrained self it conjures up, narrative threatens to enslave and objectify women. In its conclusion, as Clifford, Hepzibah, Phoebe, and Holgrave go off to take possession of Jaffrey's estate, soon to be joined by Uncle Venner, and, perhaps, even visited by young Ned Higgins, *Seven Gables* ultimately attempts to mirror the daguerreotypal parlor's vision of a classless (white) nation linked by familylike affective ties so that each can appear—or is revealed—as his or her real self to all others. With its supposedly objective combination of aesthetics and technology, art and science, daguerreotypy, rather than minstrelsy or even narrative, becomes the proper vehicle for Hawthorne to imagine a new, pure and white, Eden, a new home where (white) identity supposedly is secured. Through his daguerreotypy, Holgrave fulfills Hawthorne's national fantasy on a familial level, washing the Pyncheons and Maules' sheet white, both morally and racially.

But as critics have remarked since its initial publication, the novel's conclusion does not resolve things quite so neatly. Much of the discomfort over the end of the novel arises from the deus ex machina function that the daguerreotype and the Judge's death must play in ending the story on a positive note. In a racial register, Hawthorne's infamous attempt to "pour some setting sunshine" over this novel that "darkens damnably towards the close" becomes an attempt to remove the family from the racialized threat of the marketplace through daguerreotypy.[54] Yet daguerreotypy continued to be haunted by both its commercial nature, its ability to transform character (specifically "white" character) into an alienable and purchasable possession, and, relatedly, its dependence on racial difference for defining white respectability.[55] I want to suggest that it is for this reason that in the end Holgrave abandons not just his politics and his writing, but, presumably, the objectifying practice of daguerreotypy. Hawthorne attempts to use daguerreotypy to reimagine the bourgeois family and literary manhood by cleansing them of the racialized taint of economic exploitation, yet, unable or unwilling to embrace or imagine the transformative and emancipatory possibilities inherent to the commodification of identity in mass cultural forms, he ends his novel with no place left for artistic production or racial or class difference. The artistic failure of his novel's conclusion then rests on his failure to imagine the possibility of a more egalitarian nation or, at least, the possibility of more fluid racial boundaries, a possibility at once presented and denied in both minstrelsy and daguerreotypy.

Texts concerned with early photography's commercialization of identity often figured that commercialization, as we have seen in *Seven Gables*, in terms of race or slavery. For example, in "The Inconstant Daguerreotype" (1855), an anonymous short story in which two daguerreotypes come to life and fall in love with one another, the female daguerreotype recalls having seen "a number of our race bound together in a most conspicuous position on Broadway itself, exposed to the public gaze, and to the admiration of the lowest class of people. I remember quite shuddering with terror lest my destiny should be similar. And then, how I thanked my happy fate that placed me in the midst of elegance and a home of refinement."[56] In the female daguerreotype's eyes, the daguerreotypal gallery becomes a slave market where all of their "race" are "bound" together and exposed to the crude views of the lowest class. She fantasizes that in being removed to "a home of refinement" (as Holgrave and Phoebe are), she escapes the instability of being in public, of being a commodity. But as the story reveals, even in "a small and pretty boudoir" (820), the refinement she and her male counterpart exemplify becomes completely detachable from their original referents: the human original of the female daguerreotype falls in love with and steals the male daguerreotype when its original proves less "real." Daguerreotypy not only turns its subjects into slaves, into commodities that anyone can leer at, identify with, or desire; it transforms the "refinement" it seeks to define and protect into a transportable good, "exposed to the public gaze," that anyone can purchase (or steal) and carry away.[57]

Because of this daguerreotypal inconstancy, the way it possibly destabilized by commodifying white identity, Hawthorne has Holgrave abandon not just his radical political commitments and the multiple masks he wears in the labor economy, but both his writing and his daguerreotypy. Abandoning daguerreotypy and art, however, does not completely rescue Hawthorne from the instability of white identity, its dependence on and construction through racial difference. In the end, Holgrave's own dark "temptation" to enslave Phoebe becomes safely projected onto the dead Judge's "swarthily white" visage, thus cleansing Holgrave of his own passions, clearing the way for their marriage, and apparently creating a new homogeneous Eden. Those passions, however, simultaneously become revivified in the "dark, alien countenance" (294) of the Italian organ-grinder who returns to the house to see "the pleasant face of Phoebe" (292–93). The "dark" figure of the immigrant Italian boy and his monkey, whose phallic "enormous tail" symbolizes "the deviltry of nature" (164), reembodies those racialized dangers to the white family that the Judge's death supposedly removed. Finally, the novel ends with Dixey, the choruslike common laborer who has occasionally appeared throughout the novel with his unnamed friend, commenting on the commercial nature of the final resolution— "Pretty good business" (319)—as Alice's tortured spirit escapes heavenward. Several critics have seen Dixey's final lines as the return of the class difference and economic struggle supposedly papered over by the final marriage.[58] But I want to suggest that with the emancipation of the bond-slave Alice's spirit, this final scene also hints at the return of racial difference. Although Dan Emmett's minstrel tune "Dixie's Land" did not appear until 1859, there is evidence to suggest that Dixie (or Dixey) had been used as an appellation for both black characters and blacks in general from the beginning of the decade.[59] This is not to say that Dixey is black. Rather, it is to point to the ways in which his name indicates the need for him to fill a certain "black" role of marking the limits of the new community. Mixing racial and class difference and conflict as Hawthorne does throughout the novel, Dixey, in his role as commentator on and in his position outside the final happy conclusion, suggests the ethnographic role of daguerreotypes of blacks; he helps to delineate the emergent, supposedly homogeneous middle-class nation by standing outside its boundaries even as he remains an indispensable part of that nation in demarcating its limits.[60]

Thus, despite his desire to whitewash the nation, Hawthorne, at least aesthetically, found it necessary to recognize the internal differences, the shadows and lights, of the nation, and in doing so, to acknowledge the way in which the shadows and lights define one another and bleed over into one another.[61] A decade later, in "Chiefly About War Matters," he seems to admit, in patronizing terms, the entangled and intrinsically interconnected history of race from the beginning of settlement in America to the present:

There is an historical circumstance, known to few, that connects the children of the Puritans with these Africans of Virginia in a very singular way. They are our brethren, as being lineal descendants from the Mayflower, the fated womb of which, in her first voyage, sent forth a brood of Pilgrims on Plymouth Rock, and, in a subsequent one, spawned slaves upon the Southern soil,—a monstrous birth, but with which we have an instinctive sense of kindred, and so are stirred by an irresistible impulse to attempt their rescue, even at the cost of blood and ruin. The character of our sacred ship, I fear, may suffer a little by this revelation; but we must let her white progeny offset her dark one.[62]

In his paternalism, Hawthorne points to a continuation of the master/slave dialect he notes in his *American Notebooks*. Not only does the dark race need the white progeny to offset their monstrous birth, the white progeny simultaneously need their dark kindred to offset their whiteness with their picturesque nature. Just as the Romance must "bring out . . . the lights and deepen . . . the shadows" (2), so, it seems, Hawthorne's "white" cloth of a progressive middle-class America, even in its most optimistic, sunshine moment, must be "variegated" with the "blood and ruin" of its "brethren." In tracing out the daguerreotypelike shadows and lights of the human heart, Hawthorne draws on the shadow of race and slavery, producing a racialized (and gendered) understanding of the Pyncheons' curse. Working through and finally abandoning mass cultural forms of minstrelsy and daguerreotypy for constituting and securing white identity and white literary manhood, Hawthorne withdraws into a fantastical ending still haunted by the impure nature of his native land. Attempting to escape the destabilization of identity in market society, a destabilization he figures in terms of racial difference and sexual transgression, Hawthorne necessarily ends with no place left for art, for difference, or for commerce. Yet, in his attempt at his most optimistic ending, an ending intrinsically linked to his own fantasies of a white United States, Hawthorne's romance insistently circulates through a racialized understanding of character, and, unwittingly, traces out the interconnected weave of race, gender, and mass culture in his native land.

Epilogue

Electric Chains

In *The House of the Seven Gables* Hawthorne attempts to foreclose the cross-racial identification through mass cultural forms that, I have argued, was central to an antebellum model of literary manhood. He tries to rescue a model of artistic practice and a paradigmatic bourgeois heterosexual romance from the racialized dangers of the marketplace by drawing on the daguerreotypal parlor's construction of a homogeneously white, virtuous republic. Yet, even in a space and form as thoroughly identified as white and respectable as the daguerreotypal parlor, the possibility of cross-racial identification persists, leading to Holgrave abandoning not just his politics, but his art. I close this book by considering daguerreotypy as a model for the egalitarian, democratic poetics of Walt Whitman's 1855 *Leaves of Grass*. In using daguerreotypy to imagine a distinctly masculine, expansive, and incorporative poetic self that attempts to acknowledge differences while accepting all equally, Whitman emphasizes the ever-present transgressive possibility of the intersection of mass culture and literature in the antebellum era.

Along with being a devoted fan of Edwin Forrest and minstrel shows, Walt Whitman frequently commented on the new art of daguerreotypy in his journalistic writings.[1] At most length, in an article for the *Brooklyn Eagle* from 2 July 1846, Whitman describes a visit to Plumbe's Daguerreotype Gallery.[2] In his celebration of the gallery, Whitman emphasizes the gallery pictures' capacity to give him access to "more *life* . . . more variety, more human nature, more artistic beauty . . . than in any spot" he knows of.[3] Like Hepzibah's vision of department stores, the hundreds of reflective daguerreotypes covering the walls create "the impression of an immense Phantom concourse."[4] Unlike Hawthorne's version of things, however, Whitman accentuates that this Phantom concourse conjures up the "*realities*" of "the thousand human histories, involved in those daguerreotypes" (116). Because the portraits and "the current of thoughts running riot about them" have "a sort of magnetism," "An electric chain seems to vibrate, as it were, between our brain and him or her preserved there. . . . Time, space, both are annihilated, and we identify the semblance with the reality" (116–17).[5] Through their daguerreotypal portraits, Whitman imagines a way of connecting with the reality of other people's lives and histories, of outdoing "romance" with "*fact*" (114). In this way, as Miles Orvell has demonstrated at most length, the daguerreotypal gallery provides Whitman with a model for his project in *Leaves of Grass* of "bring[ing] the spirit of any or all events and passions and scenes and persons some more and some less to bear on your individual character as you hear or read."[6]

As a number of recent critics have reminded us, in attempting to suture himself to the nation, uniting the nation together in himself and in his poetry, by bringing all persons to bear on his readers, Whitman directly confronted the slavery controversy.[7] Among the famous "multitudes" (87) that Whitman's poetic persona contains are both "the tremulous spreading hands to protect" slavery and "the stern opposition to it which shall never cease till it ceases or the speaking of the tongues and the moving of lips cease" (8). This balancing (or confusion) of the two sides on the slavery debate appears throughout Whitman's oeuvre. In his journalism and early writings, Whitman often adopted proslavery (or at least racist) positions, as late as 1858 asking in an editorial, "Who believes that Whites and Blacks can ever amalgamate in America? Or who wishes it to happen? Nature has set an impassable seal against it. Besides, is not America for Whites? And is it not better so?"[8] Yet in *Leaves of Grass* he readily identifies with blacks and Indians and seems to embrace an antislavery stance through his proclamation that "The attitude of great poets is to cheer up slaves and horrify despots" (17).

In the longest study on the subject to date, Martin Klammer has argued that we can best understand Whitman's "baffling and seemingly contradictory attitudes toward African Americans" by recognizing "Whitman's focus on slavery is a compelling force behind his quest for a new form of expression that culminates in *Leaves of Grass*."[9] Klammer, in essence, understands *Leaves of Grass*'s formal experiments as emerging from Whitman's struggle to imagine a more egalitarian, more inclusive America (and self), a form that pushed him to identify with and embrace blacks and Indians as he does not do elsewhere.[10] Most striking perhaps, in a scene that emphasizes how he stands "Both in and out of the game, and watching and wondering at it" (30), Whitman becomes an escaped slave, feeling his pain—"I am the hounded slave. . . . I wince at the bite of the dogs"—even as he remains a detached spectator—"as I lean on my cane and observe" (65). At more length, Whitman details the common humanity of black slaves in the two slave auction scenes in what he would eventually title "I Sing the Body Electric." Stripping the male slave's body in order to reveal to his readers the "swells and jets [of] his heart" and its incorporation of "all passions and desires . . . all reachings and aspirations," Whitman uses the slave body at auction as a test case for uniting all of humanity through their similar bodies (123). Asking his readers whether they "think [these passions and desires] are not there because they are not expressed in parlors and lecture-rooms," Whitman emphasizes "the same old blood . . . the same red running blood" underneath "red black or white" skins (123). In *Leaves of Grass*, and in "I Sing the Body Electric" in particular, Whitman creates a poetic persona and form that transcend his racist journalism and bind him and his readers to black slaves.

Combining Orvell's and Klammer's hypothesizes about the origins of the formally (and perhaps ideologically) revolutionary *Leaves of Grass* suggests the daguerreotypal parlor as a source of Whitman's egalitarian racial politics. Whitman only added the famous opening line (and title) to "I Sing the Body Electric" in 1867, and in later versions, he notes that "before the war I often go to the slave-mart and watch the sale" (255), implying, perhaps, his experience in New Orleans as a model for these scenes. Yet Whitman used the notion of an electric connection with other people, as in his reportage of daguerreotypy, throughout the 1855 edition of *Leaves of Grass*, suggesting a connection to his experience of photographic exhibitions. He describes the poet as opening himself up and allowing "all things [to] enter with electric swiftness softly and duly without confusion or jostling or jam" (10), the "procreant urge" behind the merging of bodies as "electrical" (26), and his body as having "instant conductors" that "seize every object and lead it harmlessly through me" (55). Whitman's description of the "electric" nature of his poetic connection with others and their bodies further links daguerreotypy to Whitman's inclusive poetics. Becoming an electric body, linked to other electric bodies through the electric chain of daguerreotypy,

Whitman imagines the erasure of racial difference. By imaginatively bringing the bodies of racial others into (daguerreotypal) "parlors and lecture-rooms," Whitman provides an electrical connection between his readers and slaves in the South, thus emphasizing the common blood running through their bodies.[11]

Abolitionist fiction and exhibitions further suggest the possibility of daguerreotypal practices providing such a model for Whitman. Because daguerreotypal practices defined respectability through a series of marks that could be reproduced and counterfeited, the "white" respectability of the daguerreotypal portrait could be transferred to black subjects iterating an antislavery point. We can see this possibility in the way both Frederick Douglass and Harriet Beecher Stowe use the new verb "daguerreotype" in their fiction to highlight and memorialize their very different heroes.[12] Further, although Whitman probably did not encounter (and certainly does not mention seeing) antislavery daguerreotypes in his visit to Plumbe's and other galleries, other daguerreotypal parlors readily utilized the daguerreotype's "electric swiftness" in creating the kind of "electric chain" Whitman imagines between white viewers and black slaves. The most striking use of daguerreotypy for abolitionist purposes, *Ball's Mammoth Pictorial Tour of the United States*, drew on daguerreotypy's ability both to "bring the spirit of any or all events and passions" to viewers and to bind viewers and daguerreotypal subjects together through a common humanity. James Ball, a black daguerreotypist whose Cincinnati establishment was the largest daguerreotypal parlor in the West (see Figure 10, previous chapter), produced and compiled the 2,400 square-foot painted panorama whose "sketches, (except the African views) were taken by the artist, upon the spots which they represent."[13] According to the 1855 descriptive pamphlet published by abolitionist Achilles Pugh, Ball transformed his individual daguerreotypes of the South into a large-scale panorama depicting slavery and its "wasteful destruction of human life" (32). Pugh's pamphlet follows the panorama, first describing native Africans "before they are unmanned and imbruted, by slavery," as "far from being the indolent and ignorant savages that many suppose them to be" (11–12). Ball's panorama, as described by Pugh's text, relied on recontextualizing and redefining blackness in terms of civilization and respectability, in terms of Africans actually being "high in the scale of civilization" (12), as Ball's own career and his "invincible power of energy" (7), which enabled him to "triumph" over poverty and prejudice (10), illustrate.[14]

While ethnographic daguerreotypes attempted to read racial character directly from black or red skins, abolitionists used the daguerreotypal production of interior subjectivity to argue for black humanity. As these portraits and the metaphorization of these techniques suggest, the daguerreotypal parlor's policing and inculcating of white respectability simultaneously revealed the instability of whiteness and the markers of respectability; its commodification of racial identity, like that of the minstrel show, opened possibilities of racial transgression and the reconfiguration of racial identities. Refiguring the United States in poetic and daguerreotypal form, both Whitman's poetry and Ball's panorama use the inherent immediacy and supposed authenticity of photography to create new cross-racial connections and to foster a sense of common humanity and equality. In imagining a "manhood untainted" (124), Whitman draws on daguerreotypal practices to identify with the passions and desires of not just male slaves, Indians, and workers, but women of all classes and races as well, in the process participating in a problematic but potentially revolutionary model of literary manhood.[15]

This book has argued that a wide range of authors, black and Indian as well as white, worked through the changing dynamics of literature's economic and social standing by drawing on this mutable model of manhood. Literary manhood and its invocation of mass cultural forms and their racial representations allowed men (and occasionally women) to secure cultural, social, and economic capital in a rapidly changing cultural marketplace. In the process, it also often allowed them to challenge dominant notions of strict racial distinctions and the politics of Indian removal and slavery, even as it reified certain ideas of blackness and Indianness as outside the market economy. Examining selected writers and institutions in depth in order to suggest a much broader cultural strategy for negotiating middle-class gender norms in the emergent market economy, this study has emphasized the ambivalent racial politics of mid-century middle-class manhood.

Hawthorne and Whitman, in this way, represent the two poles of literary manhood and its intersection with racialized mass culture. Hawthorne attempts to protect the white family from the racialized contagion of the mass cultural marketplace, implying the artist's retreat from politics, society, and art itself. Whitman revels in the possibilities of cross-racial identification that such realms opened up, drawing on his experience with a variety of popular forms to create poetry that, for all its problems, continues to provide a utopian vision of American multicultural democracy. The other authors I have examined—Cooper, Brown, Thoreau, Tubbee, Poe—oscillate between these two poles, the desire to preserve whiteness and art in all its supposed purity and the desire to incorporate the other through mass cultural renderings of blacks and Indians. In the years that followed, as high and mass culture became more and more stratified, writers such as Mark Twain and Charles Chesnutt continued to cross over and draw from mass cultural forms in questioning the racial status quo. Yet, as minstrelsy and other antebellum forms became more stabilized and provided more static, stereotyped images of difference and as the great divide between high and low widened, literary appropriations of mass culture became both more dangerous in their transgression of middle-class norms and more limited in their potential challenge to dominant ideas of class, gender, and race. The intersection of different cultural fields of production continues to offer imaginative aesthetic and political possibilities even in this age of postmodern pastiche. But the intersection of race, mass culture, and literature in the antebellum United States, with its relative fluidity between different classes of cultural commodities, provided a particularly fruitful field of possibilities for rethinking racial and gender categories. This book has attempted to demonstrate how a prominent model of literary manhood exemplifies the negotiation, broadening, and limiting of these possibilities.

Notes

Introduction

1 Herman Melville, "Hawthorne and His Mosses," *The Piazza Tales and Other Prose Pieces, 1839–1860* (Evanston, Ill.: Northwestern UP, 1987) 248. Further references will be to this edition and will be given parenthetically.

2 Anna Cora Mowatt, *Fashion* (1845), *Dramas from the American Theatre, 1762–1909*, ed. Richard Moody (Cleveland: World Publishing Co., 1966) 332.

3 For an overview of the development of the idea of "literature" in the context of an emergent capitalist economy, see Raymond Williams, *Marxism and Literature* (Oxford: Oxford UP, 1977) 48–52. As Terry Eagleton puts it, "the birth of aesthetics as an intellectual discourse coincides with the period when cultural production is beginning to suffer the miseries and indignities of commodification. The peculiarity of the aesthetic is in part spiritual compensation for this degradation: it is just when the artist is becoming debased to a petty commodity producer that he or she will lay claim to transcendent genius" (Terry Eagleton, *The Ideology of the Aesthetic* [Oxford: Basil Blackwell, 1990] 64–65).

4 Pierre Bourdieu, *The Rules of Art: Genesis and Structure of the Literary Field*, trans. Susan Emanuel (Stanford, Calif.: Stanford UP, 1995) 4. See Louis Althusser on the "relative autonomy" of such superstructural forms as literature and on the "reciprocal action" between base and superstructure in his consideration of "'determination in the last instance' by the economic base" (Louis Althusser, "Ideology and Ideological State Apparatuses," *Lenin and Philosophy and Other Essays*, trans. Ben Brewster [New York: Monthly Review Press, 1971] 135). In contrast, however, see his statement that "From the first moment to the last, the lonely hour of the 'last instance' never comes" (Louis Althusser, "Contradiction and Overdetermination," *For Marx*, trans. Ben Brewster [London: Verso, 1990] 113). Bourdieu argues that literature is both produced by "the social world" and "brings [it] to light" (47). This relationship with the social world depends on literature's emergence as an autonomous field with the birth of the modern writer as "a full-time professional, dedicated to one's work in a total and exclusive manner, indifferent to the exigencies of politics and to the injunctions of morality, and not recognizing any jurisdiction other than the norms specific to one's art" (76–77). As Lawrence Buell points out, almost all antebellum American authors saw their work as part of a moral project, yet this idea of literature as a field beholden to nothing but its own truths, the idea of the author as a "citizen of

somewhere else" as Hawthorne put it in "The Custom House," was also beginning to appear in the United States, as suggested by Melville's essay, Hawthorne's prefaces, and much of Poe's writing (Nathaniel Hawthorne, *The Scarlet Letter, The Centenary Edition of the Works of Nathaniel Hawthorne*, vol. 1 [Columbus: Ohio State UP, 1962] 44). See Lawrence Buell, *New England Literary Culture: From Revolution Through Renaissance* (Cambridge: Cambridge UP, 1986) 68–69.

5 In this way, I want to follow Frederic Jameson's idea of a dialectical relationship between mass culture and high art: "high and mass culture as objectively related and dialectically interdependent phenomena, as twin and inseparable forms of the fission of aesthetic production under capitalism" (Fredric Jameson, "Reification and Utopia in Mass Culture," *Signatures of the Visible* [New York: Routledge, 1990] 14). Jameson sees this dialectic only emerging with the modernist era, but my book strives to demonstrate its pervasiveness from the beginning of the market revolution. For another reading of the dialectic between high and mass culture in the modernist era and mass culture's figuration as feminine, see Andreas Huyssen, "Mass Culture as Woman: Modernism's Other," *After the Great Divide: Modernism, Mass Culture, Postmodernism* (Bloomington: Indiana UP, 1986) 44–62. As I hope to show, mass culture in the antebellum era was not, as has often been posited in literary studies, gendered in simply feminine terms.

6 I take this phrasing in slightly altered form from Bill Brown, who "privilege[s] literature as a mode of explaining . . . how the material past inhabited a determinate, but not wholly determinant ideology or symbology" (Bill Brown, *The Material Unconscious: American Amusement, Stephen Crane, and the Economies of Play* [Cambridge: Harvard UP, 1996] 18). I draw on Pierre Bourdieu's preface to *Outline of a Theory of Practice*, trans. Richard Nice (Cambridge: Cambridge UP, 1977), for the idea of strategy. See also his *Distinction: A Social Critique of the Judgment of Taste*, trans. Richard Nice (Cambridge: Harvard UP, 1984). Finally, Stephen Greenblatt's "What Is the History of Literature?" *Critical Inquiry* 23.3 (spring 1997): 460–81, has helped me to rethink the ways literature is both an instrument of social control and a "place where imaginings may be made real and realities may be disclosed as the products of the imagination" (478).

7 Neil Harris speaks of an "amusement explosion" in New York in the early 1840s that would eventually sweep the entire nation in *Humbug: The Art of P. T. Barnum* (Chicago: U of Chicago P, 1973) 36. Unlike David Reynolds, then, who reads the literary mass culture "beneath" the American Renaissance as so much subversive raw material that the true artists of the era turned into "symbolic, timeless literature," I focus on the visually oriented mass culture of public spaces and will attempt to avoid replicating a high/low distinction (David Reynolds, *Beneath the American Renaissance: The*

Subversive Imagination in the Age of Emerson and Melville [Cambridge: Harvard UP, 1988] 6). Instead, I will emphasize the complexity of mass culture itself by describing how mass cultural forms provided antebellum authors a different lens through which to understand and resolve the contradictions of middle-class gender ideologies and their relationship with the market revolution.

8 I abjure the term "popular culture" in favor of "mass culture" because of the ways "popular" evokes an idea of a spontaneous expression of the people, while "mass," in the tradition of the Frankfurt School, focuses our attention on the commodified nature of these cultural products.

9 See especially Eric Lott, *Love and Theft: Blackface Minstrelsy and the American Working Class* (New York: Oxford UP, 1993).

10 As Roediger acknowledges and as more recent work suggests, the minstrel show from the early 1840s on was making "special appeals to . . . some in the respectable middle classes and above" (David R. Roediger, *The Wages of Whiteness: Race and the Making of the American Working Class* [New York: Verso, 1991] 116) and was increasingly incorporated into respectable amusements dependent on drawing a middle-class cross-gendered audience. See chapter 1 for a fuller discussion of this point and of other recent work on minstrelsy that describes its incorporation into respectable, middle-class venues.

11 See Lawrence W. Levine, *Highbrow/Lowbrow: The Emergence of Cultural Hierarchy in America* (Cambridge: Harvard UP, 1988), and Peter G. Buckley, "To the Opera House: Culture and Society in New York City, 1820–1860," Ph.D. diss., SUNY Stony Brook, 1984. The two differ in that Levine argues that it was only with the Astor Place Riot in 1849 that a real split between high and low culture (and its concomitant class distinctions) began to appear in the United States while Buckley argues that the riot was the culmination of a growing disparity that first began to appear in the 1820s. My narrative is more similar to Buckley's, but focuses on the cultural and class middle ground he identifies with Barnum. See prologue.

12 For a general overview of American economic growth in the first half of the nineteenth century, see George R. Taylor, *The Transportation Revolution, 1815–1860* (New York: Rinehart, 1951); Douglass C. North, *The Economic Growth of the United States, 1790–1860* (New York: Norton, 1961); and Charles Sellers, *The Market Revolution: Jacksonian America, 1815–1846* (New York: Oxford UP, 1991). For the impact of this economic revolution, see Melvyn Stokes and Stephen Conway, eds., *The Market Revolution in America: Social, Political, and Religious Expressions, 1800–1880* (Charlottesville: UP of Virginia, 1996). For the rise of professionalism, see, in particular, Burton J. Bledstein, *The Culture of Professionalism: The Middle Class and the Development of Higher Education in America* (New York: Norton, 1976).

13 C. B. Macpherson, *The Political Theory of Possessive Individualism, Hobbes to Locke* (New York: Oxford UP, 1962) 48. I am indebted to Amy Dru Stanley's similar use of Macpherson for indicating what she means by market; Amy Dru Stanley, "Home Life and the Morality of the Market," *The Market Revolution in America*, ed. Melvyn Stokes and Stephen Conway (Charlottesville: UP of Virginia, 1996) 75.

14 See, in particular, Paul Johnson, *A Shopkeeper's Millennium: Society and Revivals in Rochester, New York, 1815–1837* (New York: Hill and Wang, 1978); Mary P. Ryan, *Cradle of the Middle Class: The Family in Oneida County, New York, 1790–1865* (Cambridge: Cambridge UP, 1981); Karen Halttunen, *Confidence Men and Painted Women: A Study of Middle-Class Culture in America, 1830–1870* (New Haven, Conn.: Yale UP, 1982); and Stuart M. Blumin, *The Emergence of the Middle Class: Social Experience in the American City, 1760–1900* (Cambridge: Cambridge UP, 1989).

15 Stuart M. Blumin, "The Hypothesis of Middle-Class Formation in Nineteenth-Century America: A Critique and Some Proposals," *American Historical Review* 90 (1985): 309.

16 As Mary Ryan puts it, "[i]n the popular mind at midcentury social space was often divided up between the 'home' and the 'streets,' warm, personal, and stable ties as opposed to cold, brutal, and threatening encounters" (*Cradle of the Middle Class* 233). See also Barbara Welter's groundbreaking "The Cult of True Womanhood: 1800–1860," *Dimity Convictions: The American Woman in the Nineteenth Century* (Athens: Ohio UP, 1976) 21–41; Nancy F. Cott, *The Bonds of Womanhood: "Woman's Sphere" in New England, 1780–1835* (New Haven: Yale UP, 1977); and Carroll Smith-Rosenberg, *Disorderly Conduct: Visions of Gender in Victorian America* (New York: Oxford UP, 1985). In literary studies, see in particular Mary Kelley, *Private Woman, Public Stage: Literary Domesticity in Nineteenth-Century America* (New York: Oxford UP, 1984); Jane Tompkins, *Sensational Designs: The Cultural Work of American Fiction, 1790–1860* (New York: Oxford UP, 1985); and the essays collected in Shirley Samuels, ed., *The Culture of Sentiment: Race, Gender, and Sentimentality in Nineteenth-Century America* (New York: Oxford UP, 1992).

17 E. Anthony Rotundo, *American Manhood: Transformations in Masculinity from the Revolution to the Modern Era* (New York: HarperCollins, 1993) 167. Rotundo's paradigmatic study outlines three different, historically specific models of nineteenth-century middle-class manhood—a communal manhood at the beginning of the century in which "a man's identity was inseparable from the duties he owed the community. . . . [most significantly] his role as the head of the household"; self-made manhood, which became hegemonic in the middle of the century; and finally, at the end of the century, a passionate manhood which "in some respects [was] an elaboration of existing beliefs about self-made manhood, but. . . . [with a more] positive

value put on male passions. . . . [as] the body itself became a vital component of manhood" (2–6). Rotundo's book provides probably the best overview of ideals of manhood in nineteenth-century America, and his strengths and weaknesses can serve to delineate those of the field more generally. See the essays collected in Mark C. Carnes and Cynthia Griffin, eds., *Meanings for Manhood: Constructions of Masculinity in Victorian America* (Chicago: U of Chicago P, 1990); J. A. Mangan and James Walvin, eds., *Manliness and Morality: Middle-Class Masculinity in Britain and America, 1800–1940* (New York: St. Martin's Press, 1987); Elizabeth H. Pleck and Joseph H. Pleck, eds., *The American Man* (Englewood Cliffs, NJ: Prentice-Hall, 1980); G. J. Barker-Benfield, *The Horrors of Half-Known Life: Male Attitudes Toward Women and Sexuality in Nineteenth-Century America* (New York: Harper and Row, 1976); Karen Halttunen, *Confidence Men and Painted Women*; Carroll Smith-Rosenberg's "Davy Crockett as Trickster: Pornography, Liminality, and Symbolic Inversion in Victorian America," *Disorderly Conduct* 90–108; David G. Pugh, *Sons of Liberty: The Masculine Mind in Nineteenth-Century America* (Westport: Greenwood Press, 1983); John G. Cawelti, *Apostles of the Self-Made Man: Changing Concepts of Success in America* (Chicago: U of Chicago P, 1965); and Michael S. Kimmel, *Manhood in America: A Cultural History* (New York: The Free Press, 1996).

18 See Bluford Adams, *E Pluribus Barnum: The Great Showman and the Making of U.S. Popular Culture* (Minneapolis: U of Minnesota P, 1997), for a discussion of Barnum as being "all things to all people." See Buckley "To the Opera House" 495 for the comment on audience composition.

19 Part of this difference (and the focus on black and Indian bodies more generally) can be understood as reflecting the different, yet equally central, roles blacks and Indians played in the growth of a capitalist economy in the United States. As Ronald Takaki has pointed out, one of the driving forces of the American market revolution was the expansion of mass gang slavery into the southwestern lands recently appropriated through Indian removal and warfare: "the removal of Indians and the expansion of black slavery made possible the Market Revolution" (Ronald Takaki, *Iron Cages: Race and Culture in Nineteenth-Century America* [1979; New York: Oxford UP, 1990] 78). During the market revolution, as historians such as George Fredrickson have demonstrated, racism, as a "rationalized ideology grounded in what were thought to be the facts of nature," "positing the innate and permanent inferiority of non-whites," first came to "fruition" (George M. Fredrickson, *The Black Image in the White Mind: The Debate on Afro-American Character and Destiny, 1817–1914* [Middletown, Conn.: Wesleyan UP, 1971] 2, xvii). See also Thomas F. Gossett, *Race: The History of an Idea in America* (Dallas: Southern Methodist UP, 1963); Reginald Horsman, *Race and Manifest Destiny: The Origins of Racial Anglo-Saxonism* (Cambridge: Harvard UP, 1981);

and William Stanton, *The Leopard's Spots: Scientific Attitudes Toward Race in America, 1815–59* (Chicago: U of Chicago P, 1960). Economic expansion, however, did not simply create new racial ideologies; rather the construction of blacks and Indians as essentially and eternally different—as necessary casualties to the march of "progress"—simultaneously served to rationalize eastern Indian removal and the expansion of plantation slavery into the southwest, and at the same time was a product of these changes. As Takaki phrases it, racial ideologies "sprang from as well as sustained the material base of the Market Revolution" (84).

20 Hortense J. Spillers forcefully underlines the interconnection between constructions of race and gender in her "Mama's Baby, Papa's Maybe: An American Grammar Book," *Diacritics* 17.2 (summer 1987): 64–81. In the last decade, a number of writers have pointed to the centrality of questions of race in American literary texts even when those texts apparently have nothing to do with race. Most importantly, see Kenneth W. Warren, *Black and White Strangers: Race and American Literary Realism* (Chicago: U of Chicago P, 1993), and Toni Morrison, *Playing in the Dark: Whiteness and the Literary Imagination* (New York: Vintage, 1993). Shelley Fisher Fishkin surveys these kind of studies in "Interrogating 'Whiteness,' Complicating 'Blackness': Remapping American Culture," *American Quarterly* 47.3 (September 1995): 428–66. Works on nineteenth-century American literature that feature this kind of approach include Dana D. Nelson, *The Word in Black and White: Reading 'Race' in American Literature, 1638–1867* (New York: Oxford UP, 1992); Eric J. Sundquist, *To Wake the Nations: Race in the Making of American Literature* (Cambridge: Harvard UP, 1993); Russ Castronovo, *Fathering the Nation: American Genealogies of Slavery and Freedom* (Berkeley: U of California P, 1995); Rafia Zafar, *We Wear the Mask: African Americans Write American Literature, 1760–1870* (New York: Columbia UP, 1997); and Jared Gardner, *Master Plots: Race and the Founding of an American Literature, 1787–1845* (Baltimore, Md.: Johns Hopkins UP, 1998). In many ways, my work approximates that of Michael North in his discussion of American modernism's "racial cross-identification" (Michael North, *The Dialect of Modernism: Race, Language, and Twentieth-Century Literature* [New York: Oxford UP, 1994] 9).

21 According to these studies, during this period of economic take-off, middle-class definitions of manhood were very similar to the Protestant ethic Max Weber described—"the summum bonum of this ethic, the earning of more and more money, combined with the strict avoidance of all spontaneous enjoyment of life" (Max Weber, *The Protestant Ethic and the Spirit of Capitalism*, trans. Talcott Parson [New York: HarperCollins, 1991] 53). On the other hand, scholars like Elliott J. Gorn have argued that large segments of a nascent working class defined their manhood through resistance to such an

ethos. According to this argument, in working-class communities, manhood continued to be defined by a certain rugged physicality, especially as displayed in traditional sports and other leisure activities such as drinking. A distinctly working-class manliness emerged in opposition to the rising bourgeois ideal of self-made manhood and its accompanying ethos of bodily denial, decorum, and hard work: the "free-and-easy cultural style" of working-class manhood stood as an anti- (or pre-) capitalist alternative to "evangelical religion and capitalist forms of business organization" and "the ascendant ethos of productivity, humanitarian reform, steady habits, sober self-control, accumulation of property, and devotion to the domestic family" (Elliott J. Gorn, *The Manly Art: Bare-Knuckle Prize Fighting in America* [Ithaca, N.Y.: Cornell UP, 1986] 29). As I will argue below, the middle class, in its incorporation of older artisanal and elite traditions and its similar experience of self-commodification through the labor market and the disciplines of capital, often imagined itself losing the kind of manhood Gorn describes and attempted to resurrect that manhood through indulging in activities, such as attending mass cultural forms, that were often associated with Gorn's vision of working-class manhood.

22   As Carroll Smith-Rosenberg has argued, the "extreme instability" of the middle class of this period, "their ambivalence about both the process of change itself and the emerging new social order," was expressed "by postulating two competing mythic dramas" of manhood, one which was identified as more middle class and another more passionate manhood embodied by white working-class men and blacks and Indians (Carroll Smith-Rosenberg, "Davy Crockett as Trickster: Pornography, Liminality, and Symbolic Inversion in Victorian America," *Disorderly Conduct* 86, 91). Smith-Rosenberg points out that the nearly pornographic "Davy Crockett myths flourished during the same years that fear of youthful masturbation [as expressed in guides such as Alcott's] reached its apex—the 1830s through the 1850s" (93). For a more theoretically sophisticated account of how individuals were simultaneously interpellated by competing and sometimes contradictory models of manhood in an earlier period, see her "Dis-Covering the Subject of the 'Great Constitutional Discussion,' 1786–1789," in *Discovering America: Essays on the Search for an Identity*, ed. David Thelen and Frederick E. Hoxie (Urbana: U of Illinois P, 1994) 7–39. Part of the instability of the middle class was the fact that it was constantly shifting, as older elites fell into new professions and rising artisans moved upward. As Michael A. Lebowitz points out, the market revolution, above all, meant displacement in geographic (toward cities) and economic (usually downward) location. See Michael A. Lebowitz, "The Jacksonians: Paradox Lost?" in *Towards a New Past: Dissenting Essays in American History*, ed. Barton J. Bernstein (New York: Vintage, 1968) 65–89. See also Bruce Laurie, *Working People of*

Philadelphia, 1800–1850 (Philadelphia: Temple UP, 1980), for a description of "revivalists," working people who identified with new middle-class decorum and respectability.

23 Georg Lukács, "Reification and the Consciousness of the Proletariat," *History and Class Consciousness: Studies in Marxist Dialectics*, trans. Rodney Livingston (1923; Cambridge: MIT Press, 1971) 100. Just as through his labor the worker "does not affirm himself but denies himself" and thus "no longer feels himself to be freely active in any but his animal functions," so the rising bourgeoisie become alienated from themselves in production and attempt to become whole again through consumption (Karl Marx, *The Economic and Philosophic Manuscripts of 1844, The Marx-Engels Reader*, 2d ed., ed. Robert C. Tucker [New York: Norton, 1978] 74). In terms of literary studies, Gillian Brown's notion of a domestic, interior, authentic self constructed in opposition to the market, but readily commodified through such things as sentimental literature, most closely approximates my point here. See Gillian Brown, *Domestic Individualism: Imagining Self in Nineteenth-Century America* (Berkeley: U of California P, 1990). My emphasis on the commodity form over class formations for understanding capitalism follows revisionary Marxist thinkers such as Moishe Postone, who argues that "the social relations and forces of domination that characterize capitalism . . . cannot be understood sufficiently in terms of class relations" and that fundamental to a better understanding of capitalism is foregrounding the "abstract social structures" (especially the commodity) that people constitute, but are in turn dominated by (Moishe Postone, *Time, Labor, and Social Domination: A Reinterpretation of Marx's Critical Theory* [Cambridge: Cambridge UP, 1993] 6).

24 As Susan Stewart points out, "within the development of culture under an exchange economy, the search for authentic experience and, correlatively, the authentic object becomes critical. As experience is increasingly mediated and abstracted, the lived relation of the body to the phenomenological world is replaced by a nostalgic myth of contact and presence. 'Authentic' experience becomes both elusive and allusive as it is placed beyond the horizon of present lived experience, the beyond in which the antique, the pastoral, the exotic, and other fictive domains are articulated" (Susan Stewart, *On Longing: Narratives of the Miniature, the Gigantic, the Souvenir, the Collection* [1984; Durham, N.C.: Duke UP, 1993] 133). In the antebellum United States, that authentic experience was figured in terms of racial difference. The construction of blacks and Indians as embodying all that was nostalgically imagined to have been lost by expanding and intensifying economic forces and bourgeois discipline has often been noted. Frantz Fanon, for example, theorized that Euro-American men "projected [their] own desires onto the Negro," thus marking the racial other as the symbol of "the biological" and "the lower emotions" (Frantz Fanon, *Black Skin, White*

Masks, trans. Charles Lam Markmann [1952; New York: Grove Press, 1967] 165, 167, 190).

25 Michael Newbury, *Figuring Authorship in Antebellum America* (Stanford, Calif.: Stanford UP, 1997) 2–3. See, in particular, William Charvat, *The Profession of Authorship in America, 1800–1870*, ed. Matthew J. Bruccoli (Columbus: Ohio State UP, 1968) and *Literary Publishing in America, 1790–1850* (Philadelphia: U of Pennsylvania P, 1959). See also Michael Gilmore, *American Romanticism and the Marketplace* (Chicago: U of Chicago P, 1985), and Terence Whalen, *Edgar Allan Poe and the Masses: The Political Economy of Literature in Antebellum America* (Princeton, N.J.: Princeton UP, 1999). Grantland Rice and R. Jackson Wilson argue for the emergence of this market relationship in the eighteenth century; as Wilson puts it, "the existence of the marketplace set inescapable problems for writers from at least the 1770s on" (R. Jackson Wilson, *Figures of Speech: American Writers and the Literary Marketplace, from Benjamin Franklin* [New York: Knopf, 1989] 17). Also see Grantland Rice, *The Transformation of Authorship in America* (Chicago: U of Chicago P, 1997). For a discussion of the economic transformation of readership and the role of reading in the economic transformation of early nineteenth-century America, see Ronald J. Zboray, *A Fictive People: Antebellum Economic Development and the American Reading Public* (New York: Oxford UP, 1993).

26 Review of *Oeuvres d'Alexandre Dumas*, *North American Review* 53 (January 1843): 109–10.

27 Stanley, "Home Life and the Morality of the Market" 84. Stanley's discussion of the role that separate spheres and antislavery ideology played in redefining the commodification of labor in gendered terms has been immensely useful to me in thinking through these relationships.

28 David Leverenz, *Manhood and the American Renaissance* (Ithaca, N.Y.: Cornell UP, 1989); Leland S. Person Jr., *Aesthetic Headaches: Women and a Masculine Poetics in Poe, Melville, and Hawthorne* (Athens: U of Georgia P, 1988); Scott S. Derrick, *Monumental Anxieties: Homoerotic Desire and Feminine Influence in Nineteenth-Century U.S. Literature* (New Brunswick, N.J.: Rutgers UP, 1997). Where Person argues that Poe, Hawthorne, and Melville tend "to deconstruct conventional masculinity, which manifests itself in objectifying power over women, in order to achieve a 'feminized' creative self, which comes into being through the surrender of power *to* women" (6), Derrick and Leverenz give more adequate consideration to how these (and other) authors struggled with notions of middle-class manhood, at times questioning some of its central tenets, but often acceding to its requirements. Leverenz's book remains the standard on the subject with its thick historicization of "three ideologies of manhood in the antebellum Northeast: patrician, artisan, and entrepreneurial" (3). He develops these models

at length (72–90), describing how an older patrician model "defined man-hood through property, patriarchy, and citizenship" while the artisanal model defined itself through "autonomous self-sufficiency" (78). For all of his historicization, however, Leverenz finally tends to erase all historical distinctions under one transhistorical idea of manhood—"my most basic thesis, that any intensified ideology [of manhood] is a compensatory re-sponse to fears of humiliation" (4); "Anyone preoccupied with manhood, in whatever time or culture, harbors fears of being humiliated, usually by other men" (72). From my perspective, this essentializing move leaves Leverenz unable to account sufficiently for the ways ideologies of manhood were particularized in terms of race. For example, in Leverenz's account, Frederick Douglass's attempt to prove his manhood is not determined by his position as a black man and a former slave in a society that defined manhood against both blackness and slavery; it is most centrally about his desire not to be humiliated by other men. Conversely, in his more recent work on Poe and Cooper (see below), Leverenz, it seems to me, avoids this essentialism in favor of better understanding manhood in terms of the competing ideals he outlines (but finally abandons) in his book.

29 Lawrence Buell, *New England Literary Culture* 54; see figures in appendix, 378. As Nicholas Bromell points out, "during the antebellum period work was understood primarily by way of a distinction between manual and mental labor," a distinction often rendered in gendered terms, so that "male writers of the period frequently" feared that "that mental labor is in essence effeminate" (Nicholas K. Bromell, *By the Sweat of the Brow: Literature and Labor in Antebellum America* [Chicago: U of Chicago, 1993] 7, 8). This distinction between manual and mental labor was central to the self-defini-tion of the middle class; the gendering of this distinction reveals the prob-lematic nature of middle-class manhood based upon achieving economic success as an (effeminate) intellectual worker, a broader cultural problematic that literary manhood struggles to resolve.

30 The works that have challenged the separate spheres hypothesis are nu-merous. To name a few, on working-class women, see Christine Stansell, *City of Women: Sex and Class in New York, 1789–1860* (New York: Knopf, 1986); on literature, see Cathy N. Davidson, "Preface: No More Separate Spheres!" *American Literature* 70.3 (September 1998): 443–63; on women in the public political sphere, Mary P. Ryan, *Women in Public: Between Banners and Ballots, 1825–1860* (Baltimore, Md.: Johns Hopkins UP, 1990); and more generally, the essays in Laura McCall and Donald Yacovone, eds., *A Shared Experience: Men, Women, and the History of Gender* (New York: New York UP, 1998).

31 As Gail Bederman has argued, histories of manhood have tended either to "recognize that manhood might be expressed differently at different times

[yet] . . . assume that its underlying meaning remains basically the same" or "to define manhood as a coherent set of prescriptive ideals, traits, or sex roles" and thus obscure "the complexities and contradictions of any historical moment" (Gail Bederman, *Manliness and Civilization: A Cultural History of Gender and Race in the United States, 1880–1917* [Chicago: U of Chicago P, 1995] 6). I take Kimmel to be representative of the first tendency, Rotundo of the second. In place of these two approaches, Bederman offers the idea of seeing manhood as a "historical, ideological process" through which "men claim certain kinds of authority, based upon their particular types of bodies," a "cultural process whereby concrete individuals are constituted as members of a preexisting social category" (7). While I will use Bederman's notion of gender as a process, I want to insist upon gender as performance, the ways that, within limited and determining parameters, individuals are not simply constituted but constitute themselves as individual men and women and thus help to reconstitute categories of gender. As Maurice Berger, Brian Wallis, and Simon Watson put it, "social and cultural constructions of the masculine and the feminine are never so inevitable and unitary" (Maurice Berger, Brian Wallis, and Simon Watson, eds., *Constructing Masculinity* [New York: Routledge, 1995] 5). Judith Butler's work, of course, is central to understanding the ways in which gender is performative. As she notes, "gender proves to be performative—that is, constituting the identity it is purported to be" (25): the process of being a man or a woman consists of "acts, gestures, enactments" that "are *performative* in the sense that the essence or identity that they otherwise purport to express are *fabrications* manufactured and sustained through corporeal signs and other discursive means" (136). Butler's comments on how actual performances (in particular drag) reveal the performative nature of gender and "possibilities for proliferating gender configurations outside the restricting frames of masculinist domination and compulsory heterosexuality" (141) have been central to my thinking about the constitution of gender and race in the mass cultural forms I examine. See Judith Butler, *Gender Trouble: Feminism and the Subversion of Identity* (New York: Routledge, 1990). Recently, in the context of nineteenth-century America, Dana Nelson has argued that ideals of manhood are "an always-remote abstraction rather than . . . an embodied practice" (Dana D. Nelson, *National Manhood: Capitalist Citizenship and the Imagined Fraternity of White Men* [Durham, N.C.: Duke UP, 1998] 19). My work seeks to complement Nelson's attention to white male citizenship by focusing on "the construction of race in the terms of professional competition for cultural authority" (26).

32 Letter to William D. Ticknor, 19 January 1855, in *Letters, 1853–1856*, vol. 17 of *The Centenary Edition of the Works of Nathaniel Hawthorne*, gen. eds. William Charvat, Roy Harvey Pearce, and Claude M. Simpson (Columbus:

Ohio State UP, 1987) 304. Despite drawing sympathetic portraits of characters like Hester Prynne and Zenobia who transgress the true woman's sphere, Hawthorne quite frequently expressed the utmost concern with maintaining strictly distinct gendered spheres. In his most explicit statement, Hawthorne argued that the only truly proper sphere for woman was "at man's side. . . . as sympathizer; the unreserved, unquestioning believer." He continues: "All the separate action of woman is, and ever has been, and ever shall be, false, foolish, vain, destructive of her own best and holiest qualities, void of every good effect, and productive of intolerable mischief! . . . woman is a monster . . . without man as her acknowledged principal! . . . if there were a chance of their attaining the end which these petticoated monstrosities have in view, I would call upon my own sex to use its physical force, that unmistakable evidence of sovereignty, to scourge them back within their proper bounds!" ("Nathaniel Hawthorne on Woman's Rights," *The Home Journal*, 15 October 1853, *American Transcendental Quarterly* 2 [1969]: 31).

33 Letter to William D. Ticknor, 19 January 1855, in *Letters, 1853–1856* 304.

34 Letter to William D. Ticknor, 2 February 1855, in *Letters, 1853–1856* 307–8. Similarly, a year earlier, Hawthorne had praised Julia Ward Howe's first volume of poetry: "Those are admirable poems of Mrs. Howe's, but the devil must be in the woman to publish them. . . . What a strange propensity it is in these scribbling women to make a show of their hearts, as well as their heads, upon your counter, for anybody to pry into that chooses" (Letter to William D. Ticknor, 17 February 1854, in *Letters, 1853–1856* 177). For women writers to garner Hawthorne's praise, in other words, they had to transgress the limits of true womanhood and expose themselves, as Hepzibah does in *Seven Gables*, to the prying eyes of the marketplace; they had to become like men. That is precisely how Fanny Fern was often read—"If Fanny Fern were a man . . . *Ruth Hall* would be a natural and excusable book. But we confess that we cannot understand how a delicate, suffering woman can hunt down even her persecutors so remorselessly" (quoted in Joyce W. Warren, ed., Fanny Fern, *Ruth Hall and Other Writings* [New Brunswick, N.J.: Rutgers UP, 1986] ix). Further references will be to this edition.

35 Nathaniel Hawthorne, letter to Horatio Bridge, 4 February 1850, in *Letters, 1843–1853*, eds. Thomas Woodson, L. Neale Smith, and Norman Holmes Pearson, vol. 16 of *The Centenary Edition of the Works of Nathaniel Hawthorne*, gen. eds. William Charvat, Roy Harvey Pearce, and Claude M. Simpson (Columbus: Ohio State UP, 1985) 312.

36 Fanny Fern, *Ruth Hall* 166. Earlier in the novel, she pokes fun at other critics who identified more blunt writing with men—some argued "Floy" (the autobiographical Ruth's pseudonym) was "a man, because she had the courage to call things by their right names" (133).

37 Fanny Fern, "Leaves of Grass," *Ruth Hall and Other Writings* 274. See also

her reply to the comment that "Mrs. Stowe's *Uncle Tom* is too graphic ever to have been written by a *woman*" (255).

38 Margaret Fuller, *Woman in the Nineteenth Century* (1845), *The Portable Margaret Fuller*, ed. Mary Kelley (New York: Penguin, 1994) 293. Throughout her writings, Fuller ascribes the poetic to the feminine: "Wherever the poet or artist gave free course to his genius, he saw the truth, and expressed it in worthy forms, for these men especially share and need the feminine principle" (*Woman* 327).

39 Margaret Fuller, *Woman in the Nineteenth Century* 246–47.

40 *Memoirs of Margaret Fuller Ossoli* (Boston: Phillips, Sampson, and Company 1852) 1: 296–97.

41 "American Literature; Its Position in the Present Time, and Prospects for the Future," *Papers on Literature and Art*, part 2 (New York: Wiley and Putnam, 1846) 130–31; quoted in Thomas Wentworth Higginson, *Margaret Fuller Ossoli* (1884; New York: Chelsea House, 1981) 188.

42 As Ann Douglas puts it, Fuller disavows "fiction for history, the realm of 'feminine' fantasy for the realm of 'masculine' reality. She recognized, moreover, that such an opposition reflected culturally imposed polarities which she disdained, although she did not always have the energy or the resources to define, or redefine, her terms adequately" (*The Feminization of American Culture* [New York: Doubleday, 1977] 262). In *Woman in the Nineteenth Century*, Fuller does cite the sentimental novelists, especially Catherine Maria Sedgwick, when she argues that "Another sign of the times is furnished by the triumphs of female authorship" (280). Yet she implicitly opposes herself to sentimentalism when she states that "Mrs. Jameson is a sentimentalist, and, therefore, suits us ill in some respects" (302). In fact, throughout her letters and occasionally in her essays, Fuller dismisses sentimentality, even as she realizes that she may become sentimental herself at times: "Sentimentality is what I most detest, yet I may, unconsciously exhibit it" (Letter to James F. Clarke, 13 May 1838, *The Letters of Margaret Fuller*, ed. Robert N. Hudspeth, 6 vols. [Ithaca, N.Y.: Cornell UP, 1983–1994] 6:304); see also her letters to Amelia Greenwood, 1:163–65, and Almira Barlow, 1:170–72, where she mocks sentimental style).

As Lora Romero points out, we need to avoid repeating Fuller's and Melville's oversimplifying binaries in defining sentimentalism. See Lora Romero, *Home Fronts: Domesticity and its Critics in the Antebellum United States* (Durham, N.C.: Duke UP, 1997) 1–10. Not only were women like Margaret Fuller and Fanny Fern seen as writing like men (or the devil), but, as Laura McCall has shown, nearly all antebellum authors, both male and female, wrote about and celebrated the domestic sphere. See Laura McCall, "'Not So Wild a Dream': The Domestic Fantasies of Literary Men and Women, 1820–1860," in *A Shared Experience* 176–94. My interest here is not so much with defining sentimentalism and domesticity more properly as with how the gendered, critical binaries invoked by Melville, Fuller, and others worked to make the idea of literary manhood comprehensible.

43 As Eve Kosofsky Sedgwick insists, "when something is about masculinity, it is not always 'about men'" ("Gosh, Boy George, You Must Be Awfully Secure In Your Masculinity," in *Constructing Masculinity* 12). As Derrick argues, manhood became a way of defining and striving for "the cultural authority of achieved authorship" (1), a way, I contend, not always directly tied to male bodies. Along these lines, Gillian Brown's and Michael Newbury's descriptions of models of "literary individualism" and "romantic authorship" constructed in opposition to a sentimental version of authorship successfully capture the gender fluidity of these categories. See Gillian Brown, *Domestic Individualism* 145. As Newbury puts it, "The final truth about both the sentimental (female) and romantic (male) authors of the mid-nineteenth century is that they work through and construct middle-class authorship upon a relatively narrow field of class similarity as much as upon gender difference" (*Figuring Authorship* 28). I do not disagree with either Brown's or Newbury's "no more separate spheres" arguments; I simply want to insist on the ways that gendered literary categories operated even as they were transgressed. Thus, I will use the term "American literary manhood" to emphasize the importance of gender to these definitions of authorship.

44 *Manifesto of the Communist Party, The Marx-Engels Reader*, 2d ed., ed. Robert C. Tucker (New York: Norton, 1978) 475–76.

45 Phillip Barrish similarly uses "the genuine article" to refer to a kind of ethnic authenticity that grants one an amount of cultural capital; see Phillip Barrish, "'The Genuine Article': Ethnicity, Capital, and *The Rise of David Levinsky*," *American Literary History* 5.4 (winter 1993): 643–62. Miles Orvell's notion of "the real thing" similarly conjures the relationship between the market and ideas of the real or genuine in American culture at the turn of the century. Orvell allows that a "tension between imitation and authenticity is a primary category in American civilization" (xv), but stresses the ways in which this tension became more prominent as commodity culture began to dominate United States culture more completely at the beginning of the twentieth century. Orvell may have a point about the intensification of this desire for authenticity, but, as I hope to show, a rhetoric of racial and gender authenticity ran through defenses and definitions of antebellum mass culture and literary manhood. See Miles Orvell, *The Real Thing: Imitation and Authenticity in American Culture, 1880–1940* (Chapel Hill: U of North Carolina P, 1989).

46 Margaret Fuller, "Entertainments of the Past Winter," *Dial* 3.1 (July 1842): 52.

47 Margaret Fuller, review of *Narrative of the Life of Frederick Douglass* (1845), *The Portable Margaret Fuller*, ed. Mary Kelley (New York: Penguin 1994) 379.

48 James K. Kennard Jr., "Who Are Our National Poets?" *Knickerbocker* 26.4 (October 1845): 332.

49 This point, in slightly different form, is one of Lott's key insights. Both Anthony Appiah and Walter Benn Michaels have described how this tension is at play in biological (essentializing) and cultural (supposedly nonessentializing) understandings of race and how these two logics are mutually constitutive in twentieth-century texts. See Anthony Appiah, "The Uncompleted Argument: Du Bois and the Illusion of Race," *Critical Inquiry* 12.1 (autumn 1985): 21–37, and Walter Benn Michaels, *Our America: Nativism, Modernism, and Pluralism* (Durham, N.C.: Duke UP, 1995).

50 George G. Foster, *New York by Gas-Light and Other Urban Sketches by George G. Foster*, ed. Stuart M. Blumin (Berkeley: U of California P, 1990) 70–72.

Prologue

1 James Fenimore Cooper, *The Last of the Mohicans; A Narrative of 1757* (1826; Albany: State University of New York Press, 1983) 1. All further citations will be to this edition and will be made parenthetically.

2 Several critics have commented on the role of gender in this preface. See especially Shirley Samuels, "Generation Through Violence: Cooper and the Making of Americans," *New Essays on* The Last of the Mohicans, ed. Daniel Peck (Cambridge: Cambridge UP, 1992) 87–114. Throughout his oeuvre, Cooper portrays the clergy as effeminate or duplicitous, as is apparent with David Gamut in *Mohicans*. And, as Ann Douglas has argued, in mid-century American culture generally, the clergy were increasingly seen in emasculated terms. See Ann Douglas, *The Feminization of American Culture* (New York: Doubleday, 1977). As James Wallace argues, Cooper's prefatory gender segregation begins to appear after the publication of the first Leatherstocking Tale, *The Pioneers* (1823): "By the time he published *The Pilot* in 1823, Cooper was ready to abandon women readers altogether" (James D. Wallace, *Early Cooper and His Audience* [New York: Columbia UP, 1986] 87). In the preface to his first historical novel, *The Spy*, he begins to describe his work as more realistic than feminine tastes desire, even as he acknowledges that it is female readers "by whose opinion it is that we expect to stand or fall" (James Fenimore Cooper, *The Spy, A Tale of the Neutral Ground* [1821; Oxford: Oxford UP, 1968] 2–3).

3 This attempt at masculinizing writing, as Nina Baym has argued, came in part as a reaction to Lydia Maria Child's covert use of Indian stories/historical fiction for the critique of gender ideologies in *Hobomok* (1824) (Nina

Baym, "Putting Women in Their Place: *The Last of the Mohicans* and Other Indian Stories," *Feminism and American Literary History: Essays* [New Brunswick, N.J.: Rutgers UP, 1992] 19–35). Importantly, while frontier romances of the period written by women—most notably Child's *Hobomok* and Catharine Sedgwick's *Hope Leslie* (1827)—provided important correctives to the racism and masculinism of Cooper's and other male writers' work, they similarly construct Anglo-American heroes and heroines in opposition to a Puritan restraint by having them take on Indian traits or take the place of Indian characters. Both Child's and Sedgwick's novels use the independent nobility of Indian characters to criticize the stultifying Puritan culture, allowing their heroines and heroes to escape limited gender constructions by learning from the Indians. And in the end, like *Last of the Mohicans*, both novels dismiss their Indian characters from the American landscape after using them to criticize gender conventions.

4 See especially Cathy Davidson's *Revolution and the Word: The Rise of the Novel in America* (New York: Oxford UP, 1986).

5 See William Charvat, *The Profession of Authorship in America, 1800–1870*, ed. Matthew J. Bruccoli (1968; New York: Columbia UP, 1992) 19. See also Michael T. Gilmore, "The Book Marketplace I," *The Columbia History of the American Novel*, gen. ed., Emory Elliott (New York: Columbia UP, 1991) 46–71, for an overview of the gendering of genres in relation to the antebellum market for books.

6 See Wallace, *Early Cooper* 85.

7 As the novel progresses, Hawk-Eye repeatedly reminds Heyward and the reader that "The rules you find in books" (204) will not be enough to secure their safety in the wilderness, that "no bookish knowledge would carry [them] through harmless," and that instead they must "undertake [their] work like men, and not like babbling women, or eager boys" (189). According to Lora Romero, Cooper's culture imagined "that civilization necessarily spells the end of archaic [balanced] proportions" (394) and thus that "only in boyhood and savagery is there an equilibrium of body (what we can get) and mind (what we want)" (395). Romero's reading and mine have much in common; however, I am interested in how Cooper (and his culture) imagined the Indian body as an alternative to new market relations and how Heyward—a figure whom she never mentions—serves as a way of negotiating these problems. See "Vanishing Americans: Gender, Empire, and New Historicism," *American Literature* 63.3 (September 1991): 385–404.

8 In the text itself, as Steven Blakemore has pointed out, Cooper describes the reality of Indian warfare and the physical dangers of the wilderness in terms of a Burkean masculine sublime, thus delimiting American literature as a distinctly male province opposed to the civilized beauty and restraints of the drawing room. See Steven Blakemore, " 'Without a Cross': The Cultural

Significance of the Sublime and Beautiful in Cooper's *The Last of the Mohicans*," *Nineteenth-Century Literature* 52.1 (June 1997): 27–57.

In his preface to *The Spy* (1821), his first novel focusing on American materials, Cooper worries that "although the English critics not only desire, but invite works that will give an account of American manners, we are sadly afraid they mean nothing but Indian manners; we are apprehensive that the same palate which can relish the cave scene in Edgar Huntly, because it contains an American, a savage, a wild cat, and a tomahawk . . . will revolt at descriptions here, that pourtray love as any thing but a brutal passion—patriotism as more than money-making—or men and women without wool" (1–2). By the time he was writing *Mohicans*, Cooper clearly had decided to identify American manners with Indian manners, but takes care to make sure the two categories do not collapse upon one another completely. For a reading of the racial politics involved in the preface to *The Spy*, see Jared Gardner, "Cooper's Vanishing American Act," *Master Plots: Race and the Founding of an American Literature, 1787–1845* (Baltimore, Md.: Johns Hopkins UP, 1998) 81–124.

9   Washington Irving, "Traits of Indian Character," *The Sketch Book of Geoffrey Crayon, Gent.* (1819–1820; New York: Penguin, 1978) 226.

10   Washington Irving, "Traits of Indian Character" 226–27; Washington Irving, "Philip of Pokanoket, An Indian Memoir," *The Sketch Book of Geoffrey Crayon, Gent.* 234. Another early expression of this desire to become "red" as a way of escaping, in part, the entanglements of a trans-Atlantic economy comes in J. Hector St. John de Crèvecoeur's last letter in *Letters from an American Farmer* (1782).

11   Elsewhere, Cooper explicitly speaks of his books as "mere articles of trade" (Letter to Henry Colburn, 17 October 1826, in *The Letters and Journals of James Fenimore Cooper*, vol. 1, 1800–1830, ed. James Franklin Beard [Cambridge: Belknap/Harvard, 1960] 165). In his preface to *The Pioneers* (1823), he was equally explicit about the importance of market success to his idea of democratic authorship, stating that if he meets his publisher "with a smiling face" he "shall at once know that all is essentially well" (*The Pioneers, or the Sources of the Susquehanna; A Descriptive Tale* [1823; Albany: State University of New York Press, 1980] 5).

12   Quoted in Wallace, *Early Cooper* 121, 123.

13   Heyward's status as cultivated and literate, yet adventurous and courageous, clearly identifies him with those men whom Cooper imagines as the natural cultural and political leaders of the nation. At least one review from 1826 essentially places the reader in Heyward's position as companion of Hawk-Eye and the Mohicans: "We swim rivers, navigate cataracts, recognise the marks of the desert, climb mountains, and penetrate fogs and armies, as easily . . . as did Hawk-Eye and the natives, whom we accompany in their

perils" (review of *The Last of the Mohicans*, by James Fenimore Cooper, *New-York Review and Atheneum* [March 1826], *Fenimore Cooper: The Critical Heritage*, ed. George Dekker and John P. McWilliams [London: Routledge and Kegan Paul, 1973] 90). As Nina Baym notes, the "only mind entered regularly is Duncan Heyward's"; he "functions in the novel as the reader's surrogate, the position from which readers would view the action if they were *in* the action" (26). Furthermore, the novel implicitly identifies Heyward with George Washington. Immediately before Heyward first enters the narrative, Cooper footnotes Washington's exploits in the French and Indian War (13), and, like Washington, Heyward comes from the South and must practice Indian warfare techniques to save the soon-to-be nation. Michael Butler argues that *Mohicans* is about "the decline of both Indian and European on the continent, and the consequent creation and rise of the American" (118), specifically in the character of Duncan Heyward, who "transforms himself from a dependent Anglo-American to a self-reliant American" (132). See Michael Butler, "Narrative Structure and Historical Process in *The Last of the Mohicans*," *American Literature* 48.2 (May 1976): 117–39.

14 See also 64, 132, 200, 213, 330, 336.

15 In this way, *Mohicans* restages the logic of substitution presented in the first Leatherstocking novel *The Pioneers* (1823). There, the aristocratic Oliver Effingham passes as the mixed-blood and lower-class Oliver Edwards in order to reclaim his inheritance and suture his claims to the land to its original inhabitants. By becoming Indian-like, without becoming too much like Hawk-Eye, Cooper's upper-class heroes lay claim to American property and to an American manhood. David Leverenz has placed Natty Bumppo at the beginning of a long line of last real men in American culture. See his "The Last Real Man in America: From Natty Bumppo to Batman," *American Literary History* 3.4 (winter 1991): 753–81. His reading helps to locate Natty's exemplary manhood in a long historical narrative of manhood; my focus on Heyward—a character who returns to the settlements—enables an investigation of Cooper's attempt to negotiate a new type of manhood, not simply lament an older form's passing.

16 While Hawk-Eye openly admires Indian culture and lifeways and educates Heyward (and Cooper's readers) in becoming more Indian-like, he makes recourse again and again to the difference between "the gift and natur of an Indian" (138) and those of white men. Jane Tompkins reads *Mohicans* "as a meditation on *kinds*, and more specifically, as an attempt to calculate exactly how much violation or mixing of its fundamental categories a society can bear" (*Sensational Designs: The Cultural Work of American Fiction, 1790–1860* [New York: Oxford UP, 1985] 106). My concern is more with the desire to cross these boundaries and the importance of crossing these boundaries in establishing other fundamental categories—specifically crossing racial and class distinctions in order to draw gender distinctions more firmly.

17 As Richard Butsch puts it, the theater of the 1820s was "a preserve of men of
    all classes" (Richard Butsch, "Bowery B'hoys and Matinee Ladies: The Re-
    Gendering of Nineteenth-Century American Theater Audiences," *American
    Quarterly* 46.3 [September 1994]: 378). Cooper had a long-standing relation-
    ship with the theater—as indicated by William Dunlap's dedication of his
    History of the American Theatre (1832) to him and by Cooper's own unsuc-
    cessful comedy of manners, *Upside Down, or Philosophy in Petticoats* (1850)—
    and throughout *Mohicans* he makes explicit (the recurring use of the vocab-
    ulary of "scenes," "players," and "actors," the Shakespearean epigraphs) and
    implicit references to the theater. In the 1820s, Dunlap produced a stage
    version of Cooper's first successful novel *The Spy* (Rosemarie K. Bank, *The-
    atre Culture in America, 1825–1860* [Cambridge: Cambridge UP, 1997] 36)
    and included a cameo appearance of Leatherstocking in his play *A Trip to
    Niagara, or Travellers in America* (1828). See their correspondence in Coo-
    per's letters and journals and Dunlap's references to their almost daily con-
    versations in *Diary of William Dunlap (1766–1839): The Memoirs of a Dra-
    matist, Theatrical Manager, Painter, Critic, Novelist, and Historian* (New
    York: The New York Historical Society, 1931). Almost every one of Cooper's
    novels was staged (see Wallace, *Early Cooper* 180), and in one of his other
    historical romances about colonial Indian warfare, *The Wept of Wish-Ton-
    Wish* (1829), set during King Philip's War, Cooper most explicitly links his
    fiction with dramatic technique: "If the pen of the compiler, like that we
    wield, possessed the mechanical power of the stage, it would be easy to shift
    the scenes of this legend as rapidly and effectively as is required for its right
    understanding, and for the proper maintenance of its interest. That which
    cannot be done with the magical aid of machinery must be attempted by less
    ambitious, and we fear by far less efficacious means" (*The Wept of Wish-Ton-
    Wish* [1829; New York: Putnam, 1896] 226). Cooper may specifically be
    referring to the widespread use of panoramas in the theater of the period,
    such as in Dunlap's *A Trip to Niagara*.
18 "American Drama," *American Quarterly Review* 1.2 (June 1827): 332–33.
    Further citations in this paragraph are from these two pages.
19 At its height, Indian melodrama dominated dramatic writing in the United
    States; between 1800 and 1859, American dramatists wrote at least one hun-
    dred and twenty plays with Indian themes and characters (Eugene H. Jones,
    Native Americans as Shown on the Stage, 1753–1916 [Metuchen, N.J.: Scare-
    crow, 1988] 84). Most of these plays fall into two categories—Pocahontas
    plays and Noble Savage plays. The Pocahontas plays, generally, allowed the
    possibility of cross-racial marriage and said less about the "fate" of the
    Indians, while Noble Savage dramas usually offered no possibility of cross-
    racial marriage and decried the Indian's fate while staging it as inevitable.
    For more on Indian drama see Jones; Richard E. Amacher, "Behind the
    Curtain with the Noble Savage: Stage Management of Indian Plays, 1825–

1860," *Theatre Survey* 7.2 (November 1966): 101–14; Marilyn J. Anderson, "The Image of the Indian in American Drama During the Jacksonian Era, 1829–1845," *Journal of American Culture* 1.4 (winter 1978): 800–810; Rosemarie K. Bank, "Staging the 'Native': Making History in American Theatre Culture, 1828–1838," *Theatre Journal* 45.4 (December 1993): 461–86; L. M. Eich, "The American Indian Plays," *The Quarterly Journal of Speech* 30.2 (April 1944): 212–15; Susan Scheckel, "Domesticating the Drama of Conquest: Pocahontas on the Popular Stage," *The Insistence of the Indian: Race and Nationalism in Nineteenth-Century American Culture* (Princeton: Princeton UP, 1998) 41–69; Priscilla Sears, *A Pillar of Fire to Follow: American Indian Dramas, 1808–1859* (Bowling Green, Ohio: Bowling Green University Popular Press, 1982); and Werner Sollors, "Romantic Love, Arranged Marriage, and Indian Melancholy," *Beyond Ethnicity: Consent and Descent in American Culture* (New York: Oxford UP, 1986) 102–30. The best commentaries on *Metamora* are Bruce McConachie, "Theatre of Yeoman Independence for Jacksonians, 1830–1855," *Melodramatic Formations: American Theatre and Society, 1820–1870* (Iowa City: U of Iowa P, 1992) 65–156; Jeffrey D. Mason, "*Metamora* (1829) and the 'Indian' Question," *Melodrama and the Myth of America* (Bloomington: Indiana UP, 1993) 23–59; Theresa Strouth Gaul, "'The Genuine Indian Who Was Brought Upon the Stage': Edwin Forrest's *Metamora* and White Audiences," *Arizona Quarterly* 56.1 (spring 2000): 1–27; and Jill Lepore, "The Curse of Metamora," *The Name of War: King Philip's War and the Origins of American Identity* (New York: Knopf, 1998) 191–226. For the classic overview of melodrama in the United States during the period, see David Grimsted, *Melodrama Unveiled: American Theater and Culture, 1800–1850* (Chicago: U of Chicago P, 1968).

20 John Augustus Stone, *Metamora, or the Last of the Wampanoags* (1829), *Dramas from the American Theatre, 1762–1909*, ed. Richard Moody (Cleveland, Ohio: World Publishing Co., 1966) 207. Further references will be to this edition and will be given parenthetically.

21 Gabriel Harrison, *Edwin Forrest: The Actor and the Man* (Brooklyn: Brooklyn Eagle Press, 1889) 37; William Rounseville Alger, *Life of Edwin Forrest, The American Tragedian* (Philadelphia: J. B. Lippincott and Co., 1877) 239, 240.

22 From the first performance of *Metamora*, Forrest became increasingly identified with the role. As he toured the nation for the next forty years, *Metamora* became the cornerstone of his repertoire; he usually performed it at least once in every town and at least once in New York each season. Jones estimates that Forrest played Metamora two hundred times over forty years (*Native Americans* 66), while McConachie posits that by 1855, over a million Americans had seen Forrest perform (*Melodramatic Formations* 77). As B. Donald Grose puts it, "Forrest's later successes as Jack Cade, Spartacus, and

King Lear were extensions of his stage Indian, Metamora transplanted to another time and place, but still the proud, doomed individual" ("Edwin Forrest, *Metamora*, and the Indian Removal Act of 1830," *Theatre Journal* [May 1985]: 185).

23   In 1834, Cooper helped to arrange a farewell dinner on Forrest's behalf before he embarked on his first European tour, and Montrose Moses claims that the two were friends (*The Fabulous Forrest: The Record of an American Actor* [Boston: Little, Brown, 1929] 24). A letter from 1846, however, seems to indicate that, despite being on the arrangements committee for the 1834 dinner and clearly admiring him, Cooper did not know Forrest personally: "I never saw Mr. Forrest but twice, and each time he was on the stage, and in the character of Othello. I certainly thought him a great actor, and I agree with you fully in thinking him entitled to receive all merited distinction from his countrymen. My mind has long been made up to attend no more public dinners. . . . Messrs. Forrest, Hackett and Placide, as Americans who have raised an honorable art to something near its just estimation, are each and all entitled to our consideration, and from certain peculiarities connected with ancient prejudices, probably possess more claims on us for public manifestations of our respect than men of almost any other class. The artist of any sort, or the literary man, has a hard time in this country, at the best; but it requires a great deal of moral courage, as well as rare talent, for an American to make such a reputation as that enjoyed by Mr. Forrest, in his particular branch of intellectual effort" (letter dated 15 October 1846, *The Letters and Journals of James Fenimore Cooper*, ed. James Franklin Beard, vol. 5, 1845–1849 [Cambridge: Harvard UP, 1968] 172–73). In this letter, Cooper suggests Forrest as deserving of the kind of cultural authority and respect he himself desired.

24   McConachie, *Melodramatic Formations* 157. See also Bank, *Theatre Culture in America*, and Peter G. Buckley, "To the Opera House."

25   As McConachie puts it, "Elite hegemony in theatres in the 1820s depended upon attendance from 'the people'" (*Melodramatic Formations* 61–62).

26   See Alan Leander MacGregor, "Tammany: The Indian as Rhetorical Surrogate," *American Quarterly* 35.4 (fall 1983): 391–405, for a fuller discussion of how the Indian was used to figure political order and authority in the early republic.

27   While, as numerous critics have noted, the image of the noble savage that Forrest and Cooper helped to produce provided a vehicle for exculpating white blame for Indian removal (see Grose and Mason, for example, on Forrest), it also provided, through its celebration of Indian manliness, a possible site for voicing opposition to Euro-American expansion. Critics of eastern Indian removal were able to draw on and reconfigure the noble savage in articulating a more truly oppositional position. For example, both

the Sauk leader Black Hawk and Pequot missionary William Apess drew on this representational tradition in 1830s texts. The figure of the noble savage that Cooper and Forrest participated in creating—and the type of identification they imagined—provided Apess, Black Hawk, and others with ways of calling for a universal *manhood* in which Indians and whites could coexist. Cooper's text and Forrest's performances depend on imagining the possibility of such brotherhood and then dismissing it; as I will explore at more length in chapter 2, however, this possibility, through the construction of Indianness as authentic manhood, could also be refigured so as to enunciate alternative, possibly oppositional, strategies and identities.

28 For more on Forrest's development as a type of protocapitalist exploitation of intellectual labor, see McConachie, *Melodramatic Formations*, chapters 3 and 4.

29 See Bank's prologue in *Theatre Culture* on "universal spaces." The following paragraphs are indebted to Bank, Buckley, Butsch, and McConachie. Although they have important differences, they provide a fairly similar narrative of the changing class and gender dynamics of commercial amusements in antebellum America.

30 When the Englishman William Macready, with whom Forrest had had a standing feud, tried to play Macbeth at the more elite Astor Place the same night as Forrest performed the role at the more democratic Broadway, Forrest's supporters forcibly made Macready stop his performance. Protests against this encroachment on the arts were rearticulated by Forrest's fans as aristocratic and anti-American. Later that week, when Macready, convinced by a petition signed by Washington Irving, M. M. Noah, and Herman Melville among others, attempted to perform again, the mob of Forrest supporters, whipped up by a week of newspaper commentary, were met by military troops. When the expected confrontation occurred, thirty-one men were killed and another forty-eight injured. The riot all but brought to an end the masculine theater culture on which Forrest's career had depended. For Cooper's reactions to the riot—he just happened to be visiting New York City at the time—see *The Letters and Journals of James Fenimore Cooper*, vol. 6, 1849–1851, ed. James Franklin Beard (Cambridge: Harvard UP, 1968) 39–46. For more on the riot and its effects, see Buckley, "To the Opera House," Richard Moody, *The Astor Place Riot* (Bloomington: U of Indiana P, 1958), and Bruce A. McConachie, " 'The Theatre of the Mob': Apocalyptic Melodrama and Preindustrial Riots in Antebellum New York," in *Theatre for Working-Class Audiences in the United States, 1830–1980*, ed. Bruce A. McConachie and Daniel Friedman (Westport, Conn.: Greenwood Press, 1985) 17–46.

31 Buckley, "To the Opera House" 31.

32 Bank, *Theatre Culture in America* 128.

33 William Alcott, *The Young Man's Guide*, 12th ed. (1833; Boston: Perkins and

Marvin, 1838) 177. Alcott then goes on to give an anecdote to prove his point. In 1831, a young journeyman printer recently immigrated to the city from Kentucky was hired by Alcott's source. Before too long, "he expressed a desire to go to the theatre. Some great actor was to perform on a certain night, and he was very anxious to see him" (180). There is no indication that this actor is Forrest, but given the setting and the background of the employee, it is easy to suppose that it is. His employer warns him of the dangers and consequences, but the young worker goes anyway. He subsequently neglects his work, is fired by his employer, and can no longer hold any job because of his bad habits. Because of his destitute situation, he is forced to join the army as a common soldier, where he is called upon to "defend our citizens from the attacks of Indians." But when cholera hits the troops, the fallen printer is among the first to desert. (This military engagement was most likely the Black Hawk War; a large portion of the United States troops transported to Illinois never saw action against Black Hawk's small band of Sauks because of rampant cholera.) He is subsequently arrested on theft charges, and together with completing his military service and punishment for desertion—all because he went to the theater—he lost "six of the most valuable years of his life" (182). In Alcott's narrative, then, the young male, by giving into the pleasures of the theater, becomes enfeebled and unable to perform his manly duties against the always manly Natives.

34 As McConachie points out, the height of Forrest's popularity occurred during the rise of the bourgeois power (1835–1855), but declined as the bourgeoisie achieved dominance (*Melodramatic Formations* 70), and as Buckley notes, Forrest's "preoccupation with his own declining powers contributed, in some measure, to the fervor of anti-Macready sentiment" ("To the Opera House" 399). McConachie and Buckley provide the fullest treatment of Forrest's relationship to the Bowery.

35 "Dramatic Literature," *American Quarterly Review* 8.15 (September 1830): 145.

36 Sally L. Jones, "The First But Not the Last of the 'Vanishing Indians': Edwin Forrest and Mythic Recreations of the Native Population," in *Dressing in Feathers: The Construction of the Indian in American Popular Culture*, ed. S. Elizabeth Bird (Boulder, Colo.: Westview, 1996) 22. This inauthenticity is underlined by the fact that increasingly any new Indian plays were burlesques of the kind of Indian manliness that Forrest's performances foregrounded. Most famously in John Brougham's *Metamora; or, The Last of the Pollywogs* (1847) and *Po-Ca-Hon-Tas, or, The Gentle Savage* (1855), the whole genre of Indian melodrama that had grown up around Forrest's most famous play was derided and refunctioned into a vehicle for more explicitly commenting on fashions and scandals of the day and satirizing Forrest's acting style and audiences.

37 Wallace, *Early Cooper* 176, Charvat 77.

38 Charvat, *Profession of Authorship* 69.

39 Ibid. 83.

40 See MacGregor, "Tammany," for a discussion of the transformation from Indian to Injin in Cooper's work.

41 See especially Butsch, "Bowery B'hoys and Matinee Ladies," but also Mc-Conachie, *Melodramatic Formations* 8–9.

42 McConachie, *Melodramatic Formations* xiii.

43 Barnum's achievement, as Buckley notes, is that he "managed to house on a single site, forms of exhibition and amusement that had previously belonged to different areas of the city and that had catered to markedly different 'tastes' " ("To the Opera House" 495).

44 See Bank, *Theatre Culture in America*, 35, for example, on the changes exemplifed by Henry Ward Beecher's reversal in an 1848 lecture.

45 McConachie, *Melodramatic Formations* 68.

1. "De Genewine Artekil": William Wells Brown,
Blackface Minstrelsy, and Abolitionism

1 I take the term and idea of the "professional fugitive"—as a way of designating those former slaves who supported themselves through abolitionist activity—from Larry Gara, "The Professional Fugitive in the Abolition Movement," *Wisconsin Magazine of History* 48 (spring 1965): 196–204. The best overall study of black abolitionists is still Benjamin Quarles's *Black Abolitionists* (New York: Oxford UP, 1969). For a general history of free blacks in the antebellum North, see Leon F. Litwack, *North of Slavery: The Negro in the Free States, 1790–1860* (Chicago: U of Chicago P, 1961).

2 William Edward Farrison, *William Wells Brown: Author and Reformer* (Chicago: U of Chicago P, 1969) 277–80.

3 Brown titled this song "A Song for Freedom" in his *The Anti-Slavery Harp: A Collection of Songs For Anti-Slavery Meetings* (Boston: Bela Marsh, 1848) 37–38. This volume compiles a range of abolitionist songs (only a few of which Brown wrote), including "Get off the Track," set to "Dan Tucker" (25–26) and, in later editions, "The North Star" set to "O, Susannah" (William W. Brown, *The Anti-Slavery Harp; A Collection of Songs*, 4th ed. [Boston: Bela Marsh, 1854] 9–10). For the fullest discussion of "Dandy Jim," one which underscores the importance of masculinity in minstrelsy, see William J. Mahar, *Behind the Burnt Cork Mask: Early Blackface Minstrelsy and Antebellum American Popular Culture* (Urbana: U of Illinois P, 1999) 208–28.

4 William Wells Brown, *The Escape; or, A Leap for Freedom* (1858), in *Black Theater, U.S.A.: Forty-Five Plays by Black Americans, 1847–1974*, ed. James V. Hatch (New York: Free Press, 1974) 47. Further references will be to this

edition and will be given parenthetically. The best discussion of *The Escape* comes in John Ernest's "The Reconstruction of Whiteness: William Wells Brown's *The Escape; or; A Leap for Freedom*," *PMLA* 113.5 (October 1998): 1108–21. Ernest's and my arguments converge at many points, primarily in our contention that "Brown attempts to force white northerners to confront themselves *as* white northerners whose identity, collective and individual, is contingent on the reciprocal performances of many other members of the national community" (1113).

5 Quoted in Farrison, *William Wells Brown* 281.

6 As Robert Toll and numerous other historians have noted, minstrelsy "swept the nation in the 1840's," becoming the "most popular entertainment form in the country" and the "first American popular entertainment form to become a national institution" (Robert C. Toll, *Blacking Up: The Minstrel Show in Nineteenth-Century America* [New York: Oxford UP, 1974] v, vi). I discuss the recent historiography of minstrelsy below.

7 Frederick Douglass, *My Bondage and My Freedom* (1855; New York: Arno, 1969) 362.

8 Quoted in Farrison, *William Wells Brown* 294.

9 Brown's construction of race as performance prefigures later formulations of black racial consciousness as a matter of double-consciousness (W. E. B. Du Bois, *The Souls of Black Folk* [1903]) and as a matter of masquerade (Frantz Fanon, *Black Skin, White Masks* [*Peau Noire, Masques Blancs*, 1952]). For a reading of Du Bois that has influenced my understanding of the relationship between cultural (or sociohistorical) and biological understandings of race, see Anthony Appiah, "The Uncompleted Argument: Du Bois and the Illusion of Race," *Critical Inquiry* 12 (autumn 1985): 21–37.

10 Much recent attention has been paid to representations of black manhood. For other considerations of manhood and antebellum black authors, see, in particular, Richard Yarborough, "Race, Violence, and Manhood: The Masculine Ideal in Frederick Douglass's 'The Heroic Slave,'" in *Frederick Douglass: New Literary and Historical Essays*, ed. Eric J. Sundquist (New York: Cambridge UP, 1990) 166–88; and Maurice Wallace, "'Are We Men?': Prince Hall, Martin Delany, and the Masculine Ideal in Black Freemasonry, 1775–1865," *American Literary History* 9.3 (fall 1997): 396–421. More generally, see R. J. Young, *Antebellum Black Activists: Race, Gender, and Self* (New York: Garland, 1996); Joan E. Cashin, "A Northwest Passage: Gender, Race, and the Family in the Early Nineteenth Century," in *A Shared Experience: Men, Women, and the History of Gender*, eds. Laura McCall and Donald Yacovone (New York: New York UP, 1998) 222–44; Jim Cullen, "'I's a Man Now': Gender and African American Men," *Divided Houses: Gender and the Civil War*, ed. Catharine Clinton and Nina Silber (New York: Oxford UP, 1992) 76–91; and James Oliver Horton, "Freedom's Yoke: Gender Conven-

tions Among Antebellum Free Blacks," *Feminist Studies* 12.1 (spring 1986): 51–76. See also the essays collected in Marcellus Blount and George P. Cunningham, eds., *Representing Black Men* (New York: Routledge, 1996). For critiques of the continued emphasis on black men achieving or proving their acquisition of dominant models of manhood, see, in particular, Philip Brian Harper, *Are We Not Men?: Masculine Anxiety and the Problem of African-American Identity* (New York: Oxford UP, 1996) and Hazel V. Carby, *Race Men* (Cambridge: Harvard UP, 1998).

11 Eric Lott notes this historical conjunction and other connections between abolitionism and minstrelsy in *Love and Theft: Blackface Minstrelsy and the American Working Class* (New York: Oxford UP, 1993) 111. In his afterword, Lott moves toward investigating black appropriations of the minstrel show, citing Martin Delany's *Blake* (1859–1861) as a text that "devises a complex reinvention of the minstrel tradition" (236). My work attempts to complicate and expand Lott's theorization of the ambivalence of the minstrel show in the direction in which this brief discussion points. Lott's work, as I will expand upon below, heads a renewed interest in the minstrel show. Some of the most important readings of the minstrel show are collected in Annemarie Bean, James V. Hatch, Brooks McNamara, eds., *Inside the Minstrel Mask: Readings in Nineteenth-Century Blackface Minstrelsy* (Hanover, Conn.: Wesleyan UP / UP of New England, 1996). This work highlights the mutable and rapidly changing nature of blackface during this period. I will be focusing on the minstrel show as it became more mainstream—more middle-class—in the 1840s and 1850s; thus my comments should not be taken as holding true for blackface throughout the early nineteenth century, let alone the nineteenth or twentieth centuries more generally.

12 Letter from John A. Collins to William Lloyd Garrison, January 1842, quoted in Gara, "The Professional Fugitive" 196. See Theodore Dwight Weld, *American Slavery As It Is: Testimony of a Thousand Witnesses* (New York: American Anti-Slavery Society, 1839). Weld's record became one of the sources for Harriet Beecher Stowe's *Uncle Tom's Cabin* (1852) and reports an incident—a slave being drowned by a mob in New Orleans—that Brown claimed to have witnessed; see *Narrative of William Wells Brown, A Fugitive Slave, written by himself* (1847), in *Puttin' On Ole Massa*, ed. Gilbert Osofsky (New York: Harper and Row, 1969) 200–201. Further references will be to this edition and will be noted parenthetically as *N*.

13 The antebellum minstrel show was not primarily based on anything that could be called "authentically" African American. Rather it drew from conventions of representing Irish and frontier characters, popular Euro-American songs (already influenced by African American culture), *and* some elements of an already hybridized African American slave culture. The minstrel show became a place where elements of American culture already marked as

black or white (although, in both cases, already a mixture of African and European influences) came together and influenced one another. For one interesting case study of the way minstrelsy emerged through a constant play of cross-racial cultural appropriation, see Howard L. Sacks and Judith Rose Sacks, *Way Up North in Dixie: A Black Family's Claim to the Confederate Anthem* (Washington, D.C.: Smithsonian Institution Press, 1993).

14 "Editor's Table: Bowery Theatre," *Knickerbocker* 16 (July 1840): 84; advertisements quoted in Carl Wittke, *Tambo and Bones: A History of the American Minstrel Show* (Durham, N.C.: Duke UP, 1930) 37.

15 Both quoted in Gara, "The Professional Fugitive" 198.

16 Toll, *Blacking Up* 101.

17 In a letter to William Lloyd Garrison, dated 17 May 1853, which describes the fanfare accompanying Stowe's arrival in England and criticizes Stowe's husband for his reconciliatory rhetoric, Brown declared that "*Uncle Tom's Cabin* has come down upon the dark abodes of slavery like a morning's sunlight, unfolding to view its enormities in a manner which has fastened all eyes upon the 'peculiar institution,' and awakening sympathy in hearts that never before felt for the slave" (*The Black Abolitionist Papers*, vol. 1, *The British Isles, 1830–1865*, ed. C. Peter Ripley et al. [Chapel Hill: U of North Carolina P, 1985] 344). See Peter A. Dorsey, "De-authorizing Slavery: Realism in Stowe's *Uncle Tom's Cabin* and Brown's *Clotel*," *ESQ* 41 (winter 1995): 256–88, for a discussion of the intertextual borrowings of these two novels, and Robert S. Levine, "*Uncle Tom's Cabin* in *Frederick Douglass' Paper*: An Analysis of Reception," *American Literature* 64.1 (March 1992): 71–93, for a more general discussion of black abolitionists' responses to Stowe's novel.

18 Traditionally, the novel has been criticized for this fragmentary and episodic character. Of late, however, critics have begun to see the fragmentary nature of Brown's novel as giving him access to a more systemic critique of slavery. See, for example, M. Giulia Fabi, "The 'Unguarded Expressions of the Feelings of the Negroes': Gender, Slave Resistance, and William Wells Brown's Revisions of *Clotel*," *African American Review* 27 (winter 1993): 639–54; John Ernest, "The Profession of Authorship and the Cultural Text: William Wells Brown's *Clotel*," *Resistance and Reformation in Nineteenth-Century African-American Literature: Brown, Wilson, Jacobs, Delany, Douglass, and Harper* (Jackson: UP of Mississippi, 1995) 20–54; and Robert S. Levine, "'Whiskey, Blacking, and All': Temperance and Race in William Wells Brown's *Clotel*," in *The Serpent in the Cup: Temperance in American Literature*, ed. David S. Reynolds and Debra J. Rosenthal (Amherst: U of Massachusetts P, 1997) 93–114.

19 See, for example, Russ Castronovo, *Fathering the Nation: American Genealogies of Slavery and Freedom* (Berkeley: U of California P, 1995) 167, 211; Carla L. Peterson, "Capitalism, Black (Under)development, and the Production

of the African-American Novel in the 1850s," *American Literary History* 4 (winter 1992): 563; and William L. Andrews, "The Novelization of Voice in Early African American Narrative," *PMLA* 105 (January 1990): 23–34. Peterson argues that fiction "enabled [African American writers] to avoid the self-commodification of the slave narrative" (562), while I contend that it is by embracing the commodification of blackness in minstrelsy that Brown inscribes himself within the terms of literary manhood. Levine argues that "Given that whites tended to write the prefaces that authorized black texts, Brown in authorizing the 'Narrative' would have been putting on 'white-face'" ("'Whiskey, Blacking, and All'" 110, note 4). I argue that he then turns to minstrelsy to reinvoke his position as a *black* author. As Ernest puts it, "The problem was not only to expose the evils of slavery. . . . The problem was to reconfigure the terms of the cultural arguments about slavery, terms that implicitly either denied Brown's own authority or limited his voice to that of a witness" ("The Profession of Authorship" 47). Conversely, in a reading that otherwise has much in common with my own, Robert Reid-Pharr argues that *Clotel* is best understood *not* "as the seminal text of the Black American novelistic tradition" because Brown attempts to use the mulatta body "to elide the 'fact of blackness'" (Robert F. Reid-Pharr, *Conjugal Union: The Body, The House, and the Black American* [New York: Oxford UP, 1999] 38).

20 William Wells Brown, *Clotel; or, The President's Daughter: A Narrative of Slave Life in the United States* (1853; New York: Carol, 1969) 48. Further references will be to this edition and will be given parenthetically.

21 See Ernest, "Profession of Authorship" 21–23, for the best analysis of this scene.

22 For the already "threadbare" nature of the tragic mulatta, see Poe's 1845 reaction to Longfellow's poem "The Quadroon Girl" (1842) (*Edgar Allan Poe: Essays and Reviews*, ed. G. R. Thompson [New York: Library of America, 1984] 763). For a comparison of Brown's "inflationary proliferation of a series of tragic mulattas" with his shinplasters, see Peterson, "Capitalism, Black (Under)Development" 569–70. Also see Reid-Pharr's compelling discussion of Brown's use of these figures as "living representative[s] of a potentially revolutionary conception of American republicanism" (*Conjugal Union* 42).

23 Fabi focuses on these "two competing plots" ("'Unguarded Expressions of the Feelings of the Negroes'" 639) while pointing to Brown's failure to depict any black female slaves in a positive light. While I am more interested in how these two plots intersect to destabilize the idea that race is legibly inscribed on the body, Fabi's point about the lack of black women is well taken. Alongside a viable representative black manhood, Brown offers multiple mulatta heroines whose mixed racial status stands as evidence against

the sexual crimes of slavery and troubles any easy racial essentialization. While the mulatta heroine can stand in, to an extent, for black women, Brown fails to offer the same critique of—or at least devotes less attention to—constructions of black womanhood as he does constructions of black manhood.

24 As Ann duCille points out, with *Clotel*, Brown "recognized and addressed the market for women's fiction, as he had earlier played the markets for first 'abolitionist propaganda' and then Civil War narratives" (*The Coupling Convention: Sex, Text, and Tradition in Black Women's Fiction* [New York: Oxford UP, 1993] 28). By combining the sentimental text with minstrelized characters, Brown simultaneously attempted to cash in on two very different markets, at the same time creating a kind of writing that would mark him as a distinctly male author.

25 As Reid-Pharr puts it, Brown uses Pompey and his blacking to illustrate "a process by which black dissimulation is commodified" (*Conjugal Union* 54).

26 In regard to gender masquerade, Judith Butler argues that "drag fully subverts the distinction between inner and outer psychic space and effectively mocks . . . the notion of a true gender identity" (137). Thus, "gender parody reveals that the original identity after which gender fashions itself is an imitation without an origin" (138). While my work is indebted to Butler's delineation of the power of masquerade, my point is that while masquerade does reveal the constructedness of race and gender, it also works to substantiate those distinctions. Butler does note that such masquerades "become domesticated and recirculated as instruments of cultural hegemony" (139), but on the whole, I believe her account (at least here) is overly celebratory of the subversive possibilities of masquerade; see Judith Butler, *Gender Trouble: Feminism and the Subversion of Identity* (New York: Routledge, 1990). In a discussion of Nella Larsen's *Passing* (1929), Butler provides a more nuanced reading of the constitution of racial and gender lines through a movement of acknowledgment and disavowal of their fluidity; see *Bodies That Matter: On the Discursive Limits of "Sex"* (New York: Routledge, 1993) 167–85.

27 I borrow the term "colorist" from Alice Walker. For her critique of Brown as a racist and sexist, see *In Search of Our Mothers' Gardens* (San Diego: Harcourt Brace Jovanovich, 1983) 297–303. See duCille, *The Coupling Convention* 17–29, for a defense of *Clotel* against charges from both black feminists and black aestheticians.

28 See Jean Fagan Yellin, *The Intricate Knot: Black Figures in American Literature, 1776–1863* (New York: New York UP, 1972) 160. Fabi also comments on Brown's "folk characters" (" 'Unguarded Expressions of the Feelings of the Negroes' " 640). Brown's blackfaced characters could be seen in the tradition of signifying which Henry Louis Gates Jr. describes in *The Signifying Monkey: A Theory of African-American Literary Criticism* (New York: Oxford

UP, 1988). My point is that this tradition is always being constructed in dialogue with and through a constant interplay of appropriation and reappropriation from and by both "white" literature and mass cultural forms such as minstrelsy.

29 As Ralph Ellison puts it in a different context, "Without arguing the point I shall say only that if it is a trickster, its adjustments to the contours of 'white' symbolic needs is far more intriguing than its alleged origins, for it tells us something of the operation of American values as modulated by folklore and literature [and, I would add, mass culture]" (Ralph Ellison, "Change the Joke and Slip the Yoke" [1958], *Shadow and Act* [New York: Random House, 1964] 51–52).

30 William Wells Brown, *A Lecture Delivered Before the Female Anti-Slavery Society of Salem At Lyceum Hall, Nov. 14, 1847* (1847), *Four Fugitive Slave Narratives*, ed. Larry Gara (Reading, Mass.: Addison-Wesley, 1969) 81–82.

31 "Speech by William Wells Brown, Delivered at the Horticultural Hall, West Chester, Pennsylvania, 23 October 1854," *The Black Abolitionist Papers*, vol. 4, *The United States, 1847–1858*, ed. C. Peter Ripley et al. (Chapel Hill: U of North Carolina P, 1991) 248.

32 Brown's statements provide an early articulation of some of the difficulties Gayatri Chakravorty Spivak enunciates in "Can the Subaltern Speak?" in *Marxism and the Interpretation of Culture*, ed. Cary Nelson and Lawrence Grossberg (Urbana: U of Illinois P, 1988) 271–313.

33 In other words, Brown is able to use the minstrelized black body as, to invoke Lauren Berlant's term, a prophylactic body in order to remain black even while entering into the essentially white male realm of the public sphere; see Lauren Berlant, "National Brands/National Body: *Imitation of Life*," in *The Phantom Public Sphere*, ed. Bruce Robbins (Minneapolis: U of Minnesota P, 1993) 173–208.

34 Brown's appropriation of minstrelsy is only one way in which he provides an important contrast in strategy and focus to Frederick Douglass. In 1849, Douglass reported on going to see Gavitt's Original Ethiopian Serenaders, a minstrel troupe "said to be composed entirely of colored people." Douglass remarks that "they, too had recourse to the burnt cork and lamp black, the better to express their characters, and to produce uniformity of complexion. Their lips, too, were evidently painted, and otherwise exaggerated. Their singing generally was but an imitation of white performers, and not even a tolerable representation of the character of the colored people." By appearing in blackface, and thus producing themselves as "uniform," the black performers fail to give "a tolerable representation of the character of the colored people." Imitating white performers, they do not reveal "the peculiarities of their race," but rather "exaggerate" them. Douglass states that "it is something gained, when the colored man in any form can appear before a

white audience," but he immediately qualifies this gain by arguing that "this company, with industry, application, and a proper cultivation of their taste, may yet be instrumental in removing the prejudice against our race. But they must cease to exaggerate the exaggerations of our enemies; and represent the colored man rather as he is, than as Ethiopian Minstrels usually represent him to be. They will *then* command the respect of both races." According to Douglass, black performers in blackface cannot succeed in fighting racism and slavery because they do not represent the black man "as he is." It is by representing the true "character of colored people" that blacks can help in the struggle for equality and freedom (Frederick Douglass, "Gavitt's Original Ethiopian Serenaders," *North Star*, 29 June 1849, *The Life and Writings of Frederick Douglass*, vol. 1, ed. Philip S. Foner [New York: International Publishers, 1950] 141–42). On the other hand, Brown, as I argue, uses minstrelsy to obscure the very notion of a "true" black character while at the same time constructing a representative black manhood.

35 See Saidiya V. Hartman, *Scenes of Subjection: Terror, Slavery, and Self-Making in Nineteenth-Century America* (New York: Oxford UP, 1997) 26–32, for one dissenting account that still reads minstrelsy as primarily a racist caricature that helped to sustain slavery. Michael Rogin makes a similar point in the prehistory to his study of blackface in early cinema, *Blackface, White Noise: Jewish Immigrants in the Hollywood Melting Pot* (Berkeley: U of California P, 1996). Another recent study that deals with blackface in twentieth-century American culture more along the Lott model of love and theft is Susan Gubar, *Racechanges: White Skin, Black Face in American Culture* (New York: Oxford UP, 1997).

36 Wittke, *Tambo and Bones* 52.

37 See David R. Roediger, *The Wages of Whiteness: Race and the Making of the American Working Class* (New York: Verso, 1991) 115–32, for a discussion of the role of the minstrel show in making the working class white. While Robert Toll's work is usually cited as an example of the post–Civil Rights condemnation of the minstrel show, I find his work much more subtle, anticipating, in more reserved form, many of Lott's arguments. See W. T. Lhamon Jr., *Raising Cain: Blackface Performance from Jim Crow to Hip Hop* (Cambridge: Harvard UP, 1998) for the most celebratory reading of early blackface. Mahar, *Behind the Burnt Cork Mask* and Dale Cockrell, *Demons of Disorder: Early Blackface Minstrels and Their World* (Cambridge: Cambridge UP, 1997) provide the most historically thick descriptions of blackface performances in the period.

38 Lott, *Love and Theft* 115.

39 Generally, middle-class manhood in this period has been identified with rising ideals of decorum and self-restraint—a more spiritualized manhood— while working-class manhood has been identified with a certain rugged,

unconstrained physicality; see, for example, E. Anthony Rotundo, *American Manhood: Transformations in Masculinity from the Revolution to the Modern Era* (New York: Basic Books, 1993), and Elliott J. Gorn, *The Manly Art: Bare-Knuckle Prize Fighting in America* (Ithaca, N.Y.: Cornell UP, 1986). Here, I find it useful to invoke this idea of middle-class manhood, but as the middle-class celebration of the physicality of the minstrel show indicates, middle-class manhood was actually more complicated in its attempt to balance middle-class decorum with a more physical manliness. As Alexander Saxton has noted, the major stars of antebellum minstrelsy "were clearly [men] of middle-class background. . . . [who] rejected the straight ways of the Protestant ethic and sought escape into the bohemianism of the entertainment world" (*The Rise and Fall of the White Republic: Class Politics and Mass Culture in Nineteenth-Century America* [New York: Verso, 1990] 167). The minstrel show provided a forum in which white men *generally* could access the pleasures of the body associated with blackness, and middle-class whites in particular could access the pleasures associated with both blackness *and* the lower classes.

40 As Toll puts it, "By focusing on caricatures of frolicking Negroes in the idealized plantation family, minstrelsy created a state of perpetual childhood that audiences could vicariously participate in and feel superior to at the same time" (*Blacking Up* 86).

41 Margaret Fuller, "Entertainments of the Past Winter," *Dial* 3.1 (July 1842): 52. I think both Lott and Lhamon miss the point in their readings of Fuller. Lott uses Fuller's denial of having seen "Jim Crow" on the stage to make a point about the split between high and low entertainments (and their class-based audiences) during the period (*Love and Theft* 66); yet in this article Fuller mentions not seeing a number of entertainments clearly not marked in terms of class. Similarly, Lhamon suggests that Fuller's acceptance of minstrelsy shows exactly how taboo it was (*Raising Cain* 132); instead, it is an early example of a common reading, by 1850 or so, of minstrelsy as the proper antidote to the overly materialistic, progressive character of the white middle class.

42 [Y. S. Nathanson], "Negro Minstrelsy—Ancient and Modern," *Putnam's Monthly* (January 1855): 72.

43 "Songs of the Blacks," *Dwight's Journal of Music*, 15 November 1856, reprinted in *What They Heard: Music In America, 1852–1881*, ed. Irving Sablosky (Baton Rouge: Louisiana State UP, 1986) 264–65.

44 Fanon quotes "a friend who was a teacher in the United States, 'The presence of the Negroes beside the whites is in a way an insurance policy on humanness. When the whites feel that they have become too mechanized, they turn to the men of color and ask them for a little human sustenance'" (Frantz Fanon, *Black Skin, White Masks* 129).

45 "Songs of the Blacks" 264.

46 The most famous account of viewers misperceiving minstrel performers as actually black is Mark Twain's story of taking his mother and aunt to a show; see *The Autobiography of Mark Twain*, ed. Charles Neider (1924; New York: Harper, 1959) 58–63.

47 For discussions of sheet music covers, see Toll, *Blacking Up* 40, and Lott, *Love and Theft* 20–21.

48 There is no evidence to indicate that Brown even knew of Lane, although they both lived in England from 1848 until Lane's death in 1852. Brown did, however, often comment on the economic hardships faced by an increasing population of fugitive slaves in England, and his celebration of one former slave and his malleable identities points to the kind of masking that Lane's performances entailed and that *Clotel* foregrounds as so essential to black identity. In roaming London, Brown encountered Joseph Jenkins as a bill-distributor, as a street-sweeper, and as a hymn-singing tract-seller. But Jenkins also was both an accomplished thespian who took advantage of "the excitement caused by the publication of 'Uncle Tom's Cabin' [which] had prepared the public for anything in the African line" by performing *Othello* to a full house and "a most eloquent" preacher to the poor of London. When Brown finally talked to this Rinehart-like figure, this "man that I had seen in so many characters," he found out he was also "the leader of a band." Jenkins' ability to negotiate various professions, almost various selves in their diversity, "impress[ed] [Brown] with the idea that he was the greatest genius that I had met in Europe" (William Wells Brown, *The American Fugitive in Europe* [1854], *The Travels of William Wells Brown*, ed. Paul Jefferson [New York: Marcus Wiener, 1991] 203–7). See Ernest, "Reconstruction" 1108–9 and Reid-Pharr, *Conjugal Union* 143–44, fn 25, for similar readings of Brown's description of Jenkins. For a description of contemporary black actor Ira Aldridge's career and use of whiteface, see Bernth Lindfors, " 'Mislike Me Not for My Complexion . . .': Ira Aldridge in Whiteface" *African American Review* 33.2 (summer 1999): 347–54.

49 Thomas L. Nichols, *Forty Years of American Life*, vol. 2 (London: John Maxwell and Co., 1864) 231–32.

50 See Lott, *Love and Theft* 113–18, for a discussion of this point and others related to accounts of Lane's performances.

51 Quoted in Marian Hannah Winter, "Juba and American Minstrelsy," *Dance Index* 6 (February 1947): 33. Winter and Lott provide the best overviews of Lane's career.

52 Charles Dickens, *American Notes* (1842; London: Oxford UP, 1957) 90–91.

53 Both comments quoted in Winter, "Juba and American Minstrelsy" 36.

54 As Homi Bhabha puts it in his discussion of the ambivalence of stereotypes, "in order to be effective, mimicry must continually produce its slippage, its

excess, its difference. The authority of . . . mimicry is therefore stricken by an indeterminacy." This "recognition and disavowal of 'difference' is always disturbed by the question of re-presentation or construction" (*The Location of Culture* [New York: Routledge, 1994] 86, 81).

55 Quoted in Sam Dennison, *Scandalize My Name: Black Imagery in American Popular Music* (New York: Garland, 1982) 56.

56 Quoted in Saxton, *Rise and Fall* 177.

57 Toll hypothesizes in *Blacking Up* that the dearth of antislavery material that he sees in the minstrel show after 1850 or so was related to a move away from slave sources: the antislavery jokes on masters performed on the minstrel stage "may be among the authentic folk materials that minstrels borrowed" (73). Saxton, while seeing less antislavery rhetoric in minstrelsy, goes further in accrediting such subversive messages to minstrelsy's dispossession of African American cultural elements: "the early borrowings of African-American music and dance carried anti-slavery connotations that sometimes persisted subliminally in traditional verses" (*Rise and Fall* 176). Again, my point is not to deny that some "authentic" black folk material containing antislavery elements might have persisted in the minstrel show, but to foreground how the minstrel show's structure required the retention (or production) of such material.

58 This is how Brown described Turner in his lecture on St. Domingo in 1854; see William Wells Brown, *St. Domingo: Its Revolutions and Its Patriots. A Lecture . . .* (1855; Philadelphia: Rhistoric, 1969) 23.

59 Lhamon, *Raising Cain* 188, 45.

60 The noise to music paradigm is Cockrell's.

61 Y. S. Nathanson cited this song as prototypically authentic in the aesthetic Republican *Putnam's Magazine* in 1855. While Nathanson contrasted this song with the fake, sentimental tunes of modern minstrelsy, he reads "Uncle Gabriel" as exemplary of "the lightness and prevailing good humor of the negro songs" (74). Nathanson's article and its invocation of "Uncle Gabriel" both represents an attempt at taming and incorporating more subversive lyrics into the new, more respectable version of minstrelsy and exemplifies the continuation of those subversive lyrics. Conversely, see Mahar's argument that "with so many historical inaccuracies, ["Uncle Gabriel"] must be a mock heroic tale that, while it appears to sanction the harsh penalty that the insurgent receives, distorts the history of Turner's insurrection so much that the significance of the slave revolts is trivialized" (*Behind the Burnt Cork Mask* 246).

62 *Christy's Plantation Melodies #2* (Philadelphia: Fisher and Brothers, 1852) 44–45.

63 As Ernest puts it, "Sam plays whiteface to the dominant culture's blackface in a great minstrel romp that demonstrates ultimately complex alliances, desires, and ambivalence behind the carefully staged show" ("Profession of

Authorship" 51). My argument differs slightly from Peterson's contention that "Although appearing to conform to a Sambo model," "below this community's surface lies a resistant and productive slave culture" ("Capitalism, Black (Under)Development" 570), and Leonard Cassuto's position that *Clotel* "unmask[s] Sambo to reveal an unwilling captive of a system that tortures and dehumanizes him" (*The Inhuman Race: The Racial Grotesque in American Literature and Culture* [New York: Columbia UP, 1997] 131). My point is not that Brown dismisses this stereotype, but that he draws on the ambivalence immanent to such stereotypes in the minstrel show.

64 Minstrel shows were rife with this kind of characterization. Stump speeches depicting blacks as incompetently trying to follow the white examples of famous speakers like Daniel Webster and scenes involving blacks failing to act as lawyers, doctors, and such were central to minstrel shows. For example, see "Sambo's Address to his Bred'ren," in Dennison, *Scandalize My Name* 41–45; the selections on the minstrel show in Richard Moody, ed., *Dramas from the American Theatre, 1762–1909* (Cleveland, Ohio: World Publishing Co., 1966) 475–500; and skits such as "The Quack Doctor," collected in Gary D. Engle, ed., *This Grotesque Essence: Plays from the American Minstrel Stage* (Baton Rouge: Louisiana State UP, 1978).

65 *The Music of Stephen C. Foster*, vol. 1 (1844–1855), ed. Steven Saunders and Deane L. Root (Washington: Smithsonian Institution Press, 1990) 216–18. Such sentimental songs became the standard fare of minstrelsy as it moved into the more middle-class and respectable realms of Broadway.

66 See Harriet Beecher Stowe, *Dred, A Tale of the Great Dismal Swamp* (1856; Boston: Houghton Mifflin, 1884) 342–43. Foster's song here serves to demonstrate the humanity of black slaves by underlining their capacity for genuine affection and emotional attachment.

67 Kristin Hoganson, "Garrisonian Abolitionists and the Rhetoric of Gender, 1850–1860," *American Quarterly* 45 (December 1993): 558–95. See also R. J. Young, *Antebellum Black Activists*. Conversely, see Donald Yacovone's work on fraternal love in the abolitionist movement and its challenge to what has been seen as the dominant mode of antebellum manhood: "'Surpassing the Love of Women': Victorian Manhood and the Language of Fraternal Love," in *A Shared Experience* 195–221.

68 The circulation of this icon as a commodity (see, for example, Bertram Wyatt-Brown's discussion in *Lewis Tappan and the Evangelical War Against Slavery* [Cleveland, Ohio: The Press of Case Western Reserve, 1969] 155) reiterates the connection between the commercialization of blackness in minstrelsy and in abolitionism.

69 Jean Fagan Yellin reads this emblem as representing the slave as "powerful and athletic," on the verge of "bursting his fetters and asserting his freedom" (*Women and Sisters: The Antislavery Feminists in American Culture* [New Haven, Conn.: Yale UP, 1989] 8). I concur with Hoganson, however, that in

such contexts "black men's bare bodies represented impotence . . . an impotence caused by the inability to resist the master" ("Garrisonian Abolitionists" 567).

70 Yarborough, "Race, Violence, and Manhood" 167–68.

71 At least early on, white abolitionists focused on finding black *men* to serve as lecturers. While black women such as Sojourner Truth and Maria Stewart had denounced slavery in public forums at least as early as the 1830s, black women did not, it seems, become antislavery agents per se until the 1850s. For black women lecturers, writers, and workers in the antislavery movement, see Carla L. Peterson, *"Doers of the Word": African-American Women Speakers and Writers in the North (1830–1880)* (New York: Oxford UP, 1995) and Yellin, *Women and Sisters*. Two quintessential, somewhat fictionalized texts of former-slave women negotiating middle-class gender expectations are Harriet Jacobs's *Incidents in the Life of a Slave Girl* (1861) and Sojourner Truth's "A'n't I a Woman" speech (1851). For a discussion of Stewart and the politics of domesticity, see Lora Romero, "Black Nationalist Housekeeping: Maria W. Stewart," *Home Fronts: Domesticity and its Critics in the Antebellum United States* (Durham, N.C.: Duke UP, 1997) 52–69.

72 Douglass, *My Bondage and My Freedom* 362.

73 See, in particular, Gates's *Figures in Black: Words, Signs, and the "Racial" Self* (New York: Oxford UP, 1987). More recently, a number of critics have pointed out the distinctly masculine nature of this literacy-freedom paradigm. As Harryette Mullen argues in describing a different paradigm of resistant orality in women's slave narratives, the slave narrative has been "associated with the literary production of black men and linking literacy with freedom and manhood" ("Runaway Tongue: Resistant Orality in *Uncle Tom's Cabin, Our Nig, Incidents in the Life of a Slave Girl,* and *Beloved,*" in *The Culture of Sentiment: Race, Gender, and Sentimentality in Nineteenth-Century America,* ed. Shirley Samuels [New York: Oxford UP, 1992] 244); or, as Jennifer Fleischner has remarked, in men's slave narratives, literacy became "the originary movement from passivity to activity, which then manifested itself in other (American) masculine terms—physical aggressiveness, economic competitiveness, and self-reliance" (*Mastering Slavery: Memory, Family, and Identity in Women's Slave Narratives* [New York: New York UP, 1996] 186, note 7).

74 *Narrative of the Life of Frederick Douglass, An American Slave. Written by Himself* (1845), in *The Classic Slave Narratives,* ed. Henry Louis Gates Jr. (New York: Mentor, 1987) 298–99.

75 See Reid-Pharr's similar reading, *Conjugal Union* 51–52. As he puts it, Brown "lampoon[s] Douglass's vaunted confrontation with Mr. Covey" (51) and thus "clearly refuses to accept Douglass's conception of an insurmountable black body" (52).

76 *Narrative* 293, 305. The most conspicuous calls for black resistance during the period forcefully play out this logic. David Walker's *Appeal* (1829) is particularly telling on this account. Walker declares that "we are *men*, notwithstanding our *improminent noses* and *woolly heads*" (25), yet like the antislavery emblem, Walker's declaration repeatedly becomes a question: "Are we MEN!!—I ask you, O my brethren! are we MEN? . . . How could we be so *submissive?*" (36). If the enslaved blacks are truly men, they would chance death rather than submit to the degradations of slavery (34, 42, 46). Only by actively resisting slavery, "meet[ing] death with glory," will they prove to themselves and "the Americans, who are waiting for us to prove to them ourselves, that we are MEN" (*David Walker's Appeal, In Four Articles . . . ,* 3rd ed. [1830; Baltimore, Md.: Black Classic Press, 1993] 48). See also Henry Highland Garnet, *Address to the Slaves of the United States of America* (1848), in *The Ideological Origins of Black Nationalism,* ed. Sterling Stuckey (Boston: Beacon Press, 1972) 165–73. Garnet's address was originally delivered at the National Colored Convention at Buffalo in 1843, where Douglass and Brown helped to defeat its adoption.

77 Douglass, *My Bondage and My Freedom* 246–47, 242. Douglass plays on "root" by referring both to the charm he was given by a fellow slave and his roots as a slave. In both cases, he explicitly is breaking with what becomes constructed as an effeminized and ineffectual slave past.

78 Fanon, *Black Skin, White Masks* 38, 69.

79 See Frances Smith Foster, "Racial Myths in Slave Narratives," *Witnessing Slavery: The Development of Ante-bellum Slave Narratives* (Westport: Greenwood Press, 1979) 127–41, for an account of the importance of mulatto spokesmen in abolitionism.

80 Both quoted in Farrison, *William Wells Brown* 259 (December 1854), 288 (September 1857). Because of this problem, white abolitionists not only desired more "plantation manner" from spokesmen like Brown, but also actively sought out the "full, unmitigated, unalleviated and unpardonable blackness" of men like Henry Highland Garnet (quoted in Jane H. Pease and William H. Pease, *They Who Would Be Free: Blacks' Search for Freedom, 1830–1861* [New York: Atheneum, 1974] 43).

81 Frederick Douglass, "The Claims of the Negro Ethnologically Considered: An Address Delivered in Hudson, Ohio, on 12 July 1854," *The Frederick Douglass Papers,* Series One: *Speeches, Debates, and Interviews, Volume 2: 1847–1854,* ed. John W. Blassingame (New Haven, Conn.: Yale UP, 1982) 510.

82 Karen Sánchez-Eppler, "Bodily Bonds: The Intersecting Rhetorics of Feminism and Abolition," *Touching Liberty: Abolition, Feminism, and the Politics of Body* (Berkeley: U of California P, 1993) 31.

83 See Judith R. Berzon, *Neither White Nor Black: The Mulatto Character in*

American Fiction (New York: New York UP, 1978), especially chapter 2, "Racist Ideologies and the Mulatto," for a rehearsal of the critiques of the tragic mulatta as a racist figure. For a defense of its effectiveness in antislavery literature, see Jules Zanger, "The 'Tragic Octoroon' in Pre-Civil War Fiction," *American Quarterly* 18 (spring 1966): 63–70. While the mulatto character was almost always imagined to be the product of a union between a black slave woman and a white man (frequently a close relative), as Sánchez-Eppler has demonstrated, the mulatta heroine also could stand in for the most unspeakable cross-racial desire, that of a white woman for a black man. See Reid-Pharr, *Conjugal Union*, for the most sophisticated treatment of the mulatta in Brown's novel.

84 See Nancy Bentley, "White Slaves: The Mulatto Hero in Antebellum Fiction," *American Literature* 65 (September 1993): 501–22.

85 Stowe's novel is the essential text for mapping out this notion of gendered racial traits, which George Fredrickson has termed "romantic racialism"; see his "Uncle Tom and the Anglo-Saxons: Romantic Racialism in the North," *The Black Image in the White Mind: The Debate on Afro-American Character and Destiny, 1817–1914* (New York: Harper, 1971) 97–129. Cynthia Griffin Wolff has attempted to qualify readings of *Uncle Tom's Cabin* that see Tom as effeminate by correctly showing how Stowe calls for a type of manhood in which being "brave, manly" is equated with being "gentle, domestic." Wolff, however, fails to take into account the ways in which Stowe bases this idea of a more "domestic" manhood on the notion that blacks *naturally* have a more "feminine" disposition that white men need to learn. See Cynthia Griffin Wolff, " 'Masculinity' in *Uncle Tom's Cabin*," *American Quarterly* 47 (December 1995): 595–618.

86 Frederick Douglass, "The Heroic Slave" (1853), in *The Oxford Frederick Douglass Reader*, ed. William L. Andrews (New York: Oxford UP, 1996) 134, 135. All further citations will be to this edition and will be given parenthetically.

87 Richard Yarborough, whose reading of "The Heroic Slave" has influenced my own thinking about the story, argues that Washington's blackness is also called into question from this opening description ("Race, Violence, and Manhood" 173–74). For more positive accounts of "The Heroic Slave" and its obviously important reconceptualization of black manhood, see Eric J. Sundquist, *To Wake the Nations: Race in the Making of American Literature* (Cambridge: Harvard UP, 1993) 115–24, and Maggie Sale, "To Make the Past Useful: Frederick Douglass' Politics of Solidarity," *Arizona Quarterly* 51 (autumn 1995): 25–60. For a positive account that links Douglass's story with *Clotel* as examples of "discursive passing," see Castronovo, *Fathering the Nation* 190–225. My point is that such passing does allow Douglass and Brown to manipulate literary conventions and be accepted as authors, but

possibly at the price of losing their ability to represent black manhood more generally. Reid-Pharr similarly contrasts Douglass's "Heroic Slave" with Brown's stratagems, *Conjugal Union* 50–52.

88 Shirley Samuels explores the ways in which sentimental antislavery fiction worked on the premise of revealing the "white" inside of black slaves; see her "The Identity of Slavery," in *The Culture of Sentiment* 157–71.

89 Harriet Beecher Stowe, *Uncle Tom's Cabin, or, Life Among the Lowly* (1852; New York: Penguin, 1981) 392.

90 In his exploration of temperance in the novel, of Brown's "damning portrayal of slavery as a patriarchal institution that stimulates, rather than restrains, the intemperate desires of the white male masters" (99), Robert Levine argues that the blackness of Turner and Picquilo "conveys [Brown's] anxieties that revolutionary violence is a form of intemperate 'blacking' in which 'low and vindictive passions' in effect enslave the individual who succumbs to them" (" 'Whiskey, Blacking, and All' " 104).

91 This construction of black resistance and rebellion as irrational or prerational was a commonplace. Perhaps the best example of this constant shift between seeing the rebel slave as admirable and as insane is T. R. Gray's *Confessions of Nat Turner* (1831).

92 For more on the Nat/Sambo dichotomy in the Southern imagination and in the slave community, see John W. Blassingame, *The Slave Community: Plantation Life in the Antebellum South* (New York: Oxford UP, 1972). Brown invokes the image of black atavism again in his lecture on St. Domingo from 1854. While Brown stresses that the educated, rational French started the violence and were far worse in their cruelties, when he explicitly connects this revolt to the southern states, his point is clear: "Let the slave-holders in our Southern States tremble when they shall call to mind these events" (25).

93 Brown notes that upon escaping, George went "but a short distance before he felt that a change of his apparel would facilitate his progress" (228), but he makes it clear that George remains in women's clothes until in the North. Both Bentley and Fabi misread this passage as indicating that George immediately reclaims his masculine appearance. Bentley argues that Brown uses the scene to set up a "contrast between the female and male Mulattoes," so that "White male bodies are spared and female bodies are sacrificed" ("White Slaves" 507); Fabi argues that George must reclaim his manliness immediately because of Brown's "evaluation of passing as unheroic" and feminine (" 'Unguarded Expressions of the Feelings of the Negroes' " 645). My point is that Brown *stresses* George's escape through masquerade because of the impossibility of heroic action and as a way of indicating the performative nature of white manhood. Levine similarly points out that "Brown celebrates [George] at the end of the novel, then, not for his 'manly' linkage with Nat Turner, nor for his 'manly' rise in the free market, but for his

womanly fidelity" (" 'Whiskey, Blacking, and All' " 106). In the end, I think Brown celebrates him for both his manly and his womanly traits, his ability to move between the two as he moves between white and black.

94 See William Craft, *Running a Thousand Miles for Freedom; or, The Escape of William and Ellen Craft from Slavery* (1860), in *Great Slave Narratives*, ed. Arna Bontemps (Boston: Beacon Press, 1969) 269–331.

2. The Indian in the Museum:
Henry David Thoreau, Okah Tubbee, and Authentic Manhood

1 *New York Herald,* 27 February 1843.

2 *Philadelphia Public Ledger and Transcript,* 7 February 1848.

3 Pamphlet from 1790 asking for contributions, quoted in Charles Coleman Sellers, *Mr. Peale's Museum: Charles Willson Peale and the First Popular Museum of Natural Science and Art* (New York: Norton, 1980) 46. For more on Peale's museum projects, see David R. Brigham, *Public Culture in the Early Republic: Peale's Museum and Its Audience* (Washington: Smithsonian Institution Press, 1995), and Laura Rigal, "Peale's Mammoth," in *American Iconology: New Approaches to Nineteenth-Century Art and Literature*, ed. David C. Miller (New Haven, Conn.: Yale UP, 1993) 18–38.

4 For more generalized histories of early museums in the United States, see Whitfield J. Bell Jr. et al., *A Cabinet of Curiosities: Five Episodes in the Evolution of American Museums* (Charlottesville: University Press of Virginia, 1967) and Joel J. Orosz, *Curators and Culture: The Museum Movement in America, 1740–1870* (Tuscaloosa: U of Alabama P, 1990).

5 As Eric Lott has argued, "the encroachment in the late 1840s of a larger female spectatorship on the minstrel show's generalized masculinism"— which largely occurred through museum-theater spaces like Barnum's— "coincided" with the "generic projection of death and sorrow onto female or 'feminized' male black victims" (*Love and Theft: Blackface Minstrelsy and the American Working Class* [New York: Oxford UP, 1993] 187). As Robert Toll puts it, "Before the mid-1850s, minstrel portrayals of blacks contained much more than the ludicrous images of incompetent Northern Negroes and of happy slaves." But this "fundamental ambivalence about slavery" disappeared as "minstrels portrayed Negroes more as emotional children to be protected and guarded for their own good than as serious threats to whites" (*Blacking Up: The Minstrel Show in Nineteenth-Century America* [New York: Oxford UP, 1974] 66, 78). In other words, as the minstrel show became a more acceptable and respectable entertainment form, largely through its incorporation into popular museums, minstrel images became more and more centered on representations of black men as sentimentalized and effeminate. See, however, my argument in the previous chapter about the continued, submerged presence of this ambivalence in middle-class minstrelsy.

6 As Richard Butsch has pointed out, through such things as matinee shows, special seating, and special admittance policies, mid-century museums opened up a consumption-oriented public sphere marked as particularly feminine. Butsch argues that these museums "were the first of several commercial establishments, including department stores and ice cream parlors, created for ['respectable'] women within the dangerous cityscape." Museums thus played a central role in what Butsch, after Ann Douglas, calls the "feminization of middle-class culture" ("Bowery B'hoys and Matinee Ladies: The Re-Gendering of Nineteenth-Century American Theater Audiences," *American Quarterly* 46.3 [September 1994]: 377, 385). See Ann Douglas, *The Feminization of American Culture* (New York: Knopf, 1977). For more on the creation of a visually oriented, specifically feminine consumer culture in the mid-nineteenth century, see Anne Friedberg, *Window Shopping: Cinema and the Postmodern* (Berkeley: U of California P, 1993) 15–44. As Peter G. Buckley has put it, Barnum's museum was "a proto-department store of entertainment" ("To the Opera House: Culture and Society in New York City, 1820–1860," Ph.D. diss., SUNY, Stony Brook, 1984, 494). For more on the relationship between museums and department stores, see Simon J. Bronner, "Object Lessons: The Work of Ethnology Museums," in *Consuming Visions: Accumulation and Display of Goods in America, 1880–1920*, ed. Simon J. Bronner (New York: Norton, 1989) 217–54; and Neil Harris, "Museums, Merchandising, and Popular Taste: The Struggle for Influence," in *Material Culture and the Study of American Life*, ed. Ian M. G. Quimby (New York: Norton, 1978) 140–74.

7 Most studies of American manhood, such as E. Anthony Rotundo's *American Manhood: Transformations in Masculinity from the Revolution to the Modern Era* (New York: HarperCollins, 1993), see such tensions only emerging at the turn of the century with the rise of commodity culture. While the end of the nineteenth century marked an intensification of such anxieties within an increasingly visible commodity culture, such studies tend to posit a monolithic middle class of Weberian male producers up until that point rather than seeing the complex interweaving rhetorics and economics of consumption/leisure and production that were present from the beginnings of industrial capitalism.

8 Here, I want to shift the emphasis of museum critics such as James Clifford who focus on how objects (and people) in the museum are "detached from their original temporal occasions, and given enduring value in a new arrangement" (231). Clifford has importantly pointed to the ways in which cultures, specifically those of "native" peoples, are constantly in flux and interchange with other cultures, but he tends to return to an essentialist position when detailing the ways in which Western collecting has taken non-Western objects from "their original" contexts, rather than focusing on how those objects and their "value in a new arrangement" produce that

"original" context so that it can be reappropriated strategically. See James Clifford, "On Collecting Art and Culture," *The Predicament of Culture: Twentieth-Century Ethnography, Literature, and Art* (Cambridge: Harvard UP, 1988) 215–52. Barbara Kirshenblatt-Gimblett begins to shift the emphasis: "Objects become ethnographic by virtue of being defined, segmented, detached, and carried away by ethnographers," and "the putative cultural wholes of which they [ethnographic fragments] are part" are also "the creation of the ethnographer" (Barbara Kirshenblatt-Gimblett, "Objects of Ethnography," in *Exhibiting Cultures: The Poetics and Politics of Museum Display*, ed. Ivan Karp and Steven D. Levine [Washington, D.C.: Smithsonian Institution Press, 1991] 387, 389). For a critique of Clifford along these lines, see Anthony Alan Shelton, "In the Lair of the Monkey: Notes Towards a Post-Modernist Museography," in *Objects of Knowledge*, ed. Susan Pearce (London: The Athlone Press, 1990) 78–102.

9 In this way, the mid-century museum was imagined to deliver, as Donna Haraway has argued in reference to turn-of-the-century natural history museums, a "prophylactic dose of nature" for embattled Anglo-Saxon masculinity ("Teddy Bear Patriarchy: Taxidermy in the Garden of Eden, New York City, 1908–1936," *Primate Visions: Gender, Race, and Nature in the World of Modern Science* [New York: Routledge, 1989] 26). I am deeply indebted to Haraway's ideas about the museum as an institution for resurrecting an overcivilized Euro-American manhood through contact with animals and "primitive" cultures.

10 See John Rickards Betts, "P. T. Barnum and the Popularization of Natural History," *Journal of the History of Ideas* 20 (1959): 353–68, for more on Barnum's tenuous relationship with the scientific community.

11 For more on the debates over the proper balance of educational and scientific goals in the establishment of the Smithsonian, see Wilcomb E. Washburn, "Joseph Henry's Conception of the Purpose of the Smithsonian Institution," in *A Cabinet of Curiosities*, 106–66. For a discussion of Indians in the Smithsonian, see Curtis M. Hinsley, *The Smithsonian and the American Indian: Making a Moral Anthropology in Victorian America* (1981 as *Savages and Scientists*; Washington, D.C.: Smithsonian Institution Press, 1994).

12 P. T. Barnum, *Struggles and Triumphs: or, Forty Years' Recollections of P. T. Barnum* (1869; New York: Arno, 1970) 120–21.

13 *Tom Pop's First Visit to the Boston Museum, with his Grandfather; Giving an Account of What He Saw, and What He Thought* (Boston: n.p., 1848) 5, 21. Bruce McConachie lucidly describes this pamphlet as "present[ing] the museum as a series of object lessons in a domestic culture which has colonized religion, society, and nature" (*Melodramatic Formations: American Theatre and Society, 1820–1870* [Iowa City: U of Iowa P, 1992] 169).

14 *Sights and Wonders in New York; including a description of the mysteries,*

miracles, marvels, phenomena, curiosities, and nondescripts, contained in that great congress of wonders, Barnum's Museum . . . (New York: J. S. Redfield, 1849) 23.

15 *An Illustrated Catalogue and Guide Book to Barnum's American Museum* (New York: n.p., n.d. [1864]) back cover, unpaged. Further citations will be given parenthetically.

16 "Places of Public Amusement: Theatres and Concert Rooms," *Putnam's Monthly* 3.14 (February 1854): 148–49.

17 See my discussion in the prologue and Peter Buckley's arguments about how "Barnum created a public," "unmapped in the contours of class interest," by taking Bowery amusements and "appropriat[ing] the assets of conventional bourgeois morality and plac[ing] them on a cash basis" ("To the Opera House" 472, 495, 538). More recently, Bluford Adams has traced Barnum's ability to construct and play to different class-marked audiences throughout his career; see *E Pluribus Barnum: The Great Showman and the Making of U.S. Popular Culture* (Minneapolis: U of Minnesota P, 1997), especially chapters 3 and 4 and their discussion of the American Museum. In a different context, see Tony Bennett's discussion of the ways in which museums and exhibitions in Victorian England "transformed the many-headed mob into an ordered crowd, a part of the spectacle and a sight of pleasure in itself," by "provid[ing] a context in which the working- and middle-class publics could be brought together and the former . . . could be exposed to the improving influence of the latter" (Tony Bennett, "The Exhibitionary Complex," *New Formations* 4 [spring 1988]: 85, 86).

18 *New York Herald*, Saturday, 23 September 1843.

19 P. T. Barnum to Moses Kimball, 26 September 1843, and 23 September 1843, Barnum's underlining. Both dated New York. Barnum-Kimball correspondence at Boston Athenaeum.

20 *Familiar Letters*, ed. F. B. Sanborn, *The Writings of Henry David Thoreau*, vol. 6 (Boston: Houghton Mifflin, 1906) 109–10.

21 For an alternative reading of Thoreau's relationship with the urban, one that reads an eighteenth-century civic urban mercantile ethic as central to Thoreau's critique of his contemporaries, see Robert Fanuzzi, "Thoreau's Urban Imagination," *American Literature* 68.2 (June 1996): 321–46.

22 *Journal*, vol. 1 (1837–1846), ed. Bradford Torrey, *The Writings of Henry David Thoreau*, vol. 7 (Boston: Houghton Mifflin; Cambridge: Riverside, 1906) 464, undated in Bradford Torrey edition; dated 24 September 1843, in slightly different form, in the new Princeton edition (*Journal*, vol. 1 [1837–1844], gen. ed. John C. Broderick [Princeton: Princeton UP, 1981] 465). Because the Princeton edition has yet to publish all volumes of the journal, to maintain consistency, all references will be to the 1906 Riverside edition and will be to journal (not collected work) volume number. See Laura

Dassow Walls, "Textbooks and Texts from the Brooks: Inventing Scientific Authority in America," *American Quarterly* 49.1 (March 1997): 11, for a reading of this passage in terms of Thoreau's rejection of the new scientific authority embodied in professionals like Louis Agassiz.

23 For Thoreau's visits to Barnum's museum, see *J* 7:76 (22 November 1854); *J* 9:133 (25 October 1856); *J* 10:443 (24 May 1858).

24 Lee Rust Brown reads Emerson's visit to the Muséum d'Histoire Naturelle as central to his elaboration of a similarly emblematic, transcendental understanding of nature; see "The Emerson Museum," *Representations* 40 (fall 1992): 57–80.

25 *The Maine Woods*, ed. Joseph J. Moldenhauer (1864; Princeton: Princeton UP, 1972) 69–71. All further references to *The Maine Woods* will be to this edition and will be given parenthetically as *MW*.

26 *Walden*, ed. J. Lyndon Shanley (1854; Princeton, N.J.: Princeton UP, 1971) 317–18. All references to *Walden* will be to this edition and will be given parenthetically.

27 For more on the close connections between museums and theaters in the period, see Kirshenblatt-Gimblett, "Objects of Ethnography" 397–407, Butsch, "Bowery B'hoys and Matinee Ladies," McConachie, *Melodramatic Formulations*, and Adams, *Pluribus Barnum*.

28 Here, Thoreau seems to anticipate Walter Benjamin's critique of the anaesthetic effects of early commodity culture of the nineteenth century. For a reconstruction of his critique, see Susan Buck-Morss, "Aesthetics and Anaesthetics: Walter Benjamin's Artwork Essay Reconsidered," *October* 62 (fall 1992): 3–41.

29 Thoreau's relationship with the market economy has received much attention of late, beginning with Michael Gilmore's "*Walden* and the Curse of Trade," in *Ideology and Classic American Literature*, ed. Sacvan Bercovitch and Myra Jehlen (Cambridge: Cambridge UP, 1986) 293–312. Gilmore notes Thoreau's critique of market forces and the relationships they entail while elucidating the ways in which Thoreau realized his own necessary involvement in the market both during his experiment at Walden Pond and in the publication of *Walden*. According to Gilmore, Thoreau makes "no attempt to disguise the fact that he is unable to emancipate himself completely from exchange relations" (298). See also Steven Fink, *Prophet in the Marketplace: Thoreau's Development as a Professional Writer* (Princeton, N.J.: Princeton UP, 1992), and Leonard N. Neufeldt, *The Economist: Henry Thoreau and Enterprise* (New York: Oxford UP, 1989). In a different vein, more similar to my own point, Michael Warner has focused on how Thoreau's critique of capitalism is part of the driving dynamic *of* capitalism. Thoreau's desire to escape the unreality of the market for some solid ground, some "hard matter," actually takes part in the driving dynamic of the market: "Thoreau's

critical-utopian impulses come from within the cultural history of capitalism itself" ("*Walden's* Erotic Economy," in *Comparative American Identities: Race, Sex, and Nationality in the Modern Text*, ed. Hortense J. Spillers [New York: Routledge, 1991] 173).

30   "The Commercial Spirit of Modern Times," *Early Essays and Miscellanies*, ed. Joseph J. Modlenhauer and Edwin Moser (Princeton, N.J.: Princeton UP, 1975) 116, 117.

31   *A Week on the Concord and Merrimack Rivers*, ed. Carl F. Hovde et al. (1849; Princeton: Princeton UP, 1980) 56; "Walking," *Excursions and Poems, The Writings of Henry David Thoreau*, vol. 5 (Boston: Houghton Mifflin, 1906) 225. Further references will be to these editions and will be given parenthetically.

32   Elsewhere, however, Thoreau praises the Indian for being not quite so intimate with nature: "If the Indian is somewhat of a stranger in nature, the gardener is too much a familiar. There is something vulgar and foul in the latter's closeness to his mistress, something noble and cleanly in the former's distance" (*J* 1:473 [undated]). Being overly intimate with nature in this case would mean being a slave to bodily sensuality, specifically a lewd sexuality. It is this oscillation over being more intimate with both nature and the body and keeping a proper distance, this erotic economy, that Michael Warner has most fully explored.

33   As Roy Harvey Pearce phrases it, for Thoreau, "Savages, in their humanity and their thought, in their harmony and their wholeness, might guide men into the happiness proper to civilization"; "He wanted civilized men to have that integrity he found in savages" (*Savagism and Civilization: A Study of the Indian and the American Mind* [1953 as *The Savages of America*; Berkeley: U of California P, 1988] 150, 149).

34   The standard description of the Indian notebooks can be found in Albert Keiser, "Thoreau—Friend of the Native," *The Indian in American Literature* (New York: Oxford UP, 1933) 209–32. See also Richard Fleck, ed., *The Indians of Thoreau: Selections from the Indian Notebooks* (Albuquerque: Hummingbird Press, 1974); Robert Sayre, *Thoreau and the American Indians* (Princeton, N.J.: Princeton UP, 1977), especially appendix; and Linck C. Johnson, "Thoreau's Earliest 'Indian Book' and His First Trip to Cape Cod," *ESQ* 28.2 (1982): 74–87. The unpublished notebooks are located in the Pierpont Morgan Library in New York. Sayre makes a case for numbering twelve volumes, while most number it as eleven; Johnson argues for dating the start of the notebooks in 1849, while most agree upon 1847.

35   Richard Fleck, "Further Selections From the 'Indian Notebooks,'" *Thoreau Journal Quarterly* 9.1 (January 1977): 4. That Thoreau actually planned to write such a book is highly debatable. See Sayre 101–22. For other, on the whole celebratory accounts of Thoreau's depiction of Indians, see Edwin S.

Fussell, "The Red Face of Man," in *Thoreau: A Collection of Critical Essays*, ed. Sherman Paul (Englewood Cliffs: Prentice-Hall, 1962) 142–60; and Philip F. Gura, "Thoreau's Maine Woods Indians: More Representative Men," *American Literature* 49.3 (November 1977): 366–84.

36 The idea of savagism is from Pearce's *Savagism and Civilization*. This is Robert Sayre's major thesis in *Thoreau and the American Indians* (one chapter is even titled "Beyond Savagism"), one reiterated by D. M. Murray, "Thoreau's Indians and His Developing Art of Characterization," *ESQ* 21. 4 (1975): 222–29; and Linda Frost, " 'The Red Face of Man,' the Penobscot Indian, and a Conflict of Interest in Thoreau's *The Maine Woods*," *ESQ* 39.1 (1993):21–47.

37 Thoreau wrote this passage (23 January 1858) after his last Maine expedition (1857) in which he met Joe Polis. Its racial logic and its date weaken the argument that Thoreau somehow drastically changed because of meeting Polis. This is not to deny that Polis affected Thoreau deeply, but simply to question the idea that Thoreau was able to transcend savagist thinking through actual contact with "real" Indians.

38 Reginald Horsman has argued that this essentializing, biological notion of race had superseded an earlier environmental understanding of race in the United States by the middle of the nineteenth century. See Reginald Horsman, *Race and Manifest Destiny: The Origins of American Racial Anglo-Saxonism* (Cambridge: Harvard UP, 1981). Also see the debate between Horsman and Francis Paul Prucha over whether an environmentalist or essentialist understanding of race held greater sway in the 1840s and 1850s. See Francis Paul Prucha, "American Indian Policy in the 1840s: Visions of Reform" and "Scientific Racism and Indian Policy," both collected in *Indian Policy in the United States: Historical Essays* (Lincoln: U of Nebraska P, 1981), and Reginald Horsman, "Scientific Racism and the American Indian in the Mid-Nineteenth Century," *American Quarterly* 27.2 (May 1975): 152–68. As I believe Okah Tubbee exemplifies (see below), race is always already defined as both cultural (performative) and essential (biological), a definition at once doubly binding and full of slippage. Walter Benn Michaels has explored the ways in which "cultural identity" always depends on an implicitly biological idea of race. See *Our America: Nativism, Modernism, and Pluralism* (Durham, N.C.: Duke UP, 1995).

39 For an insightful discussion of the history of whites taking on Indian identities, see Philip J. Deloria, *Playing Indian* (New Haven, Conn.: Yale UP, 1998). For more on the specific antebellum literary, class, and gender dynamics of becoming Indian, see my prologue.

40 See Michael Newbury's discussion of this famous passage and his description of Thoreau's desire for a more masculine (in my reading, more Indian-like) body (Michael Newbury, *Figuring Authorship in Antebellum America* [Stanford, Calif.: Stanford UP, 1997] 144–50).

41 During the 1840s, Barnum owned two museums in New York and one each in Baltimore and Philadelphia, besides carrying on a steady exchange of attractions with Boston Museum proprietor Moses Kimball. As he notes in *Struggles and Triumphs,* "For many years I had been in the habit of engaging parties of American Indians from the far West to exhibit at the Museum, and had sent two or more Indian companies to Europe, where they were regarded as very great 'curiosities' " (573).

42 See Daniel F. Littlefield Jr.'s "Introduction," *The Life of Okah Tubbee* (Lincoln: U of Nebraska P, 1988) xxxvii, for this argument. Also see Littlefield, xxxviii–xxxix, for an account of the various editions of the biography. I have relied on Littlefield's introduction to sketch out the portions of Tubbee's life not covered in his biography.

43 Tubbee probably passed as an Indian beginning in the early 1830s, but did not promote himself as Okah Tubbee until the mid-1840s. This chronology leads to the probability that he adapted his adopted name from the title character—"one of the most noble specimens of physical manhood" (208)— of William Gilmore Simms's short story "Oakatibbe, or the Choctaw Sampson," which was first published in 1841. (It is also possible Simms based his character on Okah Tubbee; as always, racial lines of cultural appropriation fail to reveal neat categories of origin and influence.) See William Gilmore Simms, "Oakatibbe, or the Choctaw Sampson" (1841), *The Wigwam and the Cabin* (1845; Ridgewood, N.J.: The Gregg Press, 1968) 190–226. In any case, Tubbee and his wife exploited racial logics similar to those expounded in Simms's tale about a failed experiment in civilizing Indians on a Mississippi plantation, if they did not consciously appropriate his new name from the story.

44 *A Thrilling Sketch of the Life of the Distinguished Chief Okah Tubbee Alias, Wm. Chubbee, Son of the Head Chief, Mosholeh Tubbee, of the Choctaw Nation of Indians. By Rev. L. L. Allen* (New York: Cameron's Steam Power Presses, 1848) 12. This is the first edition of Okah Tubbee's autobiography.

45 *The Life of Okah Tubbee,* ed. Daniel Littlefield, 3. Littlefield reproduces the fourth and last contemporary edition of the biography—*A Sketch of the Life of Okah Tubbee, (Called) William Chubbee, Son of the Head Chief, Mosholeh Tubbee, of the Choctaw Nation of Indians. By Laah Ceil Manatoi Elaah Tubbee, His Wife* (Toronto: Henry Stephens, 1852). Unless indicated otherwise, all further citations will be to the Littlefield edition and will be given parenthetically.

46 For more on the logic of the vanishing American, see Pearce, *Savagism and Civilization*; Horsman, *Race and Manifest Destiny*; Richard Drinnon, *Facing West: The Metaphysics of Indian-Hating and Empire Building* (Minneapolis: U of Minnesota P, 1980); and Brian W. Dippie, *The Vanishing American: White Attitudes and U.S. Indian Policy* (Middletown, Conn.: Wesleyan UP, 1982).

47 This was true not only for Tubbee, who particularly needed to renounce the possibility of being black. Most other Native American speakers and autobiographers of the period similarly felt it necessary to distinguish themselves from African Americans. See, for example, *Black Hawk: An Autobiography*, ed. Donald Jackson (1833; Urbana: U of Illinois P, 1990) 152–53; William Apess, *The Experiences of Five Christian Indians* [1833], *On Our Own Ground: The Complete Writings of William Apess, a Pequot*, ed. Barry O'Connell (Amherst: U of Massachusetts P, 1992) 124–25; and George Copway, *The Life, Letters and Speeches of Kah-Ge-Ga-Gah-Bowh or, G. Copway* (New York: S. W. Benedict, 1850) 169. These distinctions were already well disseminated within racial debates of the period. Both whites and blacks made similar points to bolster their positions either in favor of or against emancipation. For example, Frederick Douglass transforms the submissiveness of blacks noted in Native American texts into a positive mutability by arguing that "the Indian, dies, under the flashing glance of the Anglo Saxon. *Not* so the Negro: civilization cannot kill him. He accepts it—becomes a part of it." If, as Thoreau put it, the history of the red man is one "of fixed habits of stagnation," then that of the black race, according to Douglass, "proves them to be wonderfully adapted to all countries, all climates, and all conditions" ("The Claims of the Negro Ethnologically Considered: An Address Delivered in Hudson, Ohio, on 12 July 1854," *The Frederick Douglass Papers*, ed. John W. Blassingame, ser. 1: Speeches, Debates, and Interviews, vol. 2: 1847–1854 [New Haven, Conn.: Yale UP, 1982] 524). On the other hand, apologists for southern slavery, such as Simms, used the same opposition between African Americans and Native Americans to posit that the innate submissiveness of blacks was indicative of their "natural" role as slaves. As *DeBow's Review* argued in 1854, "It is otherwise with the negro than with the Indian. The former, in the state of slavery for which he is created . . . cannot be civilized . . . but his condition can be ameliorated. . . . But the stern, proud Indian cannot be enslaved" (quoted in Dippie, *Vanishing American* 85).

48 Allen, *A Thrilling Sketch* 20.

49 Quoted in M. R. Werner, *Barnum* (New York: Harcourt, Brace and Co., 1923) 32. See also *Struggles and Triumphs* 73–76. See Benjamin Reiss, "P. T. Barnum, Joice Heth and Antebellum Spectacles of Race," *American Quarterly* 51.1 (March 1999): 78–107, for the best discussion of the ways in which Heth's body became a site of contestation over a variety of cultural conflicts in which race often played a less than apparent role. Reiss traces how Barnum transformed his narrative of this exhibition in order to conform with different racial and class politics over the course of his career.

50 See *Illustrated Catalogue and Guide Book* 114, 111.

51 See Reiss's discussion of such exhibits, "P. T. Barnum" 84–85. For earlier

exhibits at Peale's Museum, see Brigham, *Public Culture in the Early Republic* 132–33.

52 See James W. Cook Jr., "Of Men, Missing Links, and Nondescripts: The Strange Career of P. T. Barnum's 'What is It?' Exhibition," in *Freakery: Cultural Spectacles of the Extraordinary Body*, ed. Rosemarie Garland Thomson (New York: New York UP, 1996) 139–57, and Adams, *E Pluribus Barnum* 147–63, for discussions of Barnum's negotiation of racial politics in this exhibit. See also the next chapter of this book.

53 Promotional material for "What is It?" quoted in Robert Bogdan, *Freak Show: Presenting Human Oddities for Amusement and Profit* (Chicago: U of Chicago P, 1988) 136.

54 Barnum, *Struggles and Triumphs* 623.

55 Quoted in Irving Wallace, *The Fabulous Showman: The Life and Times of P. T. Barnum* (New York: Knopf, 1959) 139–40.

56 Minstrel shows, of course, depended on conjuring up a sense of "authentic" delineations, but simultaneously depended on the audience's knowledge that the performers were actually white. A constant oscillation between masquerade and serious representation drove the minstrel show, while displays of Indians were much more dependent on maintaining a constant sense of reality.

57 Sayre makes a similar point to mine, but because of his focus—specifically on Thoreau and Indians—does not develop it further: "Their [the slaves'] pathos was a call on his manhood, but they were not his manly equals. Towards the Indians he was exactly the opposite. . . . Their natural grandeur evoked his envy and admiration. They were examples of manhood rather than calls upon it" (*Thoreau and the American Indians* 25).

58 As Michael Meyer points out, "it is remarkable that he has very little to say about blacks themselves" ("Thoreau and Black Emigration," *American Literature* 53.3 [November 1981] 387).

59 "Slavery in Massachusetts," *Reform Papers*, ed. Wendell Glick (Princeton, N.J.: Princeton UP, 1973) 91, 94.

60 "Resistance to Civil Government," *Reform Papers* 65. Further references will be given parenthetically. In "Slavery in Massachusetts," Thoreau similarly reminds his "countrymen that they are to be men first, and Americans only at a late and convenient hour" (102).

61 "A Plea for Captain John Brown," *Reform Papers* 120. In all three of his published eulogies, "The Last Days of John Brown," "A Plea for Captain John Brown," and "Martyrdom of John Brown," Thoreau spends little time on the men that Brown was attempting to help gain freedom or on their own sacrifices. Instead, Thoreau focuses on the ways in which Brown, through "manly directness and force," has "lifted [Americans] out of the trivialness and dust of politics into the region of truth and manhood" ("A Plea" 127, 125).

62 See Christopher Newfield, *The Emerson Effect: Individualism and Submission in America* (Chicago: U of Chicago P, 1996), for a discussion of the ways in which a masculine Emersonian independence and self-reliance is constructed through a model of submission that finally refuses to grant equality to others.

63 See chapter 1 for a discussion of how this slave/manhood problematic haunted antislavery rhetoric.

64 "A Plea" 134. Elsewhere, Thoreau argues that the Indians, in their manly and stoic acceptance of their fate, "teach us how to die" ("Autumnal Tints," *Excursions and Poems, The Writings of Henry David Thoreau*, vol. 5 [Boston: Houghton Mifflin; Cambridge: Riverside, 1906] 270). Furthermore, Thoreau argues that John Brown was "befriended only by Indians" ("A Plea" 116), and hence he links Brown—and his "manly directness"—more closely with Indians than the slaves he attempted to free.

65 See Adams, *E Pluribus Barnum* 41–74, for a discussion of how Barnum used his promotion of Jenny Lind to cast himself as a purveyor of respectable and sentimental middle-class products. While Lind sang sentimental songs, Thoreau celebrates music because of its ability, like nature, to act as "an elixir," lifting us "up above all the dust and mire of the universe" and awakening us to "life within life" (*J* 9:217). As Kenneth W. Rhoads argues, Thoreau's "natural sympathies, then, were aroused by a music essentially primitive and uncultivated—music, in short, possessing a wildness which corresponded both to his own nature and to that aspect of physical nature with which he felt most empathy" ("Thoreau: The Ear and the Music," *American Literature* 46.3 [November 1974]: 317). In these terms, we can extrapolate that Thoreau would have agreed with Y. S. Nathanson's critique of "modern" sentimental minstrelsy—the kind most often performed in museums—as presenting "the most glaring marks of barefaced and impudent imposition" and being "so patched and dressed up for drawing-room inspection that they look like a bumpkin who has suddenly come into possession of a fortune" ("Negro Minstrelsy—Ancient and Modern," *Putnam's Monthly* [January 1855]: 75).

66 Aitteon becomes a doubly troublesome figure for Thoreau, because Thoreau has *employed* him and is thereby culpable for his transformation from independent Indian to commodified laborer.

67 This racial distinction emerges in Thoreau's account of his final trip to Maine in his journal (but not in *The Maine Woods*). Before hiring Joe Polis as their guide, he and his companion decide against "a young, very dark-complexioned Indian" because "he was too dark-colored, as if with African blood" (*J* 9:486 [22 July 1857]). Thoreau wants a "full-blooded" Indian as close to his primitive ancestry as possible for his guide, not a degraded "half-breed" of possibly African blood.

68 Barnum, *Struggles and Triumphs* 151–52.

69 Lydia Maria Child, *Letters From New-York* (1843), in *Hobomok and Other Writings on Indians*, ed. Carolyn L. Karcher (New Brunswick, N.J.: Rutgers UP, 1986) 189. Further citations will be to this edition and will be given parenthetically.

70 Barnum, *Struggles and Triumphs* 574, 576.

71 As Kirshenblatt-Gimblett argues in "Objects of Ethnography," such exhibits "blurr[ed] the line" between "theater and living ethnographic display" (397) in their "production of wildness" (403).

72 As Susan Stewart argues, "The body of the cultural other is by [these] means . . . both naturalized and domesticated" (*On Longing: Narratives of the Miniature, the Gigantic, the Souvenir, the Collection* [1984; Durham, N.C.: Duke UP, 1993] 109–10). As Bruce McConachie puts it, Kimball's and Barnum's museums' "domestic environments for their exhibits [tended] to encourage and enhance such sentimental effects" (*Melodramatic Formulations* 169).

73 For a similar point about a novel written the same decade as *Hobomok*, see Dana Nelson's discussion of Catharine Maria Sedgwick's *Hope Leslie* (1827) in *The Word in Black and White: Reading 'Race' in American Literature, 1638–1867* (New York: Oxford UP, 1992) 65–79.

74 Thoreau goes on to repeat his charges against the museum in this same journal passage: "When some Vandal chieftain has razed to the earth the British Museum . . . the arrowheads which the museum contains will, perhaps, find themselves at home again in familiar dust, and resume their shining in new springs upon the bared surface of the earth then, to be picked up for the thousandth time by the shepherd or savage that may be wandering there, and once more suggest their story to him. . . . As for museums, I think it is better to let Nature take care of our antiquities"(*J* 12:92–93). His charge rings hollow here, though, as he boasts that he could "make a museum that would delight" from his collected relics (*J* 12:89).

75 For Thoreau seeing arrowheads at Barnum's museum, see *J* 6:76 (22 November 1854). Although his Indian notebooks contain several passages from Morton's *Crania Americana* (1839), Thoreau was disgusted by his craniometrical practices, if not always by his racialist conclusions: "What a mean and wretched creature is man! By and by some Dr. Morton may be filling your cranium with white mustard seed to learn its internal capacity. Of all ways to come at a knowledge of a living man, this seems to me the worst, as it is the most belated. You would learn more by once paring the toe-nails of the living subject. There is nothing out of which the spirit has more completely departed, and in which it has left fewer significant traces" (*J* 4:146 [25 June 1852]).

76 Thoreau's idea of the arrowheads being "fossil thoughts" that bring their

makers back to life curiously reflects on Marx's definition of the commodities as becoming "independent beings endowed with life, and entering into relation both with one another and the human race" (Karl Marx, *Capital, Vol. I* [1867], ed. Frederick Engels, trans. Samuel Moore and Edward Aveling [New York: International Publishers, 1967] 72). In capitalism, the worker sells his labor, creating products which then seem to take on a life of their own; in the museum, by paying an entrance fee, the antiquarian can regain contact with a worker from long ago through his products. It is that sense of contact that draws Thoreau to museums despite his vituperations against them.

77 Copway, a Chippewa, gained a great deal of fame in the late 1840s and early 1850s while lecturing in some of the same venues as Tubbee and similarly publishing an autobiography. For more on Copway, see Donald B. Smith, "The Life of George Copway or Kah-ge-ga-gah-bowh (1818–1869)—and a Review of His Writings," *Journal of Canadian Studies* 23.3 (fall 1988): 5–38; and Dale T. Knobel, "Know-Nothings and Indians: Strange Bedfellows?" *Western Historical Quarterly* 15.2 (April 1984): 175–98.

78 Thoreau not only used museums as a way of gaining access to the Indian's primitive wildness; he proposed using museumlike methods to preserve wild Indians as a reservoir of primitiveness for overcivilized whites. Thoreau ends "Chesuncook" by pining for a way of saving the wildness that he has found as a source of renewal for Euro-Americans—"Why should not we . . . have our national preserves, where no villages need be destroyed, in which the bear and panther, and some even of the hunter race, may still exist, and not be 'civilized off the face of the earth,'—our forests . . . not for idle sport or food, but for inspiration and our own true recreation?" (*MW* 156). Such a preserve seems at first to invoke the reservation system beginning to be implemented in the late 1840s and early 1850s. But those in favor of the reservation system, such as Indian Commissioners William Medill and Luke Lea and Native American lecturers like Copway and Tubbee, hoped that reservations would provide a way for Native peoples to be slowly assimilated into American culture without being exploited; Thoreau, on the other hand, imagined a reserve that would maintain the Indian peoples in their "traditional" lifeways, so as to create a reservoir of primitive wildness to which Euro-American culture could go to "re-create" itself, both spiritually and physically. For more on the beginnings of the reservation system and the logic underlying it, see Robert A. Trennert Jr., *Alternative to Extinction: Federal Indian Policy and the Beginnings of the Reservation System, 1846–51* (Philadelphia: Temple UP, 1975), and Prucha, "American Indian Policy in the 1840s."

79 In *Walden* Thoreau turns to the act of watching a theatrical performance to describe how "We are not wholly involved with nature," a detachment/

contact with both nature and his own body that mirrors his experience at Ktaadn (135).

3. A "*Rara Avis in Terris*": Poe's "Hop-Frog" and
Race in the Antebellum Freak Show

1 Letter to Frederick W. Thomas, 14 February 1849, *The Letters of Edgar Allan Poe*, vol. 2, ed. John Ward Ostrom (Cambridge: Harvard UP, 1948) 427–28. Further references to the letters will be to this edition and will be given with volume and page number.

2 David Leverenz has suggested that "Hop-Frog" satirizes both Southern gentry and Northern capitalist models of manhood and hints at the sort of racial identification I foreground when he talks of Poe as a Sambo-trickster figure in "Hop-Frog." My concern is more with how Poe savages a capitalist mode while relying upon mass cultural forms to do so. See David Leverenz, "Poe and Gentry Virginia: Provincial Gentleman, Textual Aristocrat, Man of the Crowd," in *Haunted Bodies: Gender and Southern Texts*, ed. Anne Goodwyn Jones and Susan V. Donaldson (Charlottesville: UP of Virginia, 1997) 100–101. As Joan Dayan has remarked, Poe "questions what it means to speak, or to love, as a *man*. . . . he ironizes the very possibility of speaking for or as a man" (Joan Dayan, "Poe's Women: A Feminist Poe?" *Poe Studies* 26.1–2 [June/December 1993]: 1). While it may be, as Dayan argues, that "the point of much of Poe's writing" was "to mutilate what his society constructed as manhood" (9), I am interested in how he implies another model of literary manhood in the place of a normative, white, Northern, middle-class manhood. See also Eliza Richards's discussion of how in his poetry and criticism Poe attempted "to carve out a specifically masculine, poetic space" by "out-feminizing the feminine in a masculine rendition that inverts female poetic practice" (Eliza Richards, " 'The Poetess' and Poe's Performance of the Feminine," *Arizona Quarterly* 55.2 [summer 1999]: 18, 8).

3 Letter to Washington Poe, 15 August 1840, *Letters* 1:143.

4 "Hop-Frog," *Edgar Allan Poe: Poetry and Tales*, ed. Patrick F. Quinn (New York: Library of America, 1984) 899, 900. Further references to Poe's poetry and tales will be to this edition and will be given parenthetically as *PT*.

5 J. R. Hammond identifies the story as "a powerful allegory: the king representing Reality, the eternal antagonist of the creative mind, and the jester representing Imagination, the creative artist who is maimed and imprisoned by the unthinking majority" (J. R. Hammond, *An Edgar Allan Poe Companion: A Guide to the Short Stories, Romances, and Essays* [Totowa, N.J.: Barnes and Noble Books, 1981] 90–91). See also Hervey Allen's reading of "sovereign Reality who makes the cripple of Imagination, whom he keeps as a jester" who, in turn, takes "terrible revenge" and escapes with " 'Fancy' "

(Hervey Allen, *Israfel: The Life and Times of Edgar Allan Poe* [New York: George H. Doran Co., 1926] 641); and, more recently, Kenneth Silverman's gloss (Kenneth Silverman, *Edgar A. Poe: Mournful and Never-Ending Remembrance* [New York: HarperCollins, 1991] 406–7).

6   Letter to Annie L. Richmond, 8 February 1849, *Letters* 2:425.

7   Letter to Edward H. N. Patterson, [30?] April 1849, *Letters* 2: 439–40.

8   "Prospectus of *The Stylus*," 4 March 1843, *Edgar Allan Poe: Essays and Reviews*, ed. G. R. Thompson (New York: Library of America, 1984) 1033; Letter to Thomas W. White, 30 April 1835, *Letters* 1: 57–58. Further references to Poe's essays and reviews will be to the above edition and will be cited parenthetically as *ER*.

9   Poe describes the "subject" of "Hop-Frog" as a "terrible one" in his letter to Annie L. Richmond, 8 February 1849, *Letters* 2: 425.

10   Terence Whalen's observation that Poe "viewed his texts as split or divided objects—one part containing literary value for the critical taste, the other part containing such matter as would render them profitable in the mass market" seems appropriate here (Terence Whalen, *Edgar Allan Poe and the Masses: The Political Economy of Literature in Antebellum America* [Princeton, N.J.: Princeton UP, 1999] 91).

11   Given Poe's infamous identification of poetic beauty with women ("the death . . . of a beautiful woman is, unquestionably, the most poetical topic in the world" [*ER* 19]; "[The Poet] feels [poetry] in the beauty of women" [*ER* 93]), it has become a commonplace to read Poe as objectifying women as simply disembodied symbols of transcendent beauty, a reading given substance, perhaps, in his description of Trippetta as nearly bodiless, both in her small size and her grace: she was "of exquisite proportions, and a marvellous dancer" and "on account of her grace and exquisite beauty," was "universally admired and petted" (*PT* 900). Yet as Joan Dayan and others have pointed out, the women in Poe's tales tend to be frighteningly and hauntingly material as they refuse to be the purely spiritual angels of domestic ideology even in death. Poe's women, as Dayan puts it, "are not mere symbols for" Beauty because "Poe does not sustain the eternal polarities, but instead analyzes the slippage in too convenient oppositions" including gendered ones (Dayan, "Poe's Women" 1). Several critics have used this refusal of immateriality on the part of Poe's female characters to argue for seeing the tales as "an enlightened deconstruction of nineteenth-century gender roles" (J. Gerald Kennedy, "Poe, 'Ligeia,' and the Problem of Dying Women," in *New Essays on Poe's Major Tales*, ed. Kenneth Silverman [Cambridge: Cambridge UP, 1993] 114). For readings of a feminist Poe, see Cynthia Jordan, *Second Stories: The Politics of Language, Form, and Gender in Early American Fictions* (Chapel Hill: U of North Carolina P, 1989), and Leland S. Person Jr., *Aesthetic Headaches: Women and a Masculine Poetics in Poe, Melville, and*

Hawthorne (Athens: U of Georgia P, 1988). My point is not to question Poe's destabilization of gender oppositions, but to argue that in challenging one dominant mode of literary manhood, he erects another model through the invocation of racial difference in the mass cultural sphere.

12 See, for example, David Reynolds's contention that unlike the sensational literature he draws on, Poe's work "transcends its time-specific referents because it is crafted in such a way that it remains accessible to generations of readers" (David S. Reynolds, "Poe's Art of Transformation: 'The Cask of Amontillado' in Cultural Context," in *New Essays on Poe's Major Tales,* ed. Kenneth Silverman [Cambridge: Cambridge UP, 1993] 101). Also see David Reynolds, *Beneath the American Renaissance: The Subversive Imagination in the Age of Emerson and Melville* (Cambridge: Harvard UP, 1988). On the other hand, see especially Terence Whalen, "Edgar Allan Poe and the Horrid Laws of Political Economy," *American Quarterly* 44.3 (September 1992): 381–417. As Whalen has explored most fully, Poe's literary career at once grew out of the market conditions that structured literature in the antebellum era and protested against those conditions: "If Poe . . . tried to defend or create an autonomous realm for literature, it was an effort simultaneously doomed and motivated by the homogenizing pressures" of antebellum economic and literary production (391). I have found Whalen's discussion here immensely enlightening and helpful in thinking through Poe and the literary market. Jonathan Elmer has also recently considered Poe in relation to literary mass culture, but rather than being concerned with the political economy of mass culture, as Whalen is, he focuses on the democratic nature of mass culture, the tension between being part of a large, anonymous cultural whole and being an individual that was central to Jacksonian America. See Jonathan Elmer, *Reading at the Social Limit: Affect, Mass Culture, and Edgar Allan Poe* (Stanford, Calif.: Stanford UP, 1995).

13 Letter to Thomas W. White, 30 April 1835, *Letters* 1: 58; review of Beverly Tucker, *George Balcombe, Southern Literary Messenger,* January 1837, *Essays and Reviews* 978.

14 Letter to Thomas W. White, 30 April 1835, *Letters* 1: 57–58.

15 Letter to Charles Anthon, ante 2 November 1844 (probably late October), *Letters* 1:266–72.

16 As Whalen argues, "Poe's persistent struggle to influence the taste of the reading public was not so much a reactionary attempt to resurrect the old standards of literary value, but rather an effort to institute some new system of measurement that would enable the articulation and sorting of a new mass of literary commodities" (Whalen, "Horrid Laws" 398).

17 Leverenz, "Poe and Gentry Virginia" 101.

18 Poe implies his own familiarity with Barnum and his display of apes in a letter published in a Philadelphia newspaper, in which he described the face

of one of his literary rivals as resembling "that of the best-looking but most unprincipled of Mr. Barnum's baboons" (quoted in Joseph Wood Krutch, *Edgar Allan Poe: A Study in Genius* [1926; New York: Russell and Russell, 1965] 129).

19 Don Francisco Hidalgo, a dwarf, like Hop-Frog, served King Ferdinand VII of Spain as a jester until the mid-1840s, when he attempted to capitalize on Tom Thumb's success by staging a tour of his own through England and the United States (Richard Altick, *The Shows of London* [Cambridge: Harvard UP, 1978] 256). As Poe says in his story, "at the date of my narrative, professing jesters had not altogether gone out of fashion at court" (*PT* 899). Further, he states that "the animals in question [orangutans] had, at the epoch of my story, very rarely been seen in any part of the civilized world" (*PT* 904); according to at least one source, Barnum displayed the first live orangutan in America in 1846. See John Rickards Betts, "P. T. Barnum and the Popularization of Natural History," *Journal of the History of Ideas* 20.3 (June–September 1959): 353.

20 This is the definition of the freak show offered by Robert Bogdan in his seminal *Freak Show: Presenting Human Oddities for Amusement and Profit* (Chicago: U of Chicago P, 1988) 9. Besides Bogdan and Altick, for discussions of the freak show more generally and the antebellum freak show in particular, see Rosemarie Garland Thomson, "The Cultural Work of American Freak Shows, 1835–1940," *Extraordinary Bodies: Figuring Physical Disability in American Culture and Literature* (New York: Columbia UP, 1997) 55–80; Thomson, ed., *Freakery: Cultural Spectacles of the Extraordinary Body* (New York: New York UP, 1996); Leslie Fiedler, *Freaks: Myths and Images of the Secret Self* (1978; New York: Anchor Books, 1993); and Leonard Cassuto, "The Racial Freak, the Happy Slave, and the Problems of Melville's Universal Men," *The Inhuman Race: The Racial Grotesque in American Literature and Culture* (New York: Columbia UP, 1997) 168–216.

21 *Sketch of the Life, Personal Appearance, Character and Manners of Charles S. Stratton, The Man in Miniature, Known as General Tom Thumb* (New York: Van Norden and Amerman, 1847) 5.

22 Neil Harris, *Humbug: The Art of P. T. Barnum* (Chicago: U of Chicago P, 1973) 49.

23 For more on the logic of the miniature, see Susan Stewart, *On Longing: Narratives of the Miniature, the Gigantic, the Souvenir, the Collection* (1984; Durham, N.C.: Duke UP, 1993).

24 Much work has been done of late on Barnum's museum and the role it played in bringing together a cross-class audience of rising artisans, merchants, and clerks and their families in an environment that brought together high and low, Broadway and the Bowery, while promoting itself as "respectable"—middle-class. See, in particular, Bluford Adams's discussion

in *E Pluribus Barnum: The Great Showman and the Making of U.S. Popular Culture* (Minneapolis: U of Minnesota P, 1997) 75–163, and Peter Buckley's chapter on Barnum in "To the Opera House: Culture and Society in New York City, 1820–1860," Ph.D. diss., SUNY Stony Brook, 1984. See also my prologue and my chapter on Thoreau.

25 For more on Thumb as feminized commodity for an increasingly feminine audience, see Lori Merish, "Cuteness and Commodity Aesthetics: Tom Thumb and Shirley Temple," in *Freakery*, ed. Thomson 185–203. As she argues, "In the performances of these diminutive prodigies, the cute emerged as a site for feminine identification as well as a strategy for domesticating (the) Otherness (of 'freak,' of child), annexing the Other to the Self" (188). According to Merish, the cute, "emerg[ing] in conjunction with the 'feminization' of commercial amusements" (195), "transforms transgressive subjects into beloved objects" (194). Poe figures the transgressive and beloved nature of the freak by splitting it into two gendered bodies, the masculine, deformed Hop-Frog and the feminine, beautiful (or cute) Trippetta.

26 Quoted in Altick, *Shows* 265. The fullest account of Barnum's "What is It?" exhibits is James W. Cook Jr.'s "Of Men, Missing Links, and Nondescripts: The Strange Career of P. T. Barnum's 'What is It?' Exhibition," in *Freakery*, ed. Thomson 139–57.

27 Altick, *Shows* 265.

28 Joseph N. Ireland, *Records of the New York Stage from 1750 to 1860*, vol. 2 (1866; New York: Benjamin Blom, 1966) 318.

29 For Jocko, see George C. D. Odell, *Annals of the New York Stage*, vol. 4 (1834–1843) (New York: Columbia UP, 1928) 482; for Bibbo, see Odell 5:135; for the Frog, see Odell 4:371.

30 Odell 4:368.

31 Henry Mayhew, *London Labour and the London Poor*, vol. 3 (1861; New York: Dover, 1968) 103.

32 Ireland 2: 319, paraphrasing Francis Wemyss, who stated that "poor Leach [was] maltreated, and died shortly afterwards" (Francis C. Wemyss, *Wemyss' Chronology of the American Stage, from 1752 to 1852* [1852; New York: Benjamin Blom, 1968] 92).

33 See such comments as " 'museum' in the American sense of the word means [simply] a place of amusement" (quoted in Louis Leonard Tucker, " 'Ohio Show-Shop': The Western Museum of Cincinnati, 1820–1867," in *A Cabinet of Curiosities: Five Episodes in the Evolution of American Museums* [Charlottesville, Va.: UP of Virginia, 1967] 73), and the idea that American museums were "full of worthless and trashy articles" (quoted in Whitfield L. Bell Jr., "The Cabinet of the American Philosophical Society," *A Cabinet of Curiosities* 22). For Agassiz's position as the most prominent scientist of the

age, see Edward Lurie, *Louis Agassiz, A Life in Science* (Chicago: Phoenix Books, 1966), especially chapter 5, "Naturalist to America." As Bogdan notes, human curiosities' strangeness at once drew scientific censure for sensationalism and at the same time "scientific interest because they represented specimens, data to be examined in quest of answers to the pressing scientific questions of the day" (*Freak Show* 151).

34 See Betts, "P. T. Barnum" 357. See Betts more fully for a discussion of Barnum's role in popularizing science.

35 In this way, as Bogdan notes, freak shows were especially "relevant to debates concerning the classification of human races and the place of various humans in the great chain of being" (*Freak Show* 27).

36 This is basically Cassuto's overarching explanation for the rise of freak shows during the period. I find this explanation a bit too facile, especially in the way it depends on seeing the freak show and abolitionist techniques as in complete opposition to one another. As Cook has recently argued in discussing Barnum's "What is It?" exhibit and Benjamin Reiss has shown in reference to Barnum's exhibition of Joice Heth in the 1830s, we should not read such exhibits so quickly and easily as strictly upholding racist and/or pro-slavery positions. See Benjamin Reiss, "P. T. Barnum, Joice Heth, and Antebellum Spectacles of Race," *American Quarterly* 51.1 (March 1999): 78–107. Both Thomson and Cassuto invoke Eric Lott's work on the minstrel show in nodding toward the ways in which the freak show depended as much on identification as objectification, but neither seems much interested in exploring the more subversive possibilities of such sympathetic lines between freakish other and supposedly normal audience member. See, for example, Cassuto, *The Inhuman Race* 197–98. For more on the nearly all-white make-up of Barnum's audience, see Adams, *E Pluribus Barnum* 107–8.

37 See *Sketch* 15, 16, for minstrel songs, and Brooks McNamara, " 'A Congress of Wonders': The Rise and Fall of the Dime Museum," *ESQ* 20.3 (1974): 217, for a pamphlet with Thumb dressed as "My Mary Ann." Also see Merish, "Cuteness and Commodity Aesthetics," on the feminization of Thumb.

38 Letter to Moses Kimball, 18 August 1846, *Selected Letters of P. T. Barnum*, ed. A. H. Saxton (New York: Columbia UP, 1983) 35. See Cook, "Of Men," for the fullest discussion of Johnson. Also see Bogdan, *Freak Show* 134–44; Adams, *E Pluribus Barnum* 157–64, for a discussion of Johnson in terms of Barnum's shifting antebellum politics (and his production of Boucicault's *The Octoroon*); and Bill Brown, *The Material Unconscious: American Amusement, Stephen Crane, and the Economies of Play* (Cambridge: Harvard UP, 1996) 215–18 on Crane's *The Monster* and its interplay between blackface minstrelsy and the bestialized black of the freak show.

39 See Cassuto, Thomson, Cook, and Reiss for the best overviews of the racial character of the freak show. See also Bernth Lindfors, "Circus Africans,"

Journal of American Culture 6.2 (1983): 9–14. Thomson goes a bit too far, perhaps, in arguing that in the freak show, "no firm distinction exists between primarily formal disabilities and racial physical features considered atypical by dominant, white standards" ("Cultural Work" 14).

40 Toni Morrison has pointed out that Poe's use of "othering" here and elsewhere reveals "unmanageable slips" indicative of the ambivalent structure of these images of blackness (Toni Morrison, *Playing in the Dark: Whiteness and the Literary Imagination* [New York: Vintage, 1993] 58–59). As I will argue more fully below, these grotesque visions point to Poe's interest in the use of race for frightening, sensationalistic purposes along with any racism they demonstrate. Poe describes the Sioux, in *Rodman*, in somewhat similar terms: "In person, the Sioux generally are an ugly ill-made race, their limbs being much too small for the trunk, according to our ideas of the human form—their cheek bones are high, and their eyes protruding and dull" (*PT* 1222). As these different racial others indicate, I think it is important to keep the exotic locale of Hop-Frog's birth indefinite as Poe does, even as we see the parallels with descriptions of blacks and Indians. From this position, Dayan, perhaps, pushes it too far, when she says "this unheard of place refers implicitly to Africa" ("Amorous Bondage: Poe, Ladies, and Slaves," *American Literature* 66.2 [June 1994]: 258).

41 Quoted in Betts, "P. T. Barnum" 353–54; in reference to Johnson, quoted in Bogdan, *Freak Show* 136. For Leach, see above.

42 For the racial nature of the orangutan in "The Murders in the Rue Morgue," see Nancy A. Horowitz, "Criminality and Poe's Orangutan: The Question of Race in Detection," in *Agonistics: Arenas of Creative Contest*, ed. Janet Lungstrum and Elizabeth Sauer (Albany: State U of New York P, 1997) 177–95; Whalen, "Horrid Laws" 401; and Dayan, "Romance and Race," in *The Columbia History of the American Novel*, gen. ed. Emory Elliott (New York: Columbia UP, 1991) 103. Similarly, in "The System of Dr. Tarr and Professor Fether" (1844), a story "Hop-Frog" possibly alludes to when one of the ministers suggests adding "feathers" to their costumes of tar (*PT* 904), Poe links the insane with orangutans through the appearance of the tarred and feathered keepers of the asylum (*PT* 716).

43 *An Illustrated Catalogue and Guide Book to Barnum's American Museum* (New York: n.p., [1864]) III. See also David R. Brigham, *Public Culture in the Early Republic: Peale's Museum and Its Audience* (Washington, D.C.: Smithsonian Institution Press, 1995) 130, for a description of the way orangutans and blacks were linked together in Peale's Museum in 1799.

44 Perhaps most infamously, Thomas Jefferson suggested the possibility of sexual relations between black women and orangutans in *Notes on the State of Virginia*: "[blacks'] own judgment in favour of the whites, declared by their preference of them, as uniformly as is the preference of the Oran-ootan

for the black women over those of his own species" (Thomas Jefferson, *Notes on the State of Virginia*, ed. William Peden [1787; New York: Norton, 1972] 138). See Cook, "Of Men," for more on the liminal, racialized status of orangutans in reference to the "What is It?" exhibits.

45 Dayan, "Romance and Race" 104. See also her "Amorous Bondage" 258.

46 Such criticism first began appearing in the late 1950s and early 60s, but then was displaced by deconstructionist versions of Poe that tore him away from any social context. For example, Leslie Fiedler, in *Love and Death in the American Novel* (1960), argues that "*theoretically* the tale of *Gordon Pym* projects through its Negroes the fear of black rebellion and of the white man's perverse lust for the Negro, while symbolizing in the red man an innocent and admirable yearning for the manly violence of the frontier; but in the working out of the plot, the two are confused. . . . Insofar as *Gordon Pym* is finally a social document as well as a fantasy, its subject is slavery; and its scene, however disguised, is the section of America which was to destroy itself defending that institution" (Leslie A. Fiedler, *Love and Death in the American Novel* [1960; London: Paladin, 1970] 368). For more recent treatments of race and *Pym*, see John Carlos Rowe, "Poe, Antebellum Slavery, and Modern Criticism," in *Poe's Pym: Critical Explorations*, ed. Richard Kopley (Durham, N.C.: Duke UP, 1992) 117–38; Sam Worley, "*The Narrative of Arthur Gordon Pym* and the Ideology of Slavery" *ESQ* 40 (1994): 219–50; Teresa A. Goddu, "The Ghost of Race: Edgar Allan Poe and the Southern Gothic," *Gothic America: Narrative, History and Nation* (New York: Columbia UP, 1997) 73–93; Jared Gardner, "Poe's 'Incredible Adventures and Discoveries Still Farther South,'" *Master Plots: Race and the Founding of an American Literature, 1787–1845* (Baltimore, Md.: Johns Hopkins UP, 1998) 125–59; and Dana Nelson, "Ethnocentrism Decentered: Colonial Motives in *The Narrative of Arthur Gordon Pym*," *The Word in Black and White: Reading "Race" in American Literature, 1638–1867* (New York: Oxford UP, 1993) 90–108. For an alternative account, which discounts the argument for Poe's authorship of the Paulding-Drayton review as outlined by Bernard Rosenthal in "Poe, Slavery, and the *Southern Literary Messenger*: A Reexamination," *Poe Studies* 7.2 (December 1974): 29–38, see Terence Whalen, "Subtle Barbarians: Poe, Racism, and the Political Economy of Adventure," in *Styles of Cultural Activism: From Theory and Pedagogy to Women, Indians, and Communism*, ed. Philip Goldstein (Cranbury, N.J.: Associated University Presses, 1994) 169–83. As in his other scholarship, Whalen calls for reading Poe in terms of an information explosion, including an explosion of information produced by exploration about exotic locales and peoples. The criticism I have found most useful on Poe and race is Dayan, "Amorous Bondage" and "Romance and Race," and Dana Nelson, "The Haunting of White Manhood: Poe, Fraternal Ritual, and Polygenesis," *American Literature* 69.3 (September 1997): 515–46.

47 Review of *Slavery in the United States* by J. K. Paulding and *The South Vindicated from the Treason and Fanaticism of the Northern Abolitionists* [William Drayton], *Southern Literary Messenger* 2.5 (April 1836): 337; Rosenthal, "Poe, Slavery" 30. As Nelson and Goddu have pointed out and as I will touch on below, Poe's racism was far less regional than it was national. Reading his racism simply from his self-identification as a Southerner helps to obscure the way in which that racism was common nationwide.

48 Joan Dayan, "Amorous Bondage" 258; "Romance and Race" 93; "Amorous Bondage" 249. Dayan's most recent comments in "Poe, Persons, and Property," *American Literary History* 11.3 (fall 1999): 405–25, bring her insights about the philosophical underpinnings of Poe's work closer to my interest in the economics of the literary. In this article, she articulates the ways in which "Poe demands a way of reading that escapes the binary bind of the racist or nonracist Poe" (412), suggesting instead that "Poe's fantasies of degeneration or disability, then, are never *only* about the enslavement of the African American" (419), but rather derive from his "obsession with possession, personal identity, and the will" (411). My concern is with how Poe's obsession with his own literary property and reputation as possessions circulated through mass cultural images of race and slavery.

49 As Whalen notes, "given the enormous quantity of [Poe's] writings, there are precious few references to slavery, and many of these are made in the heat of a broader assault on a literary enemy who is 'vulnerable' for having abolitionist tendencies" (Whalen, "Subtle Barbarians" 183 note 23).

50 Letter to George W. Eveleth, 26 June 1849, *Letters* 2: 449–50.

51 As Whalen puts it, Poe's comments suggest "how ideological and economic forces combined to determine the salability of racism" (*Poe and the Masses* 143); in Whalen's view, "Poe capitalizes on the average racism of his audience while neutralizing the sectional conflict over slavery" (142).

52 See Harris, *Humbug* 59–91 on the operational aesthetic, and 85–88 for a discussion of this aesthetic in reference to Poe's hoaxes and detective stories.

53 For example, see Barnum's account of "*White Negroes*" from 1864: "The history of this family seems almost miraculous. The father and mother both black, and distinctly African, yet each alternate child, (and they have had fifteen) has been white and black; the white children's features being so decidedly Ethiopian as to preclude the possibility of doubt as to their being purely African" (*Illustrated Catalogue and Guide Book* 114). For more on Barnum and his depictions of blackness, see Reiss, "P. T. Barnum," and my chapter on Thoreau.

54 See Stephen Jay Gould, *The Mismeasure of Man* (New York: Norton, 1981), and William Stanton, *The Leopard's Spots: Scientific Attitudes Toward Race in America, 1815–1859* (Chicago: University of Chicago Press, 1960), for the best overviews of craniometry and the American school of ethnology. As they both point out, scientific racialism and proslavery thought during this pe-

riod did not necessarily go hand-in-hand. See also George M. Fredrickson, "Science, Polygenesis, and the Proslavery Argument," *The Black Image in the White Mind: The Debate on Afro-American Character and Destiny, 1817–1914* (New York: Harper, 1971) 71–96.

55 *Sketch of Life* 8. See Bogdan, *Freak Show* 151, for a fuller discussion of this point.

56 Jared Gardner uses Poe's acceptance of phrenological tenets to support seeing his desire to hierarchize American writers through their penmanship (in "Autography") as parallel to Morton's project of ordering races through cranial measurement. While this argument provides an interesting and suggestive parallel, which I found useful for thinking through Poe's desire to become a national critic, I will argue that the empiricism of craniometry and its implicit idea of progress repelled Poe in a way phrenology itself did not. See Edward Hungerford, "Poe and Phrenology," *American Literature* 2 (1930–1931): 209–31, for the fullest discussion of Poe's interest in phrenology. As Hungerford argues, phrenology is found in much of Poe's literary criticism and plays a central role in characterizing both Ligeia and Roderick Usher. Yet, as he also notes, Poe was quick to criticize or satirize the claims of both phrenology and physiognomy in stories such as "Lionizing" (1835); "The Business Man" (1840); "The Murders in the Rue Morgue" (1841); "Diddling Considered as One of the Exact Sciences" (1843); "The Literary Life of Thingum Bob, Esq." (1844); "Some Words with a Mummy" (1845); and "The Imp of the Perverse" (1845).

57 As Nelson puts it, Poe has his mummy "tear down the modern [scientists]' sense of cultural, political, scientific, and racial progress" ("Haunting of White Manhood" 515) by "refus[ing] to be baited by an essentialist argument correlating bodily differences with intellectual and cultural ones" (535).

58 The doltish Thingum Bob is told "You have an immense head, too, and it must hold a great many brains" (*PT* 767).

59 Much of this line of thinking derives from Poe's early poem "Sonnet—To Science," where he imagines science as a vulture who preys "upon the poet's heart" (*PT* 38). But as David Van Leer argues, "Poe himself is less interested in blaming science than in understanding its effect on future poetic projects" (David Van Leer, "Nature's Book: The Language of Science in the American Renaissance," in *Romanticism and the Sciences*, ed. Andrew Cunningham and Nicholas Jardine [Cambridge: Cambridge UP, 1990] 311). See also his "Detecting Truth: The World of the Dupin Tales," in *New Essays on Poe's Major Tales*, ed. Kenneth Silverman (Cambridge: Cambridge UP, 1993) 65–92. As John Limon puts it, rather than dismissing science outright, "Poe sees the problem of science as a competition for space" (John Limon, *The Place of Fiction in the Time of Science: A Disciplinary History of American Writing* [Cambridge: Cambridge UP, 1990] 72).

60 Stanton, *Leopard's Spots* 25. This concern with uniting science and art reap-

pears throughout his criticism, where Poe claimed that the evaluation of art works should be a matter of science, of "axioms founded in reason and in truth" (*ER* 1027), and comes to a conclusion with *Eureka*, a lecture he first gave a year prior to writing "Hop-Frog," with the hope of "get[ting] the means of taking the first step" toward establishing the *Stylus* (letter to Nathaniel Parker Willis, 22 January 1848, *Letters* 2:359). In *Eureka*, Poe articulates his skepticism toward a pure empiricism and scientific principles, repeatedly deriding the idea of using "so-called 'ocular and physical proof' " in "the so-called corroboration of [a scientific] 'theory' " (*PT* 1284). In fact, he repeats at least twice that "there is, in this world at least, *no such thing* as demonstrance" (*PT* 1261; see also 1291). Instead of placing "an inferior faith" in "merely *perceptive powers*" (*PT* 1322), "true Science" emerges through "intuitive *leaps*" (*PT* 1264). It is not through "demonstration" or "corroboration" that theories emerge as truthful; it is through our own "*fancy*" (*PT* 1329) and "force of conviction" (*PT* 1318) that we realize the truth.

61 See "Philosophy of Furniture," *Collected Works of Edgar Allan Poe*, vol. 2, *Tales and Sketches, 1831–1842*, ed. Thomas Ollive Mabbott (Cambridge: Belknap Press/Harvard UP, 1978) 500 note t.

62 Cited in Dwight Thomas and David K. Jackson, *The Poe Log: A Documentary Life of Edgar Allan Poe, 1809–1849* (Boston: G. K. Hall, 1987) 201.

63 Quoted in Killis Campbell, *The Mind of Poe and Other Studies* (Cambridge: Harvard UP, 1933) 59.

64 Motley Manners, esq. [Augustine J. H. Duganne], "A Mirror for Authors" *Holden's Dollar Magazine* (January 1849): 22. See John E. Reilly's discussion of the satire, "Poe in Pillory: An Early Version of a Satire by A. J. H. Duganne," *Poe Studies* 6 (June 1973): 4–12. Reilly contends that Poe probably never saw the Duganne satire, but whether he saw Duganne's identifying him as a Mohawk or not, he was clearly familiar with the popular idea of him as a savage, scalping Comanche-like critics.

65 Letter to Frederick W. Thomas, 14 February 1849, *Letters* 2: 428, his italics.

66 Ibid. 427–28; in *A Fable for Critics*, Lowell cautions Poe that "You mustn't fling mud-balls at Longfellow so," after commenting that Poe's "heart seems all squeezed out by the mind" (James Russell Lowell, *A Fable for Critics, The Complete Writings of James Russell Lowell*, vol. 12 [Boston: Houghton, Mifflin, 1904] 68). See Sidney P. Moss, *Poe's Literary Battles: The Critic in the Context of His Literary Milieu* (1963; Carbondale: Southern Illinois UP, 1969), for an overview of Poe's critical wars with the Bostonians, including the "Longfellow War" of 1845–1846.

67 Letter to Thomas, 2: 427, his italics.

68 Ibid.

69 See letters to George W. Eveleth, 15 December 1846, and 4 January 1848, *Letters* 2: 333, 354, for both "South & West" and Frogpondians.

70 See Kenneth Alan Hovey, "Critical Provincialism: Poe's Poetic Principle in

Antebellum Context," *American Quarterly* 39.3 (fall 1987): 341–54, for an account of Poe's criticism as being based in regional controversies over notions of history that included the issue of slavery.

71 The title has other possible sources, of course. For example, Tom Thumb had played in *Hop-o'-my-Thumb* and Leach had performed as "the Frog." See Harris, *Humbug* 102, and *Sketch* 14, on *Hop-o'-my-Thumb*. As Silverman notes in *Edgar A. Poe*, Poe's "turbulent feelings about Boston involved more than literature"(264). He quotes Bernard C. Meyer's "suspicion that ultimately [Boston] represented the underside of the ambivalence he felt toward the mother who abandoned him by her untimely death" (492). Such a reading might help to complicate Marie Bonaparte's oedipal reading of "Hop-Frog" (Marie Bonaparte, *The Life and Works of Edgar Allan Poe: A Psycho-Analytic Interpretation*, trans. John Rodker [1949; New York: Humanities Press, 1971] 510–13) and suggests another way of identifying Boston as the target of Poe's overdetermined rage.

72 This connection is further suggested by the fact that when Poe finished "Hop-Frog" he almost immediately wrote to his confidante, Annie Richmond. Richmond, a resident of Lowell, Massachusetts, was one of Poe's few close friends in the area and would have understood his ironic glee at the geographic implication of his title—especially since it would be published in a cheap Boston publication—"The five prose pages I finished yesterday are called—what do you think?—I am sure you will never guess—Hop-Frog!" (Letter to Annie L. Richmond, 8 February 1849, *Letters* 2: 425).

73 Along these lines, Duganne satirized the Bostonian abolitionist poet John Greenleaf Whittier in "A Mirror for Authors," just prior to addressing Poe, "Were 't not for *darkies* sure his fame would *darkle*:. . . . But, oh! how frail 'Othello's occupation!' / When slavery falls—falls Whittier's avocation" (22).

74 See Dayan, "Poe, Persons, and Property" for an extended discussion of how "All of Poe's fiction is about property and possession" (410) and a short commentary on "Hop-Frog" as "a final joke on the gentry both North and South, who with torturous ingenuity defined property in women, workers, and slaves, fixing them and their progeny in their status and location, kept low down in the hierarchy of entitlements" (412).

4. Inward Criminality and the Shadow of Race:
The House of the Seven Gables and Daguerreotypy

1 Shawn Michelle Smith's *American Archives* appeared as I was finishing revisions to the manuscript of this book. Her discussion of *Seven Gables* resonates with mine in its focus on the daguerreotypal inscription of white middle-class interiority and privilege. See Shawn Michelle Smith, *American Archives: Gender, Race, and Class in Visual Culture* (Princeton, N.J.: Prince-

ton UP, 1999). David Anthony's appraisal of *House* in the context of minstrelsy also appeared as I finished revisions to this chapter and intersects with a number of my arguments; see David Anthony, "Class, Culture, and the Trouble with White Skin in Hawthorne's *The House of the Seven Gables*," *Yale Journal of Criticism* 12.2 (1999): 249–68.

2 *The House of the Seven Gables*, vol. 2 of *The Centenary Edition of the Works of Nathaniel Hawthorne* (1851; Columbus: Ohio State UP, 1965) 312. Further references will be to this edition and will be made parenthetically.

3 My point then is similar to the one Kenneth Warren makes in reference to American realism at the turn of the century—"concerns about 'race' may structure our American texts, even when those texts are not 'about' race in any substantive way" (Kenneth W. Warren, *Black and White Strangers: Race and American Literary Realism* [Chicago: U of Chicago P, 1993] 10). See also Toni Morrison's consideration of "whether the major and championed characteristics of our national literature—individualism, masculinity, social engagement versus historical isolation; acute and ambiguous moral problematics; the thematics of innocence coupled with an obsession with figurations of death and hell—are not in fact responses to a dark, abiding, signing African presence" (Toni Morrison, *Playing in the Dark: Whiteness and the Literary Imagination* [New York: Vintage, 1993] 5).

4 Several critics have noted the centrality of concerns about the market and the market self to *Seven Gables*, most notably Michael Gilmore, "The Artist and the Marketplace in *The House of the Seven Gables*," *American Romanticism and the Marketplace* (Chicago: U of Chicago P, 1985) 96–112; Walter Benn Michaels, "Romance and Real Estate," *The Gold Standard and the Logic of Naturalism: American Literature at the Turn of the Century* (Berkeley: U of California P, 1987) 85–112; and Gillian Brown, "Women's Work and Bodies in *The House of the Seven Gables*," *Domestic Individualism: Imagining Self in Nineteenth-Century America* (Berkeley: U of California P, 1990) 63–95. Michaels links *Seven Gables* with *Uncle Tom's Cabin* in their attempts to imagine an unalienable self in the market economy and refers to Alice as Hawthorne's "own representation of the quadroon girl" (107) but makes it clear that in doing so he does not think that Hawthorne's story really is commenting on slavery (108). See my introduction for my use of "market" to signify the changes incumbent with the transformation to a market society.

5 As Susan Williams notes, "The mock scene of consumption here emblematizes Hawthorne's ambivalence about the marketplace" (Susan S. Williams, *Confounding Images: Photography and Portraiture in Antebellum American Literature* [Philadelphia: U of Pennsylvania P, 1997] 108). Similarly, Teresa Goddu, building on Michael Newbury's work, has suggested, in a footnote, that "Hawthorne often codes the horrors of the marketplace in terms of blackness and slavery. For instance, in *The House of the Seven Gables*, the

voracious consumption of the marketplace is figured through Ned Higgins's devouring the gingerbread Jim Crow" (Teresa Goddu, *Gothic America: Narrative, History, and Nation* [New York: Columbia UP, 1997] 181). See Newbury's discussion of the ways in which antebellum authors, including Hawthorne in *The Scarlet Letter*, drew on images of slavery to figure their own concerns about celebrity. Michael Newbury, "Eaten Alive: Slavery and Celebrity in Antebellum America," *Figuring Authorship in Antebellum America* (Stanford, Calif.: Stanford UP, 1997) 79–118. Few other critics have noted the possible symbolic importance of this figure, but see Susan L. Mizruchi, "From History to Gingerbread: Manufacturing a Republic in *The House of the Seven Gables*," *The Power of Historical Knowledge: Narrating the Past in Hawthorne, James, and Dreiser* (Princeton, N.J.: Princeton UP, 1988) 83–134 and Roger S. Platizky, "Hepzibah's Gingerbread Cakes in *The House of the Seven Gables*," *American Notes and Queries* 17.7 (March 1979): 106–8.

6   See Gillian Brown's argument in *Domestic Individualism*, especially concerning *Seven Gables*, that domesticity became a key way of figuring a kind of individualism and individual privacy/interiority, in opposition to the market, during the nineteenth century. For Brown, the domestic self, for both men and women, becomes a self protected from the dangers of the marketplace, but simultaneously produced by and circulated in the marketplace. My discussion of *Seven Gables* is indebted to Brown's insightful discussion; where she is more concerned with Hawthorne's use of women's domestic labor, as exemplified by Phoebe, as providing "a fiction of safe (protected and protective) labor" and as "rescu[ing] the body from the publicity of economic processes" (81), I am more interested in how Hawthorne figures the dangers of the marketplace, of the publicity of economic processes, to which both Hepzibah and Phoebe are exposed, in terms of race, manhood, and mass culture.

7   Hawthorne's racial politics have received increasing attention of late, the prevalent view determining that he was a "pro-Union, antislavery Northerner" (Jennifer Fleischner, "Hawthorne and the Politics of Slavery," *Studies in the Novel* 23.1 [spring 1991]: 102), who "deplored the existence of slavery, but had no high opinion of blacks" (Patrick Brancaccio, " 'The Black Man's Paradise': Hawthorne's Editing of the *Journal of an African Cruiser*," *New England Quarterly* 53.1 [March 1980]: 23). When critics have examined Hawthorne's fiction, they have tended to focus on his "strategy of avoidance and denial" toward black and Indian characters and racial justice (Jean Fagan Yellin, "Hawthorne and the American National Sin," in *The Green American Tradition: Essays and Poems for Sherman Paul*, ed. H. Daniel Peck [Baton Rouge: Louisiana State UP, 1989] 97). See also Eric Cheyfitz, "The Irresistibleness of Great Literature: Reconstructing Hawthorne's Politics," *American Literary History* 6.3 (fall 1994): 539–58; and Jonathan Arac, "The Politics of *The Scarlet Letter*," in *Ideology and Classic American Literature*, ed.

Sacvan Bercovitch and Myra Jehlen (Cambridge: Cambridge UP, 1986) 247–66. For a response to Yellin and Arac, see Jay Grossman, " 'A' is for Abolition?: Race, Authorship, *The Scarlet Letter*," *Textual Practice* 7.1 (spring 1993): 13–30. Among recent Hawthorne studies, my approach most closely approximates the work of Nancy Bentley on *The Marble Faun* (1861) in "Nathaniel Hawthorne and the Fetish of Race," *The Ethnography of Manners: Hawthorne, James, Wharton* (Cambridge: Cambridge UP, 1995) 24–67; Lucy Maddox on *The Scarlet Letter* (1850) in *Removals: Nineteenth-Century American Literature and the Politics of Indian Affairs* (New York: Oxford UP, 1991) 110–30; and Anna Brickhouse on "Rappaccini's Daughter" (1844) in " 'I Do Abhor an Indian Story': Hawthorne and the Allegorization of Racial 'Commixture,' " *ESQ* 42.4 (1996): 232–53.

8   Nathaniel Hawthorne, *Life of Franklin Pierce* (1852), *Tales, Sketches, and Other Papers*, vol. 12 of *Complete Works* (Boston: Houghton Mifflin, 1886) 417. In a letter a few months later to Horatio Bridge (another classmate at Bowdoin) Hawthorne reflected that "the biography has cost me hundreds of friends . . . who drop off from me like autumn leaves, in consequence of what I say on the slavery question. But they were my real sentiments, and I do not now regret that they are on record" (Letter to Horatio Bridge, 13 October 1852, *The Letters, 1843–1853*, ed. Thomas Woodson, L. Neal Smith, and Norman Holmes Pearson, vol. 16 of *The Centenary Edition of the Works of Nathaniel Hawthorne* [Columbus: Ohio St. UP, 1985] 605).

9   In " 'The Black Man's Paradise,' " Brancaccio makes the point that, through his ghost-writing of Horatio Bridge's *Journal of an African Cruiser* (1845), Hawthorne "identifies himself with Bridge's qualified support for colonization" (23–24). As Hawthorne told his publisher, his "own share of [the *Journal*] is so amalgamated with the substance of the work" as to be indistinguishable from what Bridge wrote (Letter to E. A. Duyckinck, 7 April 1845, *Letters* 16:86). This work specifically celebrates the progress of Liberia while arguing that such achievements would be impossible in the United States: "The white man, who visits Liberia, be he of what rank he may, and however imbued with the prejudice of hue, associates with the colonists on terms of equality. This would be impossible (speaking not of individuals, but of the general intercourse between the two races) in the United States." Bridge/Hawthorne notes that "this is sad; but it shows forcibly what the colored race have to struggle against in America, and how vast an advantage is gained by removing them to another soil"; "unquestionably, it is a better country than America, for the colored race" (Horatio Bridge, *Journal of an African Cruiser* [1845; London: Dawsons of Pall Mall, 1968] 163–64).

10 Letter to Horatio Bridge, 13 February 1862, *The Letters, 1857–1864*, ed. Thomas Woodson, et al., vol. 18 of *The Centenary Edition of the Works of Nathaniel Hawthorne* (Columbus: Ohio State UP, 1987) 428.

11 This fantasy of a white nation permeated both anti- and proslavery North-

ern thought of the 1850s. For example, even among its most radical antislavery members, the idea of preserving the nation for the Anglo-Saxon race was a point of agreement for the Republican coalition. See Eric Foner, *Free Soil, Free Labor, Free Men: The Ideology of the Republican Party Before the Civil War* (New York: Oxford UP, 1970), and "Politics and Prejudice: The Free Soil Party and the Negro, 1849–1852," *Journal of Negro History* 50.4 (October 1967): 239–56. Hawthorne was a lifelong Democrat, but some of his attitudes were similar to those of a certain antiblack Free Soil contingency that became central to the Republican party. This connection is indicated by his signing of a Free-Soil document protesting the Fugitive Slave Law in 1851, not out of "the slightest sympathy for the slaves" but for "New England" (Letter to Zachariah Burchmore, 15 July 1851, *Letters* 16:456). Also see Brickhouse's discussion of how "Rappaccini's Daughter" "covertly plays out [Hawthorne's] obsession with whiteness and purity" ("I Do Abhor" 235).

12   This is, of course, basically a restatement of Marx's description of commodity fetishism: "the existence of the things *quâ* commodities, and the value-relation between the products of labour which stamps them as commodities, have absolutely no connexion with their physical properties and with the material relations arising therefrom. There is a definite social relation between men, that assumes, in their eyes, the fantastic form of a relation between things. . . . In that world the productions of the human brain appear as independent beings endowed with life, and entering into relation both with one another and the human race" (Karl Marx, *Capital*, vol. 1 [1867], ed. Frederick Engels, trans. Samuel Moore and Edward Aveling [New York: International Publishers, 1967] 72).

13   See David R. Roediger, *The Wages of Whiteness: Race and the Making of the American Working Class* (New York: Verso, 1991), for a discussion of the ways in which working-class whites were identified with racial blackness through terms such as wage slavery.

14   Ned Higgins's purchase of the Jim Crow gingerbread man does not simply destroy Hepzibah's aristocratic pretensions; it also gives her "a thrill of almost youthful enjoyment" from "the invigorating breath of a fresh outward atmosphere" (51). Commerce endangers, in fact enslaves, Hepzibah to any "gripe" with a copper coin, but by forcing Hepzibah out into the "world" and giving her "the sense of healthy and natural effort for a purpose, and of lending [her] strength—be it great or small—to the united struggle of mankind" (45), it simultaneously reinvigorates her. See Gillian Brown, *Domestic Individualism*, for the best discussion of this dynamic.

15   *The American Notebooks*, ed. Claude M. Simpson, vol. 8 of *The Centenary Edition of the Works of Nathaniel Hawthorne* (1932; Columbus: Ohio State UP, 1972) 253.

16   See Richard Brodhead's discussion of *The Blithedale Romance* (1852) and the

emergence of an antebellum entertainment industry, for more on the creation of a passive male viewer (Coverdale) consuming feminine spectacles. Richard Brodhead, "Veiled Ladies: Toward a History of Antebellum Entertainment," *American Literary History* 1.2 (summer 1989): 283–85.

17 Minstrelsy, by 1850 or so, was focusing more and more on sentimentalized representations of pastoral plantation scenes, presenting a vision of a realm outside the urban marketplace. Earlier minstrelsy, on the other hand, tended to focus on more chaotic, threateningly masculinized caricatures, but similarly implied that blacks resided outside of the market and presented an alternative to the market economy. At the same time as it represented itself as presenting antimarket features, the minstrel show became the most successful commercial entertainment of the era and was often seen as nothing but an economic activity. Minstrel routines themselves often acknowledged the commercial nature of the business, and performers like Edwin Christy bragged of the fortune they made. Hawthorne draws upon this tension between minstrelsy's highly commercial nature and its promise of an antimarket realm to figure the way in which the market fostered apparently unbourgeois behavior.

18 In this way, Hawthorne prefigures George Fitzhugh's proslavery, anticapitalist critique *Cannibals All!* (1857), wherein he argues that capitalism leads to little more than "moral Cannibalism" (*Cannibals All! Or Slaves Without Masters* [1857; Cambridge: Harvard UP, 1988] 17).

19 The novel suggests, through Holgrave's story, that at least part of the ancient Pyncheon wealth was based on slavery (187–92), and Hepzibah dreams "that the descendants of a Pyncheon who had emigrated to Virginia, in some past generation, and become a great planter there—hearing of Hepzibah's destitution, and impelled by the splendid generosity of character, with which their Virginian mixture must have enriched the New England blood—would send her a remittance of a thousand dollars" (65). Even in Hepzibah's fantasy of escaping from the market threat materialized in the Jim Crow, she reestablishes her wealth on the bodies of black slaves.

20 Boot-blacks were one of the sources of blackface minstrelsy and often were linked to the immensely popular shows. For example, one of T. D. Rice's most famous skits from the 1830s featured blacked-up boot-blacks, a link redeployed by Thoreau in *The Maine Woods* and by Mark Twain in his description of a minstrel performer in his autobiography: "His coat was sometimes made of curtain calico . . . and had buttons as big as a blacking box" (*The Autobiography of Mark Twain*, ed. Charles Neider [1924; New York: Harper, 1959] 59). As Eric Lott puts it, Twain, in this way, links minstrelsy with "one of its literal sources—Negro bootblacks" (Eric Lott, *Love and Theft: Blackface Minstrelsy and the American Working Class* [New York: Oxford UP, 1993] 30). See Lott 133 for more on the tie between boot-

blacks and minstrelsy. For Rice's skit, see *Oh, Hush! or, The Virginny Cupids, This Grotesque Essence: Plays from the American Minstrel Stage*, ed. Gary D. Engle (Baton Rouge: Louisiana State UP, 1978) 1–12. For a discussion of Thoreau's comments, see chapter 2.

21 In "Chiefly About War Matters," written ten years after *House*, Hawthorne similarly describes racial or cultural transformation in terms of polishing. Hawthorne comments that a party of contrabands were "so picturesquely natural in manners, and wearing such a crust of primeval simplicity (which is quite polished away from the northern black man), that they seemed a kind of creature by themselves, not altogether human, but perhaps quite as good" ("Chiefly About War Matters" [1862], *Tales, Sketches, and Other Papers*, vol. 12 of *Complete Works* [Boston: Houghton Mifflin, 1886] 318–19). Just as the Judge polishes over the natural and primeval moral blackness of his ancestor, so African Americans in the North polish over the "picturesque" racial blackness of their kindred in the South.

22 For a description of the relationship between the harlequin figure and blackface, see George F. Rehin, "Harlequin Jim Crow: Continuity and Convergence in Blackface Clowning," *Journal of Popular Culture* 9.3 (winter 1975): 682–701. Also see Henry Louis Gates Jr., *Figures in Black: Words, Signs, and the "Racial" Self* (New York: Oxford UP, 1987) 51–53.

23 "Race," *Webster's American Dictionary of the English Language*, 1854. This is the first definition listed, followed by "A generation" and "A particular breed." As George Stocking notes, this was a "period when almost any human group . . . might be called a 'race'" (George Stocking, *Race, Culture, and Evolution: Essays in the History of Anthropology* [New York: Free Press, 1968] 65). By the 1867 edition of *Webster's American Dictionary*, however, "a family, tribe, people, or nation, believed or presumed to belong to the same stock; a lineage; a breed" had assumed the primary slot. This more modern, biological understanding of race is reiterated by an illustration of the "Caucasian Race" and a note stating that "Naturalists and ethnographers divide mankind into several distinct varieties or races." My aim is simply to suggest the ways in which Hawthorne's use of race as family invoked emerging ethnological definitions of "racial" inheritance.

24 J. C. Nott and George R. Gliddon, eds., *Types of Mankind: or, Ethnological Researches* (Philadelphia: Lippincott, Grambo, and Co., 1854) 79.

25 Nott and Gliddon, *Types of Mankind* 69.

26 See Alan Trachtenberg, "Seeing and Believing: Hawthorne's Reflections on the Daguerreotype in *The House of the Seven Gables*," *American Literary History* 9.3 (fall 1997): 460–81, especially 470–77. Most racial science of the era actually defined the Caucasian races in terms similar to those Hawthorne uses to describe Jaffrey; they "are by nature ambitious, daring, domineering, and reckless of danger" (*Types* 67). Like Hawthorne, racial science empha-

sizes the danger those traits place the race in through conquest—"how many thousands [of whites] are [thus] sacrificed" (67)—and by intermixture—"When the inferior types of mankind shall have fulfilled their destinies and passed away, and the superior, becoming intermingled in blood, have wandered from their primitive zoological provinces, and overspread the world, what will be the ultimate result? May not that Law of nature, which so often forbids the commingling of species, complete its work of destruction, and at some future day leave the fossil remains alone of man to tell the tale of his past existence upon earth?" (80). The Caucasian traits of ambition and dominance lead them to blur the boundaries of race through intermixture, just as Jaffrey's visage (see below) reveals his own amalgamation of black and white.

27 See Colette Guillaumin's discussion of how "The theoretical discourse of the bourgeoisie" was able "for a brief period . . . to fuse together the auto-referential system and altero-referential racism" (Colette Guillaumin, *Racism, Sexism, Power, and Ideology* [New York: Routledge, 1995] 56). Guillaumin argues that an older style " 'pre-racial' notion of race" that "was legal and institutional in nature" (54) (rather than more biological) underwrote notions of aristocracy. In this system, racial difference designated the group in power (auto-referential). In the nineteenth century, as part of the bourgeois revolution, a newer, more biological notion of race arose that defined racial difference in terms of otherness, of difference from the dominant group (altero-referential). The bourgeoisie, in part because of their very amorphousness, had to define themselves against others. Guillaumin's point about the fusion of these ideas in the mid-nineteenth century helps to explain how Hawthorne begins to figure the Maule and Pyncheon races and their departure from bourgeois norms in terms of more modern notions of (altero-referential) race.

28 Several critics have argued that Holgrave simply replicates Jaffrey's character, thus undermining the supposedly happy ending of the story. For example, Cathy Davidson reads Holgrave as "not so much contesting [the Pyncheons'] power as reembodying it" (Cathy N. Davidson, "Photographs of the Dead: Sherman, Daguerre, Hawthorne," *South Atlantic Quarterly* 89.4 [fall 1990]: 675). What I am interested in is how Hawthorne imagined Holgrave escaping from the darker self that he, like Jaffrey, masks. In this way, I agree with those critics who argue that Holgrave must negotiate between the two flawed models of manhood presented by the too-feminine aesthete Clifford and the too-masculine Jaffrey. As Leland Person puts it, "Hawthorne casts Holgrave squarely between these radically opposed, but equally unsatisfactory, models of masculinity—in a position to synthesize both extremes within his own personality into a masculinity that incorporates the feminine" (Leland S. Person Jr., *Aesthetic Headaches: Women and a Masculine Poetics in Poe, Mel-*

ville, and Hawthorne [Athens: U of Georgia P, 1988] 95–96). To become the fully integrated man as defined by mid-century middle-class ideals, Holgrave has to combine and counterbalance the Judge's "bold, imperious, relentless" (123) "ability in grasping, and arranging, and appropriating to [himself], the big, heavy, solid unrealities" (229) with Clifford's "liveliest sensibility to feminine influence" (141) and "more than feminine delicacy of appreciation" (220). David Leverenz describes this dynamic this way—"Jaffrey Pyncheon vs. Clifford, with Holgrave as triumphant observer" (David Leverenz, *Manhood and the American Renaissance* [Ithaca, N.Y.: Cornell UP, 1989] 246–47). In rejecting Jaffrey's masculine passions, Holgrave, as Leverenz phrases it, "exorcises the dangerous manhood welling up inside him" (91), a manhood, which I have argued, is figured in terms of mass cultural representations of race. In terms of daguerreotypal practices, this rejection of Jaffrey as a model is marked by Holgrave's display of a portrait of Uncle Venner (who is linked with Clifford in his poetic, antibourgeois nature) outside his studio. Finally, my reading downplays the importance of Phoebe to Holgrave's transformation into a conservative, bourgeois husband. As T. Walter Herbert puts it, "Phoebe's profession of love for Holgrave redeems him from the masquerade of male selfhood," so that "womanly dispossession and subordination are asserted as the ground on which manly virtue is established" (T. Walter Herbert, *Dearest Beloved: The Hawthornes and the Making of the Middle-Class Family* [Berkeley: U of California P, 1993] 102, 105). See also Brown, *Domestic Individualism*, Mizruchi, "From History to Gingerbread," and Joel Pfister, *The Production of Personal Life: Class, Gender, and the Psychological in Hawthorne's Fiction* (Stanford, Calif.: Stanford UP, 1991), for similar discussions of Phoebe's role as "middle-class angel" (Pfister 149).

29   See James Kennard Jr., "Who Are Our National Poets?" *Knickerbocker* 26.4 (October 1845): 332, and my discussion of this article in the introduction.

30   See Michael Gilmore, *American Romanticism and the Marketplace*, for the fullest exploration of the ways in which Hawthorne and Holgrave replicate Hepzibah's entrance into and Jaffrey's success in the marketplace.

31   As many critics have pointed out, Hawthorne structures his Romantic practice through emerging defenses of daguerreotypy that saw it as revealing "the truth of the human heart" through its ability to "bring out or mellow the lights and deepen and enrich the shadows of the picture" (1). The type of knowledge through details that seems to underlie a daguerreotypal epistemology of character may at first appear to go against Hawthorne's prefatorial denomination of *Seven Gables* as a Romance—"a certain latitude both as to its fashion and material" in aiming for "the truth of the human heart"—over and against the Novel—"a very minute fidelity, not merely to the possible, but to the probable and ordinary course of man's experience" (1). But when Hawthorne was writing *Seven Gables*, the discourse supporting the daguerre-

otype's truth claims was beginning to emphasize its ability to combine art and nature (or science) over its mechanical, unmediated nature—its attention to "a very minute fidelity." By 1850, a photographic aesthetic, as practiced and theorized first and foremost in the United States by the Boston daguerreotypal firm of Albert Southworth and Josiah Hawes, had begun to dominate debates over the nature of daguerreotypy. For more on Hawthorne and Southworth and Hawes, see J. Gill Holland, "Hawthorne and Photography: *The House of the Seven Gables*," *Nathaniel Hawthorne Journal* 8 (1978): 1–10. Numerous critics have outlined this sort of argument, pointing up how Hawthorne collapses the very distinction he sets up between Novel and Romance through the daguerreotype, just as he collapses the differences between the Maules and the Pyncheons. See in particular Davidson, "Photographs of the Dead"; Trachtenberg, "Seeing and Believing"; and Williams, *Confounding Images* 96–119. Davidson ends by discussing the novel's "eugenic obsession" (694), an obsession which I want to argue is suggested in terms of race, while Trachtenberg, in this essay, argues that the mixed-nature of daguerreotypy—as modern and conservative, simply objective, yet in need of interpretation—allows Holgrave to escape the typological system of the Pyncheons and the Maules, a typological system which, I will argue, mirrors that of typological photographs of racial others.

32   The "new scope" phrase is from Harold Francis Pfister, *Facing the Light: Historic American Portrait Daguerreotypes* (Washington, D.C.: Smithsonian Institution Press, 1978) 22.

33   Williams provides an overview of how painted and daguerreotypal portraits were used by antebellum authors to negotiate their own role in the marketplace. These fictions often reveal anxieties about gender, but more often "about the circulation and easy exchange of images . . . that fictional portraits both reveal and attempt to circumvent" (*Confounding Images* 31). With respect to *Seven Gables*, Williams points out that "Hawthorne's dependence on that market was growing as he wrote *Seven Gables*" (117) and that Hawthorne attempts to work through that dependence by "assert[ing] the superiority of literature in part to protect it—and his own prophetic powers as an author—from the destabilizing proliferation of images that the market encourages" (98). For Williams, Hawthorne inverts the common understanding of portraits as static and writing as fluid, allowing the narrative to "function as a stable, controlled picture" (103). While I differ with her reading of the narrative's success at attaining such stasis, I have found her discussion of these anxieties about authorship fruitful in delineating the racial nature of those anxieties. The next few paragraphs draw upon the work of Allan Sekula and Alan Trachtenberg on the pedagogical and epistemological grounding of early photographic practices and display. See, in particular, Alan Trachtenberg, *Reading American Photographs: Images as His-*

tory, Mathew Brady to Walker Evans (New York: Hill and Wang, 1989); Trachtenberg, "Photography: The Emergence of a Keyword," in *Photography in Nineteenth-Century America*, ed. Martha A. Sandweiss (Fort Worth: Amon Carter Museum, 1991) 17–41; Trachtenberg, "Mirror in the Marketplace: American Responses to the Daguerreotype," in *The Daguerreotype: A Sesquicentennial Celebration*, ed. John Wood (Iowa City: U of Iowa P, 1989) 60–73; Allan Sekula, "The Body and the Archive," *October* 39 (winter 1986): 3–64; and Sekula, "The Traffic in Photographs," *Art Journal* 41.1 (spring 1981): 15–25.

34   Sekula, "The Body and the Archive" 10.

35   "Photography in the United States," *Photographic Art-Journal* (June 1853), *Secrets of the Dark Chamber: The Art of the American Daguerreotype*, ed. Merry A. Foresta and John Wood (Washington, D.C.: Smithsonian Institution Press, 1995) 267. An 1863 article recounts the popularity of Mathew Brady's first gallery (1845–1853): "People used to stroll in there in those days to see what new celebrity had been added to the little collection, and 'the last new portrait at Brady's' was a standing topic of conversation" ("Brady's Gallery," *Harper's Weekly*, 14 November 1863). Brady's gallery was often cited, along with Barnum's museum, as one of the two top attractions in New York (Trachtenberg, *Reading* 35). Galleries, in fact, were rather similar to popular museums of the period in their attempt to interpellate (or integrate) a wide variety of patrons into a new "respectable" audience in a domestic atmosphere. As Trachtenberg notes, galleries were simultaneously "a feminized parlor, a simulacrum of domestic space" (*Reading* 40), and "renowned as meeting place[s] where people of all classes and grades of cultivation mingled freely" (*Reading* 39). Daguerreotypal galleries were, above all, however, an "institution of urban middle-class life" (*Reading* 25), and unlike Barnum's museum, such galleries much more readily drew on aesthetic defenses of their work and tended to downplay their commercial nature. See also Barbara McCandless, "The Portrait Studio and the Celebrity," in *Photography in Nineteenth-Century America* 49–75. For more on the development of the daguerreotypal industry, see Robert Taft's classic, *Photography and the American Scene* (1938; New York: Dover, 1964).

36   There was also great anxiety that daguerreotypy was simply another commercial intercourse, an anxiety that finally haunts Hawthorne's novel and reappears (often, again, in terms of race) in much discourse surrounding early photography. For discussions of these anxieties, see Williams, *Confounding Images*, and Trachtenberg, "Mirror in the Marketplace." The emerging defenses of photography as an artistic form in the early 1850s, which Hawthorne seems to draw on, can be seen as a reaction to these anxieties about the form's commercialism.

37   Marcus Aurelius Root, *The Camera and the Pencil, or, the Heliographic Art* (1864; Pawlet, Vt.: Helios, 1971) 27.

38 "Daguerreotypes," *Littell's Living Age* 20, June 1846: 552.

39 Root, *Camera* 43–44. These two forms of picture-taking occasionally shared space; as Tom Gunning has pointed out, in the 1850s, "public display of portraits of professional criminals . . . became one of the most popular forms of photographic galleries, with tourists flocking to them as an urban sight and Barnum displaying them in his museum" (Tom Gunning, "Tracking the Individual Body: Photography, Detectives, and Early Cinema," in *Cinema and The Invention of Modern Life*, ed. Leo Charney and Vanessa R. Schwartz [Berkeley: U of California P, 1995] 24). See, for example, the description of Barnum's "Rogues' Gallery—Daguerreotypes of a number of noted criminals" in *An Illustrated Catalogue and Guide Book to Barnum's American Museum* (New York: n.p., [1864]) 73.

40 Daguerreotypal fiction reiterates the daguerreotype's moral force. See, for example, Augustine J. H. Duganne's novel *The Daguerreotype Miniature; or, Life in the Empire City* (Philadelphia: G. B. Zieber and Co., 1846), in which an affective connection forged by a daguerreotype in Plumbe's gallery across class lines—a country boy new to the city and a rich merchant's daughter—helps to secure the urban space against those who mask their true identities and motives.

41 "In warm climates, the complexion of men is universally *swarthy* or black. . . . Black; as, the *swarthy* African" ("Swarthy," *Webster's American Dictionary*, 1854). The same edition defines "dusky" as "tending to blackness in color."

42 Sekula, "Traffic" 16. Similarly, commentary on early photography repeatedly suggests a racial dimension to the faith in photography's ability to reveal underlying truth. As Richard Dyer has suggested of cinema, "there is some very interesting work to be done on the invention of photography and the development of lighting codes in relation to the white face, which results in the technicist ideology that one sometimes hears of it being 'more difficult' to photograph black people" (Richard Dyer, "White," *Screen* 29.4 [autumn 1988]: 63). Technical articles from the period make it clear that early experiments at "taking" faces were haunted by the specter of race and that a racial logic was at play in the technological innovations of photography. See, for example, "Professor Draper on the Process of Daguerreotype and its application to taking Portraits from Life," *Philosophical Magazine* (Sept., 1840), in Foresta and Wood, eds., *Secrets of the Dark Chamber* 233, a description of an early attempt at daguerreotypal portraiture that involved making the face of the sitter whiter; "Pictorial Delineations by Light," *American Journal of Science and Art* 37.1 (October 1839): 174, where the negative process is described in terms of an irreversible racial transformation; and M. Claudet, "The Progress and Present State of the Daguerreotype Art," *Journal of the Franklin Institute* (August 1845): 117, in which Claudet uses the tenets of physical geography to theorize that Northern Europeans' and Americans' faces are more easily captured by the photographic process.

43 As M. Susan Barger and William B. White have argued, "Central to the scientific applications of the daguerreotype portrait are various aspects of craniometrics, sciences based on skull and brain measurements" (M. Susan Barger and William B. White, *The Daguerreotype: Nineteenth-Century Technology and Modern Science* [Washington, D.C.: Smithsonian Institution Press, 1991] 78). These links have been most fully elaborated, often using a Foucauldian paradigm, by Sekula, John Tagg, *The Burden of Representation: Essays on Photographies and Histories* (Amherst: U of Massachusetts P, 1988), and Brian Wallis, "Black Bodies, White Science: Louis Agassiz's Slave Daguerreotypes" *American Art* 9 (summer 1995): 39–61.

44 An 1849 ad for the "Spread Eagle Daguerrian Gallery" in New York suggests how most galleries exhibited daguerreotypes of Indians and blacks: "the attention of strangers visiting the city, and others . . . [is called] to the fine Likenesses of the Chippewa Indian Chief and his Sons, on the door posts and in their Gallery; they are dressed in full Indian costume, the same in which they appeared before all the crowned heads of Europe during their travels with Geo. Catlin, Esq." (advertisement reproduced in Floyd Rinhart and Marion Rinhart, *The American Daguerreotype* [Athens: U of Georgia P, 1981] 132). The placement of the Indians at the edge of the exhibit, on the door posts, replicates the ethnographic logic of the daguerreotypes, which placed the Indians on the outskirts of a humanity defined at its center by the respectability displayed in the portraits of eminent citizens and statesmen within the gallery.

45 As with Holgrave's daguerreotype of Jaffrey, the distinctions are already known before the daguerreotype is made, despite arguments that the daguerreotype itself disclosed the facts. As a number of critics have noted, the technology of the daguerreotype is "insufficient to the truth" in *House of Seven Gables* (Carol Shloss, *In Visible Light: Photography and the American Writer: 1840–1940* [New York: Oxford UP, 1987] 44). See also Charles Swann, "*The House of the Seven Gables*: Hawthorne's Modern Novel of 1848," *Modern Language Review* 86 (January 1991): 14; Davidson, "Photographs of the Dead," and Trachtenberg, "Seeing and Believing." Holgrave must use his knowledge of the Pyncheon family history and, in particular, the bloody facts of their racially transmitted bad passions in order to read the apparently revelatory daguerreotype of Jaffrey, just as racial scientists already knew the facts that their daguerreotypes supposedly disclosed.

46 For more on Agassiz and his role as natural scientist to the nation, see Edward Lurie, *Louis Agassiz: A Life in Science* (Chicago: U of Chicago P, 1960), especially chapter 5, "Naturalist to America." See Agassiz's introduction to *Types of Mankind*, "Sketch of the Natural Provinces of the Animal World and Their Relation to the Different Types of Man" lviii–lxxvi.

47 See Wallis, "Black Bodies, White Science," for the fullest discussion of the

Agassiz daguerreotypes; also see Elinor Reichlin, "Faces of Slavery: A Historical Find," *American Heritage* 28.4 (June 1977): 4–10, and Trachtenberg, *Reading* 53–56.

48 At the same time that Agassiz tried to use daguerreotypy to establish the eternal, essential difference of the races, government expeditions began to employ daguerreotypists to photograph the still "uncivilized" Native inhabitants of the West. As noted earlier, galleries occasionally displayed these daguerreotypes or those of Indians brought to urban museums as ethnographic exhibits. As in Agassiz's daguerreotypes, these photographs produced difference not simply through the display of "skin color," but through the accessories, the "full Indian costume" (or lack of any costumery), which marked the Indians as uncivilized. The most famous group of such daguerreotypes was the touring Fitzgibbon "collection of Indian warriors very fine, which we understand is to be forwarded to the Ethnological Society of London, to have copies and busts made from them" (quoted in Rinhart and Rinhart, *American Daguerrotype* 127). For example, see the 1853 daguerreotype of Kno-Shr, Kansas Chief, by Fitzgibbon, reproduced in *Secrets of the Dark Chamber* 77. On the other hand, while Merry Foresta argues that there were "many daguerreotypes made of freed slaves and abolitionists" (Merry A. Foresta, "Secrets of the Dark Chamber: The Art of the American Daguerreotype," in Foresta and Wood, eds., *Secrets of the Dark Chamber* 23), I have found little evidence to suggest that portraits of black abolitionists and Indian activists were shown in portrait galleries. All of the known portraits of Frederick Douglass, for example, are of a sixth plate (approximately 3.25 inches by 2.75 inches), much smaller than the half (5.5 by 4.5) or whole (8.5 by 6.5) plate portraits usually displayed in galleries. One exception that I have seen is an 1844 advertisement for the National Miniature Gallery on Broadway that mentions in its lengthy list of famous "American Statesmen, And other distinguished characters" "John Ross, Cherokee," the leader of resistance to removal in the 1830s (advertisement reproduced in Rinhart and Rinhart, *American Daguerrotype* 83). See my epilogue, "Electric Chains," however, for a discussion of abolitionist use of daguerreotypal parlors.

49 Dion Boucicault, *The Octoroon* (1859), *Representative American Plays*, 7th rev. ed., ed. Arthur Hobson Quinn (New York: Appleton-Century-Crofts, 1953) 396. The best discussion of Boucicault's play appears in Joseph Roach, "One Blood," *Cities of the Dead: Circum-Atlantic Performances* (New York: Columbia UP, 1996) 179–237. Roach adroitly addresses the racial politics of the play, but does not deal with the role of daguerreotypy. See Harley Erdman, "Caught in the 'Eye of the Eternal:' Justice, Race, and the Camera, from *The Octoroon* to Rodney King" *Theatre Journal* 45.3 (1993): 333–48, for a discussion of race and photography in the play.

50 While both Zoe's beloved owner, George Peyton, and Scudder are attracted

to her, only M'Closky desires to force his will upon her by owning her. Conversely, both George and Scudder identify themselves with the black slaves: George offers to "sell [him]self" (386) by marrying a woman whom he does not love in order to save the plantation and protect Zoe and the other slaves; Scudder similarly wishes "they could sell *me*. . . . I deserve to be a nigger this day—I feel like one, inside" (388) because he has not been able to save the plantation. Like Zoe, who would "rather be a slave with a free soul, than remain free with a slavish, deceitful heart" (388), George's and Scudder's willingness to enslave or sell themselves to help others actually proves that they are not "niggers" on the "inside."

51 I thank John Rickard for raising this point in regard to the racial coding of M'Closky's Irishness. For more on the ways in which the Irish were seen as racially different in Victorian England, see L. Perry Curtis Jr., *Apes and Angels: The Irishman in Victorian Caricature*, rev. ed. (Washington, D.C.: Smithsonian Institution Press, 1997). For a discussion of how immigrant Irish became "white" in the United States by differentiating themselves from blacks, see Noel Ignatiev, *How the Irish Became White* (New York: Routledge, 1995).

52 This dynamic between race, gender, and daguerreotypy in the moral universe of the romance emerges in succinct form in Hawthorne's short story "The Birth-Mark" (1843). In this story, Aylmer, the scientist/husband who is attempting to purify his wife Georgiana of the "Bloody Hand" (38) upon her cheek, amuses her by taking "her portrait by a scientific process. . . . effected by rays of light striking upon a polished plate of metal" ("The Birth-Mark" [1843], *Mosses from an Old Manse*, vol. 10 of *The Centenary Edition of the Works of Nathaniel Hawthorne* [1846; Columbus: Ohio State UP, 1974] 38, 45). But this daguerreotype of Georgiana blurs her features, while emphasizing the birthmark. Daguerreotypy then helps to bring out this "symbol of [Georgiana's] liability to sin," "the ineludible gripe, in which mortality clutches the highest and purest of earthly mould, degrading them into kindred with the lowest, and even with the very brutes" (39). In "The Birth-Mark," Hawthorne figures this brutishness in the racialized character Aminadab: "With his vast strength, his shaggy hair, his smoky aspect, and the indescribable earthiness that incrusted him, he seemed to represent man's physical nature; while Aylmer's slender figure, and pale, intellectual face, were no less apt a type of the spiritual element" (43). The tiny hand on her cheek, "the ineludible gripe," emblematizes that part of Georgiana that is like Aminadab's "smoky aspect," in particular her physical nature. And it is this nearly hidden aspect of her self that the daguerreotype, deployed as a toy, displays in startling emphasis.

53 Again, on this point, see Colette Guillaumin's *Racism, Sexism, Power and Ideology*.

54 Letter to J. T. Fields, 29 November 1850, *Letters* 16:376. Brook Thomas

similarly connects the ending of *Seven Gables* with Hawthorne's comments on slavery in the Franklin Pierce autobiography—"Like the evil Judge Pyncheon, slavery will magically be removed from the world" (Brook Thomas, *Cross Examinations of Law and Literature: Cooper, Hawthorne, Stowe, and Melville* [Cambridge: Cambridge UP, 1987] 89)—but does not flesh out the significance of this similarity.

55 See Trachtenberg, "Mirror in the Marketplace" 62, for more on these anxieties about daguerreotypy's commercial nature. Philip Hone's reaction to the new technology hints at daguerreotypy's breaking down of "natural" barriers that, I argue, implicitly includes race: "It appears to me a confusion of the very elements of nature" (quoted in Trachtenberg, "Mirror in the Marketplace" 60).

56 "The Inconstant Daguerreotype," *Harper's New Monthly Magazine* (May 1855): 822. Further references will be given parenthetically.

57 See Williams, *Confounding Images*, for a discussion of some of these anxieties about daguerreotypal destabilization of identity in daguerreotypal fiction. While Hawthorne attempts to use daguerreotypy to police Jaffrey's false respectability, to remove his mask, many felt that daguerreotypy simply produced another mask; as Melville put it, the daguerreotype was simply another pasteboard mask (see Shloss, *In Visible Light* 30), or as Emerson vituperated, it produced "the portrait of a mask instead of a man" (*Journals of Ralph Waldo Emerson*, vol. 6 [1841–1844], ed. Edward Waldo Emerson and Waldo Emerson Forbes [Boston: Houghton Mifflin, 1906] 100–101).

58 See, for example, Mizruchi, "From History to Gingerbread" 122–23 and Swann, "*House*" 17–18.

59 For example, a play performed in New England in 1850 featured a black mail-carrier named Dixie (Hans Nathan, *Dan Emmett and the Rise of Early Negro Minstrelsy* [Norman: U of Oklahoma P, 1962] 264–66).

60 See Homi Bhabha's argument about how the nation constitutes itself through internal differentiation against those on the margins of the nation (yet still a part of it), in Homi K. Bhabha, "DissemiNation: Time, Narrative, and the Margins of the Modern Nation," in *Nation and Narration*, ed. Homi K. Bhabha (New York: Routledge, 1990) 291–322.

61 As Hawthorne implies in his preface to his final romance, *The Marble Faun* (1860), romance is dependent upon picturesque and gloomy exploitation, a picturesqueness he connects in "Old News" and "Chiefly About War Matters" to racial difference: "No author, without a trial, can conceive of the difficulty of writing a Romance about a country where there is no shadow, no antiquity, no mystery, no picturesque and gloomy wrong, nor anything but a common-place prosperity, in broad and simple daylight, as is happily the case with my dear native land" (Nathaniel Hawthorne, *The Marble Faun: or, The Romance of Monte Beni*, vol. 4 of *The Centenary Edition of the*

Works of Nathaniel Hawthorne [1860; Columbus: Ohio State UP, 1968] 3). By imaginatively erasing not just racial difference but "gloomy wrong[s]" from his native land, *Seven Gables* pushes Hawthorne to abandon his native land as a fitting topic for narrative. It would be his last complete novel set in the United States. As noted above, in "Chiefly About War Matters," Hawthorne speaks of a party of contrabands as being "so picturesquely natural in manners, and wearing such a crust of primeval simplicity (which is quite polished away from the northern black man), that they seemed a kind of creature by themselves, not altogether human, but perhaps quite as good." Similarly, in his sketch "Old News" (1835), Hawthorne scans newspapers from a century earlier, commenting that "New-England was then in a state incomparably more picturesque than at present" largely because "there were the slaves, contributing their dark shade to the picture of society. The consequence of all this was, a great variety and singularity of action and incident" ("Old News" [1835], *The Snow-Image and Uncollected Tales*, vol. 11 of *The Centenary Edition of the Works of Nathaniel Hawthorne* [Columbus: Ohio State UP, 1974] 134). In his sketches, then, Hawthorne suggests that ethnic and racial others contribute a "wild" picturesqueness to Puritan New England, the kind of "shade" a Romance required for its play of shadows and lights. As Nancy Bentley has argued, the romantic picturesqueness of *The Marble Faun* is a product of the indistinctly racialized landscape of Italy. Hawthorne's view of the "common-place prosperity" of the United States in this preface then imagines, as his letter to Bridge does a few years later, the erasure of the "shadow" of race and with it the instability of identity it represents and the possibility of art itself.

62 "Chiefly About War Matters" 319.

Epilogue

1 Minstrelsy and Indian melodrama provide another model for Whitman's identification with blacks and Indians. As he would recall late in his life, the "influence of. . . . certain actors and singers"—he specifically notes T. D. Rice's blackface minstrelsy and Forrest "as Metamora"—"undoubtedly enter'd into the gestation of 'Leaves of Grass' " (*Specimen Days, Walt Whitman, Complete Poetry and Collected Prose* [New York: Library of America, 1982] 703, 704). Unless otherwise noted, further references to Whitman's poetry and prose will be to this edition and will be given parenthetically. Elsewhere Whitman notes that attending their performances "affected me for weeks; or rather I might say permanently filter'd into my whole nature" ("The Old Bowery: A Reminiscence of New York Plays and Acting Fifty Years Ago," *November Boughs, Walt Whitman, Complete Poetry and Collected Prose* 1188). Here, Whitman is specifically speaking of the first time he saw Forrest. In

constructing his own vision of not simply the American poet, but a decidedly "manly" poet, Whitman turns to the type of racial performance both Rice and Forrest were famous for in order to "enter the essences of the real things." David Reynolds specifically argues for reading "I Sing the Body Electric" (the poem I will focus on here) in the context of minstrelsy. See David S. Reynolds, *Walt Whitman's America: A Cultural Biography* (New York: Knopf, 1995) 186. For more on the influence of the theater on Whitman, see Alan L. Ackerman Jr., "Character of Stage: Walt Whitman and American Theater," *The Portable Theater: American Literature and the Nineteenth-Century Stage* (Baltimore, Md.: Johns Hopkins UP, 1999) 42–88.

2   For more on Plumbe, his short-lived chain of the late 1840s, and his *National Plumbeotype Gallery* (1847) of lithographs of famous Americans' daguerreotypes, see Robert Taft, *Photography and the American Scene* (1938; New York: Dover, 1964) 49–52; Beaumont Newhall, *The Daguerreotype in America*, 3rd rev. ed. (New York: Dover, 1976) 38–41; and Floyd Rinhart and Marion Rinhart, *The American Daguerreotype* (Athens: U of Georgia P, 1981) 67–75.

3   Walt Whitman, "Visit to Plumbe's Gallery" (2 July 1846), *The Gathering of the Forces*, vol. 2, ed. Cleveland Rodgers and John Black (New York: G. P. Putnam's Sons, 1920) 113. Further references will be given parenthetically.

4   This "Phantom" image recurs in "Pictures," one of Whitman's early attempts at what would become the style of *Leaves of Grass*. In this poem, unpublished until 1925, Whitman imagines his brain as "a little house" where he keeps "on the walls hanging, portraits of women and men," which create "Phantoms, countless, men and women, after death, wandering" (Walt Whitman, *Leaves of Grass*, Comprehensive Reader's Edition, ed. Harold W. Blodgett and Sculley Bradley [New York: New York UP, 1965] 642, 645). Ruth Bohan contends that the Brooklyn Art Union, rather than daguerreotypal parlors, provided the model for this poem; see Ruth L. Bohan, " 'The Gathering of Forces': Walt Whitman and the Visual Arts in Brooklyn in the 1850s," in *Walt Whitman and the Visual Arts*, ed. Geoffrey M. Sill and Roberta K. Tarbell (New Brunswick, N.J.: Rutgers UP, 1992) 1–27. More important to me is the way that images of slaves are transformed in the process of "Pictures" developing into *Leaves of Grass*—rather than objectifying "my slave-gangs . . . clumsy, hideous, black, pouting, grinning, sly, besotted, sensual, shameless" ("Pictures" 646), Whitman identifies with (while objectifying) the slave and his pain and passions.

5   Whitman's description of the daguerreotype echoes the way in which, in *House of the Seven Gables*, the telegraph allows Clifford to overcome his aesthetic distance, "selfish in its essence" (Nathaniel Hawthorne, *The House of the Seven Gables*, vol. 2 of *The Centenary Edition of the Works of Nathaniel Hawthorne* [1851; Columbus: Ohio State UP, 1965] 109), by enabling him to be "conscious of an electric thrill" (264) of human sympathy and connec-

tion. As in Clifford's vision of the telegraph, the daguerreotype's "electric chain" did not simply foster emulation (as photographic theorists like Marcus Root figured it), but also worked on a more personal level to suture society together by collapsing time and space. Importantly, in *Seven Gables*, Hawthorne holds out the revolutionary potential of new technologies breaking down old barriers and reorganizing communities and identities, only to withdraw from such possibilities in his conservative conclusion.

6 Preface to 1855 edition of *Leaves of Grass*, *Walt Whitman, Complete Poetry and Collected Prose* 12–13. Orvell argues that the daguerreotypal parlor provided Whitman with a place to learn not only "the art of observation" but the "art of organization" and "an organizational model for *Leaves of Grass* . . . a microcosm of the diversity of American society, a way of gathering into one whole the plurality of peoples and types that composed America" (Miles Orvell, *The Real Thing: Imitation and Authenticity in American Culture, 1880–1940* [Chapel Hill: U of North Carolina P, 1989] 16, 17).

7 As a starting point, see Allen Grossman, "The Poetics of Union in Whitman and Lincoln: An Inquiry Toward the Relationship of Art and Policy," in *The American Renaissance Reconsidered*, ed. Walter Benn Michaels and Donald E. Pease (Baltimore, Md.: Johns Hopkins UP, 1985) 183–208.

8 Quoted in Alexander Saxton, *The Rise and Fall of the White Republic: Class Politics and Mass Culture in Nineteenth-Century America* (New York: Verso, 1990) 154. See Dana Phillips, "Nineteenth-Century Racial Thought and Whitman's 'Democratic Ethnology of the Future,'" *Nineteenth-Century Literature* 49.3 (December 1994): 289–320, for a discussion of Whitman's poetic representations of racial others in terms of antebellum racial science.

9 Martin Klammer, *Whitman, Slavery, and the Emergence of* Leaves of Grass (University Park: Pennsylvania State UP, 1993) 2–3.

10 As Klammer puts it, "throughout *Leaves of Grass* Whitman is looking to break down barriers of race through 'the merge'" (121).

11 Critics such as Wai Chee Dimock and Philip Fisher have seen this disappearance of racial difference as exemplifying Whitman's inability to deal fully with difference, of representing the way he can only imagine an egalitarian United States by erasing differences. See Wai Chee Dimock, "Whitman, Syntax, and Political Theory," in *Breaking Bounds: Whitman and American Cultural Studies*, ed. Betsy Erkkila and Jay Grossman (New York: Oxford UP, 1996) 62–79; and Philip Fisher, "Democratic Social Space: Whitman, Melville, and the Promise of American Transparency," *Representations* 24 (fall 1988): 60–101. For a discussion of Whitman's racial politics more similar to mine, see Karen Sánchez-Eppler, "To Stand Between: Walt Whitman's Poetics of Merger and Embodiment," *Touching Liberty: Abolition, Feminism, and the Politics of the Body* (Berkeley: U of California P, 1993) 50–82.

12 After describing the domestic interior of Uncle Tom's cabin, Stowe stops to "daguerreotype" her hero for her readers, using a metaphor of the new technology and its ability to reveal character to create him as a subject, whose interior, like his cabin's, is like her readers' (Harriet Beecher Stowe, *Uncle Tom's Cabin or, Life Among the Lowly* [1852; New York: Penguin, 1981] 68). As Susan Williams puts it, Stowe "encourages [her] readers to picture him as an individual hero rather than as a slave: a hero whose picture might occupy the parlor table along with their other friends and relatives" (Susan S. Williams, *Confounding Images: Photography and Portraiture in Antebellum American Literature* [Philadelphia: U of Pennsylvania P, 1997] 47); or as Amy Schrager Lang argues, "The very fact that Tom is the subject of a portrait, albeit a photographic one, suggests, of course, that this is no 'thing' but a man. . . . Like other features of Tom's representation, the daguerreotype operates to assure us of Tom's humanity" (Amy Schrager Lang, "Class and the Strategies of Sympathy," in *The Culture of Sentiment: Race, Gender, and Sentimentality in Nineteenth-Century America*, ed. Shirley Samuels [New York: Oxford UP, 1992] 131–32).

Similarly, in Douglass's "Heroic Slave," Madison Washington's "black, but comely" face is "daguerreotyped" on Listwell's memory (Frederick Douglass, "The Heroic Slave" [1853], *The Oxford Frederick Douglass Reader*, ed. William Andrews [New York: Oxford UP, 1996] 134, 138). As I have argued, Listwell's reading of Washington's character through his physiognomy, like daguerreotypal portraits of Douglass, attempts to render him a black hero, doing so by playing up his nearly white features and his difference from the majority of the black slaves.

13 [Achilles Pugh], *Ball's Splendid Mammoth Pictorial Tour of the United States, Comprising Views of the African Slave Trade; of Northern and Southern Cities; of Cotton and Sugar Plantations; of the Mississippi, Ohio and Susquehanna Rivers, Niagara Falls, &C.* [Cincinnati, Ohio: Achilles Pugh, Printer, 1855] 7.

14 Like much antislavery material, the panorama, at least as represented by Pugh, did participate in a type of ethnographic distanciation (speaking of "heathenish" [25] and "horrid" [26] African rites in both Africa and America) as well as a type of sentimental identification. Deborah Willis provides the fullest discussion of Ball and his career in her *Reflections in Black: A History of Black Photographers, 1840 to the Present* (New York: Norton, 2000) 5–9. For a short discussion of the panorama, see Rinhart and Rinhart, *American Daguerrotype* 140–41, 243 note 31. For a contemporary description of his gallery (which does not mention Ball's race) see "Daguerrian Gallery of the West," *Gleason's Pictorial Drawing-Room Companion* (1 April 1854): 208. For a recent discussion of the politics of objectification in relation to photographic images of black men, see Kobena Mercer, "Skin Head Sex

Thing," in *How Do I Look?: Queer Film and Video*, ed. Bad Object-Choices (Seattle: Bay Press, 1991) 169–210.

15 See Vivian R. Pollak, " 'In Loftiest Spheres': Whitman's Visionary Feminism," in *Breaking Bounds* 92–111, for a discussion of the possibilities and limits of Whitman's feminism (and racial egalitarianism).

Bibliography

Ackerman, Alan L., Jr. *The Portable Theater: American Literature and the Nineteenth-Century Stage*. Baltimore: Johns Hopkins UP, 1999.

Adams, Bluford. *E Pluribus Barnum: The Great Showman and the Making of U.S. Popular Culture*. Minneapolis: U of Minnesota P, 1997.

Agassiz, Louis. "Sketch of the Natural Provinces of the Animal World and Their Relation to the Different Types of Man." In *Types of Mankind: or, Ethnological Researches*. Ed. J. C. Nott and George R. Gliddon. Philadelphia: Lippincott, Grambo and Co., 1854. lviii–lxxvi.

Alcott, William. *The Young Man's Guide*. 12th ed. Boston: Perkins and Marvin, 1838.

Alger, William Rounseville. *Life of Edwin Forrest, The American Tragedian*. Philadelphia: J. B. Lippincott and Co., 1877.

Allen, Hervey. *Israfel: The Life and Times of Edgar Allan Poe*. New York: George H. Doran Co., 1926.

Allen, L. L. *A Thrilling Sketch of the Life of the Distinguished Chief Okah Tubbee Alias, Wm. Chubbee, Son of the Head Chief, Mosholeh Tubbee, of the Choctaw Nation of Indians*. New York: Cameron's Steam Power Presses, 1848.

Althusser, Louis. "Contradiction and Overdetermination." *For Marx*. Trans. Ben Brewster. London: Verso, 1990. 87–128.

——. "Ideology and Ideological State Apparatuses." *Lenin and Philosophy and Other Essays*. Trans. Ben Brewster. New York: Monthly Review Press, 1971. 127–86.

Altick, Richard. *The Shows of London*. Cambridge: Harvard UP, 1978.

Amacher, Richard E. "Behind the Curtain with the Noble Savage: Stage Management of Indian Plays, 1825–1860." *Theatre Survey* 7.2 (November 1966): 101–14.

"American Drama." *American Quarterly Review* 1.2 (June 1827): 331–42.

Anderson, Marilyn J. "The Image of the Indian in American Drama During the Jacksonian Era, 1829–1845." *Journal of American Culture* 1.4 (winter 1978): 800–810.

Andrews, William L. "The Novelization of Voice in Early African American Narratives." *PMLA* 105.1 (January 1990): 23–34.

Anthony, David. "Class, Culture, and the Trouble with White Skin in Hawthorne's *The House of the Seven Gables*." *The Yale Journal of Criticism* 12.2 (1999): 249–68.

Apess, William. *On Our Own Ground: The Complete Writings of William Apess, a Pequot*. Ed. Barry O'Connell. Amherst: U of Massachusetts P, 1992.

Appiah, Anthony. "The Uncompleted Argument: Du Bois and the Illusion of Race." *Critical Inquiry* 12.1 (autumn 1985): 21–37.

Arac, Jonathan. "The Politics of *The Scarlet Letter.*" In *Ideology and Classic American Literature.* Ed. Sacvan Bercovitch and Myra Jehlen. Cambridge: Cambridge UP, 1986. 247–66.

Bank, Rosemarie K. "Staging the 'Native': Making History in American Theatre Culture, 1828–1838." *Theatre Journal* 45.4 (December 1993): 461–86.

——. *Theatre Culture in America, 1825–1860.* Cambridge: Cambridge UP, 1997.

Barger, M. Susan, and William B. White. *The Daguerreotype: Nineteenth-Century Technology and Modern Science.* Washington: Smithsonian Institution Press, 1991.

Barker-Benfield, G. J. *The Horrors of Half-Known Life: Male Attitudes Toward Women and Sexuality in Nineteenth-Century America.* New York: Harper and Row, 1976.

Barnum, P. T. *Selected Letters of P. T. Barnum.* Ed. A. H. Saxton. New York: Columbia UP, 1983.

——. *Struggles and Triumphs: or, Forty Years' Recollections of P. T. Barnum.* 1869. New York: Arno, 1970.

Barrish, Phillip. " 'The Genuine Article': Ethnicity, Capital, and *The Rise of David Levinsky.*" *American Literary History* 5.4 (winter 1993): 643–62.

Baym, Nina. "Putting Women in Their Place: *The Last of the Mohicans* and Other Indian Stories." *Feminism and American Literary History: Essays.* New Brunswick, NJ: Rutgers UP, 1992. 19–35.

Bean, Annemarie, James V. Hatch, and Brooks McNamara, eds. *Inside the Minstrel Mask: Readings in Nineteenth-Century Blackface Minstrelsy.* Hanover, Conn.: Wesleyan UP/UP of New England, 1996.

Bederman, Gail. *Manliness and Civilization: A Cultural History of Gender and Race in the United States, 1880–1917.* Chicago: U of Chicago P, 1995.

Bell, Whitfield J., Jr. "The Cabinet of the American Philosophical Society." In *A Cabinet of Curiosities: Five Episodes in the Evolution of American Museums.* Charlottesville: UP of Virginia, 1967. 1–34.

Bell, Whitfield J., Jr., et al. *A Cabinet of Curiosities: Five Episodes in the Evolution of American Museums.* Charlottesville: UP of Virginia, 1967.

Bennett, Tony. "The Exhibitionary Complex." *New Formations* 4 (spring 1988): 73–102.

Bentley, Nancy. "Nathaniel Hawthorne and the Fetish of Race." *The Ethnography of Manners: Hawthorne, James, Wharton.* Cambridge: Cambridge UP, 1995. 24–67.

——. "White Slaves: The Mulatto Hero in Antebellum Fiction." *American Literature* 65.3 (September 1993): 501–22.

Berger, Maurice, Brian Wallis, and Simon Watson, eds. *Constructing Masculinity.* New York: Routledge, 1995.

Berlant, Lauren. "National Brands/National Body: *Imitation of Life*." In *The Phantom Public Sphere*. Ed. Bruce Robbins. Minneapolis: U of Minnesota P, 1993. 173–208.

Berzon, Judith R. *Neither White Nor Black: The Mulatto Character in American Fiction*. New York: New York UP, 1978.

Betts, John Rickards. "P. T. Barnum and the Popularization of Natural History." *Journal of the History of Ideas* 20 (1959): 353–68.

Bhabha, Homi K. "DissemiNation: Time, Narrative, and the Margins of the Modern Nation." In *Nation and Narration*. Ed. Homi K. Bhabha. New York: Routledge, 1990. 291–322.

——. *The Location of Culture*. New York: Routledge, 1994.

Black Hawk. *Black Hawk: An Autobiography*. 1832. Ed. Donald Jackson. Urbana: U of Illinois P, 1955.

Blakemore, Steven. " 'Without a Cross': The Cultural Significance of the Sublime and Beautiful in Cooper's *The Last of the Mohicans*." *Nineteenth-Century Literature* 52.1 (June 1997): 27–57.

Blassingame, John W. *The Slave Community: Plantation Life in the Antebellum South*. New York: Oxford UP, 1972.

Bledstein, Burton J. *The Culture of Professionalism: The Middle Class and the Development of Higher Education in America*. New York: Norton, 1976.

Blount, Marcellus, and George P. Cunningham, eds. *Representing Black Men*. New York: Routledge, 1996.

Blumin, Stuart M. *The Emergence of the Middle Class: Social Experience in the American City, 1760–1900*. Cambridge: Cambridge UP, 1989.

——. "The Hypothesis of Middle-Class Formation in Nineteenth-Century America: A Critique and Some Proposals." *American Historical Review* 90 (1985): 299–338.

Bogdan, Robert. *Freak Show: Presenting Human Oddities for Amusement and Profit*. Chicago: U of Chicago P, 1988.

Bohan, Ruth L. " 'The Gathering of Forces': Walt Whitman and the Visual Arts in Brooklyn in the 1850s." In *Walt Whitman and the Visual Arts*. Ed. Geoffrey M. Sill and Roberta K. Tarbell. New Brunswick: Rutgers UP, 1992. 1–27.

Bonaparte, Marie. *The Life and Works of Edgar Allan Poe: A Psycho-Analytic Interpretation*. Trans. John Rodker. 1949. New York: Humanities Press, 1971.

Boucicault, Dion. *The Octoroon*. 1859. *Representative American Plays*. 7th rev. ed. Ed. Arthur Hobson Quinn. New York: Appleton-Century-Crofts, 1953. 369–98.

Bourdieu, Pierre. *Distinction: A Social Critique of the Judgment of Taste*. Trans. Richard Nice. Cambridge: Harvard UP, 1984.

——. *Outline of a Theory of Practice*. Trans. Richard Nice. Cambridge: Cambridge UP, 1977.

——. *The Rules of Art: Genesis and Structure of the Literary Field.* Trans. Susan Emanuel. Stanford, Calif.: Stanford UP, 1995.

"Brady's Gallery." *Harper's Weekly* 14 November 1863.

Brancaccio, Patrick. " 'The Black Man's Paradise': Hawthorne's Editing of *The Journal of an African Cruiser.*" *New England Quarterly* 53.1 (March 1980): 23–41.

Brickhouse, Anna. " 'I Do Abhor an Indian Story': Hawthorne and the Allegorization of Racial 'Commixture.' " *ESQ* 42.4 (1996): 232–53.

Bridge, Horatio. *Journal of an African Cruiser.* 1845. London: Dawsons of Pall Mall, 1968.

Brigham, David R. *Public Culture in the Early Republic: Peale's Museum and Its Audience.* Washington, D.C.: Smithsonian Institution Press, 1995.

Brodhead, Richard H. "Veiled Ladies: Toward a History of Antebellum Entertainment." *American Literary History* 1.2 (summer 1989): 283–85.

Bromell, Nicholas K. *By the Sweat of the Brow: Literature and Labor in Antebellum America.* Chicago: U of Chicago P, 1993.

Bronner, Simon J. "Object Lessons: The Work of Ethnology Museums." In *Consuming Visions: Accumulation and Display of Goods in America, 1880–1920.* Ed. Simon J. Bronner. New York: Norton, 1989. 217–54.

Brown, Bill. *The Material Unconscious: American Amusement, Stephen Crane, and the Economies of Play.* Cambridge: Harvard UP, 1996.

Brown, Gillian. *Domestic Individualism: Imagining Self in Nineteenth-Century America.* Berkeley: U of California P, 1990.

Brown, Lee Rust. "The Emerson Museum." *Representations* 40 (fall 1992): 57–80.

Brown, William Wells. *The American Fugitive in Europe.* 1854. In *The Travels of William Wells Brown.* Ed. Paul Jefferson. New York: Marcus Wiener, 1991. 71–235.

——. *Clotel; or, the President's Daughter: A Narrative of Slave Life in the United States.* 1853. New York: Carol, 1969.

——. *A Description of William Wells Brown's Panoramic Views.* 1850. In *The Black Abolitionist Papers.* Ed. C. Peter Ripley. Vol. 1. Chapel Hill: U of North Carolina P, 1985. 190–224.

——. *The Escape; or, A Leap for Freedom.* 1858. In *Black Theater, U.S.A.: Forty-Five Plays by Black Americans, 1847–1974.* Ed. James V. Hatch. New York: The Free Press, 1974. 34–58.

——. *A Lecture Delivered Before the Female Anti-Slavery Society of Salem at Lyceum Hall, Nov. 14, 1847.* 1847. In *Four Fugitive Slave Narratives.* Ed. Larry Gara. Reading, Mass.: Addison-Wesley, 1969. 79–98.

——. *Narrative of William Wells Brown, A Fugitive Slave, written by himself.* 1847. In *Puttin' On Ole Massa.* Ed. Gilbert Osofsky. New York: Harper and Row, 1969. 173–224.

——. "Speech by William Wells Brown Delivered at the Horticultural Hall,

West Chester Pennsylvania, 23 October 1854." 1854. In *The Black Abolitionist Papers*. Ed. C. Peter Ripley. Vol. 4. Chapel Hill: U of North Carolina P, 1991. 245–55.

——. *St. Domingo: Its Revolutions and Its Patriots. A Lecture.* 1855. Philadelphia: Rhistoric, 1969.

——, ed. *The Anti-Slavery Harp: A Collection of Songs.* 4th ed. Boston: Bela Marsh, 1854.

——, ed. *The Anti-Slavery Harp: A Collection of Songs For Anti-Slavery Meetings.* Boston: Bela Marsh, 1848.

Buck-Morss, Susan. "Aesthetics and Anaesthetics: Walter Benjamin's Artwork Essay Reconsidered." *October* 62 (1992): 3–41.

Buckley, Peter G. "To the Opera House: Culture and Society in New York City, 1820–1860." Ph.D. Diss. SUNY: Stony Brook, 1984.

Buell, Lawrence. *New England Literary Culture: From Revolution Through Renaissance.* Cambridge: Cambridge UP, 1986.

Butler, Judith. *Bodies That Matter: On the Discursive Limits of "Sex".* New York: Routledge, 1993.

——. *Gender Trouble: Feminism and the Subversion of Identity.* New York: Routledge, 1990.

Butler, Michael. "Narrative Structure and Historical Process in *The Last of the Mohicans.*" *American Literature* 48.2 (May 1976): 117–39.

Butsch, Richard. "Bowery B'hoys and Matinee Ladies: The Re-Gendering of Nineteenth-Century American Theater Audiences." *American Quarterly* 46.3 (September 1994): 374–405.

Campbell, Killis. *The Mind of Poe and Other Studies.* Cambridge: Harvard UP, 1933.

Carby, Hazel V. *Race Men.* Cambridge: Harvard UP, 1998.

Carnes, Mark C., and Cynthia Griffin, eds. *Meanings for Manhood: Constructions of Masculinity in Victorian America.* Chicago: U of Chicago P, 1990.

Cashin, Joan E. "A Northwest Passage: Gender, Race, and the Family in the Early Nineteenth Century." In *A Shared Experience: Men, Women, and the History of Gender.* Ed. Laura McCall and Donald Yacovone. New York: New York UP, 1998. 222–44.

Cassuto, Leonard. *The Inhuman Race: The Racial Grotesque in American Literature and Culture.* New York: Columbia UP, 1997.

Castronovo, Russ. *Fathering the Nation: American Genealogies of Slavery and Freedom.* Berkeley: U of California P, 1995.

Cawelti, John G. *Apostles of the Self-Made Man: Changing Concepts of Success in America.* Chicago: U of Chicago P, 1965.

Charvat, William. *Literary Publishing in America, 1790–1850.* Philadelphia: U of Pennsylvania P, 1959.

——. *The Profession of Authorship in America, 1800–1870.* Ed. Matthew J. Bruccoli. New York: Columbia UP, 1968.

Cheyfitz, Eric. "The Irresistibleness of Great Literature: Reconstructing Hawthorne's Politics." *American Literary History* 6.3 (fall 1994): 539–58.

Child, Lydia Maria. *Hobomok and Other Writings on Indians.* Ed. Carolyn L. Karcher. New Brunswick, NJ: Rutgers UP, 1986.

Christy's Plantation Melodies #2. Philadelphia: Fisher and Brothers, 1852.

Claudet, M. "The Progress and Present State of the Daguerreotype Art." *Journal of the Franklin Institute* (July 1845): 45–51; (August 1845): 113–18.

Clifford, James. *The Predicament of Culture: Twentieth-Century Ethnography, Literature, and Art.* Cambridge: Harvard UP, 1988.

Cockrell, Dale. *Demons of Disorder: Early Blackface Minstrels and Their World.* Cambridge: Cambridge UP, 1997.

Cook, James W., Jr. "Of Men, Missing Links, and Nondescripts: The Strange Career of P. T. Barnum's 'What is It?' Exhibition." In *Freakery: Cultural Spectacles of the Extraordinary Body.* Ed. Rosemarie Garland Thomson. New York: New York UP, 1996. 139–57.

Cooper, James Fenimore. *The Last of the Mohicans; A Narrative of 1757.* 1826. Albany: State U of New York P, 1983.

——. *The Letters and Journals of James Fenimore Cooper.* Ed. James Franklin Beard. 6 vols. Cambridge: Harvard UP, 1960–1968.

——. *The Pioneers, or, The Sources of the Susquehanna: a Descriptive Tale.* Albany: State U of New York P, 1980.

——. *The Spy, A Tale of the Neutral Ground.* 1821. Oxford: Oxford UP, 1968.

——. *The Wept of Wish-Ton-Wish.* 1829. New York: Putnam, 1896.

Copway, George. *The Life, Letters, and Speeches of Kah-Ge-Ga-Gah-Bowh or, G. Copway.* New York: S. W. Benedict, 1850.

Cott, Nancy F. *The Bonds of Womanhood: "Woman's Sphere" in New England, 1780–1835.* New Haven, Conn.: Yale UP, 1977.

Craft, William. *Running a Thousand Miles for Freedom; or, The Escape of William and Ellen Craft from Slavery.* 1860. In *Great Slave Narratives.* Ed. Arna Bontemps. Boston: Beacon Press, 1969.

Cullen, Jim. " 'I's a Man Now': Gender and African American Men." In *Divided Houses: Gender and the Civil War.* Ed. Catharine Clinton and Nina Silber. New York: Oxford UP, 1992. 76–91.

Curtis, L. Perry, Jr. *Apes and Angels: The Irishman in Victorian Caricature.* Rev. ed. Washington: Smithsonian Institution Press, 1997.

"Daguerreotypes." *Littell's Living Age* (20 June 1846): 551–52.

"Daguerrian Gallery of the West." *Gleason's Pictorial Drawing-Room Companion* 6.13 (1 April 1854): 208.

Davidson, Cathy N. "Photographs of the Dead: Sherman, Daguerre, and Hawthorne." *The South Atlantic Quarterly* 89.4 (fall 1990): 667–701.

——. "Preface: No More Separate Spheres!" *American Literature* 70.3 (September 1998): 443–63.

——. *Revolution and the Word: The Rise of the Novel in America.* New York: Oxford UP, 1986.

Dayan, Joan. "Amorous Bondage: Poe, Ladies, and Slaves." *American Literature* 66.2 (June 1994): 239–73.

——. "Poe, Persons, and Property." *American Literary History* 11.3 (fall 1999): 405–25.

——. "Poe's Women: A Feminist Poe?" *Poe Studies* 26.1–2 (June/December 1993): 1–12.

——. "Romance and Race." In *The Columbia History of the American Novel.* Gen. Ed. Emory Elliott. New York: Columbia UP, 1991. 89–109.

Deloria, Philip Joseph. *Playing Indian.* New Haven, Conn.: Yale UP, 1998.

Dennison, Sam. *Scandalize My Name: Black Imagery in American Popular Music.* New York: Garland, 1982.

Derrick, Scott S. *Monumental Anxieties: Homoerotic Desire and Feminine Influence in Nineteenth-Century U.S. Literature.* New Brunswick, NJ: Rutgers UP, 1997.

Dickens, Charles. *American Notes.* 1842. New York: Oxford UP, 1957.

Dimock, Wai Chee. "Whitman, Syntax, and Political Theory." In *Breaking Bounds: Whitman and American Cultural Studies.* Ed. Betsy Erkkila and Jay Grossman. New York: Oxford UP, 1996. 62–79.

Dippie, Brian W. *The Vanishing American: White Attitudes and U.S. Indian Policy.* Middletown: Wesleyan UP, 1982.

Dorsey, Peter A. "De-authorizing Slavery: Realism in Stowe's *Uncle Tom's Cabin* and Brown's *Clotel.*" *ESQ* 41.4 (1995): 256–88.

Douglas, Ann. *The Feminization of American Culture.* New York: Doubleday, 1977.

Douglass, Frederick. "The Claims of the Negro Ethnologically Considered: An Address Delivered in Hudson, Ohio, on 12 July 1854." In *The Frederick Douglass Papers.* Series One: *Speeches, Debates, and Interviews.* Ed. John W. Blassingame. Volume 2: 1847–1854. New Haven, Conn.: Yale UP, 1982. 497–524.

——. "Gavitt's Original Ethiopian Serenaders." *North Star.* 29 June 1849. In *The Life and Writings of Frederick Douglass.* Ed. Philip S. Foner. Vol. 1. New York: International Publishers, 1950. 141–42.

——. "The Heroic Slave." 1853. In *The Oxford Frederick Douglass Reader.* Ed. William L. Andrews. New York: Oxford UP, 1996. 131–63.

——. *My Bondage and My Freedom.* 1855. New York: Arno, 1969.

——. *Narrative of the Life of Frederick Douglass, An American Slave. Written By Himself.* 1845. In *The Classic Slave Narratives.* Ed. Henry Louis Gates Jr. New York: Mentor, 1987. 243–331.

"Dramatic Literature." *American Quarterly Review* 8.15 (September 1830): 134–61.

Drinnon, Richard. *Facing West: The Metaphysics of Indian-Hating and Empire Building*. Minneapolis: U of Minnesota P, 1980.

Du Bois, W. E. B. *The Souls of Black Folk*. 1903. In *W. E. B. Du Bois: Writings*. Ed. Nathan Huggins. New York: Library of America, 1986. 357–547.

DuCille, Ann. *The Coupling Convention: Sex, Text, and Tradition in Black Women's Fiction*. New York: Oxford UP, 1993.

Duganne, Augustine J. H. *The Daguerreotype Miniature; or, Life in the Empire City*. Philadelphia: G. B. Zieber and Co., 1846.

Dunlap, William. *Diary of William Dunlap (1766–1839): The Memoirs of a Dramatist, Theatrical Manager, Painter, Critic, Novelist, and Historian*. New York: New York Historical Society, 1931.

Dyer, Richard. "White." *Screen* 29.4 (autumn 1988): 44–64.

Eagleton, Terry. *The Ideology of the Aesthetic*. Oxford: Basil Blackwell, 1990.

"Editor's Table: Bowery Theatre." *Knickerbocker* 16.1 (July 1840): 84.

Eich, L. M. "The American Indian Plays." *The Quarterly Journal of Speech* 30.2 (April 1944): 212–15.

Ellison, Ralph. "Change the Joke and Slip the Yoke." 1958. *Shadow and Act*. New York: Random House, 1964. 45–59.

Elmer, Jonathan. *Reading at the Social Limit: Affect, Mass Culture, and Edgar Allan Poe*. Stanford, Calif.: Stanford UP, 1995.

Emerson, Ralph Waldo. *Journals of Ralph Waldo Emerson*. Ed. Edward Waldo Emerson and Waldo Emerson Forbes. 10 vols. Boston: Houghton Mifflin, 1909–1914.

Engle, Gary D., ed. *This Grotesque Essence: Plays from the American Minstrel Stage*. Baton Rouge: Louisiana State UP, 1978.

Erdman, Harley. "Caught in the 'Eye of the Eternal:' Justice, Race, and the Camera, from *The Octoroon* to Rodney King." *Theatre Journal* 45.3 (1993): 333–48.

Ernest, John. "The Profession of Authorship and the Cultural Text: William Wells Brown's *Clotel*." *Resistance and Reformation in Nineteenth-Century African-American Literature: Brown, Wilson, Jacobs, Delany, Douglass, and Harper*. Jackson: UP of Mississippi, 1995. 20–54.

——. "The Reconstruction of Whiteness: William Wells Brown's *The Escape; or; A Leap for Freedom*." *PMLA* 113.5 (October 1998): 1108–21.

Fabi, M. Giulia. "The 'Unguarded Expressions of the Feelings of the Negroes': Gender, Slave Resistance, and William Wells Brown's Revisions of *Clotel*." *African American Review* 27.4 (winter 1993): 639–54.

Fanon, Frantz. *Black Skin, White Masks*. 1952. Trans. Charles Lamm Markmann. New York: Grove Press, 1967.

Fanuzzi, Robert. "Thoreau's Urban Imagination." *American Literature* 68.2 (June 1996): 321–46.

Farrison, William Edward. *William Wells Brown: Author and Reformer.* Chicago: U of Chicago P, 1969.

Fern, Fanny [Sara Willis Parton]. *Ruth Hall and Other Writings.* Ed. Joyce W. Warren. New Brunswick, N.J.: Rutgers UP, 1986.

Fiedler, Leslie. *Freaks: Myths and Images of the Secret Self.* 1978. New York: Anchor Books, 1993.

——. *Love and Death in the American Novel.* 1960. London: Paladin, 1970.

Fink, Steven. *Prophet in the Marketplace: Thoreau's Development as a Professional Writer.* Princeton, N.J.: Princeton UP, 1992.

Fisher, Philip. "Democratic Social Space: Whitman, Melville, and the Promise of American Transparency." *Representations* 24 (fall 1988): 60–101.

Fishkin, Shelley Fisher. "Interrogating 'Whiteness,' Complicating 'Blackness': Remapping American Culture." *American Quarterly* 47.3 (September 1995): 428–66.

Fitzhugh, George. *Cannibals All! Or Slaves Without Masters.* 1857. Cambridge: Harvard UP, 1988.

Fleck, Richard. "Further Selections From the 'Indian Notebooks.'" *Thoreau Journal Quarterly* 9.1 (January 1977): 2–23.

——, ed. *The Indians of Thoreau: Selections from the Indian Notebooks.* Albuquerque, N.M.: Hummingbird Press, 1974.

Fleischner, Jennifer. "Hawthorne and the Politics of Slavery." *Studies in the Novel* 23.1 (spring 1991): 96–106.

——. *Mastering Slavery: Memory, Family, and Identity in Women's Slave Narratives.* New York: New York UP, 1996.

Foner, Eric. *Free Soil, Free Labor, Free Men: The Ideology of the Republican Party Before the Civil War.* New York: Oxford UP, 1970.

——. "Politics and Prejudice: The Free Soil Party and the Negro, 1849–1852." *Journal of Negro History* 50.4 (October 1967): 239–56.

Foresta, Merry A. "Secrets of the Dark Chamber: The Art of the American Daguerreotype." In *Secrets of the Dark Chamber: The Art of the American Daguerreotype.* Ed. Merry A. Foresta and John Wood. Washington, D.C.: Smithsonian Institution Press, 1995. 15–30.

Foresta, Merry A., and John Wood, eds. *Secrets of the Dark Chamber: The Art of the American Daguerreotype.* Washington, D.C.: Smithsonian Institution Press, 1995.

Foster, Frances Smith. *Witnessing Slavery: The Development of Ante-bellum Slave Narratives.* Westport, Conn.: Greenwood Press, 1979.

Foster, George G. *New York by Gas-Light and Other Urban Sketches by George G. Foster.* Ed. Stuart M. Blumin. Berkeley: U of California P, 1990.

Foster, Stephen C. *The Music of Stephen C. Foster.* Ed. Steven Saunders and Deane L. Root. Vol. 1 (1844–1855). Washington, D.C.: Smithsonian Institution Press, 1990.

Fredrickson, George M. *The Black Image in the White Mind: The Debate on Afro-American Character and Destiny, 1817–1914*. New York: Harper, 1971.

Friedberg, Anne. *Window Shopping: Cinema and the Postmodern*. Berkeley: U of California P, 1993.

Frost, Linda. " 'The Red Face of Man,' the Penobscot Indian, and a Conflict of Interest in Thoreau's *The Maine Woods*." *ESQ* 39.1 (1993): 21–47.

Fuller, Margaret. "American Literature; Its Position in the Present Time, and Prospects for the Future." *Papers on Literature and Art*. Part 2. New York: Wiley and Putnam, 1846. 121–59.

——. "Entertainments of the Past Winter." *Dial* 3.1 (July 1842): 46–72.

——. *The Letters of Margaret Fuller*. Ed. Robert N. Hudspeth. 6 vols. Ithaca, N.Y.: Cornell UP, 1983–1994.

——. *Memoirs of Margaret Fuller Ossoli*. 2 vols. Boston: Phillips, Sampson and Company, 1852.

——. *Woman in the Nineteenth Century*. 1845. In *The Portable Margaret Fuller*. Ed. Mary Kelley. New York: Penguin, 1994. 228–362.

Fussell, Edwin S. "The Red Face of Man." In *Thoreau: A Collection of Critical Essays*. Ed. Sherman Paul. Englewood Cliffs, NJ: Prentice-Hall, 1962. 142–60.

Gara, Larry. "The Professional Fugitive in the Abolition Movement." *Wisconsin Magazine of History* 48.3 (spring 1965): 196–204.

Gardner, Jared. *Master Plots: Race and the Founding of an American Literature, 1787–1845*. Baltimore, Md.: Johns Hopkins UP, 1998.

Garnet, Henry Highland. *Address to the Slaves of the United States of America*. 1848. In *The Ideological Origins of Black Nationalism*. Ed. Sterling Stuckey. Boston: Beacon Press, 1972. 165–73.

Gates, Henry Louis, Jr. *Figures in Black: Words, Signs, and the 'Racial' Self*. New York: Oxford UP, 1987.

——. *The Signifying Monkey: A Theory of African-American Literary Criticism*. New York: Oxford UP, 1988.

Gaul, Theresa Strouth. " 'The Genuine Indian Who Was Brought Upon the Stage': Edwin Forrest's *Metamora* and White Audiences." *Arizona Quarterly* 56.1 (spring 2000): 1–27.

Gilmore, Michael T. *American Romanticism and the Marketplace*. Chicago: U of Chicago P, 1985.

——. "The Book Marketplace I." In *The Columbia History of the American Novel*. Gen. ed. Emory Elliott. New York: Columbia UP, 1991. 46–71.

——. "*Walden* and the Curse of Trade." In *Ideology and Classic American Literature*. Ed. Sacvan Bercovitch and Myra Jehlen. Cambridge: Cambridge UP, 1986. 293–312.

Goddu, Teresa A. *Gothic America: Narrative, History, and Nation*. New York: Columbia UP, 1997.

Gorn, Elliott J. *The Manly Art: Bare-Knuckle Prize Fighting in America.* Ithaca: Cornell UP, 1986.

Gossett, Thomas F. *Race: The History of an Idea in America.* Dallas: Southern Methodist UP, 1963.

Gould, Stephen Jay. *The Mismeasure of Man.* New York: Norton, 1981.

Gray, Thomas R. *The Confessions of Nat Turner.* 1831. In *The Confessions of Nat Turner and Related Documents.* Ed. Kenneth S. Greenberg. Boston: Bedford, 1996. 37–58.

Greenblatt, Stephen. "What Is the History of Literature?" *Critical Inquiry* 23.3 (spring 1997): 460–81.

Grimsted, David. *Melodrama Unveiled: American Theater and Culture, 1800–1850.* Chicago: U of Chicago P, 1968.

Grose, B. Donald. "Edwin Forrest, *Metamora,* and the Indian Removal Act of 1830." *Theatre Journal* (May 1985): 181–91.

Grossman, Allen. "The Poetics of Union in Whitman and Lincoln: An Inquiry Toward the Relationship of Art and Policy." In *The American Renaissance Reconsidered.* Ed. Walter Benn Michaels and Donald E. Pease. Baltimore, Md.: Johns Hopkins UP, 1985. 183–208.

Grossman, Jay. " 'A' is for Abolition?: Race, Authorship, *The Scarlet Letter.*" *Textual Practice* 7.1 (spring 1993): 13–30.

Gubar, Susan. *Racechanges: White Skin, Black Face in American Culture.* New York: Oxford UP, 1997.

Guillaumin, Colette. *Racism, Sexism, Power and Ideology.* New York: Routledge, 1995.

Gunning, Tom. "Tracking the Individual Body: Photography, Detectives, and Early Cinema." In *Cinema and the Invention of Modern Life.* Ed. Leo Charney and Vanessa R. Schwartz. Berkeley: U of California P, 1995. 15–45.

Gura, Philip F. "Thoreau's Maine Woods Indians: More Representative Men." *American Literature* 49.3 (November 1977): 366–84.

Halttunen, Karen. *Confidence Men and Painted Women: A Study of Middle-Class Culture in America, 1830–1870.* New Haven, Conn.: Yale UP, 1982.

Hammond, J. R. *An Edgar Allan Poe Companion: A Guide to the Short Stories, Romances, and Essays.* Totowa, NJ: Barnes and Noble Books, 1981.

Haraway, Donna. "Teddy Bear Patriarchy: Taxidermy in the Garden of Eden, New York City, 1908–1936." *Primate Visions: Gender, Race, and Nature in the World of Modern Science.* New York: Routledge, 1989. 26–58.

Harper, Philip Brian. *Are We Not Men?: Masculine Anxiety and the Problem of African-American Identity.* New York: Oxford UP, 1996.

Harris, Neil. *Humbug: The Art of P. T. Barnum.* Chicago: U of Chicago P, 1973.

——. "Museums, Merchandising, and Popular Taste: The Struggle for Influence." In *Material Culture and the Study of American Life.* Ed. Ian M. G. Quimby. New York: Norton, 1978. 140–74.

Harrison, Gabriel. *Edwin Forrest: The Actor and the Man.* Brooklyn: Brooklyn Eagle Press, 1889.

Hartman, Saidiya V. *Scenes of Subjection: Terror, Slavery, and Self-Making in Nineteenth-Century America.* New York: Oxford UP, 1997.

Hawthorne, Nathaniel. *The Centenary Edition of the Works of Nathaniel Hawthorne.* Gen. eds. William Charvat, Roy Harvey Pearce, and Claude M. Simpson. 23 vols. to date. Columbus: Ohio State UP, 1962–.

———. "Chiefly About War Matters." 1862. *Tales, Sketches, and Other Papers.* Vol. 12 of *Complete Works.* Boston: Houghton Mifflin, 1886. 299–345.

———. *Life of Franklin Pierce.* 1852. *Tales, Sketches, and Other Papers.* Vol. 12 of *Complete Works.* Boston: Houghton Mifflin, 1886. 349–438.

———. "Nathaniel Hawthorne on Woman's Rights." *The Home Journal.* 15 October 1853. *American Transcendental Quarterly* 2 (1969): 31.

Herbert, T. Walter. *Dearest Beloved: The Hawthornes and the Making of the Middle-Class Family.* Berkeley: U of California P, 1993.

Higginson, Thomas Wentworth. *Margaret Fuller Ossoli.* 1884. New York: Chelsea House, 1981.

Hinsley, Curtis M. *The Smithsonian and the American Indian: Making a Moral Anthropology in Victorian America.* Washington, D.C.: Smithsonian Institution Press, 1994. Rev. ed. of *Savages and Scientists.* 1981.

Hoganson, Kristin. "Garrisonian Abolitionists and the Rhetoric of Gender, 1850–1860." *American Quarterly* 45.4 (December 1993): 558–95.

Holland, J. Gill. "Hawthorne and Photography: *The House of the Seven Gables.*" *Nathaniel Hawthorne Journal* 8 (1978): 1–10.

Horowitz, Nancy A. "Criminality and Poe's Orangutan: The Question of Race in Detection." In *Agonistics: Arenas of Creative Contest.* Ed. Janet Lungstrum and Elizabeth Sauer. Albany: SUNY Press, 1997. 177–95.

Horsman, Reginald. *Race and Manifest Destiny: The Origins of Racial Anglo-Saxonism.* Cambridge: Harvard UP, 1981.

———. "Scientific Racism and the American Indian in the Mid-Nineteenth Century." *American Quarterly* 27.2 (May 1975): 152–68.

Horton, James Oliver. "Freedom's Yoke: Gender Conventions Among Antebellum Free Blacks." *Feminist Studies* 12.1 (spring 1986): 51–76.

Hovey, Kenneth Alan. "Critical Provincialism: Poe's Poetic Principle in Antebellum Context." *American Quarterly* 39.3 (fall 1987): 341–54.

Hungerford, Edward. "Poe and Phrenology." *American Literature* 2 (1930–1931): 209–23.

Huyssen, Andreas. "Mass Culture as Woman: Modernism's Other." *After the Great Divide: Modernism, Mass Culture, Postmodernism.* Bloomington: Indiana UP, 1986. 44–62.

Ignatiev, Noel. *How the Irish Became White.* New York: Routledge, 1995.

An Illustrated Catalogue and Guide Book to Barnum's American Museum. New York: n.p., 1864.

"The Inconstant Daguerreotype." *Harper's New Monthly Magazine* (May 1855): 820–26.

Ireland, Joseph N. *Records of the New York Stage from 1750 to 1860.* 1866. Vol. 2. New York: Benjamin Blom, 1966.

Irving, Washington. *The Sketch Book of Geoffrey Crayon, Gent.* 1819–1820. New York: Penguin, 1978.

Jameson, Fredric. "Reification and Utopia in Mass Culture." *Signatures of the Visible.* New York: Routledge, 1990. 9–34.

Jefferson, Thomas. *Notes on the State of Virginia.* Ed. William Peden. 1787. New York: Norton, 1972.

Johnson, Linck C. "Thoreau's Earliest 'Indian Book' and His First Trip to Cape Cod." *ESQ* 28.2 (1982): 74–87.

Johnson, Paul. *A Shopkeeper's Millennium: Society and Revivals in Rochester, New York, 1815–1837.* New York: Hill and Wang, 1978.

Jones, Eugene H. *Native Americans as Shown on the Stage, 1753–1916.* Metuchen, N.J.: Scarecrow, 1988.

Jones, Sally L. "The First But Not the Last of the 'Vanishing Indians': Edwin Forrest and Mythic Recreations of the Native Population." In *Dressing in Feathers: The Construction of the Indian in American Popular Culture.* Ed. S. Elizabeth Bird. Boulder, Colo.: Westview, 1996. 13–27.

Jordan, Cynthia. *Second Stories: The Politics of Language, Form, and Gender in Early American Fictions.* Chapel Hill: U of North Carolina P, 1989.

Keiser, Albert. "Thoreau—Friend of the Native." *The Indian in American Literature.* New York: Oxford UP, 1933. 209–32.

Kelley, Mary. *Private Woman, Public Stage: Literary Domesticity in Nineteenth-Century America.* New York: Oxford UP, 1984.

Kennard, James K., Jr. "Who Are Our National Poets?" *Knickerbocker* 26.4 (October 1845): 331–41.

Kennedy, J. Gerald. "Poe, 'Ligeia,' and the Problem of Dying Women." In *New Essays on Poe's Major Tales.* Ed. Kenneth Silverman. Cambridge: Cambridge UP, 1993. 113–29.

Kimmel, Michael S. *Manhood in America: A Cultural History.* New York: The Free Press, 1996.

Kirshenblatt-Gimblett, Barbara. "Objects of Ethnography." In *Exhibiting Cultures: The Poetics and Politics of Museum Display.* Ed. Ivan Karp and Steven D. Levine. Washington, D.C.: Smithsonian Institution Press, 1991. 386–443.

Klammer, Martin. *Whitman, Slavery, and the Emergence of* Leaves of Grass. University Park: Pennsylvania State UP, 1993.

Knobel, Dale T. "Know-Nothings and Indians: Strange Bedfellows." *Western Historical Quarterly* 15.2 (April 1984): 175–98.

Krutch, Joseph Wood. *Edgar Allan Poe: A Study in Genius.* 1926. New York: Russell and Russell, 1965.

Lang, Amy Schrager. "Class and the Strategies of Sympathy." In *The Culture of*

Sentiment: Race, Gender, and Sentimentality in Nineteenth-Century America. Ed. Shirley Samuels. New York: Oxford UP, 1992. 128–42.

Review of *The Last of the Mohicans,* by James Fenimore Cooper. *New-York Review and Atheneum* 2 (March 1826): 285–92. In *Fenimore Cooper: The Critical Heritage.* Ed. George Dekker and John P. McWilliams. London: Routledge and Kegan Paul, 1973. 89–96.

Laurie, Bruce. *Working People of Philadelphia, 1800–1850.* Philadelphia: Temple UP, 1980.

Lebowitz, Michael A. "The Jacksonians: Paradox Lost?" In *Towards a New Past: Dissenting Essays in American History.* Ed. Barton J. Bernstein. New York: Vintage, 1968. 65–89.

Lepore, Jill. "The Curse of Metamora." *The Name of War: King Philip's War and the Origins of American Identity.* New York: Knopf, 1998. 191–226.

Leverenz, David. "The Last Real Man in America: From Natty Bumppo to Batman." *American Literary History* 3.4 (winter 1991): 753–81.

——. *Manhood and the American Renaissance.* Ithaca, N.Y.: Cornell UP, 1989.

——. "Poe and Gentry Virginia: Provincial Gentleman, Textual Aristocrat, Man of the Crowd." In *Haunted Bodies: Gender and Southern Texts.* Ed. Anne Goodwyn Jones and Susan V. Donaldson. Charlottesville: UP of Virginia, 1997. 79–108.

Levine, Lawrence W. *Highbrow/Lowbrow: The Emergence of Cultural Hierarchy in America.* Cambridge: Harvard UP, 1988.

Levine, Robert S. "*Uncle Tom's Cabin* in *Frederick Douglass' Paper*: An Analysis of Reception." *American Literature* 64.1 (March 1992): 71–93.

——. "'Whiskey, Blacking, and All': Temperance and Race in William Wells Brown's *Clotel.*" In *The Serpent in the Cup: Temperance in American Literature.* Ed. David S. Reynolds and Debra J. Rosenthal. Amherst: U of Massachusetts P, 1997. 93–114.

Lhamon, W. T., Jr. *Raising Cain: Blackface Performance from Jim Crow to Hip Hop.* Cambridge: Harvard UP, 1998.

Limon, John. *The Place of Fiction in the Time of Science: A Disciplinary History of American Writing.* Cambridge: Cambridge UP, 1990.

Lindfors, Bernth. "Circus Africans." *Journal of American Culture* 6.2 (1983): 9–14.

——. "'Mislike Me Not for My Complexion . . .': Ira Aldridge in Whiteface." *African American Review* 33.2 (summer 1999): 347–54.

Littlefield, Daniel F., Jr., ed. *The Life of Okah Tubbee.* 1852. Lincoln: U of Nebraska P, 1988.

Litwack, Leon F. *North of Slavery: The Negro in the Free States, 1790–1860.* Chicago: U of Chicago P, 1961.

Lott, Eric. *Love and Theft: Blackface Minstrelsy and the American Working Class.* New York: Oxford UP, 1993.

Lowell, James Russell. *A Fable for Critics. The Complete Writings of James Russell Lowell.* Vol. 12. Boston: Houghton Mifflin, 1904. 1–88.

Lukács, Georg. "Reification and the Consciousness of the Proletariat." *History and Class Consciousness: Studies in Marxist Dialectics.* Trans. Rodney Livingston. 1923. Cambridge: MIT P, 1971. 83–222.

Lurie, Edward. *Louis Agassiz: A Life in Science.* Chicago: U of Chicago P, 1960.

MacGregor, Alan Leander. "Tammany: The Indian as Rhetorical Surrogate." *American Quarterly* 35.4 (fall 1983): 391–405.

Macpherson, C. B. *The Political Theory of Possessive Individualism, Hobbes to Locke.* New York: Oxford UP, 1962.

Maddox, Lucy. *Removals: Nineteenth-Century American Literature and the Politics of Indian Affairs.* New York: Oxford UP, 1991.

Mahar, William J. *Behind the Burnt Cork Mask: Early Blackface Minstrelsy and Antebellum American Popular Culture.* Urbana: U of Illinois P, 1999.

Mangan, J. A., and James Walvin, eds. *Manliness and Morality: Middle-Class Masculinity in Britain and America, 1800–1940.* New York: St. Martin's, 1987.

Manners, Motley [Augustine J. H. Duganne]. "A Mirror for Authors." *Holden's Dollar Magazine* January 1849: 20–22.

Marx, Karl. *Capital: A Critique of Political Economy.* 1867. Vol. 1. Ed. Frederick Engels. Trans. Samuel Moore and Edward Aveling. New York: International Publishers, 1967.

———. *The Economic and Philosophic Manuscripts of 1844. The Marx-Engels Reader.* 2nd ed. Ed. Robert C. Tucker. New York: Norton, 1978. 66–125.

Marx, Karl, and Frederick Engels. *Manifesto of the Communist Party. The Marx-Engels Reader.* 2nd ed. Ed. Robert C. Tucker. New York: Norton, 1978. 469–500.

Mason, Jeffrey D. "*Metamora* (1829) and the 'Indian' Question." *Melodrama and the Myth of America.* Bloomington: Indiana UP, 1993. 23–59.

Mayhew, Henry. *London Labour and the London Poor.* 1861. Vol. 3. New York: Dover, 1968.

McCall, Laura, and Donald Yacovone, eds. *A Shared Experience: Men, Women, and the History of Gender.* New York: New York UP, 1998.

McCandless, Barbara. "The Portrait Studio and the Celebrity." In *Photography in Nineteenth-Century America.* Ed. Martha A. Sandweiss. Fort Worth, Tex.: Amon Carter Museum, 1991. 49–75.

McConachie, Bruce. *Melodramatic Formations: American Theatre and Society, 1820–1870.* Iowa City: U of Iowa P, 1992.

———. " 'The Theatre of the Mob': Apocalyptic Melodrama and Preindustrial Riots in Antebellum New York." In *Theatre for Working-Class Audiences in the United States, 1830–1980.* Ed. Bruce A. McConachie and Daniel Freeman. Westport, Conn.: Greenwood Press. 1985. 17–46.

McNamara, Brooks. "'A Congress of Wonders': The Rise and Fall of the Dime Museum." *ESQ* 20.3 (1974): 216–32.

Melville, Herman. "Hawthorne and His Mosses." *The Piazza Tales and Other Prose Pieces, 1839–1860*. Evanston: Northwestern UP, 1987. 239–53.

Mercer, Kobena. "Skin Head Sex Thing." In *How Do I Look?: Queer Film and Video*. Ed. Bad Object-Choices. Seattle: Bay Press, 1991. 169–210.

Merish, Lori. "Cuteness and Commodity Aesthetics: Tom Thumb and Shirley Temple." In *Freakery: Cultural Spectacles of the Extraordinary Body*. Ed. Rosemarie Garland Thomson. New York: New York UP, 1996. 185–203.

Meyer, Michael. "Thoreau and Black Emigration." *American Literature* 53.3 (November 1981): 380–96.

Michaels, Walter Benn. *Our America: Nativism, Modernism, and Pluralism*. Durham, N.C.: Duke UP, 1995.

——. "Romance and Real Estate." *The Gold Standard and the Logic of Naturalism: American Literature at the Turn of the Century*. Berkeley: U of California P, 1987. 85–112.

Mizruchi, Susan L. "From History to Gingerbread: Manufacturing a Republic in *The House of the Seven Gables*." *The Power of Historical Knowledge: Narrating the Past in Hawthorne, James, and Dreiser*. Princeton, N.J.: Princeton UP, 1988. 83–134.

Moody, Richard. *The Astor Place Riot*. Bloomington: U of Indiana P, 1958.

——, ed. *Dramas from the American Theatre, 1762–1909*. Cleveland: World Publishing Co., 1966.

Morrison, Toni. *Playing in the Dark: Whiteness and the Literary Imagination*. New York: Vintage, 1993.

Moses, Montrose J. *The Fabulous Forrest: The Record of an American Actor*. Boston: Little, Brown, 1929.

Moss, Sidney P. *Poe's Literary Battles: The Critic in the Context of His Literary Milieu*. 1963. Carbondale: Southern Illinois UP, 1969.

Mowatt, Anna Cora. *Fashion*. 1845. In *Dramas from the American Theatre, 1762–1909*. Ed. Richard Moody. Cleveland: World Publishing Co., 1966. 317–47.

Mullen, Harryette. "Runaway Tongue: Resistant Orality in *Uncle Tom's Cabin, Our Nig, Incidents in the Life of a Slave Girl*, and *Beloved*." In *The Culture of Sentiment: Race, Gender, and Sentimentality in Nineteenth-Century America*. Ed. Shirley Samuels. New York: Oxford UP, 1992. 244–64.

Murray, D. M. "Thoreau's Indians and His Developing Art of Characterization." *ESQ* 21.4 (1975): 222–29.

Nathan, Hans. *Dan Emmett and the Rise of Early Negro Minstrelsy*. Norman: U of Oklahoma P, 1962.

[Nathanson, Y. S]. "Negro Minstrelsy—Ancient and Modern." *Putnam's Monthly* (January 1855): 72–88.

Nelson, Dana D. "The Haunting of White Manhood: Poe, Fraternal Ritual, and Polygenesis." *American Literature* 69.3 (September 1997): 515–46.

——. *National Manhood: Capitalist Citizenship and the Imagined Fraternity of White Men.* Durham, N.C.: Duke UP, 1998.

——. *The Word in Black and White: Reading 'Race' in American Literature, 1638– 1867.* New York: Oxford UP, 1992.

Neufeldt, Leonard N. *The Economist: Henry Thoreau and Enterprise.* New York: Oxford UP, 1989.

Newbury, Michael. *Figuring Authorship in Antebellum America.* Stanford, Calif.: Stanford UP, 1997.

Newfield, Christopher. *The Emerson Effect: Individualism and Submission in America.* Chicago: U of Chicago P, 1996.

Newhall, Beaumont. *The Daguerreotype in America.* 3d rev. ed. New York: Dover, 1976.

Nichols, Thomas L. *Forty Years of American Life.* Vol. 2. London: John Maxwell and Co., 1864.

North, Douglass C. *The Economic Growth of the United States, 1790–1860.* New York: Norton, 1961.

North, Michael. *The Dialect of Modernism: Race, Language, and Twentieth- Century Literature.* New York: Oxford UP, 1994.

Nott, J. C., and George R. Gliddon, eds. *Types of Mankind: or, Ethnological Researches.* Philadelphia: Lippincott, Grambo and Co., 1854.

Odell, George C. D. *Annals of the New York Stage.* 15 vols. New York: Columbia UP, 1927–1949.

Review of *Oeuvres d'Alexandre Dumas. North American Review* 53 (January 1843): 109–37.

Orosz, Joel J. *Curators and Culture: The Museum Movement in America, 1740– 1870.* Tuscaloosa: U of Alabama P, 1990.

Orvell, Miles. *The Real Thing: Imitation and Authenticity in American Culture, 1880–1940.* Chapel Hill: U of North Carolina P, 1989.

Pearce, Roy Harvey. *Savagism and Civilization: A Study of the Indian and the American Mind.* Berkeley: U of California P, 1988. Rev. ed. of *Savages of America.* 1954.

Pease, Jane H., and William H. Pease. *They Who Would Be Free: Blacks' Search for Freedom, 1830–1861.* New York: Atheneum, 1974.

Person, Leland S., Jr. *Aesthetic Headaches: Women and a Masculine Poetics in Poe, Melville, and Hawthorne.* Athens: U of Georgia P, 1988.

Peterson, Carla L. "Capitalism, Black (Under)development, and the Production of the African-American Novel in the 1850s." *American Literary History* 4.4 (winter 1992): 559–83.

——. *"Doers of the Word": African-American Women Speakers and Writers in the North (1830–1880).* New York: Oxford UP, 1995.

Pfister, Harold Francis. *Facing the Light: Historic American Portrait Daguerreotypes.* Washington, D.C.: Smithsonian Institution Press, 1978.

Pfister, Joel. *The Production of Personal Life: Class, Gender, and the Psychological in Hawthorne's Fiction.* Stanford, Calif.: Stanford UP, 1991.

Phillips, Dana. "Nineteenth-Century Racial Thought and Whitman's 'Democratic Ethnology of the Future.'" *Nineteenth-Century Literature* 49.3 (December 1994): 289–320.

"Photography in the United States." *Photographic Art-Journal* (June 1853). Reprinted in *Secrets of the Dark Chamber: The Art of the American Daguerreotype.* Ed. Merry A. Foresta and John Wood. Washington, D.C.: Smithsonian Institution Press, 1995. 267–71.

"Pictorial Delineations by Light." *American Journal of Science and Art* 37.1 (October 1839): 169–85.

"Places of Public Amusement: Theatres and Concert Rooms." *Putnam's Monthly* (February 1854): 141–52.

Platizky, Roger S. "Hepzibah's Gingerbread Cakes in *The House of the Seven Gables.*" *American Notes and Queries* 17.7 (March 1979): 106–8.

Pleck, Elizabeth H., and Joseph H. Pleck, eds. *The American Man.* Englewood Cliffs, N.J.: Prentice-Hall, 1980.

Poe, Edgar Allan. *Edgar Allan Poe: Essays and Reviews.* Ed. G. R. Thompson. New York: Library of America, 1984.

——. *Edgar Allan Poe: Poetry and Tales.* Ed. Patrick F. Quinn. New York: Library of America, 1984.

——. *The Letters of Edgar Allan Poe.* Ed. John Ward Ostrom. 2 vols. Cambridge: Harvard UP, 1948.

——. "The Philosophy of Furniture." 1840. In *Tales and Sketches, 1831–1842.* Ed. Thomas Ollive Mabbott. Vol. 2 of *Collected Works of Edgar Allan Poe.* Cambridge: Belknap Press/Harvard UP, 1978. 494–504.

Pollak, Vivian R. "'In Loftiest Spheres': Whitman's Visionary Feminism." In *Breaking Bounds: Whitman and American Cultural Studies.* Ed. Betsy Erkkila and Jay Grossman. New York: Oxford UP, 1996. 92–111.

Postone, Moishe. *Time, Labor, and Social Domination: A Reinterpretation of Marx's Critical Theory.* Cambridge: Cambridge UP, 1993.

"Professor Draper on the Process of Daguerreotype and its application to taking Portraits from Life." *Philosophical Magazine* (September 1840). Reprinted in *Secrets of the Dark Chamber: The Art of the American Daguerreotype.* Ed. Merry A. Foresta and John Wood. Washington, D.C.: Smithsonian Institution Press, 1995. 233–35.

Prucha, Francis Paul. *Indian Policy in the United States: Historical Essays.* Lincoln: U of Nebraska P, 1981.

[Pugh, Achilles]. *Ball's Splendid Mammoth Pictorial Tour of the United States, Comprising Views of the African Slave Trade; of Northern and Southern Cities;*

of Cotton and Sugar Plantations; of the Mississippi, Ohio and Susquehanna
  Rivers, Niagara Falls, &C. Cincinnati: Achilles Pugh, Printer, 1855.

Pugh, David G. Sons of Liberty: The Masculine Mind in Nineteenth-Century
  America. Westport, Conn.: Greenwood Press, 1983.

Quarles, Benjamin. Black Abolitionists. New York: Oxford UP, 1969.

Rehin, George F. "Harlequin Jim Crow: Continuity and Convergence in Blackface Clowning." Journal of Popular Culture 9.3 (winter 1975): 682–701.

Reichlin, Elinor. "Faces of Slavery: A Historical Find." American Heritage 28.4
  (June 1977): 4–10.

Reid-Pharr, Robert F. Conjugal Union: The Body, The House, and the Black
  American. New York: Oxford UP, 1999.

Reilly, John E. "Poe in Pillory: An Early Version of a Satire by A. J. H. Duganne." Poe Studies 6 (June 1973): 4–12.

Reiss, Benjamin. "P. T. Barnum, Joice Heth and Antebellum Spectacles of
  Race." American Quarterly 51.1 (March 1999): 78–107.

Reynolds, David S. Beneath the American Renaissance: The Subversive Imagination in the Age of Emerson and Melville. Cambridge: Harvard UP, 1988.

——. "Poe's Art of Transformation: 'The Cask of Amontillado' in Cultural Context." In New Essays on Poe's Major Tales. Ed. Kenneth Silverman. Cambridge:
  Cambridge UP, 1993. 93–112.

——. Walt Whitman's America: A Cultural Biography. New York: Knopf, 1995.

Rhoads, Kenneth W. "Thoreau: The Ear and the Music." American Literature
  46.3 (November 1974): 313–28.

Rice, Grantland. The Transformation of Authorship in America. Chicago: U of
  Chicago P, 1997.

Richards, Eliza. " 'The Poetess' and Poe's Performance of the Feminine." Arizona Quarterly 55.2 (summer 1999): 1–29.

Rigal, Laura. "Peale's Mammoth." In American Iconology: New Approaches to
  Nineteenth-Century Art and Literature. Ed. David C. Miller. New Haven,
  Conn.: Yale UP, 1993. 18–38.

Rinhart, Floyd, and Marion Rinhart. The American Daguerreotype. Athens: U of
  Georgia P, 1981.

Ripley, C. Peter, gen. ed. The Black Abolitionist Papers. 5 vols. Chapel Hill: U of
  North Carolina P, 1985–1992.

Roach, Joseph. "One Blood." Cities of the Dead: Circum-Atlantic Performances.
  New York: Columbia UP, 1996. 179–237.

Roediger, David R. The Wages of Whiteness: Race and the Making of the American
  Working Class. New York: Verso, 1991.

Rogin, Michael Paul. Blackface, White Noise: Jewish Immigrants in the Hollywood
  Melting Pot. Berkeley: U of California P, 1996.

Romero, Lora. Home Fronts: Domesticity and its Critics in the Antebellum United
  States. Durham, N.C.: Duke UP, 1997.

——. "Vanishing Americans: Gender, Empire, and New Historicism." *American Literature* 63.3 (September 1991): 385–404.

Root, Marcus Aurelius. *The Camera and the Pencil*. 1864. Pawlet, Vt.: Helios, 1971.

Rosenthal, Bernhard. "Poe, Slavery, and the *Southern Literary Messenger*: A Re-examination." *Poe Studies* 7.2 (December 1974): 29–38.

Rotundo, E. Anthony. *American Manhood: Transformations in Masculinity from the Revolution to the Modern Era*. New York: HarperCollins, 1993.

Rowe, John Carlos. "Poe, Antebellum Slavery, and Modern Criticism." In *Poe's Pym: Critical Explorations*. Ed. Richard Kopley. Durham, N.C.: Duke UP, 1992. 117–38.

Ryan, Mary P. *Cradle of the Middle Class: The Family in Oneida County, New York, 1790–1865*. Cambridge: Cambridge UP, 1981.

——. *Women in Public: Between Banners and Ballots, 1825–1860*. Baltimore: Johns Hopkins UP, 1990.

Sacks, Howard L., and Judith Rose Sacks. *Way Up North in Dixie: A Black Family's Claim to the Confederate Anthem*. Washington, D.C.: Smithsonian Institution Press, 1993.

Sale, Maggie. "To Make the Past Useful: Frederick Douglass' Politics of Solidarity." *Arizona Quarterly* 51.3 (autumn 1995): 25–60.

Samuels, Shirley. "Generation Through Violence: Cooper and the Making of Americans." In *New Essays on* The Last of the Mohicans. Ed. Daniel Peck. Cambridge: Cambridge UP, 1992. 87–114.

——. "The Identity of Slavery." In *The Culture of Sentiment: Race, Gender, and Sentimentality in Nineteenth-Century America*. Ed. Shirley Samuels. New York: Oxford UP, 1992. 157–71.

——, ed. *The Culture of Sentiment: Race, Gender, and Sentimentality in Nineteenth-Century America*. New York: Oxford UP, 1992.

Sánchez-Eppler, Karen. *Touching Liberty: Abolition, Feminism, and the Politics of Body*. Berkeley: U of California P, 1993.

Saxton, Alexander. *The Rise and Fall of the White Republic: Class Politics and Mass Culture in Nineteenth-Century America*. New York: Verso, 1990.

Sayre, Robert. *Thoreau and the American Indians*. Princeton, N.J.: Princeton UP, 1977.

Scheckel, Susan. "Domesticating the Drama of Conquest: Pocahontas on the Popular Stage." *The Insistence of the Indian: Race and Nationalism in Nineteenth-Century American Culture*. Princeton, N.J.: Princeton UP, 1998. 41–69.

Sears, Priscilla. *A Pillar of Fire to Follow: American Indian Dramas, 1808–1859*. Bowling Green, Ohio: Bowling Green University Popular Press, 1982.

Sedgwick, Eve Kosofsky. "Gosh, Boy George, You Must Be Awfully Secure in

Your Masculinity." In *Constructing Masculinity*. Ed. Maurice Berger, Brian Wallis, and Simon Watson. New York: Routledge, 1995. 11–20.

Sekula, Allan. "The Body and the Archive." *October* 39 (winter 1986): 3–64.

——. "The Traffic In Photographs." *Art Journal* 41.1 (spring 1981): 15–25.

Sellers, Charles Coleman. *Mr. Peale's Museum: Charles Willson Peale and the First Popular Museum of Natural Science and Art*. New York: Norton, 1980.

Sellers, Charles G. *The Market Revolution: Jacksonian America, 1815–1846*. New York: Oxford UP, 1991.

Shelton, Anthony Alan. "In the Lair of the Monkey: Note Towards a Post-Modernist Museography." In *Objects of Knowledge*. Ed. Susan Pearce. London: The Athlone Press, 1990. 78–102.

Shloss, Carol. *In Visible Light: Photography and the American Writer: 1840–1940*. New York: Oxford UP, 1987.

Sights and Wonders in New York; including a description of the mysteries, miracles, marvels, phenomena, curiosities, and nondescripts, contained in that great congress of wonders, Barnum's Museum. New York: J. S. Redfield, 1849.

Silverman, Kenneth. *Edgar A. Poe: Mournful and Never-Ending Remembrance*. New York: HarperCollins, 1991.

Simms, William Gilmore. "Oakatibbe, or the Choctaw Sampson." 1841. *The Wigwam and the Cabin*. 1845. Ridgewood, N.J.: The Gregg Press, 1968. 190–226.

Sketch of the Life, Personal Appearance, Character and Manners of Charles S. Stratton, The Man in Miniature, Known as General Tom Thumb. New York: Van Norden and Amerman, 1847.

Review of *Slavery in the United States* by J. K. Paulding and *The South Vindicated from the Treason and Fanaticism of the Northern Abolitionists* [William Drayton]. *Southern Literary Messenger* 2.5 (April 1836): 336–39.

Smith, Donald B. "The Life of George Copway or Kah-ge-ga-gah-bowh (1818–1869)—and a Review of his Writings." *Journal of Canadian Studies* 23.3 (fall 1988): 5–38.

Smith, Shawn Michelle. *American Archives: Gender, Race, and Class in Visual Culture*. Princeton, N.J.: Princeton UP, 1999.

Smith-Rosenberg, Carroll. "Dis-Covering the Subject of the 'Great Constitutional Discussion,' 1786–1789." In *Discovering America: Essays on the Search for an Identity*. Ed. David Thelen and Frederick E. Hoxie. Urbana: U of Illinois P, 1994. 7–39.

——. *Disorderly Conduct: Visions of Gender in Victorian America*. New York: Oxford UP, 1985.

Sollors, Werner. "Romantic Love, Arranged Marriage, and Indian Melancholy." *Beyond Ethnicity: Consent and Descent in American Culture*. New York: Oxford UP, 1986. 102–30.

"Songs of the Blacks." *Dwight's Journal of Music* 15 November 1856. Reprinted in

What They Heard: Music In America, 1852–1881. Ed. Irving Sablosky. Baton Rouge: Louisiana State UP, 1986. 264–65.

Spillers, Hortense J. "Mama's Baby, Papa's Maybe: An American Grammar Book." *Diacritics* 17.2 (summer 1987): 64–81.

Spivak, Gayatri Chakravorty. "Can the Subaltern Speak?" In *Marxism and the Interpretation of Culture*. Ed. Cary Nelson and Lawrence Grossberg. Urbana: U of Illinois P, 1988. 271–313.

Stanley, Amy Dru. "Home Life and the Morality of the Market." In *The Market Revolution in America*. Ed. Melvyn Stokes and Stephen Conway. Charlottesville: UP of Virginia, 1996. 74–96.

Stansell, Christine. *City of Women: Sex and Class in New York, 1789–1860* . New York: Knopf, 1986.

Stanton, William. *The Leopard's Spots: Scientific Attitudes Toward Race in America, 1815–59*. Chicago: U of Chicago P, 1960.

Stewart, Susan. *On Longing: Narratives of the Miniature, the Gigantic, the Souvenir, the Collection*. 1984. Durham, N.C.: Duke UP, 1993.

Stocking, George. *Race, Culture, and Evolution: Essays in the History of Anthropology*. New York: The Free Press, 1968.

Stokes, Melvyn, and Stephen Conway, eds. *The Market Revolution in America: Social, Political, and Religious Expressions, 1800–1880*. Charlottesville: UP of Virginia, 1996.

Stone, John Augustus. *Metamora, or the Last of the Wampanoags*. 1829. In *Dramas from the American Theatre, 1762–1909*. Ed. Richard Moody. Cleveland: World Publishing Co., 1966. 199–228.

Stowe, Harriet Beecher. *Dred, A Tale of the Great Dismal Swamp*. 1856. Boston: Houghton Mifflin, 1884.

———. *Uncle Tom's Cabin or, Life Among the Lowly*. 1852. New York: Penguin, 1981.

Sundquist, Eric J. *To Wake the Nations: Race in the Making of American Literature*. Cambridge: Harvard UP, 1993.

Swann, Charles. "*The House of the Seven Gables*: Hawthorne's Modern Novel of 1848." *Modern Language Review* 86 (January 1991): 1–18.

Taft, Robert. *Photography and the American Scene*. 1938. New York: Dover, 1964.

Tagg, John. *The Burden of Representation: Essays on Photographies and Histories*. Amherst: U of Massachusetts P, 1988.

Takaki, Ronald. *Iron Cages: Race and Culture in Nineteenth-Century America*. 1979. New York: Oxford UP, 1990.

Taylor, George R. *The Transportation Revolution, 1815–1860*. New York: Rinehart, 1951.

Thomas, Brook. *Cross Examinations of Law and Literature: Cooper, Hawthorne, Stowe, and Melville*. Cambridge: Cambridge UP, 1987.

Thomas, Dwight, and David K. Jackson. *The Poe Log: A Documentary Life of Edgar Allan Poe, 1809–1849.* Boston: G. K. Hall, 1987.

Thomson, Rosemarie Garland. "The Cultural Work of American Freak Shows, 1835–1940." *Extraordinary Bodies: Figuring Physical Disability in American Culture and Literature.* New York: Columbia UP, 1997. 55–80.

——, ed. *Freakery: Cultural Spectacles of the Extraordinary Body.* New York: New York UP, 1996.

Thoreau, Henry David. "The Commercial Spirit of Modern Times." In *Early Essays and Miscellanies.* Ed. Joseph J. Modlenhauer and Edwin Moser. Princeton, N.J.: Princeton UP, 1975. 115–18.

——. *Excursions and Poems.* Vol. 5 of *The Writings of Henry David Thoreau.* Boston: Houghton Mifflin, 1906.

——. *Familiar Letters.* Vol. 6 of *The Writings of Henry David Thoreau.* Boston: Houghton Mifflin, 1906.

——. *Journal.* Ed. Bradford Torrey. 14 vols. Vols. 7–20 of *The Writings of Henry David Thoreau.* Boston: Houghton Mifflin, 1906.

——. *Journal.* Vol. 1. Ed. John C. Broderick. Princeton, N.J.: Princeton UP, 1981.

——. *The Maine Woods.* Ed. Joseph J. Moldenhauer. Princeton, N.J.: Princeton UP, 1972.

——. *Reform Papers.* Ed. Wendell Glick. Princeton, N.J.: Princeton UP, 1973.

——. *Walden.* Ed. J. Lyndon Shanley. Princeton, N.J.: Princeton UP, 1971.

——. *A Week on the Concord and Merrimack Rivers.* Ed. Carl F. Hovde, et al. Princeton, N.J.: Princeton UP, 1980.

Toll, Robert. *Blacking Up: The Minstrel Show in Nineteenth-Century America.* New York: Oxford UP, 1974.

Tompkins, Jane. *Sensational Designs: The Cultural Work of American Fiction, 1790–1860.* New York: Oxford UP, 1985.

Tom Pop's First Visit to the Boston Museum, with his Grandfather; Giving an Account of What He Saw, and What He Thought. Boston: n.p. 1848.

Trachtenberg, Alan. "Mirror in the Marketplace: American Responses to the Daguerreotype." In *The Daguerreotype: A Sesquicentennial Celebration.* Ed. John Wood. Iowa City: U of Iowa P, 1989. 60–73.

——. "Photography: The Emergence of a Keyword." In *Photography in Nineteenth-Century America.* Ed. Martha A. Sandweiss. Fort Worth, Tex.: Amon Carter Museum, 1991. 17–41.

——. *Reading American Photographs: Images as History, Mathew Brady to Walker Evans.* New York: Hill and Wang, 1989.

——. "Seeing and Believing: Hawthorne's Reflections on the Daguerreotype in *The House of the Seven Gables.*" *American Literary History* 9.3 (fall 1997): 460–81.

Trennert, Robert A., Jr. *Alternative to Extinction: Federal Indian Policy and the Beginnings of the Reservation System, 1846–51.* Philadelphia: Temple UP, 1975.

Tubbee, Laah Ceil Manatoi Elaah. *The Life of Okah Tubbee.* 1852. Ed. Daniel F. Littlefield Jr. Lincoln: U of Nebraska P, 1988.

Tucker, Louis Leonard. " 'Ohio Show-Shop': The Western Museum of Cincinnati, 1820–1867." *A Cabinet of Curiosities: Five Episodes in the Evolution of American Museums.* Charlottesville: UP of Virginia, 1967. 73–105.

Twain, Mark. *The Autobiography of Mark Twain.* Ed. Charles Neider. 1924. New York: Harper, 1959.

Van Leer, David. "Detecting Truth: The World of the Dupin Tales." In *New Essays on Poe's Major Tales.* Ed. Kenneth Silverman. Cambridge: Cambridge UP, 1993. 65–92.

——. "Nature's Book: The Language of Science in the American Renaissance." In *Romanticism and the Sciences.* Ed. Andrew Cunningham and Nicholas Jardine. Cambridge: Cambridge UP, 1990. 307–21.

Walker, Alice. *In Search of Our Mothers' Gardens.* San Diego: Harcourt Brace Jovanovich, 1983.

Walker, David. *David Walker's Appeal in Four Articles . . .* 3d ed. 1830. Baltimore: Black Classic Press, 1993.

Wallace, Irving. *The Fabulous Showman: The Life and Times of P. T. Barnum.* New York: Knopf, 1959.

Wallace, James D. *Early Cooper and His Audience.* New York: Columbia UP, 1986.

Wallace, Maurice. " 'Are We Men?' Prince Hall, Martin Delany, and the Masculine Ideal in Black Freemasonry, 1775–1865." *American Literary History* 9.3 (fall 1997): 396–421.

Wallis, Brian. "Black Bodies, White Science: Louis Agassiz's Slave Daguerreotypes." *American Art* 9 (summer 1995): 39–61.

Walls, Laura Dassow. "Textbooks and Texts from the Brooks: Inventing Scientific Authority in America." *American Quarterly* 49.1 (March 1997): 1–25.

Warner, Michael. "*Walden's* Erotic Economy." In *Comparative American Identities: Race, Sex, and Nationality in the Modern Text.* Ed. Hortense J. Spillers. New York: Routledge, 1991. 157–74.

Warren, Joyce, ed. *Ruth Hall and Other Writings.* By Fanny Fern. New Brunswick, N.J.: Rutgers UP, 1986.

Warren, Kenneth W. *Black and White Strangers: Race and American Literary Realism.* Chicago: U of Chicago P, 1993.

Washburn, Wilcombe E. "Joseph Henry's Conception of the Purpose of the Smithsonian Institution." *A Cabinet of Curiosities: Five Episodes in the Evolution of American Museums.* Charlottesville: UP of Virginia, 1967. 106–66.

Weber, Max. *The Protestant Ethic and the Spirit of Capitalism.* Trans. Talcott Parsons. New York: HarperCollins, 1991.

Weld, Theodore Dwight. *American Slavery As It Is: Testimony of a Thousand Witnesses.* New York: American Anti-Slavery Society, 1839.

Welter, Barbara. "The Cult of True Womanhood: 1800–1860." *Dimity Convictions: The American Woman in the Nineteenth Century.* Athens: Ohio UP, 1976. 21–41.

Wemyss, Francis C. *Wemyss' Chronology of the American Stage, from 1752 to 1852.* 1852. New York: Benjamin Blom, 1968.

Werner, M. R. *Barnum.* New York: Harcourt, Brace, and Co., 1923.

Whalen, Terence. "Edgar Allan Poe and the Horrid Laws of Political Economy." *American Quarterly* 44.3 (September 1992): 381–417.

——. *Edgar Allan Poe and the Masses: The Political Economy of Literature in Antebellum America.* Princeton, N.J.: Princeton UP, 1999.

——. "Subtle Barbarians: Poe, Racism, and the Political Economy of Adventure." In *Styles of Cultural Activism: From Theory and Pedagogy to Women, Indians, and Communism.* Ed. Philip Goldstein. Cranbury, N.J.: Associated UP, 1994. 169–83.

Whitman, Walt. "Pictures." *Leaves of Grass.* Comprehensive Reader's Edition. Ed. Harold W. Blodgett and Sculley Bradley. New York: New York UP, 1965. 642–49.

——. "Visit to Plumbe's Gallery." 1846. In *The Gathering of the Forces.* Ed. Cleveland Rodgers and John Black. Vol. 2. New York: G. P. Putnam's Sons, 1920. 113–17.

——. *Walt Whitman, Complete Poetry and Collected Prose.* New York: Library of America, 1982.

Williams, Raymond. *Marxism and Literature.* Oxford: Oxford UP, 1977.

Williams, Susan S. *Confounding Images: Photography and Portraiture in Antebellum American Literature.* Philadelphia: U of Pennsylvania P, 1997.

Willis, Deborah. *Reflections in Black: A History of Black Photographers, 1840 to the Present.* New York: Norton, 2000.

Wilson, R. Jackson. *Figures of Speech: American Writers and the Literary Marketplace, from Benjamin Franklin.* New York: Knopf, 1989.

Winter, Marian Hannah. "Juba and American Minstrelsy." *Dance Index* 6.2 (February 1947): 28–47.

Wittke, Carl. *Tambo and Bones: A History of the American Minstrel Show.* Durham, N.C.: Duke UP, 1930.

Wolff, Cynthia Griffin. " 'Masculinity' in *Uncle Tom's Cabin.*" *American Quarterly* 47.4 (December 1995): 595–618.

Worley, Sam. "*The Narrative of Arthur Gordon Pym* and the Ideology of Slavery." *ESQ* 40 (1994): 219–50.

Wyatt-Brown, Bertram. *Lewis Tappan and the Evangelical War Against Slavery.* Cleveland: The Press of Case Western Reserve, 1969.

Yacovone, Donald. " 'Surpassing the Love of Women': Victorian Manhood and the Language of Fraternal Love." In *A Shared Experience: Men, Women, and the History of Gender.* Ed. Laura McCall and Donald Yacovone. New York: New York UP, 1998. 195–221.

Yarborough, Richard. "Race, Violence, and Manhood: The Masculine Ideal in Frederick Douglass's 'The Heroic Slave.'" In *Frederick Douglass: New Literary and Historical Essays.* Ed. Eric Sundquist. Cambridge: Cambridge UP, 1990. 166–88.

Yellin, Jean Fagan. "Hawthorne and the American National Sin." In *The Green American Tradition: Essays and Poems for Sherman Paul.* Ed. H. Daniel Peck. Baton Rouge: Louisiana State UP, 1989. 75–97.

——. *The Intricate Knot: Black Figures in American Literature, 1776–1863.* New York: New York UP, 1972.

——. *Women and Sisters: The Antislavery Feminists in American Culture.* New Haven, Conn.: Yale UP, 1989.

Young, R. J. *Antebellum Black Activists: Race, Gender, and Self.* New York: Garland, 1996.

Zafar, Rafia. *We Wear the Mask: African Americans Write American Literature, 1760–1870.* New York: Columbia UP, 1997.

Zanger, Jules. "The 'Tragic Octoroon' in Pre-Civil War Fiction." *American Quarterly* 18.1 (spring 1966): 63–70.

Zboray, Ronald J. *A Fictive People: Antebellum Economic Development and the American Reading Public.* New York: Oxford UP, 1993.

Index

Brodhead, Richard H., 224 n.16
Bromell, Nicholas K., 166 n.29
Brougham, John, 179 n.36
Brown, Bill, 158 n.6
Brown, Gillian, 164 n.23, 170 n.43, 222 n.6
Brown, John, 86–88, 205 n.61
Brown, William Wells, 2, 7, 17–18, 20, 37–46, 49, 52–66, 69, 80, 95, 156; *The Anti-Slavery Harp*, 37, 56, 180 n.3; *Clotel; or, The President's Daughter*, 17–18, 37, 41–46, 49, 52–55, 58, 60–66; *A Description of William Wells Brown's Panoramic Views*, 41, 56, 57; *The Escape; or, A Leap for Freedom*, 37–38, 53; *Narrative of William Wells Brown, A Fugitive Slave*, 41, 44, 58
Browning, Tod, 108
Buckley, Peter G., 4, 31, 159 n.11, 180 n.43, 199 n.17
Buell, Lawrence, 10, 157 n.4
Butler, Judith, 167 n.31, 185 n.26
Butsch, Richard, 197 n.6

Capitalism, 3, 5, 15, 23, 48, 70, 78, 90, 128, 158 n.5, 161 n.19, 164 n.23, 208 n.76. *See also* Commodity culture; Literature: and the marketplace; Market revolution
Cassuto, Leonard, 109, 191 n.63, 214 n.36
Channing, William Ellery, 121–22, 124
Charvat, William, 9
Child, Lydia Maria, 41, 91–92, 96, 171 n.3
Christy, Edwin, 40, 52
Class distinctions: and blackness, 130–33, 137–38; and daguerreotypy, 19, 127, 139–43; and Indianness, 17, 25–33; and manhood, 2, 5, 6, 162 n.21; and mass culture, 2, 4, 6, 7, 18, 34–35; and minstrel shows, 4, 46–48, 52, 127, 188 n.39; and museums, 73, 109, 212 n.24; and race, 2, 4, 6, 7,

15–20, 25–33, 46–48, 52, 55–61, 109, 125–27, 129–33, 137–38, 143–44, 146; and theater culture, 6, 29–32, 34; and whiteness, 4, 7, 32. *See also* Middle class
Clifford, James, 197 n.8
Cockrell, Dale, 47
Commodity culture, 1, 22–23, 78–80
Cooper, James Fenimore, 13, 17, 21–33, 35, 78, 156; and authorship as profession, 22–24, 32–33; and class, 22–30, 32–33; and Edwin Forrest, 27–30, 177 n.23; *The Last of the Mohicans*, 17, 21–30, 125; and literary manhood, 22–24; *The Pioneers*, 21, 173 n.11, 174 n.15; *Precaution*, 22; *The Redskins*, 33; *The Spy*, 173 n.8; *The Wept of Wish-Ton-Wish*, 175 n.17
Copway, George, 94, 208 n.77
Craft, William and Ellen, 64
Craniometry, 93, 115–16, 123, 143, 217 n.54. *See also* Morton, Samuel George
Cummins, Maria, 11

Daguerreotypy, 2, 4, 17, 19–20, 35, 125–27, 134, 139–55; and blackness, 127, 143–44, 154–55; and class, 19, 127, 139–43; and families, 125, 127, 139–40, 146; and gender, 139–40, 145; and Indianness, 127, 143–44; and literature, 19–20; and the marketplace, 139–41, 147–49; as pedagogical 140–42; and race, 19–20, 126–27, 142–46, 151–56, 231 n.42, 232 n.44, 233 n.48; and respectability, 19; and scientific racialism, 143–44; and whiteness, 19, 126–27, 142–47, 231 n.42
Davidson, Cathy N., 227 n.28
Dayan, Joan, 111–12, 209 n.2, 210 n.11, 217 n.48, 220 n.74
Deloria, Philip Joseph, 202 n.39
Derrick, Scott S., 9, 165 n.28

Indianness (*cont.*)

    and blackness, 6, 18, 67–69, 80,
84–92, 99, 161 n.19, 204 n.47; and
class, 17, 25–33; as commodity, 14,
80, 85, 90–91, 94–97; in daguerreotypy, 127, 143–44; as hypermasculine, 7; and literature, 18, 22–
26, 30, 80, 96–97; and manhood,
17, 18, 21–33, 68, 77–80, 84–90,
92–97, 155–56; and masculine passions, 14, 17, 18, 26–33, 68, 80; in
melodrama, 6, 17, 26–32; in museums, 7, 18, 67–71, 74, 78, 85–86,
90–97, 109; as performative, 27–33;
and Poe, 110, 118–19; and savagism,
78, 83; and sentimentalism, 91; and
the vanishing American, 30, 83; and
whiteness, 25–30, 78–79; and wildness, 18, 21–22, 27–28, 32, 68, 78–
80, 83, 86, 91, 94–97. *See also* Forrest, Edwin; Tubbee, Okah

Indian removal, 16, 23, 30, 32, 155, 161
n.19, 177 n.27

Irving, Washington, 23

Jackson, Andrew, 30
Jameson, Fredric, 158 n.5
Jefferson, Thomas, 43, 215 n.44
Johnson, William Henry, 85, 109–10

Kennard, James K, Jr., 15, 138
Kimball, Moses, 71, 74, 203 n.41
Kimmel, Michael S., 167 n.31
Kirshenblatt-Gimblett, Barbara, 198
n.8
Klammer, Martin, 152–53

Lane, William Henry, 49–51, 64, 65,
86, 131, 189 n.48
Lang, Amy Schrager, 239 n.12
Leach, Harvey, 19, 106–10, 114–15
Leverenz, David, 9, 104, 165 n.28, 174
n.15, 209 n.2, 228 n.28
Levine, Lawrence W., 4, 159 n.11
Levine, Robert S., 184 n.19, 195 nn.90,
93

Lewis, Matthew (Monk), 113
Lhamon, W. T., Jr., 47, 52, 188 n.41
Limon, John, 218 n.59
Lind, Jenny, 89, 206 n.65
Literary manhood, 1–3, 8–13, 12–27,
42, 69, 98–100, 103, 108, 119, 121,
129, 138, 147–48, 151, 155–56; as
antimarket, 1, 69, 80–81, 100, 103,
112, 125; and blackness, 39, 43, 46,
65–66, 69; and cultural authority,
22–35; and daguerreotypy 139, 147–
48, 151; defined, 2–3; and Indianness, 69, 80, 94–95; and the marketplace, 34, 137–38, 147, 155–56;
and mass culture, 14, 16, 33–35, 125,
155–56; and middle-class manhood,
13, 16, 19, 42, 127, 129, 155–56; and
minstrel shows, 39, 65–66; and professionalism, 8–13, 32–35, 69; and
race, 14, 19, 125, 137–38, 155–56; and
theater culture, 26–30; and women
writers, 9–13, 155

Literature: and blackness, 17–18; and
capitalism, 3; and class, 1; as commodity 15, 16, 19, 24, 34–35, 103–4,
108, 123, 126, 137–38, 147, 157 n.3; as
feminine 9–10, 21–24, 26, 35, 80,
120–21; and gender, 2, 8–13, 18, 22–
24; and Indianness, 18, 22–26, 30,
80, 96–97; and manhood, 17, 22–
24, 26, 98; and the marketplace, 2,
9, 10, 18, 19, 20, 23–24, 69; and
mass culture, 14–16; and professionalism, 2, 3, 8–10, 33–35, 98, 157
n.4

Littlefield, Daniel F., Jr., 203 n.42
Longfellow, Henry Wadsworth, 116,
117, 119–24
Lott, Eric, 2, 4, 41, 46–47, 182 n.11, 188
n.41, 196 n.5, 225 n.20
Lowell, James Russell, 98, 119–20, 124
Lukács, Georg, 8

Macpherson, C. B., 5
Macready, William, 31

Minstrel shows (*cont.*)
196 n.5; and literature, 14–15; and
market society, 7, 19; and masculine
embodiment, 48–49, 64, 127–29,
133, 136–39; and museums, 68, 109,
115; and respectability, 47–48; and
sentimentalism, 7, 47, 53, 206 n.65;
and white manhood, 17–18, 37, 43,
47, 48–51, 132–33
Morrison, Toni, 214 n.40, 221 n.3
Morton, Samuel George, 93, 115, 143,
207 n.75
Mowatt, Anna Cora, 1
Mullen, Harryette, 192 n.73
Museums, 2, 4, 17, 35, 67–74, 80, 84–
97, 99, 104–5, 108–9, 112–13, 124, 197
n.8, 198 n.9; audiences of, 67, 70–74;
blackness in, 67, 85–86, 115; and
class, 73, 109, 212 n.24; and families,
71–74, 109, 114; as feminizing or domestic, 71–74, 77, 80, 90; gender in,
70–74; and guidebooks, 71–74, 96;
Indianness in, 7, 8, 67, 71, 74, 78, 85–
86, 90–97, 109; minstrels shows in,
68, 109, 115; and race, 99, 108–9; and
respectability, 68, 212 n.24; and sentimentalism, 68, 91–92, 96–97; and
theater culture, 73, 76; whiteness in,
67, 99–100, 109, 114. *See also*
Barnum, P. T.; Freak shows

Nathanson, Y. S., 46
Native Americans, representations of.
See Indianness
Nelson, Dana D., 116, 167 n.31, 217
n.47
Newbury, Michael, 9, 170 n.43, 202
n.40, 222 n.5
Noah, M. M., 28

Orvell, Miles, 152–53, 170 n.45

Panoramas, 130–31, 154–55
Peale, Charles Willson, 67, 104–5
Person, Leland S., Jr., 9, 165 n.28, 227
n.28

Peterson, Carla L., 184 n.19, 191 n.63
Pierce, Franklin, 129
Poe, Edgar Allan, 2, 13, 19, 98–124,
156; and Barnum, 211 n.18; black
characters of, 110; *Eureka*, 117, 219
n.60; "Hop-Frog," 98–124; Indian
characters of, 110; and literary market, 19, 98–100, 101–4, 108, 112–13,
117, 119; *Narrative of Arthur Gordon
Pym*, 110–12; racial politics of, 99,
111–12, 116–18, 122; and savageness,
98, 118–19, 121–22; *Stylus*, 98, 101,
104, 112, 113, 119, 121
Popular culture, 47, 159 n.8
Postone, Moishe, 164 n.23
Prucha, Francis Paul, 202 n.38
Pugh, Achilles, 154

Race: as authentic, 2–4, 14, 15, 35, 38,
44–45, 51, 68–69, 78–79; as biological, 78–79, 84–85, 95, 114, 135; and
class, 2, 4, 6, 7, 15–20, 25–33, 46–
48, 52, 55–61, 109, 125–27, 129–33,
137–38, 143–44, 146; as commodity,
2, 14, 19, 87, 95–97, 99–100, 112–
14, 123–24, 125, 147–48, 155–56; and
daguerreotypy, 19–20, 126–27, 142–
46, 152–56, 231 n.42, 232 n.44, 233
n.48; definitions of, 135, 145, 226
n.23; and freak shows, 19, 99–100,
105–106, 108–18, 121–24; and gender, 39, 43, 46, 51, 55–66, 68–69, 81,
87, 89–90; and literature, 1, 14; and
manhood, 2, 4, 7, 14, 16, 19–20, 38,
52, 59, 99–100, 126–27, 133–38; and
market revolution, 164 n.24; in
mass culture, 2–4, 14–16, 125; and
middle class, 1–2, 4, 59, 133–38; in
minstrel shows, 18; and museums,
99, 108–9; as performative, 3, 14, 15,
35, 38, 43–46, 51, 60–66, 68–69. *See
also* Blackness; Indianness; Whiteness
Reid-Pharr, Robert F., 184 n.19, 192
n.75

Walker, David, 40, 193 n.76
Warner, Michael, 200 n.29
Warren, Kenneth W., 221 n.3
Weber, Max, 162 n.21
Whalen, Terence, 9, 103–4, 211 n.12, 216 n.46
"What is It?" (Barnum exhibition), 85, 99, 105–11, 114–15, 117, 124, 214 n.36
Whiteness: and blackness, 38–39, 42, 46–51, 58–66, 85, 126–29, 133–39, 142, 149–50; and class, 4, 7, 32; as commodity, 147–49; and commodity culture, 130–31, 134, 137–38, 156; and daguerreotypy, 19–20, 142–47, 231 n.42; and freak shows, 99–100, 105, 109, 111, 114; and gender, 59–61, 68, 109; and Indianness, 25–30, 32, 78–79, 85, 131; and manhood, 4, 7, 15–16, 51, 58–65, 127, 133–39; and mass culture, 4; and middle-class identity, 2, 4, 6, 7, 15–20, 55–61, 109, 125–27, 129, 143–44, 146; and minstrel shows, 17–18, 37, 40–41, 43, 46–51, 132–33; in mu-

seums, 18–19, 67–68, 99–100, 109, 114
Whitman, Sarah Helen, 121
Whitman, Walt, 20, 151–56; and daguerreotypy, 151–56; and Edwin Forrest, 151; and minstrel shows, 151; and slavery, 152–53
Williams, Susan S., 140, 221 n.5, 229 n.33, 235 n.57, 239 n.12
Women: and blackness, 60; as commodities, 128, 132, 138; and literary manhood, 9–13, 155; and literature, 21–24; and market revolution, 8–9; and mass culture, 18, 68–74; middle-class identity, 5–6, 32, 60, 68–74, 126; and Poe, 210 n.11; as readers, 21–24, 43, 137–38; and respectability, 34–35, 68–69; and whiteness, 68–69, 127–28; as writers, 9–13, 22–24

Yarborough, Richard, 56, 194 n.87
Yellin, Jean Fagan, 45, 191 n.69

Zealy, J. T., 143–44

Paul Gilmore is Assistant Professor of English
at Bucknell University.

Library of Congress Cataloging-in-Publication Data

Gilmore, Paul
The genuine article : race, mass culture, and American literary
manhood / Paul Gilmore.
p. cm. — (New Americanists)
Includes bibliographical references (p.   ) and index.
ISBN 0-8223-2754-6 (alk. paper)
ISBN 0-8223-2764-3 (pbk. : alk. paper)
1. American literature—Male authors—History and criticism.
2. American literature—19th century—History and criticism.
3. Popular culture—United States—History—19th century. 4. Race
awareness—United States—History—19th century. 5. Masculinity—
United States—History—19th century. 6. Men—United States—
History—19th century. 7. Race awareness in literature. 8. Masculinity
in literature. 9. Race in literature. 10. Men in literature. I. Title.
II. Series.
PS153.M3 G55 2002
810.9'9286'09034—dc21   2001033777